LOWELL D. HOLMES, Ph.D., Northwestern University, is Professor and Head of the Department of Anthropology at Wichita State University. He was formerly the Chairman of the Department of Sociology at Missouri Valley College. Dr. Holmes has conducted anthropological research in American Samoa under the sponsorship of the Tri-Institutional Pacific Program and the University of Hawaii and has investigated leadership and decision-making in Samoan society under the sponsorship of the National Science Foundation. Dr. Holmes is a Fellow of the American Anthropological Association.

ANTHROPOLOGY

AN INTRODUCTION

LOWELL D. HOLMES
Wichita State University

THE RONALD PRESS COMPANY • NEW YORK

Library of Congress Catalog Card Number 65–27071

To the Memory of
RANDALL BOCK

Preface

This book is designed for introductory courses in anthropology. A major task has been the selecting from a great volume of material those facts and concepts that will best reveal the nature of anthropology as a science. To this end I have endeavored to communicate the valuable contributions of hundreds of dedicated anthropologists and other investigators in the behavioral sciences who over the years have painstakingly built up a vast body of literature concerning the unique ways of man.

Every effort has been made to cover adequately all pertinent aspects necessary for an introductory textbook. At the same time considerable emphasis is placed on the American cultural configuration. This has been done through extensive comparisons of the lifeways of primitive people with those of representatives of Western civilization, through selected studies of modern American culture, and through discussions of cultural relativism and the problems that Americans face today. The book borrows data from other disciplines, such as political science, history, geography, psychology, sociology, and education, when they are enlightening, but care is taken to show in what ways the methods of anthropology are distinctive to it and what role it plays among the behavioral sciences.

In presenting to the student the bases of anthropology I hope that these materials will aid him, functioning as a citizen, to make a more rational appraisal of the peoples and cultures that share his world and are destined to demand his attention.

On completion of any textbook an author finds himself much the debtor. My thanks, appreciation, and admiration go first to the many anthropologists and other social scientists from whose work I have so liberally drawn. Much of the theoretical frame of reference has without doubt come from the inspiration and tutelage of my mentors William Bascom, Richard Waterman, Francis Hsu, and the late Melville J. Herskovits. Equally effective as mentors were the people of American Samoa, who taught me the meaning of culture and provided me with the opportunity of observing that people can live noble and happy lives according to traditional standards quite different from my own. To them I must express my *fa'afetai lava*. Thanks are also due to my students who asked the questions and demanded the interpretations that form the bulk of this book.

My debt of gratitude also extends to my colleagues at Wichita State University, to my artist, Valerie Kiste, to George Holcomb of the University of North Carolina for his comments on Chapter 4, and to my wife Jeanette, who served as literary critic, proofreader, and typist.

LOWELL D. HOLMES

Wichita, Kansas
July, 1965

Contents

ANTHROPOLOGY
AN INTRODUCTION

1

The Meaning of Anthropology

Anthropology is the study of man—the total man. There is no other academic discipline that examines man as thoroughly. It deals with man's physical makeup and his patterns of social and cultural behavior in the present day and in the historic and prehistoric yesterdays. The study of these many aspects of such a complex organism as man represents a considerable undertaking, and it is therefore not surprising that anthropology has many facets. It is at the same time a natural, social, and historical science; it is also the science of culture and, in some aspects of its study, one of the humanities.

Anthropology may be considered a natural science in that it studies man as a member of the animal kingdom, recognizing that he is a vertebrate, a mammal, a primate, and finally, because of his superior brain and culture-building capacity, a Hominid, or human being. Man not only resembles other animals in certain anatomical features but he also shares a number of behavioral characteristics with a great group of social animals. Humans, like many other animals, find comfort, strength, and security in group living. Although much has been made of the concept of survival of the fittest in explaining man's development on this planet, one must also keep in mind that if it had not been for the aid he received from his fellow man, he might have become as extinct as the dinosaur or the sabre tooth tiger. Anthropology's analysis of man's group orientation and affiliations definitely aligns it with the social sciences.

Man has inhabited this globe for at least one million years, struggling with nature, fashioning various patterns of living in an effort to survive. An important phase of anthropology is the attempt to trace man's cultural development through this vast period and thereby provide an historical perspective for the study of modern man. While anthropologists believe that it is possible to learn a great deal about the nature of the human animal by merely viewing the contemporary scene, much more can be learned if man is viewed in the light of history. The situation might be likened to that of the drama critic who has arrived at the theater in time to view only the final act of a play. Although he might appreciate the acting and the prose, it is impossible for him to catch the full meaning of the play, having missed the initial acts.

If there has been any unique contribution of anthropology to the behavioral sciences it is the concept of culture. Culture denotes the patterns of shared values and behavior which are passed on from generation to generation in a given society through the means of symbolic communication. Since culture shapes the lives of individuals and gives form and stability to societies, it lies at the heart of all anthropological research.

Although anthropology is commonly recognized as a scientific discipline, some areas of anthropological interest fall more naturally within the area of the humanities. Such topics as language, art, and religion, often ignored by other scientific disciplines, traditionally have been regarded as legitimate areas for anthropological research, since they represent aspects of the total range of human activity.

THE DIVISIONS OF ANTHROPOLOGY

Because of the magnitude of the task anthropology has chosen for itself, it has become virtually impossible for any one person to function as a complete anthropologist. Rather, it has become necessary for students of this discipline to be aware of broad understandings concerning the whole man while concentrating on one or two of its many subdivisions, or areas of specialization. Basically, there are only two major divisions of anthropology—physical and cultural. Physical anthropology developed out of the study of human anatomy and became a recognized scientific discipline early in the nineteenth century. Cultural anthropology, on the other hand, developed out of social philosophy and did not become an established academic discipline until almost the turn of the present century. Although cultural anthropology has had a shorter history of growth, it is now more widely taught in American universities and colleges, and cultural anthropologists outnumber physical anthropologists by about fifteen to one.

The Field of Physical Anthropology

HUMAN EVOLUTION. Perhaps the most important branch of physical anthropology is that which deals with the study of human evolution. This area of research came of age in the year 1859 when Charles Darwin published his startling thesis, *The Origin of Species*. In this scientific work man was ushered, once and for all, to his place in the animal kingdom. He was presented to the world as the product of many of the same evolutionary processes which have shaped the anatomy and behavior of all animal organisms. Darwin felt that man's ancestor had been a primitive apelike animal, and that both modern man and modern apes developed their present forms through a series of adaptations to the physical environment. With the Darwinian theory to orient their research, anthropologists began to look for the fossil relics (sometimes called "missing links") with which to fill in the sequence of something less than human to something resembling modern man. The search was well rewarded by the discovery of the million-year-old South African Man-Apes (Australopithecine) and the Ice Age fossils of Java Man (Pithecanthropus erectus), China Man (Pithecanthropus pekinensis), Neanderthal, Cro-Magnon, and scores of others.

Painstakingly the evidence was put together—a broken primitive skull from here and a jawbone from there. It was like putting a jigsaw puzzle together fully realizing that pieces were missing. As more and more fossils were fitted into the picture of man's development, it was apparent that slowly but surely through the ages man has become progressively more erect in stature, larger brained, and more adept at tool-making and culture-building. Instead of being more and more adapted to a given environment, his physical form represents a conquest over environment.

Today the field of human evolution stands as one of the most dynamic of scientific studies. New discoveries are constantly being made, bringing about re-evaluations and adjustments of the story of man's rise from ape man to "wise man" (*Homo sapiens*).

PRIMATOLOGY. The overwhelming fossil evidence of man's development from an apelike ancestor has resulted in a great amount of interest in the anatomy and behavior of modern apes and monkeys. Anthropologists generally have felt that through the study of these very

ANTHROPOLOGY

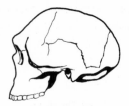

PRE-MOUSTERIAN MAN
100,000-200,000 Years

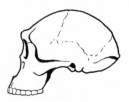

PITHECANTHROPUS
200,000-500,000 Years

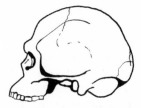

EARLY MOUSTERIAN MAN
50,000-100,000 Years

AUSTRALOPITHECUS
500,000-1,000,000 Years

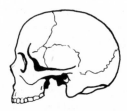

MODERN
EUROPEAN

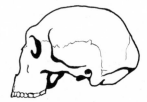

NEANDERTHALENSIS
about 50,000 Years

Fig. 1—1 (after Le Gros Clark).

complex animals some insight might be gained into man's prehistoric behavior and, indeed, into man's behavior today. During the nineteenth century the behavior of monkeys and apes played a great part in speculative theories concerning the origins of family, property, and society. Since man was believed to have been not unlike these lower primates at one period of his development, anthropologists of the past century asked such questions as "Are apes and monkeys monogamous or polygamous?" "Are these animals communistic or individualistic?" "Do they have social organization?" "Can apes and monkeys communicate?" "How do they solve problems?"

Primatologists are still asking these questions, although there is little interest today in speculating on the origins of institutions. Present interest stems from the realization that while men are quite different from apes and monkeys in their capacities, a knowledge of the anatomical and behavioral nature of these lower animals does provide some insight into the biological nature of man.

SOMATOLOGY OR CONSTITUTIONAL ANTHROPOLOGY. Even in ancient times men believed that different body builds produced different types of behavior or personality. In the Shakespearean play, *Julius Caesar*, Mark Antony makes the statement, quite characteristic of his times, that he does not trust Cassius because he has a "lean and hungry look." Interest in the relationship between behavior and physique exists even today, and physical anthropology has tackled the problem on a scientific basis. Somatology classifies various body builds and studies how they correlate with certain types of behavior and personality and with tendencies toward mental and physical illness. A pioneer in this type of anthropology, W. H. Sheldon, classified body types into three categories—ectomorphic, endomorphic, and mesomorphic. He claimed that while everyone actually represents a combination of the three body types, everyone also tends to lean more toward one type than the others. Sheldon maintained that a pronounced ectomorph is excessively slender, lacks muscular development, and tends to be fragile. The endomorph is heavy-set, with a large stomach and liver and a general softness to his body. The mesomorph, on the other hand, is heavily muscled, large boned, and exhibits a firm upright posture.

While the Sheldon classifications are important in understanding the physical variability of man, the most interesting aspect of this study has been the attempts to correlate types of personality with the various body builds. He concluded from his research that the slender ectomorph tends to be oversensitive and inhibited, shrinking from social occasions whenever possible. He has trouble getting to sleep, but once asleep he is hard to awaken. Our fleshy friend, the endomorph, is sociable—loving people, food, and polite society. He can go to sleep in the middle of a conversation. The mesomorph, often a good athlete, is extremely vigorous in all of his activities, having great courage, a will to dominate, and often an insensitivity for the feelings of others. Getting up early to play a round of golf or just to do daily exercises is his meat.

Most modern anthropologists view the Sheldon studies with a degree of suspicion in that they attempt to explain personality in terms of but a single variable—physical type—while ignoring both social and cultural factors.

RACE. Since the scientific study of race deals primarily with the classification of mankind according to physiological differences and not language, religion, or cultural capacity, it has always been an area of major concern for physical anthropology. Scientists who work in this area have pretty well documented the fact that the major races known today originally came into existence during the latter part of the great Ice Age (c. 50,000 years ago) when populations of *Homo sapiens* migrated to various parts of the world and became differentiated in respect to skin color, hair form, skull form, etc., as a result of mutation (changes in genes) and adaptation to their particular natural environment. Dark skin tended to appear in the hot sunny areas of the world where special protection from the sun was essential to survival; eye folds developed in populations that had to survive extreme cold and thus required special protection for the orbits; and light skin developed in the overcast northern climes where those with less skin pigmentation could better absorb the beneficial qualities of the sun's rays.

Although the term race refers strictly to physical characteristics, the word is frequently confused with such extraneous matters as religion, language, nationality, and culture. An example of the confusion that often arises in this area concerns the racial classification of Jews. Jews are not a race, but merely people who worship in the Judaistic tradition. Such religiously affiliated people may be found today in the Middle East and Europe and also, surprisingly enough, in Northern China and Ethiopia. Thus, Jews may be found in each of the major racial divisions of mankind—Caucasian, Mongoloid, and Negroid.

The term Aryan, which was used so convincingly by the Nazis to designate their supposedly pure and superior "race," is actually a term that refers to a group of Indo-European languages and has nothing to do with physical appearance. A linguistic term cannot be used to designate race because a given language can be learned by anyone regardless of racial type.

Nationality represents a similar situation. To refer to the Italian race is wrong because an Italian is a person who is a citizen of the country known as Italy, and one might be reasonably certain that Italy does not give citizenship only to Caucasians. Just as nationality is not synonymous with race, neither is culture. People do not practice polygamy, worship Allah, or eat grubs because they belong to a certain race, but because these customs have traditionally been practiced by the society in which they were raised and educated. During the frontier days of the West white children were occasionally stolen and raised as Indians. The fact that they were Caucasian rather than Mongoloid did not prevent them from learning to speak an Indian language, worship an Indian deity, or live their lives according to Indian standards of value. A given way of life may be learned by anyone regardless of racial type.

Even when attention is focused on the proper criterion of race—physical features—there still is not complete agreement on what constitutes a race. Some scholars have divided mankind into three great races—Caucasians, Mongoloids, and Negroids—while others have added a fourth category, Australoid, or even a fifth, Pygmoid, to take care of people who do not fit neatly into the threefold classification. For instance, it is quite valid to ask where one places the Polynesians, who are a mixture of three great racial stocks, or where one places the Semang and Sakai of Malaya, who are a pygmy-sized people with a mixture of Mongoloid and Negroid features. Actually, the existence of these hybrid people points up a rather important fact about race. Race is not a static thing, and there is not now, nor was there ever, any such thing as a pure race. As representatives of different racial stocks have come into contact and produced offspring, new combinations of physical features have resulted. With modern racial theory centering its attention on a dynamic rather than a static view of race, there has been less and less emphasis placed on three- or fourfold classifications and more on classifications of individual racial populations. Such populations, perhaps numbering only a few hundred individuals, are made up of people who tend to resemble one another because as a group they share a common fund of genes—a fund of genes that might produce individuals that are not characteristically Negroid, Mongoloid, or Caucasian, as the types have been traditionally defined, but perhaps represent a mixture of characteristics of all the major racial types.

Scholars of race have not been satisfied with merely establishing methods of classifying man. They have also been interested in such problems as whether or not there is any justifiable grounds for statements that certain races are superior to others. This has been an immensely complex problem since all known tests of intelligence do not measure innate mental capacity so much as they record differences

**Table 1. Physical characteristics of the three main races of mankind.
(UNESCO 1952)**

Trait	Caucasoid	Mongoloid	Negroid	Hybrid Type (Polynesian)
Skin color	Pale reddish white to olive brown, some dark brown.	Pale yellow to yellow-brown; some reddish brown.	Brown to brown-black; some yellow-brown.	Olive to brown.
Stature	Medium to tall.	Medium tall to medium short.	Tall to very short.	Tall.
Head form	Long to broad and short; medium high to very high.	Predominantly broad; height medium.	Predominantly long; height low to medium.	Predominantly broad; medium high to high.
Face	Narrow to medium broad; no projecting jaw.	Medium broad to very broad, cheekbones "high" and flat.	Medium broad to narrow; frequent projecting jaws.	High narrow forehead, wide and massive face; prominent cheekbones.
Hair	Head hair: color light blond to dark brown; texture fine to medium, form straight to wavy. Body hair: moderate to profuse.	Head hair: color brown to brown-black; texture coarse; form straight. Body hair: sparse.	Head hair: color brown-black; texture, coarse; form light curl to woolly or frizzly. Body hair: slight.	Head hair: color black; texture coarse; form straight to wavy. Body hair: sparse.
Eye	Color: light blue to dark brown; occasional side eye fold.	Color: brown to dark brown; fold of flesh in inner corner very common.	Color: brown to brown-black; vertical eye fold common.	Color: dark brown; eye fold usually absent.
Nose	Bridge usually high; form narrow to medium broad.	Bridge usually low to medium; form medium broad.	Bridge usually low; form medium broad to very broad.	Bridge medium; form large and broad.
Body build	Slim to broad; slender to rugged.	Tends to be broad; occasional slimness.	Tends to be broad and muscular, but occasional slimness.	Broad and muscular, robust.

in social and cultural environment. To date, there is no proof whatsoever that any one race is superior to any other.

Further scientific interest has been focused on the results of race-crossing. Although racial determinists once maintained that interracial mating produced inferior offspring, controlled studies of race-crossing by modern scholars show that just the reverse is true. Harry Shapiro's study of the descendants of Bounty mutineers and Tahitian women shows that a form of heterosis, or hybrid vigor, was apparently

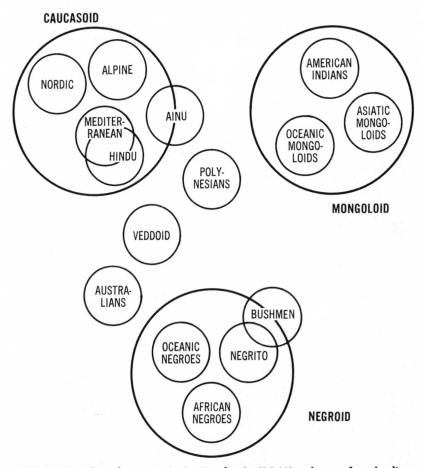

Fig. 1–2. The above is A. L. Kroeber's (1948) scheme for dealing with the classification of hybrid populations. Distances between the centers of circles are representative of the degree of relationship. Note the position of the Polynesians, Ainu, and Australian aborigines. (From *Anthropology* by A. L. Kroeber. © 1923, 1948, by Harcourt, Brace and World, Inc., and reproduced with their permission.)

operative in these interracial matings, producing individuals larger, stronger, and more fertile than could be found in either of the parent stocks.

Another topic of interest to students of race has been the extent to which climate and other aspects of the physical environment affect body build, pigmentation, nose form, and other racial characteristics. As the science of human genetics has increasingly revealed the mystery of the mechanics of heredity, physical anthropologists have been learning more about the racial questions we have cited. They have been able to overthrow more and more of the superstitions concerning race and have moved ever closer to a rational and scientific position on racial differences.

ANTHROPOMETRY. If the average layman were asked to describe the

Dr. Wilfrid D. Hambly utilizing anthropometry in the study of African racial distribution. (Courtesy of Chicago Natural History Museum.)

activities of the physical anthropologist he would probably say that he measures skulls. Physical anthropology does often involve the measuring of skulls, but there are many other measurements that are just as important. With the help of calipers and various specialized instruments, the student of man analyzes and records the physical dimensions—cephalic index, cranial capacity, nasal index, limb ratios, standing and sitting height—of living men and fossil skeletons. This activity is known as anthropometry. Actually, anthropometry is a set of techniques and methods rather than a separate division of physical anthropology—techniques and methods extremely useful in the study of race, human evolution, somatology, growth, and even primatology.

GROWTH STUDIES. Anthropologists who study the physical characteristics of living populations find that an important aspect of their research concerns the patterns of growth and maturation that mark the periods of infancy, childhood, and adolescence. The maturing human child represents a growth phenomenon paralleled in few other animals.

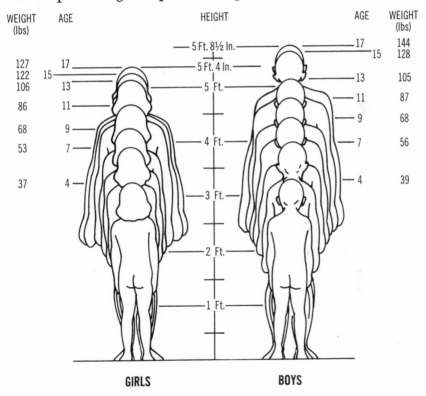

Fig. 1–3. Growth and weight chart of American young people (Bayley 1956).

He is born with an extremely large head, a long slender body, and very short arms and legs. Then growth occurs in intermittent spurts, with different rates of growth occurring in different parts of the body, until the final result is a properly proportioned adult. Through an intensive study of these patterns of growth, physical anthropologists have been able to predict within reasonable limits many of the patterns of development of children in this and in other cultures. It is the growth experts who construct the tables (often found in doctor's offices) that tell mothers when their children should cut their first teeth, when the soft spot on their baby's head should close, and how much a child of a given age should measure and weigh. Of course, maturation rates depend upon diet, climate, patterns of work, and exercise. Therefore, the growth specialist believes that if he is ever to understand completely the phenomenon of growth in the human animal, comparative studies must be made in a variety of cultures and geographical locations.

Table 2. Approximate age of tooth eruption (as developed by growth specialists).

Milk dentition (20 teeth)	
Lower central incisors	6–9 months
Upper incisors	8–10 months
Lower lateral incisors and first molars	15–21 months
Canines	16–20 months
Second molars	20–24 months
Permanent dentition (32 teeth)	
First molars	6th year
Central incisors	7th year
Lateral incisors	8th year
First premolars	9th year
Second premolars	10th year
Canines	11th–12th year
Second molars	12th–13th year
Third molars	17th–25th year

DEMOGRAPHY. A comparatively new area of anthropological concern is that of demography. Although population statistics such as birth rates, death rates, morbidity, and infant mortality rates have long interested students of sociology, it is only recently that their interests have been taken over by anthropologists and focused on primitive man. As anthropology has become more and more quantitative in its approach, it is only natural that interest should turn to the vital statistics of a people under study. Colonial and trusteeship governments have come to realize that any form of planning for the future must take into consideration such matters as population resources and medical and health problems, and, therefore, administrators have enlisted the aid of anthropologists in collecting and interpreting these facts.

Through the cross-cultural efforts of anthropological demographers we are beginning to have greater comprehension of man's span of life, the nature and cause of his illnesses, and the conditions under which societies grow or diminish in numbers.

The Field of Cultural Anthropology

ARCHEOLOGY. There is a good deal of confusion about the position of archeology in relation to cultural anthropology. The layman often thinks that every anthropologist is an archeologist, and some archeologists tend to think of archeology as a separate and distinct discipline from cultural anthropology. Archeology is definitely a branch or subdivision of cultural anthropology, the one that attempts to reconstruct the past history of nonliterate peoples by digging up the material products (artifacts) of their culture—their tools, houses, and art works. Archeology is the area of anthropology that seems to have greatest public appeal. In fact, one writer has referred to archeologists as "the glamor boys" of the anthropological world.

Anthropological archeology is known as prehistoric archeology because it tends to investigate ancient people who never developed a written history of their own. Hence, anthropologists dig up American Indian villages or South Sea island ceremonial centers but leave Greek and Roman ruins to the classical archeologists and Egyptian tombs to Egyptologists. There is a great deal of interest in archeology in this country, as Americans are quite naturally curious about the cultures and civilizations of the native peoples that inhabited North America as early as 35,000 B.C. Hundreds of excavations have provided evidence that the American Indians developed not a uniform culture in all parts of the New World (as our movies and television programs lead us to believe) but, rather, infinitely varied ways of life. As archeologists have studied the remains of ancient cultures they have come to realize that every primitive culture has a unique history of its own; and in order to understand why people have different economies, hold different religious values, and perceive the world in different ways, something must be known of their cultural histories.

The archeologist is not just a collector of arrowheads and other Indian lore. He is a trained scientist who carefully excavates and records the material effects of ancient people as to location and level.

Complete notes are a vital part of any archeological project, and after a location (called a site) has been dug it would actually be possible for the archeologist to put everything back exactly where he found it. It is important to record the exact position of every artifact taken from the site because various levels of material usually represent various stages of cultural development.

Using a variety of tools, students of archeology carefully remove sections of earth containing ancient Indian artifacts. (Courtesy of Chicago Natural History Museum.)

Whenever possible, the archeologist attempts to assign definite dates to his finds, and a number of techniques of relative and absolute dating have been developed. One of the most interesting methods of dating ancient settlements is dendrochronology—tree ring dating. This technique, developed by A. E. Douglass, involves comparison of patterns of annual rings of growth in living trees with those of timbers from ruins of ancient habitations. It was through dendrochronology that the

Mesa Verde site in Colorado was dated at 1206 A.D. Although this method has been limited primarily to the Southwestern part of the country, it has been very valuable in providing knowledge of the sequence of development of the Pueblo Indian cultures.

The most recent and effective method of absolute dating has been given to the archeologist by the atomic scientist. In the late 1940's Willard Libby discovered that there is a constant amount of a mildly radioactive substance, carbon 14, present at all times in our atmosphere and in the tissues of all living matter. At death, however, the radioactive carbon begins to disintegrate at a fixed rate. With the use of a special ultrasensitive Geiger counter it is possible to measure the amount of carbon present at any given time in the tissues of anything that ever lived. Then, through fairly simple calculations it is possible to determine the precise year of its death.

ETHNOGRAPHY. While archeology explores man's prehistoric past, ethnography is concerned with the details of the cultural configurations of contemporary peoples. The term ethnography refers to the empirical, fact-finding activities—observation and interview—carried out by cultural anthropologists in the field. For many years cultural anthropologists were armchair theorists speculating on the nature of man from the accounts of native peoples that filtered in from missionaries, colonial administrators, and explorers. Often this material was highly inaccurate, biased, and lacking in the intricate details that would make them valuable or even useable in a scientific study of man. It was soon recognized that scientific facts relating to man must be collected by the anthropologists themselves, and late in the nineteenth century and early in the twentieth the first effective ethnographers began to leave the comfort of their armchairs and go to distant lands, living among primitive peoples, sometimes for years, eating native dishes, dwelling in native housing, learning native tongues, attempting to understand the values and motivations of their native hosts, and, above all, recording every detail, no matter how insignificant, of the foreign way of life.

ETHNOLOGY. Take the facts of ethnography, add a pinch of theory and you come up with the cross-cultural study of human behavior, better known as ethnology. It is commonly felt that the student of man should not only have the experience of living and working in a culture other than his own, but that he should be familiar with the ethnographic details of a variety of cultures. In this way he can gain the perspective for making the generalizations necessary in a scientific theory of man. Ethnology is comparative—comparative in the sense that it looks at man's culture at many prehistoric and historic periods and in many places in an attempt to formulate statements about similarities and differences among all men and about the ability of human beings as a species to adapt to a variety of physical and cultural environments. When a number of cultures or aspects of those cultures are compared on a common time level the studies are labeled *synchronic*. Comparative studies of the nature of man's religions or his many forms of family around the world would be of this stripe. On the other hand, if an anthropologist should concern himself with a single cultural tradition and its characteristics over an extended period of time—e.g., an analysis of a Plains Indian culture through successive periods of hunting and gathering, agriculture, horse-oriented hunting, and finally reservation life—the ethnological research is then referred to as being of the *diachronic* ("through time") variety.

SOCIAL ANTHROPOLOGY. In Great Britain ethnologists have come to be known as social anthropologists rather than cultural anthropologists. The social anthropologist, unlike his American counterpart, actually pursues a course of study that might better be called comparative sociology. He is mainly interested in studying structures and functions of groups rather than such phenomena as material culture, language, the arts, or religion. The scholars who work in terms of this social frame of reference have made many valuable contributions to the science of man, but most of their studies have been limited in their scope to analyses of kinship and political or economic structures of nonliterate peoples. Like cultural anthropology, social anthropology utilizes worldwide comparisons and employs many of the same field techniques in the collection of data.

LINGUISTICS. A few cultural anthropologists have chosen to study the way in which men communicate through the spoken word and through gestures and other symbols. This aspect of man's behavior, perhaps more than any other, sets him apart from the lower animals and makes possible the existence of culture. Although man has studied the phenomenon of language for many years through the disciplines of philology and etymology, anthropological linguistics is unique because it concentrates on the more exotic languages of the world such as African Swahili and Bantu, American Indian Algonkian and Athabascan, and South Sea island Malayo-Polynesian, to mention but a few. Most of these languages are not written and therefore require quite different methods of recording and analysis. The study of hundreds of languages of primitive peoples has shown that no two languages have been put together in exactly the same way, and sounds used to convey meaning in some tongues sound quite strange to our ears. For example, the Bantu and Bushman people of South Africa utilize lip and tongue noises, called "clicks," as Americans use consonants. Polynesians assign special meaning to no sound at all when it is used to interrupt a word. For example, in the Samoan language *"sao"* means "to escape," while *"sa'o"* means "straight." The latter word contains a glottal stop (indicated by ') which is executed by choking off sound by closing the glottis.

In addition to the analysis of structure—i.e., the way significant sounds and words are put together—anthropological linguistics has concentrated on the historical development of languages and the relationship of language patterns to cultural values. Historical linguistics does not attempt to tell us how language began, but it has provided valuable insights into historical contacts of various societies by analyzing similarities and differences in their languages. By ascertaining the percentage of affinity of two languages it is possible to make quite positive statements as to whether they might represent offshoots from a common mother tongue.

One of the outstanding contributions of anthropological linguistics has been the research on the topic of language and culture. Linguists point out that language largely influences our philosophy of life, our values, and even our perception of reality. People can hardly hold values that cannot be described or communicated. Within each culture, thoughts and actions follow channels that have already been dredged by language. Thomas Jefferson, who was a very fine amateur anthropologist and linguist, once made the statement that he doubted if American Indians could be converted to Christianity as it was impossible to translate the rather abstract concepts of that religion into the Indian languages. There just were no words for such ideas.

Anthropological linguistics has made a great contribution to the understanding of the nature of primitive man by showing that it is impossible to defend the superiority of one language over another. While some peoples have larger vocabularies than others, every group has developed a language adequate for its communication needs. Although Western man has a huge stock of words for tools, machines, and mechanical processes, he has only one word for coconut (Tokelau Islanders have nine, indicating various degrees of ripeness) and one word for potato (Peruvian and Bolivian Indians have over two hundred words for potatoes indicating differences in size and quality). No matter how simple or primitive a culture may appear, one can be certain that they have a way of getting across the ideas that they feel are vital.

The study of human communication involves more than just human speech and its meaning. It must not be overlooked that shrugs of the shoulders, movements of the head, and motions of the hands and arms also convey meaning and are a vital part of any communication system.

FOLKLORE. At one time folklorists were people interested in the queer customs and superstitions of peasant people, but by modern anthropological definition folklorists have come to be known as people who study the artistic creations of man—oral literature, music, the dance, and the graphic and plastic arts. Ethnographic studies have shown that there is no people in the world who do not tell tales, sing

The study of music and the dance is an integral part of cultural anthropology.

songs, and create art objects. While there are anthropologists who specialize entirely in this area of human activity, it is rare indeed to find an anthropologist returning from the field without a collection of myths, tales, and riddles or without information concerning the role and status of the artist, the nature of the art products, and the processes used in their manufacture.

PERSONALITY AND CULTURE. One of the more recently developed areas of anthropological research is that known as "Personality and Culture." This specialty developed from a wedding of cultural anthropology and psychoanalytic theory, and, since its inception in the late 1920's, has worked toward a better understanding of how personality development is influenced by the cultural environment. The discipline differs somewhat from psychology in that it concentrates less on individual personality than on the extent to which personality types are shared within given societies or nations. Starting with such pioneer studies as Margaret Mead's investigation of adolescent personality difficulties in Samoa and America (as presented in *Coming of Age in Samoa*) and Ruth Benedict's application of psychological labels to primitive cultures in her book *Patterns of Culture*, workers in this area have increasingly contributed to the understanding of the nature and causes of mental illness, the influence of childhood experiences on adult personality, and the extent to which common cultural and ideological forces tend to produce similar personality types among the citizens of modern industrial nations.

The Field of Applied Anthropology

Every scientific discipline has its pure and applied aspects. Medicine has its Dr. Salks and its general practitioners. Geology has researchers and oil and mineral prospectors. Anthropology also has its theoretical and practical sides. Although many anthropologists are interested in merely finding things out about the biological and cultural nature of man, others—the applied anthropologists—draw upon the findings of cultural anthropology, physical anthropology, and also upon the discoveries of many other social, natural, and physical sciences and apply their findings to social, political, and economic problems in this and other cultures. This problem-solving phase of anthropology, sometimes referred to as "action anthropology" or "human engineering," can perhaps, because of the nature of its activities, be classified here as a separate and special type of anthropology although it enlists the help of both cultural and physical anthropologists.

A perusal of *Human Organization*, the official journal of the Society for Applied Anthropology, can quickly acquaint the beginning student of anthropology with the many types of work done in this area, but the following types of activities are a sample of those commonly undertaken by applied anthropologists.

Applied anthropologists have long been utilized in Great Britain's colonial system as advisors on government policy for native populations. Because of suggestions from anthropologically trained people the British adopted the policy of "indirect rule" in the colonial governments of West Africa. This was a method of ruling through local hereditary leaders. Government anthropologists often worked in the colonies themselves where they served as liaison personnel between the native populations and the colonial administrators (District Officers and District Commissioners).

Fig. 1–4. The difference between applied and theoretical anthropology.

Applied anthropologists have also been very useful in our own dealings with native peoples. At the end of World War II the United States was given a Trusteeship Charter by the United Nations to govern many of the Micronesian islands—the Carolines, the Marshalls, the Marianas and others. As the United States had had little experience in dealing with native peoples, its first step was to conduct a massive cultural survey of the area. The services of nearly every top anthropologist available were enlisted in this effort. By using this survey material as a guide, an administrative program was drawn up designed to help and encourage the Micronesian people wherever possible without forcing them to give up or drastically alter the basic principles underlying their cultural systems. The Trust Territory administration still employs anthropologists as resident advisors on many of the larger islands.

The Bureau of Indian Affairs similarly has utilized the services of trained anthropologists in dealing with social and cultural problems on the many Indian reservations scattered throughout the United States. Henry Schoolcraft, John Collier, and many other able anthropologists have contributed their knowledge and insight to the solutions of the almost overwhelming problems facing the American Indian in his struggle to adjust to the ways of the white man's world.

The whole area of Public Health has been another arena for anthropological activities. Both at home and abroad the Public Health Officer is faced with cultural patterns, often quite different from his own, that serve as deterrents to programs directed at improving the health conditions of communities or neighborhoods. Schools of Public Health frequently employ anthropologists to teach students the importance of taking the cultural factor into consideration when working among foreign peoples or even when working in rural areas or among minority groups in the United States. The Public Health worker not only must be made aware of the cultural values of the people with whom he is to work, but he must also be made aware that he too has a certain set of values that might possibly be detrimental to his program if he is too rigid in adhering to them.

Industry has also profited from the insights of anthropology, particularly in the area of labor-management relations. The first important industrial study undertaken by applied anthropologists was carried out at the Hawthorne Western Electric Plant just outside Chicago in 1933. This study, using anthropological research methods, discovered ways in which better relations between management and staff could be developed, thus improving working conditions, morale, and also production. A similar analysis of administrative policies, carried out in hospitals, showed that morale is often lower among employees in medical institutions than in industry in general. A thorough study pointed up the fact that many of the problems stemmed from the fact that there are usually two sets of bosses to be satisfied—the doctors and the hospital administrators. Another phenomenon further complicated the situation. Medical workers could not look forward to promotions up through the ranks because each higher status was not achieved so much through industry and ability as through having the right qualifications and schooling. A ward aide could not look forward to someday becoming a nurse; a nurse could not look forward to becoming a doctor. The hospital personnel was actually organized in a hierarchy of castelike occupational statuses and therefore had no opportunity for upward mobility. This, of course, was extremely discouraging to the employees, since our culture definitely values promotions as a symbol of success and hard work.

Although most of the activities thus far cited have involved cultural anthropologists, it must not be overlooked that the talents of the physical anthropologists have also been brought to bear in solving a variety of problems in our own and other cultures. A very good example of this is the research that has greatly altered the nature of the garment industry in the past few years. After careful studies of the physical characteristics of the American public, recommendations were made to clothing manufacturers so that they might better meet the size demands of the consumer. The recent trend toward "tall," "short," and "stout" sizes represents an awareness by the manufacturer of the variability of the human physique in America.

In 1945 a Harvard research team under the direction of the late Ernest Hooton undertook a similar type of anthropometric study—this time of American postures and posteriors. The result was a design for a more comfortable seat for trains, buses, and airplanes.

Probably the most interesting application of the knowledge of physical anthropology to twentieth-century problems has been the work of W. M. Krogman, who has sometimes been referred to as "the anthropological detective." Dr. Krogman has become well known for the aid he has given to police departments in all parts of the country in analyzing skeletal material for age, sex, race, and evidence of injury. His scientific efforts have been instrumental in resolving a number of murder and missing person cases. Similar types of identification were made of skeletal material of men killed in action in World War II, by students of physical anthropology working in Graves Registration Divisions. It was a grim job but it quite naturally was given to those who know the nature of the human skeleton, the physical anthropologists.

Today the physical anthropologists are being called upon to make even more unusual applications of their knowledge of the anatomy of man. The science fiction of yesterday has become the reality of today as man stands on the brink of an era of space exploration. Travel in space must be prefaced by highly precise studies of the human organism—its plasticity and limits of endurance. Just as the engineer who designs the space ship must know the strengths and weaknesses of the materials to be used, so the physical anthropologist must be able to predict the qualities of the men who will pilot these machines into the far reaches of the universe.

ANTHROPOLOGY STUDIES "PRIMITIVE" PEOPLES

Although anthropology studies the physical, social, and cultural aspects of man, it should be pointed out that the discipline is somewhat restricted in scope by the fact that it has traditionally studied primitive peoples. The word "primitive" has become so misused and misunderstood that anthropologists have often substituted the word "nonliterate" to refer to the subjects of their study. When the anthropologist speaks of "primitive" people, he refers to those societies of aboriginal America, Africa, the Pacific, and Asia which, in contrast to Western "civilized" societies, generally have (1) an absence of a written language of their own, (2) a relatively simple technology, (3) social institutions (particularly economics and political organization) that are relatively less complex, (4) small populations, (5) a relatively isolated habitat, and consequently, (6) a slower rate of cultural change. It must be kept in mind, however, that not all "primitive" peoples satisfy all of these criteria. Some West Africans, for example, live in urban communities and have elaborate and complex political organizations.

The emphasis on primitive societies stems from early interest in the oddities of native cultures described by explorers, missionaries, and traders, and in the use of primitive cultures for documentation of the schemes of social and cultural evolutionists of the nineteenth century who saw such primitive societies as representing stages in a great evolution of mankind from savagery to civilization.

Today anthropologists continue to concentrate on primitives with the view that they represent many experiments in human living under various environmental conditions, and also because they are more representative of human culture, as it has existed for a million years or more, than people who live in modern industrial nations. While primitive societies have been their primary concern, modern anthropologists certainly have not neglected the more industrialized civilizations of the world. Recent anthropological studies have documented the culture of such nations as Yugoslavia, Japan, England, the United States, Soviet Russia, and Germany.

The thing about anthropology that is frequently misunderstood is that studies of primitives are not just descriptions of the exotic and bizarre. These studies are used to establish generalizations or principles of human behavior that apply to men everywhere regardless of whether they are "primitive" or "civilized."

SUGGESTED READINGS

BOAS, FRANZ. "Anthropology," *Encyclopedia of the Social Sciences,* 1944. (Describes the scope of anthropological inquiry.)

BROOM, ROBERT. "The Ape-Men," *Scientific American,* November, 1949. (The characteristics and significance of Australopithecus fossils.)

COON, C. S. "What is Race?" *Atlantic Monthly,* October, 1957. (A summary of existing knowledge on racial origins and race classification.)

DEBORHEGYI, S. F. "Aqualung Archeology," *Natural History,* March, 1958. (Describes a new wrinkle in archeology and its value in collecting Pre-Columbian artifacts.)

GREENBERG, JOSEPH. "Current Trends in Linguistics," *Science,* 130:1165, 1959. (Describes the subject matter and methods of linguistic science and its interdisciplinary value.)

HARDING, C. F. "The Social Anthropology of American Industry," *American Anthropologist,* 57:1218, 1955. (An anthropological analysis of the characteristics of modern industry.)

HOWELLS, W. W. "The Distribution of Man," *Scientific American,* September, 1960. (Discusses the racial distribution in the world at various periods and comments on the factors producing changes in racial populations.)

KROGMAN, W. M. "How Your Children Grow," *Saturday Evening Post,* July 14–21, 1962. (Reveals new methods of predicting the rate and amount of children's growth.)

LIBBY, W. F. "Radiocarbon Dating," *Science,* 133:621, 1961. (How archeologists determine the age of materials through carbon 14 analysis.)

MURDOCK, G. P. "Anthropology and its Contribution to Public Health," *American Journal of Public Health,* 42:7, 1952. (Explains how anthropologists can make a valuable contribution to the field of public health.)

PURSGLOVE, S. D. "Science takes the Measure of Man," *Popular Mechanics,* July, 1961. (How the U.S. Air Force is using anthropometry in space research.)

REDFIELD, ROBERT. "The Folk Society," *American Journal of Sociology,* 52:293, 1947. (Describes the characteristics of the "ideal" primitive society.)

SNYDER, RICHARD G. "Manned Space Flight Vehicles and the Physical Anthropologist," *American Journal of Physical Anthropology,* 19:185–94, 1961. (Anthropology's contributions to space research.)

STRUMER, LOUIS M. "History of a Dig," *Scientific American,* March, 1955. (How archeologists located and excavated a site on the coast of Peru.)

THIEME, F. P. "The Population as a Unit of Study," *American Anthropologist,* 54:504, 1952. (Stresses the importance of studying populations in studies of evolution and race.)

WISSLER, CLARK. "How Science Deciphers Man's Past," *Natural History,* March, 1943. (Excellent summary of the activities of archeologists; well illustrated.)

Paperbound Books

BENEDICT, RUTH. *Race: Science and Politics.* Viking Press. (Deals with race and racism.)

CLARK, GRAHAME. *Archaeology and Society.* Barnes and Noble. (Describes methods and interpretations in European prehistoric archeology.)

COON, CARLETON (ed.). *Anthropology—A to Z.* Grosset and Dunlap. (Deals mostly with physical anthropology.)

KLUCKHOHN, CLYDE. *Mirror For Man.* Fawcett Publications, Inc. (A classic introduction to cultural anthropology.)

LEGROS CLARK, W. E. *History of the Primates, an Introduction to the Study of Fossil Man.* University of Chicago. (An excellent introduction to human evolution.)

OLIVER, DOUGLAS. *Invitation to Anthropology.* Doubleday. (A brief outline of anthropology's scientific interests.)

SAPIR, EDWARD. *Language.* Harcourt, Brace and Company. (The sounds, structure, and meaning of languages around the world.)

TAX, SOL (ed.). *Anthropology Today.* University of Chicago Press. (Summary of the state of knowledge in major areas of anthropological inquiry.)

2

Anthropology and
Its Related Fields

After being introduced to someone in our culture, the first question that usually enters our mind is "What does he do?" If we know a person's occupation, we also know something of the role he plays in society. We know what kinds of contributions he makes to the community and to a certain extent, we have a good idea of what his interests are and what positions he will take on certain issues. Having now been introduced to the discipline of anthropology, the reader should be interested in the role of anthropology in the community of scholarly disciplines and what contributions it has made and is making to the study of human behavior.

ANTHROPOLOGY'S CONTRIBUTIONS

Perhaps the most important of anthropology's contributions to the study of human behavior has been its role in integrating the various disciplines dealing with man. It has tended to draw together the data and theory from the humanities, the natural and behavioral sciences, and focus them upon the human animal. With the concept of culture at the heart of all its varied activities, anthropology has tended to concentrate on the overall problems, feeling that studying man in terms of special aspects of behavior impedes the following of problems wherever they might lead. Anthropology has drawn heavily on the findings and formulations of sociology, economics, history, biology, and countless other disciplines but has refused to study man within the narrow confines of any single specialized field.

While anthropology recognizes the great advantage of specialization and is grateful to the several disciplines for their contributions, the science of man is more interested in the total configuration of culture— i.e., in its organic wholeness—than it is in the minute details of every facet of man's life. To put it in another way, the anthropologist, if forced to do so, will sacrifice detail for form.

Not only has anthropology refused to atomize the study of man's behavior but it has also refused to concentrate on the people of any one part of the world for its studies. Since its very inception anthropology has taken a cross-cultural approach to man. By comparing peoples in all parts of the world the science of man seeks to discover common denominators among cultures and to document the range of variability in human behavior. The anthropologist is, to this extent, a citizen of the world, not specializing in a single culture but trying to understand all facets of *Homo sapiens* everywhere.

Because anthropology has not built its theory on a single system of values, and because of its interest in all cultures whether labeled "primitive" or "civilized," it has encouraged objective and rational thinking. Ignorance of the way of life of other peoples tends to foster the belief that one's own way is the only way, and such an attitude does little to promote universal understanding. Anthropology helps to make people aware of other varieties of culture and therefore helps to clarify thinking about other peoples by making people realize that any culture that satisfies the needs of its members is as good and efficient as any other.

Understanding Ourselves

Not only does the science of man help us understand the ways of other people; it also helps us understand ourselves. A number of years ago the French author, André Gide, wrote a book entitled *The Counterfeiters*. In this book Gide has his characters (university students) engage in a scientific discussion about a certain fish that, due to its physical structure, is unable to rise to the surface, nor is it able to descend to the bottom of the ocean. Such a fish, it will be realized, has no knowledge of its surroundings. It does not know that it is swimming in water because it has never seen anything else. It has experienced neither sand nor air. Many people today are in the same situation as that fish. These people have no insight into their own way of life, because they have never been exposed to any other. Anthropology helps this sort of person break out of his shell of intellectual isolation and get some insight into his own and other ways of life. As Clyde Kluckhohn put it, "Anthropology holds up a great mirror to man and lets him look at himself in his infinite variety" (1957:16).

Anthropology and Determinism

The facts and findings of anthropology have also proved to be a mighty weapon against deterministic thinking. An analysis of the history of social and cultural thought reveals that all too frequently, scholars, without a full acquaintance with the facts (or perhaps without the desire to take all the facts into consideration), have arrived at oversimplified explanations of social and cultural phenomena. In America, for example, Madison Grant (1916) maintained that the degree of racial purity and percentage of Nordic blood in a population were all that need be considered in assessing its relative superiority or inferiority. In Germany Karl Marx (1867) saw the evolution of society largely in terms of a long economic struggle between "haves" and "have nots." In France Montesquieu (1748) postulated that the form of institutions of any society was determined by the geographical setting. These are but a few of the many formulations of geographical, racial, economic, social, and cultural determinism which have cluttered men's minds for centuries. When the historical and cross-cultural facts of anthropology are brought to bear on these inadequate theories their errors of oversimplification may easily be seen.

For example, Montesquieu's theory that desert climates produce monotheistic religions can immediately be quashed by the anthropologists who can give multiple examples of desert cultures where polytheistic religions have existed from the very beginning. Claims of white superiority seem ridiculous indeed when anthropology produces evidence that African negroes smelted iron and lived in urban communities when the ancestors of Western Europeans were living in brush shelters and caves and manufacturing stone tools. In like manner the study of prehistoric culture development by archeologists has exposed the fallacy of Marx's economic deterministic thesis that human civilization evolved through revolution and class struggle.

The above, then, are some of the unique contributions that anthropology makes to the knowledge of human behavior. Now that we know something of the scope and flavor of the study let us look at what kind of company it keeps. In other words let us look at how it is related to other scientific disciplines which are also interested in the nature of the animal Man.

ECONOMICS

Although anthropology frequently draws upon the theories that have been developed in the field of economics, it can generally be stated that the anthropologist has found great difficulty incorporating the major part of economic theory into a cross-cultural approach to man. The main reason for this is that economics is probably the most culture bound of any of the social sciences. Economic theory not only deals almost entirely with economic activities in European society, but, with the exception of the specialty known as economic history, with the economics of modern or present day Europeans. All of the models and instruments of analysis, such as the price system or market phenomenon, have been developed in terms of a European set of values. Economics is very much a matter of values. No one ever has the means for getting everything that he wants. Therefore he must choose to do those things, or get those things that he will enjoy the most. Economists call this "maximizing one's satisfactions." Economic behavior then is a matter of making rational choices. People who have grown up in the Western, or European, tradition tend to make a certain type of choices. Their decisions are rational in terms of their value orientation, but these same choices might seem exceedingly irrational to someone from another culture. Therefore, since many of the formulations economists use to predict economic behavior and its consequences are based on European value systems, they will be of little use when applied to a South Sea island people or a West African people.

Some economists have maintained that their economic theories cannot be applied to primitive peoples since Western industrial civilization is so complex and primitive culture is so simple. They say that, after all, primitives do not have banks, capital, business cycles, dividends, interest, rent, wages, or any of the things economists should concern themselves with. More liberal economists, however, see the value of analyses of primitive economic systems and welcome attempts on the part of anthropologists to develop generalizations about economic behavior that will apply not only to Western man but to man in general. They have felt that perhaps primitives do have equivalents of banks, capital, business cycles, etc., but they have not been heretofore recognized as such because the anthropological accounts of primitive societies have not been detailed enough in this area and also because the economists have not done a great deal of this kind of research themselves.

Still another very fundamental difference separates economics and anthropology. Economics studies but one aspect of modern European culture and, while this specialization has its advantages, it also has its disadvantages. The discipline, in its efficiency of specialization, often loses sight of the greater picture—i.e., the way economic life relates to other facets of living such as art, religion, and sex and family behavior. On the other hand, the anthropologist with a more general approach is likely to more readily see form and interrelation of institutions but is often pathetically inept at describing and analyzing purely economic phenomena. His remarks about economics are more often than not descriptive rather than analytical, and he borrows terms from economics and uses them to make his study seem more scientific and erudite. Both disciplines could profit from excursions into one another's territory.

POLITICAL SCIENCE

Like economics, political science has tended to center its attention on the behavior of Western man, but there are indications today that political scientists are beginning to think more in terms of a truly worldwide perspective. Modern scholars in this area have often directed their attention to nativistic movements in Africa and Asia, and the current interest in underdeveloped countries has presented a new challenge to the student of government. There have also been other changes in the approach of political science that have drawn its interests closer to those of anthropology. Whereas this discipline formerly studied only forms and theories of government, it now studies political behavior of groups and individuals as well.

Although there are trends that indicate a more cross-cultural approach in the future, most political science departments in American universities continue to dwell upon American and European modes of political behavior. Courses in comparative government are rarely comparative in the anthropological sense. Such courses usually study political systems and behavior of, say, the United States, Great Britain, France, and the U.S.S.R. but ignore several thousand governmental systems to be found among primitive and non-Western peoples. One critic of political science (not an anthropologist) maintains that even when foreign institutions are studied the methodological frame of reference is to a great extent set by concepts derived from English or American constitutional experience. Thus we find that most courses in comparative government do little with political organizations based on kinship and family affiliation.

Political science is not to be criticized for dealing with problems that press for solution. Americans must understand their system of government and the nature of political behavior in their society. When so much remains to be understood about the nature of government in our own society, we can hardly expect political scientists to go chasing off to far corners of the world to accommodate anthropologists who would like to see more studies of non-Western government. In drawing this comparison between political science and anthropology the intention is to point out that while both disciplines are concerned with human behavior the scopes and approaches are different. Political scientists are studying different things, not the wrong thing.

Since anthropology is concerned with all aspects of human behavior, anthropologists are also students of government, but there are few who feel adequate in this area. Anthropological discussions of political life have in the past been most unscientific and shallow. Often they have involved only description of systems utilized by peoples at various subsistence levels or have shown how societies use real or imagined kinship as the basis of their political loyalties. Some headway has been made in the study of primitive law, but for the most part studies of primitive and non-Western government have been few in number and far from adequate.

HISTORY

The statement was once made by Maitland (1911) that anthropology had the choice of being history or nothing. This was, of course, an expression of the opinion that laws of human behavior could never be discovered, and, therefore, anthropology would be forced to be a particularizing rather than a generalizing discipline.

While anthropologists in many of the large universities find themselves in combined departments with sociologists, they sometimes feel ill at ease in this association and would prefer affiliation with the historians. Actually, the nature of the two disciplines, anthropology and history, provides considerable justification for this feeling. To begin with, Herodotus has been referred to as the father both of history and of anthropology. The activities and theoretic position of Franz Boas and other pioneers in American anthropology have frequently been referred to collectively as the American Historical School of anthropology, and even today anthropologists take pride in the somewhat antiquarian flavor of their discipline.

While the American anthropologist uses scientific procedures in his approach to human phenomena, he often thinks of himself as doing "contemporary cultural history" from primary rather than secondary (literary) sources. When the anthropologist is in the field studying a primitive or foreign people, he notes significant behavior trends and values much as the cultural historian tries to present an account of the significant events and attitudes of let us say the Elizabethan or Victorian eras of England so that we might have a better understanding of particular cultural periods. A strong advocate of anthropology as history rather than science is Evans-Pritchard, who refers to ethnologists as the historians of primitive people. In his book *Social Anthropology* he extends a challenge.

One has a right, I think, to ask those who assert that the aim of social anthropology is to formulate sociological laws similar to the laws formulated by natural scientists to produce formulations which resemble what are called laws in these sciences. Up to the present nothing even remotely resembling what are called laws in the natural sciences has been adduced . . . The generalizations which have so far been attempted have, moreover, been so vague and general as to be, even if true, of little use, and they have rather easily tended to become mere tautologies and platitudes on the level of common sense deduction. (1956:57)

While few anthropologists would reject the statement that to date the literature of anthropology could be considered "contemporary cultural history" and that their generalizations concerning man and culture are not in the nature of "laws" as found in the physical and natural sciences, the majority of anthropologists would hastily add that the goal toward which they are working is the ability to make more valid generalizations and predictions concerning the human and cultural nature of man and the dynamics of culture.

GEOGRAPHY

Another discipline kindred to anthropology is geography. While the older variety of geography—that is, physical geography—deals with such matters as climatic zones, varieties of soils, topographic features such as mountains, steppes, plateaus, etc., and the relationship of land masses to bodies of water, modern geography, known as human geography, is man-centered rather than nature-centered and is interested in many of the same problems that concern anthropology. The primary interest of human geography is the study of how man adjusts to the variety of environmental problems that face him in various parts of the world. It is, so to speak, the study of man-nature relationships. If one were asked to point out the basic differences between human geography and cultural anthropology, the answer would probably be that the former is primarily concerned with the natural environment and the manner in which it shapes culture, while anthropology gives equal attention to the factors of man's geographical setting, his biological makeup, his traditions, social situation, and the nature of his contacts with other peoples.

Human geographers share a definite interest in the concept of culture and their studies are often cross-cultural. It is not unusual, therefore, that human geography is referred to in many circles as anthropogeography. Geographers have both drawn upon and contributed to the knowledge that anthropology has developed concerning man and the nature of his cultures in all parts of the world.

SOCIOLOGY

Anthropology and sociology have long been considered sister sciences, but most students have had a much greater opportunity to familiarize themselves with sociology because of the greater availability of these courses in college curriculums. Therefore, when students first discover the less popular sister, anthropology, they are interested in learning precisely how the two differ. It is especially difficult for the beginning student to understand where the two disciplines differ because anthropologists and sociologists often confuse the issue themselves by invading one another's territory. For example, W. Lloyd Warner, an anthropologist, moved from his initial study of Australian aborigines to a lifetime study of social stratification in America. William Foote Whyte, the author of *Street Corner Society*, identifies himself as a sociologist but admits that most of his research methods might be labeled "anthropological" rather than "sociological." Sociologists Robert and Helen Lynd studied "Middletown" using participant observation and other traditional anthropological techniques of investigation. In spite of the fact that interests or research methods may be hard to label as either sociological or anthropological, both anthropologists and sociologists seem quick to claim professional distinctness, although intellectually the two fields should be complementary sciences. As John W. Bennett and Kurt H. Wolff have stated:

They [sociology and anthropology] behave somewhat like political parties; they possess professionalized bodies and ideologies, are organized for the protection of their members and prerogatives, and carry on propaganda to please the voters. (1956:329)

It might also be added that like political parties they both have man's interests at heart but have somewhat different ideas as to how to serve them best.

Because of the overlapping nature of anthropology and sociology any discussion that attempts to explain the differences between the two sciences runs the danger of drawing the lines too sharply and dwelling on minor details. In many cases anthropologists and sociologists may be found studying the same kinds of phenomena with the same methods and therefore we shall think in terms of general emphases in the two disciplines. Of course, physical anthropology, with its close relationship to the biological sciences, is quite distinct from sociology, except perhaps in the area where they have mutual interest, i.e., demography. On the other hand, cultural anthropology and sociology are very similar in interests and procedures, but differences do exist.

Perhaps the most basic difference between sociology and anthropology is that anthropology has concentrated to a greater extent on the simpler and more isolated societies of the world, while sociology (at least in America) has been primarily concerned with Western European civilization, particularly that of the United States. Sociology has sometimes been defined as the "anthropology" of particular civilized societies. Partly as a result of this tendency to work in primitive societies, the "science of man" works more in terms of whole cultures whereas the "science of society" operates more in terms of aspects of complex civilized society.

Of course, the relatively smaller size and greater isolation of most primitive societies allows for a more holistic or functional approach, which is difficult or impossible to accomplish in modern European society. Any study that would document all aspects of a European civilization and their interrelationships would take a lifetime to complete. Booth's study (1891) of workmen's living conditions in London filled four volumes in describing only one segment of London society.

While there is great variation in the activities of research workers in sociology, the discipline represents a more statistical and detached approach to man and society than does anthropology, and because of its more quantitative and impersonal nature it has frequently been referred to as the "science of probabilities." The sociologist tends to submerge man in his environment, explaining many of his actions in terms of his social or economic milieu. On the other hand, anthropologists have attempted to view their objects of study as fellow human beings, finding explanations for their actions in cultural values and personal motivations. As the dean of American anthropology, A. L. Kroeber has put it:

> We want face-to-face experience with our subjects. The anonymity of the sociological questionnaire seems to us bloodless, even though its specificity and quantifiability are obvious assets to which we cannot easily attain by our methods. (1959:400)

Anthropology has traditionally worked in terms of a worldwide perspective, emphasizing similarities and differences among men everywhere. Although sociology has used anthropological data as a kind of comparative documentation for its findings, until very recently few sociologists have engaged in worldwide comparative research themselves. In Europe they have tended more toward the cross-cultural approach, but this interest, to date, has not been widely shared by American sociologists.

Sociology stresses that man is a social animal and its prime objects for study are social institutions such as family organization, economics, education, and political organization. Anthropology also deals with man as a social animal, but in viewing man as a builder of culture it touches on aspects of human behavior that frequently do not involve social organization—the arts, language, and religion.

Matters of time perspective also set the two disciplines apart, in that modern sociology deals primarily with events that have occurred within the last few hundred years, whereas anthropology attempts to reconstruct history and analyze its effect on culture back to the very dawn of time. Because of this, anthropologists have frequently been labeled antiquarians, and it is interesting to note that while there are numerous anthropological museums there are no sociological ones.

The Laboratories of Sociologists and Anthropologists

Because of the difference in frames of reference and conception of problems, field methods in the two sciences have likewise developed along different lines. Since most anthropological research has been carried out in smaller and more isolated groups, the investigators in this field have seen little need for sampling techniques or schedules as they are known in sociology. Instead, they have utilized the techniques of observation, participation, and interview. The field investigator selects a few key informants familiar with the culture as a whole or its specialized aspects and utilizes the information provided by these people in developing his analysis of the culture.

The social scientist frequently speaks of his field situation as his "laboratory." Sociology, which is very quantitative in its approach, attempts to control its laboratory situation by statistical methods. Through the use of multiple correlations, various factors are held constant while others are shifted about in order to ascertain the relative importance of each. In some respects the anthropologist's situation is less complex. When he has a hypothesis to test, he locates a tribe that has the conditions for experimental observation ready-built into the culture. This procedure is well exemplified by the Samoan study of Margaret Mead. In the introduction to *Coming of Age in Samoa* Mead states the characteristics of her laboratory situation for testing E. Stanley Hall's thesis that adolescent personality difficulties have a physiological basis. Believing that such adolescent difficulties were culturally determined (generated) Margaret Mead chose:

. . . to go to a different civilization and make a study of human beings under different cultural conditions in some other part of the world. For such studies the anthropologist chooses quite simple peoples, whose society has never attained the complexity of our own. In this choice of primitive people . . . the anthropologist is guided by the knowledge that the analysis of a simpler civilization is more possible of attainment. (1959:14)

From such societies, different in historical development, language, and religious ideas "it is possible to learn many things about the effect of a civilization upon the individuals within it" (*ibid.*:15).

In drawing comparisons between sociology and anthropology in matters of frame of reference and methods, it is not the intention of the author to cast one discipline in a more favorable light than the other. Each discipline has its own perspective and its own techniques of study. Social science needs both approaches.

There is also an increasing tendency for the disciplines of anthropology and sociology to draw closer together and share an identity of interests and methods. Many anthropologists have taken a great interest in studies of American culture and subculture, thereby refusing to be restricted to the study of certain kinds of people in certain areas of the world. As primitive people become more Westernized and industrialized, anthropologists have been turning more and more to sociological methods of investigation. On the other hand, sociology has been expanding its interests to include cross-cultural comparisons in such areas as the study of aging, group behavior, and social change.

PSYCHOLOGY

It would not be proper to conclude our discussion of the relationship of anthropology to the other social and behavioral sciences without considering how it relates to the disciplines of psychology and social psychology.

Psychology is sometimes referred to as a social science but is more commonly known as a behavioral science. It is concerned with the study of sensory, motor, and cognitive behavioral characteristics of human beings. It is the study of the individual and his unique pattern of responses to stimuli of many kinds, including cultural and social.

Social psychology, an outgrowth of both sociology and psychology, tends to place great emphasis on the influence of the group (family, crowd, or community) on individual behavior and personality development. Although the cultural factor is taken into consideration, it is not as highly stressed as the influence of the social environment. Neither psychologists nor social psychologists have been as prone to deal cross-culturally with man as have culture and personality specialists whose research into man's psychological makeup has been carried on as a part of cultural anthropology.

SUGGESTED READINGS

American Council of Learned Societies, *Newsletter*, "Out of Context," 3:11 (Summer), 1952. (How anthropology and history can complement one another.)

BENEDICT, RUTH. "Anthropology and the Humanities," *American Anthropologist*, 50:585, 1948. (How the methods of the sciences and of the humanities can combine to produce better anthropological studies.)

BERNARD, J. "Observation and Generalization in Cultural Anthropology," *The American Journal of Sociology*, 50:284, 1945. (Critique of anthropological field methods.)

BIERSTEDT, R. "Limitations of Anthropological Methods in Sociology; with Comments by C. Kluckhohn," *American Journal of Sociology*, 54:22, 1948. (Stresses the inadequacy of anthropological methods in studying Western society; article is followed by a rejoinder by Clyde Kluckhohn.)

KROEBER, A. L. "The History of the Personality of Anthropology," *American Anthropologist*, 61:398, 1959. (Similarities and differences between anthropology and sociology.)

REDFIELD, ROBERT. "The Art of Social Science," *American Journal of Sociology*, 54:181, 1948. (The relationship of social sciences to the humanities.)

————. "A Contribution of Anthropology to the Education of the Teacher," *School Review*, November, 1945. (The importance of the concept of integrated culture to the public school teacher.)

ROSENSTIEL, A. "Anthropology and Childhood Education," *School and Society*, 87:482, 1959. (How anthropology can help the classroom teacher better understand the problems and need of her students.)

SPINDLER, GEORGE. "Anthropology in the Social Studies Curriculum," *National Education Journal*, 47:626, 1958. (What anthropology can contribute to elementary and secondary school social studies curriculums.)

TOMARS, A. "Some Problems in the Sociologist's Use of Anthropology," *American Sociological Review*, 8:625, 1943. (An evaluation of the field of anthropology by a sociologist. This article is followed (p. 635) by a rejoinder, "What Price Glory? The Counterplaint of an Anthropologist" by Loren Eiseley.)

Paperbound Books

BOAS, FRANZ. *Anthropology and Modern Life.* W. W. Norton and Company. (How a knowledge of anthropology enables one to look with greater freedom at the problems confronting our civilization.)

HOSELITZ, BERT. *A Reader's Guide to the Social Sciences.* Free Press. (The scope and interests of anthropology and other social sciences; excellent annotated bibliography for each discipline.)

SPINDLER, GEORGE. *Education and Culture: Anthropological Approaches.* Holt, Rinehart and Winston. (Problems of American education considered cross-culturally.)

ZNANIECKI, FLORIAN. *Cultural Sciences: Their Origin and Development.* University of Illinois Press. (History of the development of sociology as a cultural science.)

3

The History of Anthropological Thought

In order to understand the perspective of anthropology today it is necessary to trace the historical development of its scope and theory. Anthropology, like all disciplines, has gone through a long period of growth wherein various theoretical "schools" of thought flourished. Although "school" thinking is seldom found in modern anthropology, many individuals and groups of scholars have contributed to the scientific position of anthropology today.

ANCIENT WRITINGS

While descriptive accounts of primitive cultures date back a long way, anthropology as a science is a mere youngster among the behavioral sciences. Long before anyone conceived of such a discipline, ancient scholars were turning out detailed descriptions of the peoples and cultures that occupied the then known world. In the fifth century B.C. Herodotus qualified as the "father of anthropology" by documenting Egyptian patterns of dress, division of labor, religious ceremony, racial type, and language. This material, published in a book entitled *Euterpé*, is but part of his total writings, which included ethnographic descriptions of Babylonians, Scythians, and other Mediterranean peoples.

The Roman philosopher Lucretius (98–55 B.C.) equally qualified as an anthropologist when he speculated on such theoretical questions as the origin of speech, religion, and the arts. Concerning the latter, he wrote:

A garment tied on the body was in use before a dress of woven stuff. Woven stuff comes after iron, because iron is needed for weaving a web; and in no other way can such finely polished things be made, as heddles and spindles, shuttles and ringing yarnbeams. And nature impelled men to work up the wool before womankind; for the male sex in general far excels the other in skill and is much more ingenious; until the rugged countrymen so upbraided them with it, that they were glad to give it over into the hands of the women and take their share in supporting hard toil. (1873)

Lucretius' speculations concerning the sequence of metal and weaving, the origin of a division of labor, and the natural aptitudes of the sexes, while grossly in error, represent an intriguing chapter in the development of scholarly interest in the nature of man and culture.

Less speculative and more descriptive in nature was the work of the Roman historian Tacitus, who wrote a splendid ethnographic account of the German people. While this 98 A.D. account deals with nearly all aspects of indigenous German culture, a single example of his work—that dealing with family life—will reveal an approach very much like that found in modern anthropological monographs.

Their marriage code . . . is strict, and indeed no part of their manners is more praiseworthy. Almost alone among barbarians they are content with one wife, except a very few among them, and these not from sensuality, but because their noble birth procures for them many offers of alliance. The wife does not bring a dower to the husband but the husband to the wife . . . [The bride] is reminded by the ceremony which inaugurates marriage that she is her husband's partner in toil and danger, destined to suffer and to dare with him alike both in peace and in war . . . Very rare for so numerous a population is adultery, the punishment for which is prompt, and in the husband's power . . .
In every household the children, naked and filthy grow up with those stout frames and limbs which we so much admire. Every mother suckles her own offspring, and never entrusts it to servants and nurses. The master is not distinguished from the slave by being brought up with greater delicacy. Both live amid the flocks and lie on the same ground till the freeborn are distinguished by age and recognized by merit. The young men marry late, and their vigour is thus unimpaired . . . Nor are the maidens hurried into marriage . . . sister's sons are held in as much esteem by their uncles as by their fathers . . . but every man's own children are his heirs and successors, and there are no wills . . . The more relatives he has, the more numerous his connections, the more honoured is his old age. (1942:717–19)

Anthropological writings were not restricted to European authors but were also produced by Chinese scholars of the Han dynasty who made detailed studies of many tribal groups living in the more isolated regions of their country.

All of these ancient accounts seem naive and impressionistic by modern anthropological standards, but they do point to an early interest in the nature of man and in the diversity of his cultures. While scholars of many periods recorded the quaint customs of primitives they met in their travels, it was not until the eighteenth and nineteenth centuries that the travel accounts of explorers, traders, and missionaries began to give rise to speculation about the nature of human variability and the origins of culture.

EXPLORERS AND NATURALISTS

It was during this period that the vast boundaries of the discipline of anthropology were established. It was not uncommon for many of the early voyagers to carry natural scientists as part of their expedition. These naturalists—such as Forster, who traveled with Cook on his second exploratory voyage—besides being interested in the flora and fauna they observed on the various islands and continents, were extremely interested in the aboriginal peoples they encountered. They recorded their strange customs and manners, but they also concerned themselves with describing the racial peculiarities of these exotic people. Through an analysis of these racial characteristics they felt that the mysteries of geographic origins of these native peoples could better be unraveled. Thus it was that many accounts of primitives included not only descriptions of culture but of physical type as well, thereby foreshadowing the development of the science of anthropology with its interest in both the cultural and physical characteristics of man.

AMATEUR ANTHROPOLOGISTS

The eighteenth and nineteenth centuries were without doubt times when there was growing interest in the peculiarities of primitive societies. Concerning this development Clyde Kluckhohn wrote:

The first systematic anthropologists were gifted amateurs—physicians, natural historians, lawyers, businessmen—to whom anthropology was a hobby. They applied common sense, the habits they had learned in their professions, and the fashionable scientific doctrines of their day to the growing knowledge about "primitive" peoples. (1949:3)

Thomas Jefferson is a good example of this group of pioneers in the field of anthropology. Jefferson had lived among Indians and had developed a keen interest in their history, physical type, language, culture, and welfare. His greatest interest was the comparative study of languages, and he personally collected vocabularies of about fifty Indian tribes. Jefferson's interest in Indian prehistory prompted him to engage in considerable archeological research, and it is believed that it was Jefferson who first employed the concept of stratigraphy, a major concern in nearly all modern excavation. A fascinating, but little known, fact is that the ethnographic data collected by the Lewis and Clark expedition perhaps would not have been obtained had it not been for President Jefferson. In a section of Meriwether Lewis' orders marked "Ethnographic Information Desired," Jefferson classified the kinds of information he wanted the party to gather and gave full directions, including certain questions to ask, for the recording of the details of American Indian cultures.

MUSEUMS

Because anthropology began as the study of curiosities it is logical that museums played a large part in the formulation and encouragement of the science of man. Men have always enjoyed bringing together the artifacts of foreign people. Museums existed in Babylonia, Alexandria, and Rome. But in the mid-1800's it was demonstrated that the products of non-Western peoples could lend themselves to scientific treatment. In 1850, the Museum of Ethnology was established in Hamburg, Germany, and in 1866 the Peabody Museum of Archeology and Ethnology came into being at Harvard University for the purpose of collecting and analyzing cultural materials.

In 1851, A. H. Pitt-Rivers, working at the University Museum of Oxford, arranged the tools and weapons of contemporary peoples according to quality of workmanship and complexity, in an attempt to illustrate how man had evolved or progressed in his technical abilities. The mere problem of how to display primitive artifacts forced museum people to develop theoretical frames of reference for the classification of materials. Whereas early European museums often chose to display materials according to a developmental or evolutionary sequence, American museums in the early part of the present century classified materials according to geographical regions—a procedure that ultimately led to the concept of culture areas (regions of common culture).

SOCIAL, CULTURAL, AND BIOLOGICAL EVOLUTION

It is impossible to discuss the growth of the science of anthropology without noting the nineteenth century philosophical and scientific concept—evolution. Between 1840 and 1860 evolutionary ideas were popping up everywhere. In 1858 Charles Darwin learned that Alfred

Russel Wallace, a botanist working in the East Indies, had independently developed a theory of biological evolution much like his own. As early as 1855 the sociologist Herbert Spencer maintained that societies are like organisms and they progress from simple to complex forms according to "invariable laws." During this same period a third scholar in the United States, Lewis Henry Morgan, developed his own scheme of cultural evolution apparently unaware of the work of Spencer and Darwin.

With the development of this evolutionary frame of reference and a fund of data about primitive peoples available in museums and in the accounts of various travelers, missionaries, and government administrators, all of the ingredients were now available for the scientific study of man, to be known as anthropology. *The Origin of Species* (Darwin 1859) had established man as an animal, subject to many of the same drives and needs that motivate other social animals, and Spencer had defined the task of the social scientist as that of tracing the development of human society from its most savage to its most civilized state.

The force of evolutionary thought was not to be denied and the result was the first theoretical formulation of cultural anthropology, the "school" of cultural evolution.

Tylor and Morgan

Although many scholars were instrumental in formulating and advancing this school of thought, the names Edward B. Tylor and Lewis Henry Morgan stand out above all others. Edward B. Tylor, an Englishman, was learning his father's brass foundry business when, as a result of a trip to Mexico, he became interested in the nature of primitive man. On the other side of the Atlantic, Morgan, an upstate New York lawyer handling a land claims case for the Iroquois Indians, became so intrigued by their unique family organization that he spent the rest of his life studying Indian groups and speculating on the growth and development of man's culture.

Although there is little evidence that Tylor and Morgan were ever in contact, the theories that they developed were remarkably similar and may be summarized as follows:

Culture had evolved in successive stages, from a condition of savagery to one of civilization. This succession of stages was essentially the same in all parts of the world. There had been, so to speak, a *unilineal* development of culture.

This development was quite natural since progress from simple to complex was the natural destiny of man. Not only was progress inevitable, but so was the order of stages of development, because all men had the same mental equipment and the same thought processes. This common endowment was referred to as the *psychic unity* of man.

In the scheme of the cultural evolutionists contemporary primitive cultures were considered representatives of the various stages of evolution of human culture. In his book *Primitive Culture* Edward Tylor describes his methods as follows:

By simply placing [European] nations at one end of the social series and savage tribes at the other, [and] arranging the rest of mankind between these limits . . . ethnographers are able to set up at least a rough scale of civilization . . . [representative of] a transition from the savage state to our own. (1871:26–27)

In their discussions of the development of culture the evolutionists pointed to the Australian aborigines (a hunting culture with stone tools) as being a living example of the *savage* stage of man's development, while a people like the Hopi (a village Indian group with pottery) represented the stage of *barbarism*. A people like the Western Europeans with an alphabet and a science of metallurgy fully qualified as occupying the final stage of development—*civilization*.

A characteristic activity of the cultural evolutionists was speculation on the origins of such institutions as the family, law, private property, and religion. Equally important in their method was the search for survivals—i.e., elements in modern cultures that represent holdovers from former stages of culture. "Old folklore themes" and "superstitions" were construed as evidence of earlier stages of development. They believed that survivals revealed the history of man's cultural growth just as biologists used to believe that the growing human embryo revealed the many prehuman stages in the biological evolution of man.

Although the reconstruction of human history according to the evolutionary principles of Tylor and Morgan has been rejected by most modern scholars, this school of thought made a number of valuable contributions to the discipline of anthropology. These are the *comparative method* (cross-cultural comparisons of cultures), the concept of *culture* (developed by Tylor), the framework for the analysis of social organization (Morgan's concepts of *affinity* and *consanguinity*), and the idea of the mental equality of all men (implied in the *psychic unity* principle), which was a rather unique idea for its time. In addition to the above contributions to anthropological thought it must be pointed out that Tylor, although not a university-trained scholar himself, held the first chair in anthropology at Oxford University and was responsible for training a number of British anthropologists. It must also be pointed out that Tylor was not as rigid a cultural evolutionist as

Morgan. His scientific attitude and knowledge of primitive peoples prevented this. Although he did believe in various cultural stages, he was always willing to weigh evidence even though it may have run contrary to his general theoretical position. In general, however, the cultural evolutionists—McLennan, Maine, Bachofen, Morgan, and others—had a tendency to neglect evidence of cultural borrowing as well as all facts not compatible with their evolutionary scheme. It was this shortcoming that brought violent negative reaction to evolutionary thought in Great Britain, Germany, and the United States.

THE DIFFUSIONISTS

In Great Britain certain scholars completely rejected the psychic unity principle and viewed man as extremely uninventive. They claimed that most of the elements that make up the cultures of the world had diffused from a single source. Two extreme advocates of this type of thinking, G. Elliot Smith and W. J. Perry, postulated that a number of cultural ideas such as kingship, irrigation, cremation, navigation, etc., derived from Egypt, their worldwide diffusion taking place when voyagers from this land circled the globe in search of precious gems.

G. Elliot Smith (1871–1937) had made an outstanding name for himself as an anatomist and physical anthropologist, but he made the mistake of going to Egypt to make a study of the brains of mummies. While in that country he became so impressed with the accomplishments of the ancient Egyptians that he credited all of the cultural accomplishments in the world to them. These ideas were developed into a body of theory referred to as the Manchester or Heliocentric (sun-centered) school of thought. Robert Lowie has summarized the diffusionist position as follows

1. Man is uninventive; hence culture arises only in exceptionally favorable circumstances, practically never twice independently.
2. Such circumstances existed only in ancient Egypt; hence elsewhere culture, except some of the simplest elements, must have spread from Egypt with the rise of navigation.
3. Civilization is naturally diluted as it spreads to outposts; hence decadence has played a tremendous role in human history. (1937:161)

Smith and Perry maintained that nearly every important cultural trait known to man came from the ancient Egyptians but, as Lowie (*ibid.*: 167) points out, they never quite explained how the Egyptians acquired the knowledge necessary to teach Eskimos how to build igloos or Siberians how to ski. While Smith and Perry had their day in England and even, surprisingly, attracted some good anthropologists to their theory, their school soon collapsed for want of supporting scientific data. In Germany, however, a much more convincing school of diffusionist thought was developing.

The German Diffusionists

The German diffusionist school commonly known as the "cultural historical" or *Kulturkreis* school gained recognition about 1925 through the writings of Robert F. Graebner and Father Wilhelm Schmidt. In comparison with the position of the cultural evolutionists and the British diffusionists the *Kulturkreis* school was scientific and scholarly. This school maintained that the cultures of the world had been built up by the spread of several core cultures (groups or clusters of traits) that diffused out of the Old World at various periods. For example, in the South Seas one complex of traits consisted of conical roofed huts, dugouts, spears, spearthrowers, and totemism, while a later unit was composed of yam cultivation, planked boats, gabled huts, heavy clubs, and the worship of the dead. The study of the cultural history of any particular group therefore necessitated making an analysis of its inventory of cultural traits. While modern day anthropologists credit this school with developing effective methods for assessing culture contacts, they deplore its disregard for geographical and psychological factors in the transmission of culture traits, its insistence on migration as the sole agent of diffusion, and its general tendency to utilize data supporting its theories while ignoring counterevidence. Although the culture-historical school scholars at one time exerted great influence on the work of German, Austrian, and Scandinavian anthropologists, their views are generally felt to be inadequate today by former adherents.

America's Historical Diffusionists

In America Franz Boas, the father of American anthropology, and others, had rejected the cultural evolution school and were establishing a body of anthropological theory themselves. Boas, his students, and colleagues, while different in their points of view and in their anthropological activities, have frequently been described as representing a school of thought that has sometimes been called either the American diffusionist or the American historical school. Some of these pioneers in American cultural anthropology were museum men while others were professors of anthropology at various universities, but they all had one important thing in common: They were not armchair theorists. All believed in comprehensive field observation. Boas, for example, made prolonged field trips to the Eskimos of Baffin Island and worked with Northwest Coast Indians almost every summer for about thirty years. He constantly impressed upon his students at Columbia University that every aspect of culture, no matter how insignificant, should be recorded. He knew that he had left many gaps in his study of the Eskimos and was determined that his students should profit from his mistakes. American ethnographers felt that mastery of the native language was essential and that not only should the anthropologist speak like the people but ideally he should learn to think like the people so that culture could be studied from the people's point of view.

Anthropologists working in the early part of the twentieth century were especially concerned with the fact that American Indian groups, and indeed, primitives all over the world, were losing their cultural identity through contact with the West. Thus, there was a feeling of urgency, a desire to get out and record what still remained of the "old" cultures. Because many of the aboriginal customs had already been lost, there was an attempt to reconstruct the precontact culture by working with old people who remembered how things had been done in the more traditional past. These interviews were supplemented by archeological data, by analysis of folklore, and by delving into historical documents written by traders, missionaries, "squaw men," and explorers.

AGE-AREA CONCEPT. Where these methods were not adequate, some American scholars developed hypothetical schemes such as the "age-area" concept for the reconstruction of cultural histories. The "age-area" method involved the study of trait diffusion and it is partly from this method that the American scholars got their "diffusionist" label. It assumed that cultural traits diffuse out from their point of origin in concentric circle patterns. By determining the areas of disribution of given traits, it was believed that their source and comparative age could be established. It was also believed that if the history of a number of traits could be established they would add up to the history of a particular culture.

BOAS' HISTORICAL APPROACH. While the diffusionist label has been given to the work and theory of Boas and other pioneers in American cultural anthropology, it should be pointed out that their preoccupation with the diffusion of particular cultural traits was merely part of an historical approach to culture. Actually, the discovery of evidence of cultural borrowing from one tribe to another was but the first step in the development of a cultural history of a given tribe. Boas maintained that culture must primarily be understood in an historical context. In Boas' view, Hopi Indians do not live in permanent villages and farm because they have moved up the evolutionary ladder to that point but rather because of a unique set of historical circumstances—opportunities and limitations—coming from both within and from outside the culture which have shaped their lives.

BOAS' GOAL FOR ANTHROPOLOGY. The American historical school has, of course, greatly influenced the growth and development of American anthropology. This is only natural since many American anthropologists have been greatly influenced by the work and teachings of Boas. More than just an influential teacher, Franz Boas made a number of major contributions to the growing discipline of anthropology. To begin with, Boas' insistence on exhaustive studies of cultures has provided modern anthropologists with valuable field data with which to test and document modern theoretical formulations concerning the nature of culture. He and his colleagues are largely responsible for the establishment of a systematic and orderly approach to the study of culture. Such concepts as culture traits, complexes, patterns, and areas have proved to be valuable research tools.

While there was a tendency in the American historical school to study separately the multiplicity of elements that make up a culture, these scholars constantly stressed a holistic approach to culture and warned against thinking of culture as anything but a configuration of interrelated traits and complexes.

Although Boas and others were scientific in their methods and approach (Boas often used statistical analysis of data), they were not scientific in the sense that they were trying to discover "laws" of human behavior. Boas was often criticized for his failure to generalize on his findings. To such critics Boas replied that the ultimate goal of anthropology *was* the formulation of general laws of human behavior and cultural growth, but he maintained that first it would be necessary to have more detailed studies of tribal cultures and histories. Without all of these facts no valid generalizations could be ventured. As early as 1896 Boas' theoretical point of view had been crystallized. He knew where he was going and how to get there. In a speech in that year he stated:

It will be well to restate at this place one of the principal aims of anthropological research. We agreed that certain laws exist which govern the growth of human culture, and it is our endeavor to discover these laws. The object of our investigation is to find the processes by which certain stages of culture have developed. The customs and beliefs themselves are not the ultimate objects of research. We desire to learn the reasons why such customs and beliefs exist. (1948:276)

Boas was always concerned with why certain traits found their way into a culture and others didn't. He also wanted to know how traits were incorporated into a new cultural context. In every case he thought that the reasons were historical, growing out of the unique cultural development of the group.

FUNCTIONALISM

Any discussion of modern anthropological perspective must of necessity note the contribution of two European schools of theory which, in spite of their theoretical differences, have both been labeled *functionalism*. The earlier of these was the French sociological school of functionalism, which originated just prior to World War I with the work of the British anthropologist A. R. Radcliffe-Brown. Radcliffe-Brown had been a student of the French sociologist Émile Durkheim and the anthropological theory that he developed was strongly influenced by Durkheim's analysis of Australian aboriginal society. The functionalism of Radcliffe-Brown stressed the importance of group or societal behavior and all but dropped the concept of culture. It is interesting to note that the best statement of this theoretical position, Radcliffe-Brown's *Andaman Islanders*, does not even list the word culture in its index. Tribal custom was interpreted in terms of social cohesion and integration and the individual was virtually ignored in an attempt to discover *laws* of group interaction. The function or purpose of such customs as funerals, puberty ceremonies, and feasts was to contribute to group solidarity and survival. All systems existed primarily to maintain the social structure and enhance social integration. A good example of A. R. Radcliffe-Brown's position may be seen in his interpretation of mourning in the Andaman Island study:

> For the society a death is the loss of one of its members, one of its constituent parts. A person occupies a definite position in society, has a certain share in social life, is one of the supports of the network of social relations. His death constitutes a partial destruction of the social cohesion, the normal social life is disorganized, the social equilibrium is disturbed. (1948:285)

Thus, Radcliffe-Brown takes the position that death is less of a personal tragedy than a group tragedy. The response, therefore, is institutionalized mourning. This and many other human cultural habits were seen to grow out of the nature of group life. The group was stressed in his theories often at the expense of the individual. Functionalist theory looked upon society as something not unlike a biological organism and often drew analogies from biological terminology. For example, the form or structure of society was often referred to as its "social morphology," whereas the nature of its activities or operations was referred to as its "social physiology."

It is primarily from this school of functionalism that the modern discipline of social anthropology developed, with its emphasis on social organization and social function. Anthropologists today are indebted to this school of thought for its theoretical and methodological contributions in the realm of family, kinship, and political organization analysis.

Malinowski's Functionalism

Although the theory of the British anthropologist Bronislaw Malinowski has also been labeled *functionalism*, his point of view was quite different from that of A. R. Radcliffe-Brown. The most basic difference was that Malinowski was concerned with cultural traditions whereas Brown was primarily interested in society and the interaction of its members. Malinowski maintained that individual cultures have a unity or equilibrium wherein every cultural trait is dependent upon, and interrelated with, every other, making it possible for society to function like a machine with every gear and cog in the proper place.

In one study of the Trobriand Islanders, *Argonauts of the Western Pacific,* he shows how economic activities are related to other facets of life such as folklore, religion, social organization, etc. This study was but one of his many exhaustive treatments of the Trobriand Island people, a group with which he spent a number of years doing first hand field research. Like Franz Boas, Malinowski laid importance on field investigation stressing that the anthropologist must see the culture from the native's point of view or, in Malinowski's own words, the anthropologist must "get inside the native's skin."

Malinowski not only emphasized the interrelated quality of the items in culture but maintained that the main function of each and every custom and institution was the satisfaction of biological, psychological, and social and cultural needs. While Malinowski's functionalism was psychological in approach, taking into consideration the factors molding individual personality and considering the conflict points in family and social life, he is often accused of being antihistorical. However, Malinowski is known to have emphasized the value of scientifically derived history in training his students; but he repeatedly went on record as opposing the kind of conjectural history that was utilized by the diffusionists and cultural evolutionists.

Not only did Malinowski refrain from engaging in historical reconstruction, but he almost totally disregarded evidence of diffusion. His
interest was the here and now, not the processes of cultural growth
that produced the culture. Kardiner sums up the Malinowski position
when he states:

> The history of an institution, its form and distribution, its evolution and
> diffusion—all these problems are of secondary importance. The important
> questions are, How does an institution function now? How does it satisfy
> individual and cultural needs in a given society, and How is it related to
> other institutions? (1961:174)

Without doubt, the work of Malinowski added materially to the
growing young discipline of anthropology in the late 1920's and the
1930's. He was, to begin with, the layman's anthropologist. He lectured
widely and his books, always carrying catchy titles, were widely read.
For the professionals he had shown the value of a field worker totally
submerging himself in the culture. Malinowski's own field methods—
his use of interview, observation, and careful analysis of the native
language—set a pattern for much research to follow. By spotlighting
the unity of culture, Malinowski did much to correct the misimpression
of many, that culture is a fabric made up of "shreds and patches," i.e.,
traits massed haphazardly as the result of diffusion.

Configurationalism

Some anthropologists would claim that there was still a third functional school, that of the poet-anthropologist, Ruth Benedict. While her
approach has been termed configurationalism, it had many things in
common with that of Bronislaw Malinowski. She approached culture in
terms of its holistic and integrated quality, but unlike Malinowski she
concentrated on whole cultures and not their component institutions.
The book Patterns of Culture illustrates clearly her approach to
culture. In this study she attempted to show how four cultures,
Kwakiutl, Dobu, Zuni, and Plains, had a particular "pattern" or
"theme" (terms borrowed from her background in aesthetics) that ran
through all institutions and customs and tended to mold the personalities of the society members to a particular, homogeneous form.
Just as the many cells of the body contain identical sets of chromosomes and genes, Benedict maintained that the many traits that make
up a culture reflect the characteristics of the whole. All the traits work
together to produce a certain type of culture and at the same time a
common personality type. Culture, to her, had a master plan.

Benedict's writing not only emphasized the organic unity of culture
but added still another dimension to the study of culture—the psycho-

logical aspect. With the use of such labels as Dionysian, Apollonian, paranoid, and megalomanian, Benedict attempted to characterize the *ethos* or psychological emotional set of a culture.

NEO-EVOLUTIONISTS

By 1945, many anthropologists were of the opinion that in rejecting unilinear evolution Boas and others had "thrown out the baby with the bath." Re-evaluations of the concept of cultural evolution were being made by Julian Steward, Leslie White, Robert Redfield, and the British archeologist V. Gordon Childe. Most of the new theories that developed did not hold that all cultures in their processes of growth had gone through a series of identical stages, but maintained that as men of various cultures developed their technology, broad trends, or similarities, in cultural development could be noted.

Multilinear Evolution

Julian Steward held, for example, that similar (but not identical) stages of development could be recognized in the cultural growth of such civilizations as the Inca, the Maya, the Mesopotamian, the Egyptian, and the Chinese. Steward's position, sometimes referred to as *multilinear evolution,* stressed the fact that similar institutions may develop independently under similar conditions and with similar sequences of events.

General Evolution

Leslie White, V. Gordon Childe, and Robert Redfield shared slightly different ideas concerning the development of culture. Their theories, sometimes referred to as *general evolution,* postulated a general trend in cultural growth toward more complex and heterogeneous forms. The formulations of general evolution differ from those of Steward in that they refer to culture as a whole and do not single out individual societies or cultures.

Evaluation of Evolution Today

Present-day anthropologists are far from reaching an agreement on the usefulness of the concept of "evolution" as a frame of reference. The more traditional American anthropologists prefer to speak of "cultural change" and not "cultural evolution," believing the latter smacks too much of Tylor and Morgan and is all too often associated with biological evolution or with ideas involving value judgments such as "progress." One thing is certain; cultural evolution is once again on the anthropological horizon and will not easily be put down.

CURRENT ANTHROPOLOGY

Although the discussion thus far has stressed "schools" of theory developed by individuals or groups of anthropologists, there is little evidence that "school" thinking is present to any great extent in modern American anthropology. Social anthropology, which has found its greatest following in England, has been greatly influenced by the work of Durkheim, Malinowski, and Radcliffe-Brown, but cultural anthropology seems to have selected the best contributions from the various "schools" of anthropological thought and combined them in a rounded, comprehensive study of man and his works. At its best, modern anthropology is functional, historical, diffusionist, psychological, and comparative; in other words, it has developed into an eclectic discipline.

Whether it is labeled cultural evolution or cultural change, the study of the dynamics of culture has, without doubt, become the most important consideration in present-day anthropology. With the ever-increasing modification of primitive culture by Western contact it is felt that the task of anthropology is to analyze the processes and effects of cultural borrowing and assimilation. Because of this modification some anthropologists have even questioned the value of continuing to regard anthropology as the study of "primitives." There has been a developing emphasis on the cross-cultural aspect of the discipline and a decreasing insistence that anthropology should be concerned only with one kind of people. It is not unusual today to find anthropologists studying peasant, folk, and even complex Western societies.

While the older approaches to the study of man and his works asked such questions as "What did he do?" and "When did he do it?" the more modern approach is deeper and more searching. Now the question most frequently asked about the behavior of man is "Why did he do it?" Thus the areas of values, beliefs, and motivations have become prime subjects for anthropological research. Along with this trend there has been an increasing cooperation between anthropology and psychology, sociology, and social psychology in order to better investigate such topics as human interaction, personality formation, and value orientation.

The trend toward working more closely with other disciplines may also be seen in the recent emphasis on the relationship between human biology and culture. This research has, of course, been directed at explaining the existence of cultural universals (cultural items found in all cultures) in terms of the biological nature of man. The titles of many new areas of anthropological specialization—ethnomusicology, ethnohistory, ethnobotany, chemical anthropology, ethnolinguistics— indicate the degree to which modern anthropology has joined forces with still other scientific and humanistic disciplines in order to explore ever deeper the biological, psychological, and sociological dimensions of man.

SUGGESTED READINGS

BARTON, D. R. "Biographer of the Indian; Clark Wissler," *Natural History,* April, 1940. (The ethnographic activities of Clark Wissler of the American Museum of Natural History.)

GOLDENWEISER, A. A. "Diffusionism and the American School of Historical Ethnology," *American Journal of Sociology,* 31:19, 1925. (Discussion of British and German diffusionism and the theoretical orientation of Franz Boas and his disciples.)

_____. "Social Evolution," *Encyclopedia of the Social Sciences,* 1937. (Describes the climate of social thought in Europe which gave rise to the school of cultural evolution in anthropology.)

HERSKOVITS, M. J. "Past Development and Present Currents in Ethnology," *American Anthropologist,* 61:389, 1959. (Survey of "schools" of anthropological thought.)

KROEBER, A. L. "Anthropology, 1900–1950," *Scientific Monthly,* September, 1950. (Discusses the progress of anthropology in clarifying the concept of culture over a fifty-year period.)

LOWIE, ROBERT H. "Franz Boas, Anthropologist," *Scientific Monthly,* February, 1943. (A summation of Boas' research and teaching activities.)

_____. "American Contributions to Anthropology," *Science,* 100:321, 1944. (Survey of outstanding studies by Americans in all areas of anthropology.)

MALINOWSKI, BRONISLAW. "The Group and the Individual in Functional Analysis," *American Journal of Sociology,* 44:938, 1939. (A brief outline of the functional approach to anthropological field work.)

ROBERTS, F. H. H. "One Hundred Years of Smithsonian Anthropology," *Science,* 104:119, 1946. (Contributions of museum workers in the advancement of anthropology.)

SARGEANT, W. "Profiles: Margaret Mead," *New Yorker,* December 30, 1961. (An intimate portrait of America's most widely read anthropologist.)

STEWARD, JULIAN. "Cultural Evolution," *Scientific American,* May, 1956. (Statement of the neo-evolutionary position.)

Paperbound Books

BENEDICT, RUTH. *Patterns of Culture.* New American Library of World Literature, Inc. (An anthropological classic; reveals Benedict's configurational position.)

DURKHEIM, ÉMILE. *Elementary Forms of Religious Life.* Collier Books. (Presents the sociological theory that gave rise to Radcliffe-Brown's functionalism.)

EISELEY, LOREN. *Darwin's Century.* Doubleday. (Currents of philosophical thought which led to Darwin's evolutionary thesis.)

FIRTH, RAYMOND (ed.). *Man and Culture,* Harper and Row. (An evaluation of Malinowski's functionalism.)

GOLDSCHMIDT, WALTER (ed.). *The Anthropology of Franz Boas.* Chandler Publishing Company. (Deals with Boas' contributions to anthropology as teacher, statistician, ethnographer, linguist, and human growth specialist.)

HAYS, H. R. *From Ape to Angel: An Informal History of Social Anthropology.* Putnam. (Discoveries, theories, and anecdotes of such anthropologists as Schoolcraft, Morgan, Frazer, Boas, Malinowski, and Mead.)

KARDINER, ABRAM, and PREBLE, EDWARD. *They Studied Man.* New American Library of World Literature, Inc. (Theoretical contributions of such anthropologists as Tylor, Frazer, Boas, Malinowski, Kroeber, and Benedict.)

MORGAN, LEWIS HENRY. *Ancient Society.* World Publishing Company. (Classic statement of the theory of cultural evolution.)

TYLOR, EDWARD BURNETT. *Origins of Culture.* Harper and Row. (Part one of Tylor's major work on cultural evolution, *Primitive Culture.*)

4

The Emergence of Man

Physical anthropologists generally agree that human beings evolved from a primitive apelike ancestor which they refer to as a proto-hominoid. While there is much controversy as to the exact sequence of forms that constitutes man's line of development, the frame of reference that generally orients scientific thinking is one derived from concepts developed by Linnaeus, Charles Darwin, Gregor Mendel, and Hugo de Vries and literally scores of other dedicated scientists. There is much that is speculative about man's developmental history, but evolution is a fact rather than a theory. The term *evolution*, commonly associated with the work of Darwin, is still much maligned but little understood. Darwin is responsible for the concept of natural selection but not evolution. Evolution means nothing more than change—change in the morphological characteristics of an organism over a period of time. Organisms *have* changed through time and are still doing so. In the case of man, for example, we find that in recent generations sons are on the average about one inch taller than their fathers, and judging from the size of suits of armor decorating European castles and museums, man has been growing steadily taller for several hundred years. Any dentist will confirm the fact that jaws are growing progressively smaller. Much of their time is spent straightening teeth in overcrowded jaws and removing wisdom teeth that have no room to develop. The jaws of man in the twentieth century can rarely accommodate a full compliment of 32 teeth. Since changes in the biological characteristics of man can be seen to be occurring today, scientists have no reason to believe that they have not always taken place. The question of whether an apelike animal can be transformed

into a man may, however, present difficulty to nonscientists. Some
theologians object strongly to the concepts of evolution, natural selection, and the idea of having a primate ancestry, but others of all
denominations agree with the position put forth by William W.
Howells that "as an explanation of creation, natural selection is purely
mechanical in its workings, and it showed God moving in a more
mysterious way than had ever previously been allowed for" (1946:8).[1]

For purposes of our study, let us follow the position of Howells and
look at the scientific frame of reference used by physical anthropologists in sketching the developmental history of man.

NATURAL SELECTION AND ADAPTATION

Of basic importance to our understanding of man's emergence from
the world of nonhuman primates are the concepts of natural selection
and adaptation. The natural selection concept presented initially by
Darwin and subsequently modified by genetic researchers maintains
that in every generation of animals there will be a struggle with the
environment with the prize being survival. This struggle for existence
partly involves the ability to escape one's predators or the ability to
compete successfully for scarce food with other members of the
species, but more important, it is a struggle with the environment itself.
Animals struggle with the cold by developing heavier pelts or a habit
of hibernation. Plants struggle with an arid climate by developing deep
roots or spines instead of leaves. Struggle may even involve developing
a pattern of cooperation and mutual aid rather than a competitive
system where only the most aggressive and cunning are at an advantage.

The important key to natural selection is reproduction. The animal
that lives long enough to reproduce will influence the form of future
generations, whereas the one who never reaches the mating age will
not. The constant struggle of organisms with environment and with
each other and its accompanying loss of less fit animals will over a
period of many generations be responsible for producing alterations in
the form and habits of given populations of animals.

Many of Darwin's statements recorded in *The Origin of Species*
were derived from observations he made while on a scientific expedition in 1835 on HMS *Beagle*. In the Galapagos Islands, for example, he
discovered that from a common fossil ancestor had evolved thirteen
varieties of finches. This radiation of types was believed to be the result

[1] From *Mankind So Far* by William W. Howells. Copyright 1944 by Doubleday
& Company, Inc. Reprinted by permission of the author and the publisher.

of adaptation to slight differences in environment. He remarked on this discovery, "I never dreamed that islands about 50 to 60 miles apart, placed under a quite similar climate, would have been differently tenanted. One might really fancy that from an original paucity of birds in this archipelago one species has been taken and modified for different ends" (1846: Chap. 17 *passim*).

Although Darwin was a good observer and documented the phenomenon of natural selection and adaptation of basic species of plants and animals under varying climatic and ecological conditions, he did not understand the mysteries of their heredity. Darwin believed that variation within a population was essential if there was to be natural selection, but he did not understand how it could be maintained. His view of heredity has sometimes been referred to as the "blood theory," i.e., that parents with varying characteristics would produce an offspring that was a blend of the two and thus make for greater uniformity rather than difference in a population.

MENDELIAN PRINCIPLES

A partial explanation of how natural selection could operate was provided in 1865 (but not appreciated until 1900) when Mendel discovered the units that determine the hereditary characteristics (genotypes) of individuals. These units—called genes and chromosomes—are found in all living cells. Through experimentation with pea plants in a monastery garden in Brunn, Czechoslovakia, the Augustinian abbot Gregor Mendel found that hereditary characteristics are passed on from generation to generation, not as blends but as stable features that maintain their identity for generations. To understand the nature of Mendel's methods let us look at one experiment involving giant (six-foot) and dwarf (two-foot) pea plants. By cross-pollinating these plant's flowers the result was not a blend of the two parents—i.e., a plant of intermediate height—but rather all tall plants. When the seeds of this generation of tall plants were planted, however, the result was a generation of three tall plants for every short one. After observing many more generations Mendel concluded that when a unit for tallness appeared in combination with a unit for shortness the unit for tallness overruled the effects of the unit for shortness. Thus he arrived at the concept of dominant and recessive hereditary units, or what we know today as *genes*. His experiments also corrected the basic error in Darwin's thinking by showing that variation in a population is not eliminated through blending but that variation will persist.

Additional research by other investigators established that genes are linked together on threadlike units that they labeled *chromosomes*. It is

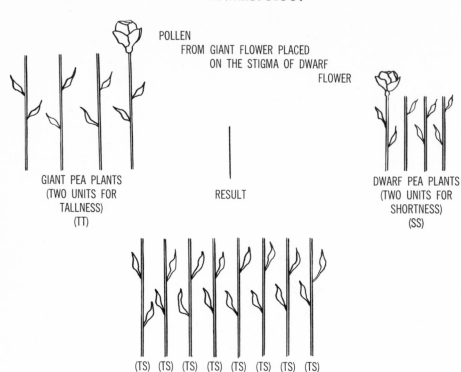

POLLEN
FROM GIANT FLOWER PLACED
ON THE STIGMA OF DWARF
FLOWER

GIANT PEA PLANTS
(TWO UNITS FOR
TALLNESS)
(TT)

RESULT

DWARF PEA PLANTS
(TWO UNITS FOR
SHORTNESS)
(SS)

(TS) (TS) (TS) (TS) (TS) (TS) (TS) (TS)
ALL GIANT
BUT EACH IS A HYBRID, THAT
IS IT CARRIES A HEREDITARY
UNIT FOR TALLNESS (T) AND
ONE FOR SHORTNESS (S)

SEEDS FROM THESE SELF FERTILIZING HYBRID PLANTS
PRODUCED

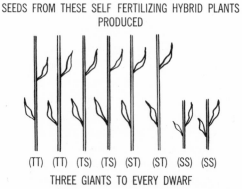

(TT) (TT) (TS) (TS) (ST) (ST) (SS) (SS)
THREE GIANTS TO EVERY DWARF

Fig. 4–1. Mendel's experimental method in the study of heredity.

the coming together of the male and female sex cells at conception with their chance selection of gene-laden chromosomes that establishes the heredity, or genotype of the resulting offspring.

MUTATION AND RECOMBINATION

Even the discovery of the Mendelian principles of heredity did not completely explain how Darwin's concept of natural selection and adaptation could operate. The formulation of the theory of gene *mutation* by Hugo de Vries provided additional scientific insight. This scientist maintained that genes occasionally undergo a permanent change in character and thus introduce an entirely new and different hereditary characteristic into a plant or animal population. The concept of mutation helped scientists to understand, for example, how it was possible for quite different varieties of finches (observed by Darwin) to have evolved in the relatively similar environment of the several Galapagos Islands. We know today that mutations can occur naturally or they can be produced by certain environmental factors such as exposure to X-rays, ultraviolet light, or certain chemicals. Investigators have also found that even a greater number of new features can arise through the recombinations of genetic materials when fragments of chromosomes break off and get lost or reattached to a different part of the same chromosome or unite with another. The interaction of natural selection, mutation, and recombinations of genetic material explains how the physical characteristics of a population may change over many generations. Mutations and recombinations alone would have a tendency to produce a population of freaks, but the genetic variability they produce is given order and direction by the forces of natural selection.

Mutant genes or gene recombinations are often lethal and prevent their carriers from surviving to reproductive age, but some gene changes or realignments that are introduced into the hereditary endowments of a population will be useful in some environments, and they will sometimes be particularly useful in a changing environment. A good example of this is the portion of a population of flies that had inherited a mutant gene rendering them resistant to DDT. Prior to the development of this insecticide these flies had no special advantage over "normal" flies, but their unique heritage meant that they could survive a DDT barrage while others could not. It should be noted that the insecticide did not bring about the gene change but that the potential to resist this kind of chemical was already present in a certain percentage of the fly population. In this case, first documented in Sweden and Italy in 1947, we have a very dramatic example of evolution resulting from an interaction of mutation and natural selection. When the environment was altered (by the introduction of DDT), a large number of flies were killed off leaving only those that had inherited a special mutant gene. Thus, in a very short time, there was a radical alteration of a population—i.e., one resistant to DDT.

While biologists believe that man is a product of the same basic forces of organic evolution (Mendelian inheritance, mutation, recombination, natural selection) which have produced other animal species, it must also be recognized that man is a unique creation. As Dobzhansky puts it:

> The leading forces of human evolution are intelligence, ability to use linguistic symbols, and the culture which man has developed. These exclusively, or nearly exclusively, human phenomena affect the biological evolution of man so profoundly that it cannot be understood without taking them into account. Conversely, human society and culture are products of the biological evolution of our species. Human evolution is wholly intelligible only as an outcome of the interaction of biological and social forces. (1955:320)

With this in mind let us examine the evidence and interpretations concerning the development of man's capacity for culture and how culture has in turn influenced man's physical characteristics. We shall concern ourselves only with the more recent developments within the primate order of the animal kingdom and discuss theories of how and when one variety of primate became significantly differentiated from others of his order in physical appearance and culture-building abilities to be recognized as a human being.

Most theories of man's development hold that both he and the great apes (gorillas, chimpanzees, orangutans, and gibbons) descended from a common ancestor. No modern scientist believes that man's forebears were apes such as the modern gibbon, orangutan, chimpanzee, or gorilla, for these animals are much too specialized for tree life to be ancestral to a generalized creature like man.

The usual interpretation is that man developed from a *proto-hominoid* (hominoid is a term that includes all fossil and living men and apes but not monkeys). In other words, man's ancestor is believed to have been something more advanced than a monkey but less developed and less specialized than any modern ape. The creature is assumed, however, to have been somewhat apelike in its general physical characteristics and intelligence. There is a general indication that the home of man's forebears was the tropical Old World (probably Africa or India).

FIVE STAGES OF MAN'S DEVELOPMENT

The evolution of modern man may be analyzed in terms of five developmental stages. They are:

1. An early prehuman stage—represented by proto-hominoids.
2. A late prehuman stage—represented by Australopithecines.
3. An early human stage—represented by *Homo habilis.*
4. A late human stage—represented by *Homo erectus.*
5. The modern human stage—represented by *Homo sapiens.*

Stage I (Early Prehuman)

Hockett and Ascher in a speculative article (1964) on the descent of man conceive of the proto-hominoid ancestor as having the following characteristics:

1. Keen vision, a de-emphasized sense of smell, freely movable arms with manipulative hands, and brains larger than the average for land mammals.
2. Band organization; the group consisting of a few adult males, females and offspring—ten to thirty individuals in all—but with no permanent form of family.
3. Mixed arboreal and ground life. They were equally at home in the trees or on the ground; nests were built in trees but the proto-hominoid ancestor was not an expert brachiator. On the ground they could stand or run with a semi-erect posture but bipedal walking was not their usual habit.
4. Ability to use objects of nature as tools, but unable to fashion tools to meet their needs.
5. Largely vegetarian in eating habits.
6. No power of speech. Perhaps some rudimentary call system such as that within the capacity of modern apes and monkeys was employed but no system of communication that might be called language.

OUT OF THE TREES. Geological evidence suggests that during the Miocene period there were climatic changes that converted the African tropical forests into an area of savannah grasslands with but few trees. Thus the proto-hominoid forebears of man were forced to spend the major share of their time on the ground. In time the challenge of the new environment brought about significant changes in both their morphology and living habits.

Stage II (Late Prehuman)

Sherwood Washburn (1960) believes that the descent of man from the proto-hominoid ancestor described above hinges on two all-important developments—tool use and bipedal locomotion. Even limited bipedal posture, he maintains, would leave the hands free to carry and use sticks and stones as tools. As proto-hominoids gradually established a successful pattern of life using tools, natural selection pressures brought changes in teeth, hands, brain, and pelvis. Wood and stone tools became weapons of defense instead of teeth, thus making possible an evolutionary trend toward the reduction in the size of canine teeth and jaws. Increased bipedal locomotion brought about changes in the pelvis. Washburn believes that one important development was the reduction of the size of the birth canal in the modified pelvis. This, combined with a selective trend toward larger brains brought on by tool use, resulted in a much shorter gestation period and thus a more immature and helpless offspring. Not only did the necessity of carrying this premature child bring about a greater use of the hands and arms and a greater necessity for bipedal locomotion, but it also tended to establish a closer bond between male and female. The necessity of the male providing for the helpless child and the slow-moving, burdened female imposed a pattern of family organization on the emerging human species.

AUSTRALOPITHECINE. An example of the late prehuman animal that emerged as a result of tool use and bipedal locomotion is *Zinjanthropus*. This fossil, whose name was derived from the Arabic word for "East Africa," was discovered by L. S. B. Leakey in Tanganyika in 1959. Very clearly it is a variety of Australopithecine (Southern ape). These animals whose skeletons have been found mainly in South Africa are not apes at all but a variety of primate that resembles an ape in certain cranial features but is very manlike from the neck down. The bulk of Australopithecines (*Paranthropus, Telanthropus, Australopithecus*) are believed to be less than one million years old, but for *Zinjanthropus* the established date (reckoned by potassium-argon dating) is approximately 1,750,000 years ago.

Although there is some variation in these late prehuman fossils, generally we can describe them as having skulls with low foreheads and chinless protruding muzzles and brains only a trifle larger than those of chimpanzees. They were, however, bipedal upright walkers with the pelvis and lower limbs resembling those of modern man. There is some evidence that Australopithecines were tool-makers and had a uniform method of hunting, probably in coordinated groups. Whether or not they had fire is unknown and, of course, we have no idea as to how they communicated with one another.

Stage III (Early Human)

The discovery of *Homo habilis* by L. S. B. Leakey in East Africa in April, 1964, provided evidence that the dividing line between pre-human and human forms was crossed as early as two million years ago. Experts from England and South Africa have examined parts of seven individuals and have concluded that *Homo habilis* was about the size of modern pygmies. They walked completely erect on feet in which the arrangement of the big toe and the arch system resembled that of modern man. Their brain size is estimated at about 700 cc. and their crania have been described as more manlike than those of the Australopithecines.

Students of anthropology are in general agreement that man had truly been created when he (1) assumed erect posture, (2) became a meat eater, (3) developed tool-making and -using abilities, and (4) developed symbolic communication. There are indications that all of these criteria are satisfied in *Homo habilis*.

Definitely associated with the bones of this early variety of man are bones of large mammals, which have been cracked open to extract the marrow, and the remains of small mammals, reptiles, and fish that apparently had also made up his bill of fare. Instead of having to eat continuously as did the vegetarian primates, this protein diet freed *Homo habilis* to spend a greater amount of time in hunting and tool-making. His tools were fabricated out of stone and bone and further evidence of his ingenuity in modifying his environment is to be seen in a semicircular structure of piled stones which may have served as a wind break.

Both *Zinjanthropus* and *Homo habilis* fossils come from Olduvai Gorge in Tanganyika, and it is believed that they were contemporaries. Leakey postulates that *Homo habilis* is in a direct ancestral line to present-day man while *Zinjanthropus* ultimately became extinct, thus representing one unsuccessful attempt by nature to produce man.

CLASSIFICATION	TYPE	SKULL	AGE (in thousands of years)	 CULTURAL STAGE
HOMO SAPIENS	MODERN MAN	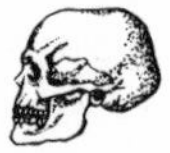	0-80?	ADVANCED
	LATE NEANDERTHAL	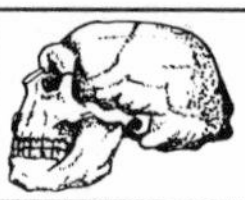	30-150?	STONE TOOLS
	SWANSCOMBE	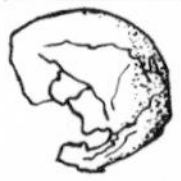	250	FLINT AXES FIRE
	STEINHEIM	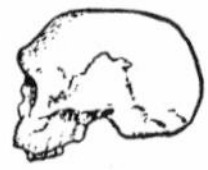	250	?
HOMO ERECTUS	HEIDELBERG		350	?
	CHELLEAN		350	STONE TOOLS
	ATLANTHROPUS		400	STONE TOOLS
	PEKIN (SINANTHROPUS)	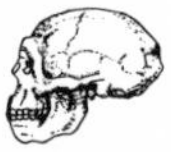	400	STONE TOOLS FIRE
	JAVA (PITHECANTHROPUS)	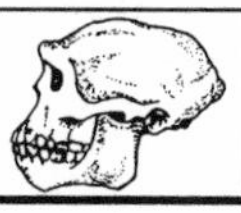	400-700?	POSSIBLY BONE TOOLS
HOMO HABILIS			1750	STONE AND BONE TOOLS
AUSTRALO – PITHECINAE	AUSTRALOPITHECUS	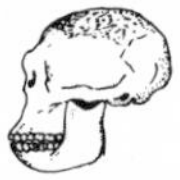	1000 (time span about 500?)	?
	ZINJANTHROPUS		1750	?
MODERN APE	GORILLA		present day	—

Fig. 4–2. Fossil men and their characteristics.

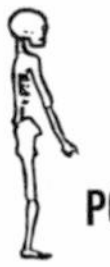 POSTURE	 FEET AND LEGS	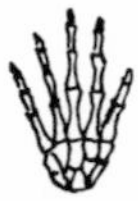 HANDS	 TEETH	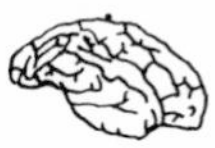 BRAIN SIZE (cc)
ERECT	MODERN	MODERN	MODERN	1400
ERECT 5-6 FOOT	SHORT ROBUST	SHORT ROBUST	LARGE	1400-1600
?	?	?	?	1325
?	?	?	?	1150?
?	?	?	'HUMAN'	?
?	?	?	?	1100?
?	?	?	LARGE MOLARS	?
ERECT	?	?	LARGE MOLARS	1000-1200
ERECT 5-6 FOOT	'HUMAN LEGS'	?	LARGE MOLARS	775-900
ERECT 4 FOOT	'NEAR-MAN' FOOT	STRONG GRIP RATHER SHORT THUMB?	LARGE MOLARS FRONT TEETH IN PROPORTION	680?
ERECT NOT GOOD WALKER	?	?	VERY LARGE MOLARS SMALL FRONT TEETH	300-600
ERECT POOR WALKER	?	?	VERY LARGE MOLARS SMALL FRONT TEETH	300-600?
NORMALLY QUADRUPEDAL	TYPICAL ANTHROPOID FEET	STRONG LONG FINGERS RELATIVELY SHORT THUMB	LARGE MOLARS AND CANINES	MAX. ABOUT 700

Fig. 4-2. (Continued.)

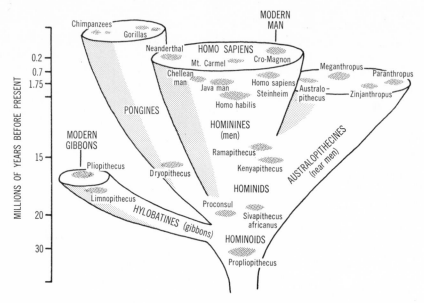

Fig. 4–3. Schematic relationship of fossils (after Napier 1964).

Stage IV (Late Human)

Fossils discovered in Java, China (near Pekin), Africa, and possibly Germany represent a somewhat more advanced stage of development than the Australopithecines, but in many respects they were more primitive than other modern human forms which are believed by some to have been living about the same time in Europe. *Pithecanthropus erectus* (the Java ape-man who walked erect) and *Pithecanthropus pekinensis* (the Pekin ape-man) are very similar in type, but the latter is believed to be a somewhat more recent and more modern representative of a common genus and species, *Homo erectus*. Their cranial capacity of approximately 1000 cc. places them midway between the apes and modern man. The skulls of these ape-men are heavy and have prominent brow ridges. Although the jaw has no chin, it can positively be stated that the skull is more manlike than apelike. Furthermore, the representatives of this fossil type walked completely erect. They produced stone tools of a hand axe variety and Pekin specimens are known to have used fire.

Wilfrid E. Le Gros Clark postulates a direct line of evolution from Australopithecines to *Homo erectus*. He points out that *Homo erectus* was not merely an Asiatic species but that there were representatives of

this type in Africa and possibly Europe at the same period. The fossils *C2/05*
Atlanthropus (discovered in Algeria), *Africanthropus* and *Chellean 3*
(both from East Africa), and possibly Heidelberg man (known only by
a massive lower jaw discovered near the village of Mauer in Germany)
share many of the physical characteristics of Java and Pekin man and
are believed to have lived between 350,000 to 700,000 years ago.
Napier (1964), on the other hand, postulates an early branching off of
Australopithecines and therefore sees no link between them and *Homo
erectus*. The former are, he feels, too specialized to be in a direct
evolutionary line.

Stage V (Modern Human)

Professor Leakey believes that representatives of the *Homo habilis*
type of man spread into Europe and ultimately evolved into an early
form of *Homo sapiens*. The earliest representatives of this modern
human type are two fragmentary skulls from Europe known to scientists as Swanscombe and Steinheim.

In 1935 two cranial bones were discovered at a depth of twenty-six
feet in Pleistocene gravel deposits at Swanscombe in Kent, England.
These bones indicate that Swanscombe man (actually a twenty-year-
old woman) was definitely of the genus *Homo*. Although the bones are
quite thick they are almost identical with modern English female skulls
with respect to the forward position of the foramen magnum (the large
aperture at the base of the skull where the spinal column is attached),
shape of cranial curves, and cranial capacity (1,325 cc.). Some scientists have considered this fossil a contemporary of Java man, but the
more common date assigned to it is 250,000 years.

The Steinheim skull, discovered at Steinheim, Germany, in 1933, is
of approximately the same antiquity as Swanscombe but the cranial
capacity is less (1100–1175 cc.). The skull has massive brow ridges and
a low vault, but the forehead and back of the skull are quite round,
and in the region of the ear Steinheim was remarkably modern. Some
physical anthropologists feel that the skull has a Neanderthal look
about it and thus might represent an early branching off of the Neanderthal strain from the *Homo sapiens* family tree.

France has also produced an early Neanderthaloid fossil. Parts of
two skulls discovered at Fontéchevade belong to individuals with
cranial capacities of 1470 cc., reduced brow ridges, and completely
modern faces.

Modern human forms of great antiquity have also been found in
Africa. A portion of a lower jaw discovered at Kanam, Kenya, could

possibly be as old as 600,000 years. Although the general shape of this mandible is completely modern, the presence of a cancerous growth makes it impossible to judge whether or not it had a chin. Kanjera, Kenya, has been the source of parts of four skulls and a limb bone of individuals contemporary with Swanscombe man. The bones are definitely of modern type.

One of the most puzzling discoveries of modern human fossils is the collection from caves on Mt. Carmel in Palestine which has been dated 100,000 years old. An analysis of the several skeletons reveals that they represent a highly varied population. Some of the individuals are much like the *Homo sapiens* of the Upper Paleolithic period in Europe while others possess primitive Neanderthaloid features. The Mt. Carmel population might very well represent a situation where an early form of Neanderthal lived side by side with true *Homo sapiens,* interbreeding to produce a hybrid population.

HOMO NEANDERTHALENSIS. Contrary to common belief, the Neanderthal men who became abundant and widely dispersed throughout Europe and the Middle East during the first part of the fourth glacial period were not grotesque animals with bullish necks, knock-knees and a stooped posture. *Homo neanderthalensis,* who was named after the Neanderthal Valley near Düsseldorf, Germany, where the first specimen was found in 1856, tends to exhibit a low forehead, receding chin, heavy brow ridges, and a large bunlike skull, but in posture, skeletal structure, and general intelligence he was not greatly different from modern man. He fashioned tools with precision and skill, hunted in organized groups, and had a rudimentary religion. When this variety of man disappeared during the Upper Paleolithic, it is quite likely that he was absorbed by Cro-Magnon populations rather than exterminated by them.

HOMO SAPIENS. The Upper Paleolithic period in Europe, which began about 50,000 years ago, witnessed the rise of large populations of completely modern *Homo sapiens.* Perhaps the best known variety was Cro-Magnon, but he was not the only type. Even in his native France this ancestor of the modern Caucasian had to share the scene with varieties such as Combe Capelle, Chancelade, and perhaps Grimaldi man.

Cro-Magnon men were tall and robust with erect posture and straight necks. Their heads were domed and featured high foreheads. Their faces were delicate and they had prominent noses and chins. They still exhibited fairly distinguishable brow ridges, but their cranial bones were only about half as thick as those of *Homo erectus.* These men undoubtedly lived in well-organized societies, produced tailored clothing and cave paintings, and hunted cooperatively. Their tools of antler, bone, and stone were skillfully fashioned and have been classified as constituting three major tool industries—the Aurignacian, Solutrian, and Magdelenian.

Combe Capelle may represent an earlier variety of modern *Homo sapiens* than Cro-Magnon. He and a similar variety of man discovered in Brunn, Czechoslovakia, were shorter than Cro-Magnon, had narrower faces and heads and more prominent brow ridges. It is possible that they reflect a Neanderthaloid physical heritage.

Another *Homo sapiens* fossil that comes from the same region of France as Cro-Magnon has been labeled Chancelade. This variety of early European has been pronounced Eskimo-like in that it has a narrow skull, a broad face, strong jaws, and a special feature of the palate that is common in Eskimos. Chancelade man, however, differs little from other Upper Paleolithic men and its identification as "Eskimo" might very well have been influenced by the fact that the tools he made (Magdelenian) greatly resemble those manufactured by Eskimo peoples.

A cave on the shores of the Mediterranean in the principality of Monaco has produced another variety of Upper Paleolithic man which has also been the subject of some debate. Skeletons of two individuals from this site have been referred to as Grimaldi man. The name Grimaldi, incidentally, was that of the ruling prince of Monaco at the time of the discovery (1901). The limb proportions, the shape of the upper jaw, and the high degree of prognathism of these skeletons have prompted scientists to suspect Grimaldi man of being a Negro. However, all of the "Negro" features present in the Grimaldi skeletons can be found in other European fossils of this period, and there is little reason for this interpretation. Generally, it is believed that the differentiation of mankind into different racial varieties is a relatively recent phenomenon (late Pleistocene) and thus there is a great temptation to interpret the Chancelade and Grimaldi finds as being evidence of this early racial dispersion.

The problem of deciphering the ancestry of man is difficult at best. In many cases the antiquity of fossils is uncertain and therefore their relationship to others cannot be ascertained. An example is the date of Swanscombe man, which some have claimed to be 650,000 while others see it as only 250,000 years old. Also, there is the difficulty that the fossils that have been discovered are not "missing links" in a direct linkage of individuals, but are rather representatives of populations in which there undoubtedly was a great deal of variation. We do not know therefore how typical these fossils are of their species. The picture of man's development will become clearer as new fossil discoveries are made. Physical anthropologists today feel that the basic pattern of man's development is known and the precise details will soon be added as additional evidence comes to light.

SUGGESTED READINGS

COON, CARLETON S. "Man Against the Cold," *Natural History*, January, 1961. (Study of man's adaptation to the subpolar climate of Tierra del Fuego.)

DOBZHANSKY, THEODOSIUS. "The Genetic Basis of Evolution," *Scientific American*, January, 1950. (Discusses Mendelian principles of inheritance, mutation, isolation, and adaptation as forces in race and species formation.)

————. "The Present Evolution of Man," *Scientific American*, March, 1960. (How modern technology and science are influencing the direction of man's development.)

EISELEY, LOREN. "Antiquity of Modern Man," *Scientific American*, July, 1948. (Fossil discoveries indicate that *Homo sapiens* is as old as Neanderthal man.)

HOCKETT, CHARLES F. "The Origin of Speech," *Scientific American*, September, 1960. (Man's communication with symbols has roots in communication in lower animals.)

KROGMAN, W. M. "The Scars of Human Evolution," *Scientific American*, December, 1951. (The price man pays for walking erect.)

LEAKEY, L. S. B. "Man's Beginnings," *The World Book Year Book*, 1965. (Leakey's theory of man's development from *Homo habilis* to *Homo sapiens*.)

SHAPIRO, HARRY L. "Portrait of the American People," *Natural History*, June, 1945. (The evolution of physical type in America in recent generations.)

SINGER, RONALD. "Emerging Man in Africa," *Natural History*, November, 1962. (Recent fossil finds in Africa and the information they provide concerning man's ancestry.)

WASHBURN, SHERWOOD L. "Tools and Human Evolution," *Scientific American*, September, 1960. (How use of tools by prehuman primates gave rise to *Homo sapiens*.)

WECKLER, J. E. "Neanderthal Man," *Scientific American*, December, 1957. (Relationship of Neanderthal to *Homo sapiens*.)

Paperbound Books

BRODRICK, ALAN H. *Man and His Ancestry*. Fawcett Publications. (A general treatment of human evolution from *Zinjanthropus* through *Homo sapiens*.)

CLARK, W. E. LE GROS. *Antecedents of Man: An Introduction to the Evolution of the Primates*. Harper and Row. (Man's place within the primate order.)

DARWIN, CHARLES. *The Origin of Species*. New American Library of World Literature, Inc. (The classic work on natural selection.)

DOBZHANSKY, THEODOSIUS. *Mankind Evolving: The Evolution of the Human Species*. Yale University Press. (Prize winning volume on mankind as a product of evolution.)

DUNN, L. C., and DOBZHANSKY, TH. *Heredity, Race and Society*. Mentor Books, New American Library of World Literature, Inc. (Group differences, how they arise, and the influences of heredity and environment.)

HOGARTH, PAUL, and JEAN-JACQUES SALOMON. *Prehistory*. Dell Publishing Co. (Beautifully illustrated introduction to the biological and cultural evolution of mankind.)

MONTAGU, ASHLEY. *Human Heredity*. New American Library of World Literature, Inc. (Genetic inheritance and how it is affected by environment.)

———— (ed.). *Culture and the Evolution of Man*. Oxford University Press. (Collection of essays stressing the relationship between cultural and physical factors in the evolution of man.)

SIMPSON, GEORGE GAYLORD. *The Meaning of Evolution*. New American Library of World Literature, Inc. (The concept of evolution and its ethical implications for mankind.)

5

The Concept of Culture

Culture is defined in anthropology as the learned, shared behavior that man acquires as a member of society. Although culture is a key concept in many of the social sciences, it has been anthropology, more than any other discipline, that has led the way in defining and studying this abstract concept which is such a great factor in determining man's behavior and personality. As the definition implies, it has been impossible to study culture without also studying the nature of society. Thus we can see the importance of maintaining a close relationship between anthropology and sociology; the former focuses its attention on culture, while the latter emphasizes the study of society.

In order to understand fully the concept of culture and, indeed, society, it will be useful to break down our definition of culture and analyze its several parts. First of all, culture is learned behavior; it is not biologically inherited. Nearly everything that man does he must learn from others. As the infant grows into the child and then into the adult, he will begin to think and act like those around him—the members of his family, his neighborhood play group, his community. If the members of his group eat with knives and forks, worship in the Christian tradition, and speak English, he will learn to do the same. When he has fully learned his culture, he will behave very much like his contemporaries and not too much differently from his ancestors.

Not too many years ago psychologists attributed a number of instincts to man—mother love, pugnacity, gregariousness. But, one by one, these have been stripped away and today it is known that man comes into the world with very little that will predetermine his behavior and allow him to fend for himself. Within minutes, a newly

74

hatched chick can get onto its feet and go looking for food, but a human child must learn to get food and even to walk from its parents or other members of its group. The importance of learning for human animals is quite dramatically stated by A. L. Kroeber:

> Take a couple of ant eggs of the right sex—unhatched eggs, freshly laid. Blot out every individual and every other egg of the species. Give the pair a little attention as regards warmth, moisture, protection, and food. The whole of ant "society," every one of the abilities, powers, accomplishments, and activities of the species . . . will be reproduced, and reproduced without diminution, in one generation. But place on a desert island or in a circumvallation two or three hundred human infants of the best stock from the highest class of the most civilized nation; furnish them the necessary incubation and nourishment; leave them in total isolation from their kind; and what shall we have? . . . only a pair or a troop of mutes, without arts, knowledge, fire, without order or religion. Civilization would be blotted out within these confines—not disintegrated, not cut to the quick, but obliterated in one sweep. (1917:177–78)

Secondly, our definition of culture states that culture is shared. Let us imagine that we are all anthropologists newly arrived in a West African village. Our purpose in being there is to describe the culture, or traditional customs, of the people. The people we encounter will probably be inhabiting a common territory (in this case, the village), they will be interacting with one another (rubbing shoulders, so to speak) in order to achieve a common set of goals. If these conditions are present, we can say that the people we see form a society. What about their culture? At first we see the people of this West African community engaged in a variety of daily activities. In one part of the village a man is busy thatching his roof; in another, a woman is disciplining a child. Outside the village a man is hoeing his garden. After we have lived in the village for some time, we begin to see that there is a tendency for all men to use much the same methods in roof-thatching; the majority of women seem to discipline their children in much the same way and for the same reasons; and that all farmers seem to use the same tools, the same motor behavior, and the same methods in hoeing their fields. These uniformities or consensuses of behavior are what the anthropologist is referring to when he speaks of the culture of a people.

Culture is an abstraction just as a map is an abstraction. A map depicts only the most important characteristics of a geographical region, and culture refers only to the most significant aspects of a people's behavior. Every anthropologist is, of course, interested in more than just the main characteristics of a culture. He knows that there are always deviants who do not completely follow the traditional customs, but the idiosyncratic behavior of deviants, while it is also learned, is not shared by the members of the society, and therefore it cannot be classed as cultural behavior. When the anthropologist describes a culture, he is interested in characterizing the true nature of that way of life and not in showing the exceptions to the rule. The purpose of a map is to guide and direct people, to increase a person's knowledge of an area. To do this the map must be accurately and scientifically constructed. Similarly, an accurate analysis of a culture makes it possible to find one's way around in a society, anticipating what the people will do in a given situation and understanding curious ceremonies and customs.

In defining cultural behavior as shared behavior, one caution must be observed. There are some types of behavior that are shared by all men but are not learned, and therefore cannot be labeled cultural behavior. For example, if a flash gun went off in the faces of a number of people there would be a common response. The pupils of all of their eyes would grow smaller. If the light flash were accompanied by a loud report, the people would jump or show some sort of startle response. If a number of individuals are tapped with a mallet at a certain spot on the knee, we can expect their legs to jerk. These reactions are reflex responses and are a product of the human organism. They are shared but not learned and therefore they do not fit into our definition of cultural behavior.

The final part of our definition of culture maintains that one acquires culture as a member of society. Without society it is impossible to have culture, and without culture it is impossible for any human group to survive because culture provides established, traditional means for solving certain basic human problems such as securing food, keeping warm, and producing and raising young. Although it is possible to study culture without reference to people (archeologists do it every day in their analysis of the material effects of past civilizations), it must be remembered that without people carrying a set of ideas in their heads, without people being incensed by infractions of the cultural values, culture could not exist.

CULTURE AND COMMUNICATION

Most social scientists would agree that culture is unique to man. Although there is some evidence that lower animals may learn certain types of behavior through imitation, most animal behavior is pretty much determined by the nature of the organism. Men, on the other hand, do not have to grow heavy pelts to live in the arctic or grow wings in order to fly through the air like birds. Their culture has provided them with ways of accomplishing these things. While animals have given us a great deal of evidence that they are intelligent, in some respects more intelligent than men, they fall down in one area. This is the area of abstract, symbolic communication. Language is essential to the development and transmission of culture. It is well known that lower animals are capable of a low level of communication. Howler monkeys can convey their feelings of anger, fear, danger, and sexual desire by various types of cries or hoots, but these are responses to immediate situations or emotional states. They can only react to a here-and-now situation or feeling. The monkey can utter a mating call, but he can hardly make a date for next Saturday night. He cannot warn his young of things that might happen in the future. He cannot tell others the solutions to problems that he has worked out and that they might face during their lives. On the other hand, many a college professor has learned that it is unwise to give the same examination to two different sections of a course if one meets at eight o'clock and the other meets at ten. Humans can communicate the solutions to problem situations, and the ten o'clock class can, in this situation, be expected to do better on the examination, provided they have friends in the eight o'clock class.

There is a vast difference between the signal of a gibbon telling his group that he has found the way through the jungle and the rapid series of meaningful grunts coming from the mouth of the minister discussing a theological principle in the Sunday morning sermon or the grunts of the college professor explaining Aristotelian logic. It is the ability to store up knowledge, speculate on future events, and then, most important of all, communicate through a series of abstract sound symbols, ideas of things seen, unseen, and unseeable that sets man apart from the lower animals and puts him into a different world—the world of culture.

Since it has been established that language is vital to culture it might be helpful in our analysis of culture to look at some of the characteristics of language. To begin with, language is a product of culture, and many of the same things that can be said about culture can also be said about language. For example, language, like culture, is shared, learned behavior. If it were not shared, there would be no reason for its existence. A man can hardly have a language all by himself, and even a language known only to two men is more of a code than a language. Language provides the communication that allows societies to work toward common goals. If men are going to get things done, they have to exchange ideas and settle among themselves on proper methods. The Bible story of the tower of Babel points up this important function of language. The story relates that when the builders of the tower no longer shared a common language all work stopped.

Human beings are born with the type of brain and vocal organs that enables them to speak, but they are not born with language. It would be ridiculous to suppose that language could be inherited biologically. That would mean that Frenchmen would have to carry a gene for French, Germans for German, and Americans for English. Language is learned within the society, and particularly within the family, through imitation and conscious teaching just as culture itself is learned. Both language and culture are found among all men, but the forms of each are infinitely varied. In spite of its many forms, language does much the same things for all men—it helps them to maintain an orderly and efficient society and to pass on their basic values to subsequent generations.

ENCULTURATION AND SOCIALIZATION

It appears that everything that sets man apart from the lower animals and makes him a unique creature—his ability to use language and develop culture—he acquires through the process of learning. In anthropology, the learning of one's language and tradition is known as *enculturation*. It is a learning process unique to man because only man has culture. It is through enculturation that the random behavior of children is directed into acceptable channels. Enculturation is, you might say, a conditioning process wherein values, conventions, and symbolic meanings of a culture are transmitted to the young or, in some cases, to new adults who have recently joined the society. As this learning process goes on, the values, ideals, and ethics of a society are internalized so that the individual will automatically operate in terms of the norms of his society even if others are not with him. The values of society become his values and make up a sort of social conscience that will then serve as the basis for what he in turn will teach his own children when the time comes.

In addition to enculturation there is another type of learning that is important in the development of a human being. This is *socialization*. It is a different kind of learning experience, but it goes hand in hand with enculturation. Unlike enculturation, socialization is not unique to man but is characteristic of social animals in general. While enculturation has to do with learning a cultural tradition, socialization refers to learning to get along with the unique personalities making up the social groups into which the individual is born or which he has joined. No two families are exactly alike; father may be strict and mother lenient, or vice versa. Both may be strict or both lenient. There are different adjustment situations for the eldest child, the youngest, or the only child. Over a period of time the child must learn to discriminate between individuals and adjust his behavior accordingly.

Differences Between Enculturation and Socialization

While we have differentiated between the processes of socialization and enculturation, it must be kept in mind that the two are intimately tied together. To a great extent one learns how to get along with the individuals that make up one's group by drawing upon the values or patterns of accepted behavior that prevail within the culture. Sociologists often lump these two types of learning experience together under the common term socialization, but the use of this single label leaves something to be desired. A good example of the difference between the processes of enculturation and socialization is to be found in the college pledge situation. Each semester the fraternities on our college campuses add new members to their groups. These new members are called pledges. For a certain period these pledges are on probation while they learn to become good fraternity members. To begin with they must be enculturated—i.e., they must learn the nationwide heritage, or traditions, of the fraternity. Secondly, the pledge must learn how to get along with the "brothers" who live with him in the fraternity house. He must learn, for example, that Joe is very sensitive about his excess weight. Pete is very easy to get along with; nothing bothers him. Jim, on the other hand, likes to sleep late in the morning and is pretty mean if disturbed. Still another "brother," Bill, is very serious about his grades and doesn't want people wandering into his room when he is studying. If the pledge is ever to become an "active," he must learn to get along with these people and their idiosyncrasies. In other words, he must be socialized. If he does not choose to learn the fraternity's traditions, or if he does not learn to adjust to the patterns of behavior that prevail within the group, he will not be allowed to become a member in full standing. Even in this situation it may be seen that enculturation and socialization are closely associated. The pledge is aided in his socialization process if he has learned the fraternity traditions well, as they tend to define how fraternity brothers should act toward one another and toward outsiders. The experiences of the fraternity pledge and the growing child are alike in this respect. The child growing up in a culture finds that he gets along much better with his parents if he follows certain norms concerning respect and obedience that are dominant in his culture. Beyond this point, it is a matter of individual differences. Some parents demand more respect or obedience than others, and the child must learn, as the pledge did, to adjust to his particular group.

MATERIAL AND NONMATERIAL CULTURE

The cultural world in which the child grows up is composed of two types of reality—nonmaterial and material. Thus far our discussion of culture has dealt primarily with the individual's nonmaterial environment—his patterns of thought and behavior, the moral code that regulates his behavior, and the values and goals that motivate it. Nonmaterial culture concerns the ideas men live by and the principles that men will die for. The nonmaterial aspects of culture are often the most difficult for the anthropologists to describe, because they often exist at the covert level—i.e., below the level of observation. It is not unusual for a people to be quite unaware of the values that motivate their behavior, and therefore, the anthropologist must try to discover them himself through prolonged observation and analysis of behavior.

The material aspects of culture, on the other hand, are much more easily observed and documented. Every society tends to produce and use a special set of material objects—houses, clothes, tools, weapons—which also must be considered as part of the traditional way of life.

Although we have recognized material and nonmaterial culture as separate and different types of phenomena, in reality, it is almost impossible to study them as separate entities. Material and nonmaterial culture are functionally related in every society and it is extremely unwise to consider the one without making reference also to the other.

A society's religion includes not only a set of spirits or deities and a set of beliefs but also a set of religious objects—altars, carved images, fetishes, shrines—which are part and parcel of the total religious configuration and can hardly be separated from the nonmaterial aspects of worship. The interrelationship of material and nonmaterial culture can also be seen when we look at the way material objects and technological processes affect the total world view of a people. Europeans who have the technical abilities and inventions to change the course of rivers, turn deserts into productive farm land, and transform swamps into cities look upon nature in a very different way from the fatalistic primitive people who must take nature as it comes and adjust to its whims. The man on the assembly line who merely turns a single nut on a truck or solders a single connection in a television set cannot help but have a different attitude toward his work and the product that he is producing from the craftsman who begins with a set of raw materials and alone fashions them into a finished product. A society that regulates its behavior by the clock has a very different pattern of living and a very different set of values from one where time is less accurately kept. Punctuality and tardiness, "saving time" or "wasting time," are significant concepts only to people who live by the clock.

The artifacts making up the material culture of a group have proved to be valuable objects of study for anthropologists concerned with the reconstruction of the history of prehistoric cultures. The various diffusionist schools of anthropological thought dealt almost entirely with the material products of primitive people. House and canoe types, weapons, and tools served them as evidence in their efforts to trace the spread of peoples and ideas about the world. One of the main objections to diffusionists' schemes, however, is that even identical artifacts do not always have the same function in different societies. This is a very important principle to keep in mind in studying the relationship between material and nonmaterial culture. A paddle that propels a canoe in one society may serve as a dance baton in another. To know a people's way of life one must know not only about their artifacts but also how they put them to use. Every aspect of life—economics, religion, family, government—has its material equipment as well as its principles and modes of behavior. All are tied together in a meaningful and consistent whole.

CULTURE AND BIOLOGY

If the anthropologist were asked for a simple statement of why man has culture, he would probably say that it provides him with certain time-tested methods or procedures for satisfying basic biological, psychological, and sociological needs. It provides man with a pattern for behavior that will ensure or greatly enhance his chances for survival. Culture provides man with ready-made solutions for keeping himself fed and sheltered, satisfying his sex drive, understanding the mysteries of his universe, and regulating his society. Life without culture would be very much like putting a hi-fi kit together without instructions. Each step would have to be worked out through trial and error rather than by depending on a prescribed procedure.

Once a man has been thoroughly enculturated, his behavior becomes highly automatic. He develops habits of eating, driving cars, putting on clothes, lighting cigarettes. If a man were to stop and think about each of his actions, life would indeed be complicated and filled with no end of confusion. The situation would be not unlike that of the centipede.

who, upon being asked what foot he put out first, became so confused that he couldn't manage his many legs at all.

Although culture ordinarily makes life easier and is, in general, a response to a set of biological as well as other derived needs, it certainly cannot be said that the various aspects of culture are precisely determined by the biological necessities of man. Culture often modifies or even inhibits purely biological needs. Rather than always seeing to man's comfort, culture often complicates his life and disciplines his efforts to satisfy his needs. For example, every culture provides for some method whereby the need for nourishment is satisfied, but almost every culture stipulates what foods should be eaten, how they will be prepared, and when they can be eaten. There are probably few if any societies in the world that do not have a concept of "meal time." Polynesians eat twice a day, at 10 A.M. and 7 P.M., while Americans eat three times a day, at 8 A.M., 12 noon, and 6 P.M. In each case these meal times represent a regulation of eating. In no society is man able to satisfy his hunger in the simplest and most direct manner. Depending on his culture, he must manage knives and forks, chopsticks, or, if no utensils are used, he must eat with his hands in a special "polite manner." Although man has a more diverse diet than any other animal, every society considers certain foods unpalatable or actually taboo.

Similar regulations are imposed on man's attempts to satisfy other biological needs. The drive for sexual satisfaction is also controlled by a myriad of special restrictions. There is always a time and place for sex activity. Some societies restrict sex to marriage while others do not. Strict rules regulate whom the partners may be. There are often special taboos in regard to sex relations with relatives, members of different castes, or persons below a certain legal age.

While culture provides man with means for protecting himself from the elements, it frequently clothes him in styles and materials that are not in tune with his geographical environment or his activities. Men in European societies, regardless of the heat, are expected to wear coats and ties in public, while women, for the sake of fashion, are often grossly underclothed in the most frigid temperatures. Many an American salesgirl has remarked at the end of the day that her feet are killing her or that she has a headache. Her problem usually stems from the fact that she has spent long hours wearing shoes that, because of extremely high and slender heels, are not suited to her activities. Her grandmother also suffered discomforts in the name of beauty. She cinched in her waist so tightly that her swooning was probably more the result of lack of air than it was an affectation to be called forth in times of shock or emotional crisis.

Some cultural ideas do more than just cause discomfort, they actually reduce one's chances for survival. In time of war or other crisis, cultural values such as courage or patriotism often cause men to sacrifice their lives. If one's main purpose is to survive, one would certainly not respond to such values as courage and patriotism but would rather take the easiest and safest way out of each crisis situation.

Thus, we can see that man's behavior is more than just a response to certain physical or animal needs. The biological dimension of man represents only one influence on him. All mankind is one, biologically, but there are almost as many kinds of culture as there are societies. Therefore, it is plain that biological needs may be satisfied in a variety of ways. At this point it is quite pertinent to ask "If biology alone is not responsible for culture, what are the other factors involved?"

CULTURE AND GEOGRAPHY

Geography is always a factor to be considered in any attempt to understand the nature of a given culture. While geography does not determine what form a culture will take, it definitely has a limiting influence. Eskimos, for example, can never become farmers unless they build greenhouses (an unlikely possibility) for the arctic earth never thaws out for long enough periods to make agriculture possible. The conditions of their environment pretty much point them in the direction of hunting although there are peoples of Siberia who herd under almost exact climatic conditions. While the form of economy, and, for that matter, family and political organizations, of a people is often influenced by the nature of the region, people often persist in following customs that seem quite out of tune with their environment. These ideas are perhaps just capricious ones deriving from man's stubbornness against being controlled in a different climatic environment that persist although the people have shifted their habitat. An example of this is to be found in the division of labor ideas of the reindeer-herding people of Siberia, the Chuckchi, Koryak, and Yukighir. When their animals have exhausted the sparse tundra vegetation in one area, they must move. The men drive the herd to a new area, leaving the women to move the skin tents that make up the camp. Once the men have driven their animals to a suitable location they merely sit down and wait in the cold until the women arrive to build fires and set up the tents. Rather than engage in what they consider woman's work—building some type of crude windbreak or building a fire to warm themselves—the men sit and suffer in the cold. This perhaps doesn't make much sense to us, but the customs of many peoples seem irrational to those outside the culture.

Culture grows not only from the ideas that people originate themselves but also from the ideas they acquire from others. Using American culture as an example, we find that only a small proportion of the culture content has actually been developed by Americans. Ralph Linton estimates that at least ninety per cent of our ideas and objects have come to us from foreign sources. Since prehistoric times, societies have come into contact and have given or borrowed ideas about how men should organize their lives.

CULTURE AND HISTORICAL ACCIDENT

Nearly every culture in the world has probably at one time or another been influenced by historical accidents—events that have taken place that could not have been predicted by the people themselves and for which they were not prepared. The coming of the white man to North America greatly altered the nature of Indian cultures. The white man brought the Indian the horse, the gun, and the fur industry, but he also brought him the Indian reservation and the status of underprivileged minority group. The arrival of whites in the South Pacific was accompanied by the spread of both Christianity and influenza. Whole populations were wiped out and others, like the people of the Marquesas, were so demoralized that they almost completely lost their will to live. Earthquakes, floods, epidemics, drastic climatic changes, and a variety of other crises have drastically altered the cultural configurations of a variety of cultures around the world.

In summary it can be said that the unique history of each group determines the manner in which biological, psychological, and social needs will be satisfied. Man and societies must survive, but the manner in which they accomplish it is infinitely varied.

MAN WITH CULTURE IS LIKE A GROUP

Culture, in that it provides ready solutions for man's problems, allows each individual to face his environment as though he were a group. Even though a man may be completely alone he carries in his head the solutions to problems that have been discovered by men in many places at many times. He does not have to work out each solution for himself, but he can recall what he has read or what he has been told someone else did in a similar situation. Many an ex-serviceman is alive today because he had read one of the survival booklets published by the armed forces during World War II and the Korean War. These booklets represented a composite of knowledge known to primitive as well as civilized men about how to deal with specific problems in specific environments. Much of the knowledge that is so important to us today—how to use fire, how to farm and raise livestock—were ideas first developed by prehistoric man and perpetuated from one generation to the next for centuries through culture.

THE SUPERORGANIC

Culture is often referred to by sociologists and anthropologists as the *superorganic*. The term was first coined by the social philosopher Herbert Spencer, but more recently has been elaborated by A. L. Kroeber. The term is useful to the beginning student of anthropology, because its sheer composition tells something of the nature of culture. First we can think of "super" as meaning "other than" or "apart from." Considered in this way the word tells us that culture is not part of the organism; it is not passed on through the genes but rather through the processes of learning. Secondly, it is possible to think of "super" as meaning "greater than" or "more permanent than." Superorganic considered in this way reminds the student that culture outlives the organism—i.e., the life of culture is greater than a single generation. Culture may be considered to be "greater than" the individual organism in still another way. When we look at culture in a certain light, it almost appears to be a Frankenstein's monster. Although man created culture, in the end, culture molds and controls man. A newborn baby has little to say about what language he will learn, what religion he will observe, or how he will be disciplined. His parents have equally restricted lives. If they do not raise the child according to cultural prescription, there will be pressure from relatives and neighbors to do so. Culture seems to dictate when the child shall give up his bottle, when he shall be toilet trained, and when he shall begin to date. There may be things about culture that man does not like, but whether he likes it or not he must conform. If he deviates too far, society will take a stand and force him back in line.

The situation of man in regard to culture has been aptly described by Melville J. Herskovits, who likens culture to an escalator and society to those who ride on it. The escalator, of course, remains quite permanent while the people who ride it tend to change. People get on, ride for a time, and then get off, but the escalator goes on and on. Some people may try to walk up the steps but their efforts are insignificant compared with the movement of the escalator itself. Stepping onto the moving stairs is much like being born into a culture. For a time the riders are like the members of a society; they are part of the culture. Although, figuratively speaking, at death a person gets off the metaphorical escalator, this does not mean its end, for there are others just getting on and others in the process of riding it. The man who has just stepped off the moving stairs was a part of it for a time, but once his ride is over the escalator goes on, little changed by the fact that he was once a part of it.

Although we have made the statement that individuals do little to change the fundamental form of culture, it is important to realize that culture does change. Culture is relatively stable in its main outlines, but it is constantly changing. There is an old saying that there are two things that one can always be sure of—death and taxes. It would be valid to add still a third thing—change. The only unchanging cultures are those being studied by archeologists—i.e., dead ones. Change occurs in certain areas and within certain limits. For example, many of the basic values of American culture derive from the Judeo-Christian tradition, but there have been superficial changes. There are some areas in which changes are welcomed and other areas where new ideas and interpretations find stiff resistance. Each autumn Americans rush to showrooms to observe new automobiles with new designs and new gadgets. The inventor in American culture has high prestige. The area of technology is one in which change is desired. However, other aspects of our culture such as family organization or basic political and religious ideology are very conservative and slow to change. Innovators in these areas are often branded as immoral, subversive, or heretic.

Change comes to a culture from within the society itself, or new ideas may filter in from the outside. Although various aspects of a culture may have been added at various times, culture is not a hodge-podge of behavior patterns and nonmaterial objects. Everything that is part of a culture must be meaningful to the members of the society and all parts are related in some degree to all other parts. Although an item, such as fire, discovered nearly a million years ago, co-exists with the most modern of innovations, the many elements making up culture are knit into a consistent, intricately woven fabric.

NORMS OF SOCIETY—FOLKWAYS, MORES, AND SANCTIONS

In every society there are attitudes about the importance of follow-ing the dictates of culture, and there are attitudes about what things are right and what things are wrong. Sometimes these attitudes, which are also a part of culture, are very inconsistent. A thing may be right in one situation and wrong in another. In American culture, for example, a person may wear very scanty clothing on the beach, but, in another situation, on a downtown street, he is expected—in fact, required—to be fully clothed. It is the *mores* and *folkways* that require the citizen to walk a fine line of discretion and understand that there is a time and place for everything. The concepts of folkways and mores were developed by William Graham Sumner in 1906 but remain meaningful concepts today in spite of great advances in sociological and anthropological theory. In Sumner's theory, folkways are expected but not compulsory customs (e.g., Scotchmen wearing kilts or Americans tipping their hats) and mores are customs that are considered vital to the welfare of the society (e.g., Americans having but one wife at a time). Further insight into the operation of these principles may be seen by returning for a moment to the matter of decent or indecent dress.

Let us say that it is a very warm day and a man decides to remove his coat. No real harm is done as far as society is concerned, but we *are* entering the realm of folkways. In most places society would take no notice of this man's notion, but if he were ushering in church, a few eyebrows might be raised. This is because culture says that it is customary to wear one's coat if ushering in church. Now let us suppose that the man feels compelled to take off his tie. Again no real harm is done, but in his coatless and tieless condition he would probably be refused entrance to certain restaurants. Now let us imagine that our friend takes off his shirt. This action has restricted his movements still further. He may go without his shirt in the privacy of his home or backyard or on the beach, but if he were to walk down the street this way there certainly would be talk about his propriety. So far, we have been in the area of folkways, but we are about to enter the realm of mores. The man now takes off his pants! He is standing there only in his shorts. If these shorts were tailored in a certain way and if the design were an Hawaiian print, he could get by at the beach, but as he is now, he is pretty much restricted to his bedroom or the locker room at the YMCA. If he should go out on the street like this, he could expect to be hustled off to jail or perhaps to a mental institution, for he has broken a cardinal principle of society.

Culture carefully defines what is proper to do where, and it sets limits within which people have some latitude for deviation. These principles, which involve folkways, mores, and sanctions, perhaps are best labeled *norms*. They are the shared attitudes of what is legitimate or what is normal behavior for a given individual in a given situation. Certain individuals are expected to follow some norms more rigidly than others. The limits that culture sets for the minister or priest are much narrower than for the artist. If a clergyman were to do some of the things an artist might do, he would be considered mentally ill, for he has a well-defined role that is associated with him, restricting the types of residences he may occupy, the kind of friends he can have, the hours he must keep, and the type of family life he can enjoy.

Both men have a good deal of choice that they can exercise, but these choices are within the limits defined by culture. The choices open to the artist, while broader than those of the clergyman, do not include cutting off one's ear as Vincent Van Gogh did. There is a point where society steps in and says "You have gone far enough." Even people who are notorious for their nonconformity are operating within the safe limits that have been defined by their culture. The bearded young poet who lives in a garret is actually differing only superficially from the solid citizen who takes pride in his conformity. Both speak the same language, sit on chairs, sleep in beds, use knives and forks when they eat, and operate in terms of many of the same American cultural principles. Both want recognition—one in the area of business and the other in the area of the arts. Both will work hard and sacrifice to achieve their ends. Actually, the bearded poet is conforming as much as the business man. He is wearing a beard, living in a garret, eating bread and cheese and drinking wine because this is a recognized pattern for struggling young poets to follow. He may not be much of a poet, but he is determined to look and act like one.

REAL AND IDEAL CULTURE

The norms of society are often ideal standards of behavior that in actuality are followed by a relatively small number of people, although everyone gives lip service to them. If, for example, an anthropologist should come to the United States to study the cultural patterns of its citizens, he would find that the people would tell him that in America people get married for life, that unmarried people are completely celibate, and that there is complete equality among all Americans. In the course of his investigation he might also look into the matter of laws. His informants, for example, might explain that there are traffic laws that say that a red light means stop and a green light means go and that there are eight-sided yellow signs that do not have a light but demand a full stop from the motorist. The anthropologist would write all these responses from Americans down in his notebook and then, according to anthropological methods of study, go and observe the people living their lives. He would also go to the libraries to see what the literature could tell him about American culture.

Chances are, he would be quite surprised by what he would see and read. To begin with, he would find out that in reality there is, in a single year, about one divorce for every five marriages. If he were to look through the published works of Dr. Kinsey, he would find that unmarried people are far from celibate. If he really dug deeply into the situation of equality and equal rights, he would find that American Indians and American Negroes do not have equal opportunities with whites in getting jobs, finding adequate housing, or getting an education. He would also find, if he stood on a corner for any amount of time that the eight-sided yellow sign reading "Stop" is but haphazardly observed. His observations would no doubt be much like those of the psychologist Allport (1934). Approximately seventy-five per cent of motorists literally obey the sign and come to a complete stop. Twenty-two per cent reduce their speed and proceed very slowly. Another two per cent will slow down slightly, while about one per cent will proceed as though the sign did not exist.

Thus, it is important to realize that what people say that they do is not necessarily what they actually do. There is often a great gap between the ideal and the real patterns of culture. It is because of this discrepancy that anthropology utilizes both interview and observation techniques. Using both of these approaches in collecting data, the anthropologist has a chance to verify what is told to him and to assess the degree of conformity or nonconformity that is sanctioned by the society.

SUGGESTED READINGS

FORD, C. S. "Culture and Human Behavior," *Scientific Monthly*, December, 1942. (Comments on the problem-solving function of culture.)

HEWES, GORDON W. "The Anthropology of Posture," *Scientific American*, February, 1957. (How posture and motor behavior are influenced by culture.)

KROEBER, A. L. "The Superorganic," *American Anthropologist*, 19:163, 1917. (Explores the force of cultural tradition.)

MALINOWSKI, BRONISLAW. "Culture," *Encyclopedia of the Social Sciences*, 1931. (Defines culture and comments on how it develops in response to social, physical, and psychic needs.)

SAHLINS, MARSHALL D. "The Origin of Society," *Scientific American*, September, 1960. (Analysis of social behavior of lower primates for purposes of discovering clues to the origins of the human family and society.)

SAPIR, EDWARD. "Communication," *Encyclopedia of the Social Sciences*, 1931. (Discusses the importance of language and other forms of communication in the functioning of a society.)

———. "Culture: Genuine and Spurious," *American Journal of Sociology*, 29:401, 1924. (Varying definitions of culture; the relationship of the individual to the culture of his group.)

VOGT, EVON Z., and ROBERTS, JOHN M. "A Study in Values," *Scientific American*, July, 1956. (Comparison of value systems in various ethnic groups in the American Southwest.)

Paperbound Books

HARRIS, MARVIN. *The Nature of Cultural Things.* Random House. (Reveals how a taxonomy of cultural things can be grounded in observation of nonverbal behavior.)

KROEBER, A. L., and KLUCKHOHN, CLYDE. *Culture.* Random House. (Collection of definitions of culture.)

MALINOWSKI, BRONISLAW. *A Scientific Theory of Culture.* Oxford University Press. (The relationship of culture to biological and sociological needs.)

WHITE, LESLIE. *The Science of Culture.* Grove Press. (Presents anthropology as the science of culturology.)

6

The Units of Culture

In the previous chapter we have learned something about the importance of the concept of culture in studying the behavior of man, but culture is a very abstract and elusive idea and the anthropologist setting out to make an orderly and scientific study of any cultural system must have a basic set of theoretical tools to aid him in his research. It is all well and good to say to the student that anthropologists study culture, but when he asks "How?" he is inquiring as to the methods and procedures that are the earmarks of a scientific discipline. Over the rather short but vigorous period of its development, anthropology has devised systematic ways of breaking down total cultural configurations so that their structures may be studied more carefully.

To begin with, we must keep in mind that anthropology is a cross-cultural or comparative science. But it is difficult to handle simultaneously all the facts that have been learned about each and every culture because there are literally thousands of separate cultural systems in the world. From the very beginning of the discipline this has posed a serious problem and anthropology like every other science has had to develop methods for ordering vast quantities of data.

TRAITS AND ELEMENTS

One of the first concepts developed to make anthropological materials more comparable was that of the cultural *trait*, or cultural *element*. These have been defined as the minimal significant components of culture—i.e. the smallest identifiable units of culture.

Ordinarily, it is difficult to think in terms of traits, for nearly all reality as we perceive it is composed of bundles of interrelated elements, the individual items of which seem meaningless and insignificant when removed from their natural context. The average college student is very much aware of the colorful autumn Saturday afternoon extravaganzas that are known as "football games." The football game is actually a bundle or cluster of integrated traits, but ordinarily we do not think of it as such. We do not arrive at the stadium and set about analyzing the elements which make up the spectacle. As long as all of the right things are found in the stadium, we take the whole show pretty much for granted. The only time a fan would take notice of an individual trait would be if it were foreign to the normal state of affairs. A few years ago a professional football team appeared in a game wearing tennis shoes instead of cleated football shoes because they felt it would be easier to keep their feet on the frozen ground. This fact was written up on every sport page in the country. People were in this case made very much aware of one trait (a certain kind of footwear) in the football-game complex.

Whereas we do not ordinarily look for traits at a football game, a visiting anthropologist from another country would perhaps do so. In analyzing this great American custom he might record in his notebook such things as (1) eleven men on a team, (2) helmets, (3) jerseys, (4) cleated shoes, (5) yard markers, (6) one hundred-yard field, (7) officials with striped shirts, (8) cheers, (9) cheer leaders, (10) megaphones, (11) dozens of rules—each an individual trait of the game, (12) marching bands making clever formations during half time, (13) drum majors and majorettes, etc. A careful inventory of all the traits in the football complex would probably number into the thousands.

The concept of cultural traits or elements was one of the first theoretical tools developed in scientific anthropology. Ruth Benedict has pointed out that the reason for this is to be found in the procedures used by the early students of man. She reminds us that the early anthropologists

. . . were armchair students who had at their disposal the anecdotes of travellers and missionaries . . . It was possible to trace from these details the distribution of the custom of knocking out teeth, or of divination by entrails, but it was not possible to see how these traits were embedded in different tribes in characteristic configurations that gave form and meaning to the procedures. (1959:54–55)

Such works as Frazer's *Golden Bough* or Sumner's *Folkways* are classic examples of analytic discussions of traits that tend to ignore their integration in the total culture. While pioneers in the science of custom had little choice but to deal with traits, subsequent scholars found the concept useful and it continues to be a tool of anthropologi-

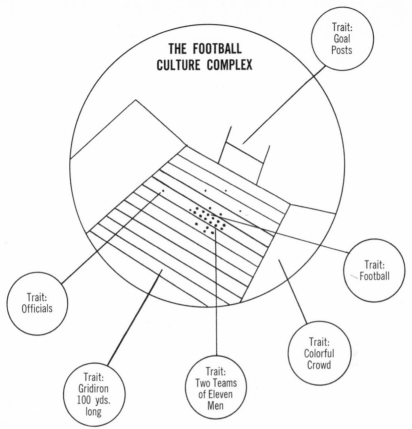

Fig. 6–1. The football culture complex.

cal research today. The cultural evolutionists Morgan and Tylor singled out certain traits found among various primitive and civilized groups as being representative of stages of either savagery, barbarism, or civilization. German, British, and American anthropologists alike were concerned during the 1920's and '30's with the spread (diffusion) of both material and nonmaterial elements of culture units over great areas of the world. Herskovits recalls how American anthropologists "traced the details of the Sun Dance among different Plains Indian tribes to ascertain with precision what elements of this complex rite were found in what cultures; studies which enabled them to draw conclusions not only as to what had been diffused, but how the elements that moved from tribe to tribe had been adapted and readapted in each new setting" (Herskovits 1953:59). In the course of research of this type elaborate distribution maps were made in terms of single traits, and Fig. 6–2, originally drawn up by Clark Wissler (1923:54), is an example of this approach.

Fig. 6–2. Variations in dress patterns among Indians of western United States (after Wissler).

In the process of drawing up a trait inventory of any group, the student of culture cannot help but be impressed with the great complexity of any cultural system. It makes him aware that in the study of man there are no simple answers and above all there are really no "simple" cultures. Even the rudest of cultures such as that of the Australian aborigines seems infinitely complex when one attempts to list the hundreds upon thousands of traits that make up the social, economic, and religious institutions of their society. William Bascom (1948) did much to change ideas about the "simpleness" of West

African culture by describing the many traits that make up such complexes as divination, folklore, medicine, cult activity, and certain aspects of art among the Yoruba of Nigeria.

In the area of divination (soothsaying) Bascom claims that no diviner can practice professionally until he has committed to memory at least one thousand verses and their accompanying sacrifices and charms. The better diviners know up to four thousand verses. Over three thousand Yoruba proverbs have been published, and it is not unusual for a Yoruba to be able to recite two hundred and fifty or more at a single sitting. Better than three thousand remedies for diseases have been recorded and about an equal number of charms and medicines having to do with wealth, good luck, safe journeys, marriage, and hunting have found their way into anthropologists' note books. The Yoruba worship some one hundred and thirty-two deities, each of which has a separate cult group presided over by approximately sixteen priests. In the area of arts and crafts, thirteen patterns of men's weaving and fourteen forms of women's hair dress are known.

THE CULTURAL COMPLEX

Although traits are useful tools for research, it must be remembered that they are not meaningful units by themselves, and, what is more, no culture is made up of just so many traits gathered up haphazardly by a society over a period of time. There is always a compatible integration of traits into complexes, patterns, and total configurations of culture.

We have mentioned the football game as a composite of associated traits—i.e., a complex. It is but one of several thousand that are part of our daily lives. The college student is quite familiar with the classroom complex, which is composed of such traits as desks, books, blackboards, lectures, a professor, a philosophy of education, students, note books, and so on. As we read on we will become acquainted with many of the cultural complexes known to people in other parts of the world—the Kula trading complex of the Trobrianders, the Sun Dance complex of the Sioux, and the Snake Dance complex of the Hopi Indians.

CULTURE PATTERNS

The culture pattern has been a significant concept ever since it was brought to the attention of the anthropological profession by Ruth Benedict in her now famous book *Patterns of Culture*. In this work she analyzed the Zuni, Dobuan, and Kwakiutl cultures and showed how specific traits and complexes fit together in a particular way to give a certain set or direction to each of these cultures. Culture patterns that have been defined as structural regularities in culture can perhaps best be illustrated by analyzing the phenomenon of language. Of course, linguistic behavior is like any other type of cultural behavior—it is learned and shared by the members of a particular society. Language is made up of sounds (traits) and combinations of sounds (complexes), but no two languages are put together in exactly the same way. The unique, but consistent, manner in which the linguistic elements are linked together represents the pattern of the language. For example, in the English language adjectives always precede the noun, plural subjects always require plural verbs, and if a "q" appears in a written word, it must be followed by the letter "u." Similar types of regularities occur in all languages.

Every society has a certain set of distinctive culture trait and culture complex linkages that set it apart from other societies. These unique combinations of cultural elements represent meaningful reality to the members of that society and tend, therefore, to persist over many generations. In every society there are, for example, shared patterns of motor behavior, family organization, dress, and ceremonial life. In our own society families are typically composed of one husband, one wife, and their offspring. Very little importance is placed on kin relationships outside this small, intimate group. The wife has equal status with the husband and their main purpose aside feom the reproductional function is the pursuit of happiness. The West African family, on the other hand, is patterned along very different lines. "Blood" or kinship ties are considered more important than marriage ties. The preferred form of family is a husband, several wives, and their children. Wives have a much lower status than do their American counterparts, and the economic function of the family is more highly emphasized than the affectional. Romantic love is an unknown concept. Men are more concerned with finding compatible, industrious childbearers than they are with finding personal companions.

Cultural Adhesions

In discussing the linkage of traits and complexes which form the patterns of culture, something should be said about those traits and complexes that naturally seem to hang together in a variety of cultures. As early as 1888 the British anthropologist Edward Tylor became aware of the fact that certain features of culture frequently are found in association with others. In a survey of three hundred fifty-nine cultures (1889) he found that where there is matrilocal residence—i.e., where a married couple resides with the wife's parents—there also tends to be a custom forbidding the son-in-law to look at, speak to, or enjoy any social relationship with his wife's mother. Subsequent investigations have demonstrated that pottery-making is frequently associated with maize cultivation; wife-purchase, with pastoral economy; infanticide and wife-lending, with hunting economy; and human sacrifice with agricultural economy. Tylor referred to these complexes that tend to go hand-in-hand as *adhesions*. His investigations not only provided anthropologists with greater insight into the way cultures are structured, but they represent the first use of correlation statistics in the study of anthropology.

Cultural Configurations

Actually it is possible to talk about patterns within patterns. A pattern may have to do with aspects of culture, such as family structure and behavior, or it may be used to refer to the total configuration of the culture. It was Benedict's point in *Patterns of Culture* that if the overall emphasis of the culture was either cooperative, materialistic, or hostile, each and every pattern within it bore the stamp of the total culture. It was her claim that "the whole determines its parts, not only their relation but their very nature" (1959:57). She also pointed out that "a culture, like an individual, is a more or less consistent pattern of thought and action" (1959:53).

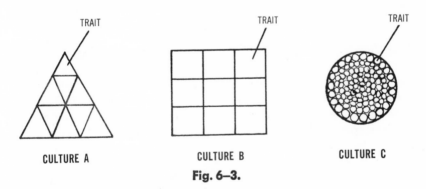

Fig. 6–3.

Figure 6–3 portrays this idea graphically. It will be noted that the form of the individual units that make up the culture is consistent with the overall configuration. In illustrating how a culture is oriented in particular directions, Benedict reveals how, in the culture of the Zuni Indians of New Mexico, there is a general consistency of patterns, which in their totality constitute a cultural configuration that places stress or importance on cooperation, group (rather than individual) action, sobriety and serenity. The nature of all of the various aspects of this culture is consistent with the overall emphasis of the culture.

The family, for example is, according to Benedict's description,[1] a highly regulated institution with little regard for individual action. Marriages are arranged; the couple's place of residence is determined by custom; and there is no place in the system for such emotions as jealousy, revenge, or deep and lasting attachment. Status is derived from clan membership rather than wealth, and even the important position of priest is determined by kin relationship rather than individual qualifications.

The typical Zuni avoids positions of leadership. If they are thrust upon him he will accept his responsibility but no Zuni enjoys being placed in the limelight. Zuni culture, however, is consistent in the fact that it does not expect its leaders to exercise individual authority over their fellows. Since everyone cooperates, leaders are not required to exert authority.

In this Pueblo society everything is done in concert, with the group's interests always paramount. Even dancing is ritualistic, orderly, and performed in unison. Worship takes the form of group ritual and prayers to the deities are mild, prescribed, and ceremonious in form. They are appeals for "orderly life, pleasant days (and) shelter from violence" (1959:66). The ideal man is one who is inconspicuous in his community, and drunkenness, crime, and other forms of violent behavior are virtually unknown.

THE CULTURE AREA

Another tool that has greatly aided the study of cultural anthropology is the concept of *culture area*. Culture areas, commonly defined as regions of common culture, allow for a systematic approach to the study of cultural similarities and differences. There are literally thousands of societies in the world, each practicing a way of life unique in certain respects even from their nearest neighbors. If cultural anthropology—the cross-cultural study of man—were to try to deal with each and every one of these cultures separately and try to compare their ways of life with all the others in the world, the task would be impossible. Therefore, some method of grouping or classifying cultures together is a necessity. The concept of culture area satisfies this need. The technique of classifying cultures is not a great deal unlike that developed by the Swedish naturalist Carolus Linnaeus in 1758, for

[1] It should be pointed out that Benedict's characterizations of Zuni life in *Patterns of Culture* have been the subject of much controversy. Other investigators who have worked among these people feel that many of her statements are oversimplifications that ignore a great deal of individual variability. See Bennett (1946) and Li An-Che (1937).

classifying the animal kingdom. In an effort to create some order in the scientific study of animals, Linnaeus developed a taxonomic system— i.e., a method of grouping animals according to the degree to which they resembled one another in their biological makeup. Of course, he divided the animal kingdom into various categories such as phyla, classes, orders, families, genera, and species, but for our purposes let us look at what he did in the case of a special group of animals that he labeled mammals.

Mammals are a class of animals having certain characteristics in common. Some of these characteristics are that the female suckles the young, they have two sets of teeth (a milk and a permanent set), they have warm blood and a hair- or fur-covered body, etc. In spite of these similarities there are thousands of varieties of mammals. Believing that systematization and order is a necessary part of scientific investigation, Linnaeus divided them into suborders (again based on common biological characterics) such as ungulates (hooved animals), rodents (gnawing animals), primates (apes, monkeys, and man), carnivores (flesh-eaters), and so on.

In similar vein, the grouping of cultures according to culture areas is in effect a taxonomy of cultures. Although culture area classification has not been developed to the degree that animal classification has, it nevertheless has proved a useful tool for acquainting students with the varieties of cultures throughout the world without resorting to a description of each and every culture. We can talk about types of cultures rather than individual cultures. Just as the suborder ungulata referred to a variety of hooved animals—giraffes, cattle, horses, camels—culture areas do not necessarily imply a complete similarity of cultural traits among the cultures of a certain area. Instead, it means that the cultures grouped together are more alike than are those groups who live farther apart. When we say, for example, that the Indians of the Northeast Woodlands of North America lived in bark longhouses, we do not mean to imply that every single tribe used this identical type of houses; we merely mean that it is characteristic of the people of that area.

It has sometimes been claimed that the concept of culture area grew out of the rather concrete problem of how to display artifacts in anthropological museums. There may, indeed, be something to this claim, as the man who is generally credited with the development of this system of classifying culture was Clark Wissler, head curator of anthropology at the American Museum of Natural History in New York. Although the first application of this technique was used in connection with American Indian societies, anthropologists have subsequently classified the cultures of nonliterates all over the world. (See Fig. 6–4, 6–5, 6–6, and 6–7.)

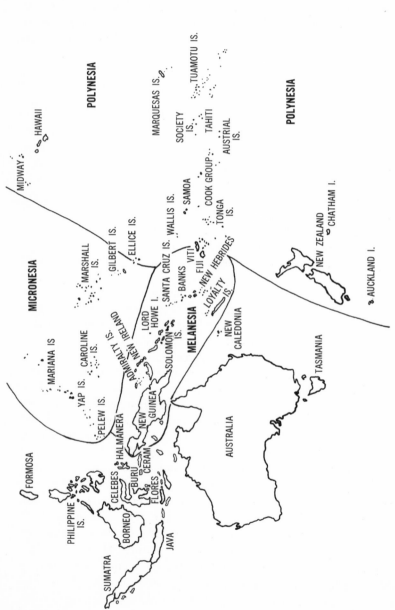

Fig. 6–4. Culture areas of the Pacific (after Linton).

In his book *Man and Culture* (1923), Wissler gives us some indication of the methods used in deriving his set of culture areas of North America. First, he made a survey or analysis of the food resources and methods of subsistence. After this information had been plotted, Wissler turned to such factors as methods of transportation, varieties of textiles, and ceramic types. The distribution of house type and other

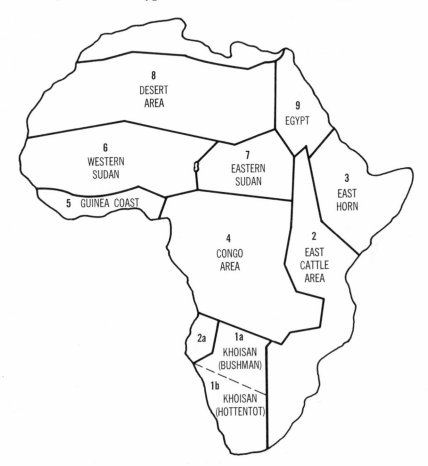

Fig. 6–5. Culture areas of Africa (after Herskovits).

forms of native architecture was then considered along with the characteristics of stone and metal work. Although Wissler did attempt to categorize the distribution of social institutions, ritual behavior, and mythology, it must be pointed out that the first culture areas were drawn up mainly according to distributions of material cultures. The fact that food resources and subsistence methods were of primary importance made geographical and climatic conditions figure heavily in the results. Boas was quick to recognize the weaknesses in this method and pointed out that "The student interested in religion, social organization or some other aspect of culture would soon discover that the culture areas based on material culture do not coincide with those

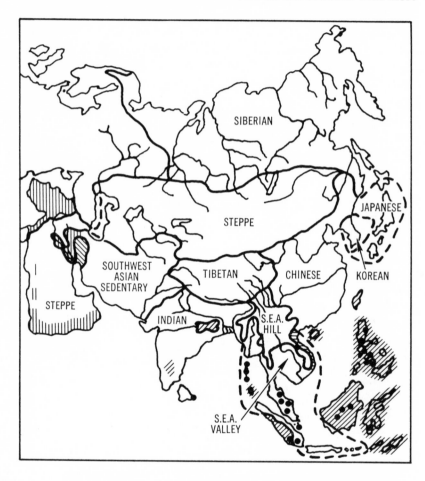

Fig. 6–6. Culture areas of Asia (after Naroll 1950).

Key to enclaves

Vertical hachures—Southwest Asian Sedentary
Diagonal hachures (NW-SE)—Steppe
Horizontal hachures—Southeast Asian Valley
Diagonal hachures (NE-SW)—Southeast Asian Hill
Solid black dots—Southeast Asian Marginal [add Palawan]

that would naturally result from his studies" (1938:671). Another feature of Wissler's methodology was the identification of culture center—i.e., the point within the culture area that best characterized the area as a whole. As one moved away from the culture center, one would find less and less of the characteristic elements of the area and "the tribal cultures lying at the boundary between two distinct culture areas are mixtures" (Wissler 1923:57).

To better understand the concept of culture area and also learn something of the variety of culture among North American Indians, let us look at the nine areas that have been differentiated. In the following presentation a traditional set of areas will be described, not only in terms of material aspects of culture, but in terms of nonmaterial factors as well.

Culture Area 1—Eskimo and Arctic

The Eskimo peoples represent the latest of the Asiatic migrants into North America. The harsh environment of this arctic region imposes certain restrictions on the cultures of the area making for a general uniformity of culture. In certain respects, however, it is possible to differentiate Eastern from Western Eskimo culture.

The major subsistence activities in most areas are sea mammal hunting in the winter when the people camp near the sea, and caribou hunting in the summer when they go inland. Common weapons include the harpoon and bow and arrow. The diet, made up mostly of fat and meat (frequently uncooked), is supplemented from time to time with fish. While men are dominant in subsistence activities, women are essential in the household as they dress hides, make clothes, and prepare the food. The realization that a man can not survive on a hunting trip without a woman greatly encourages the Eskimo custom of wife-lending.

During the summer months, skin tents are universal with all Eskimos, but in the winter Alaskan Eskimos live in rectangular earth-covered homes while the Eastern groups live in domed snow igloos. Certain objects of material culture—kayaks, woman's knives, bowdrills, snow goggles, dog sleds (fan hitch in the East, tandem hitch in Alaska)—are found throughout the entire area.

The Eskimo family is typically monogamous, but wife hospitality and wife-lending are common features. The immediate family is the significant social unit, and kinship, emphasizing kinship ties with both the male and female lines, is not unlike that found in the modern American family. Formal political organization is non-existent and

Fig. 6–7. Culture areas of North America.

group activities involving leadership are confined to activities such as communal seal hunts.

Eskimos believe that all animate and inanimate objects have souls, and there is a concept of an impersonal supernatural force known as *sila* that resembles the *manitou* concept of Indian groups or the *mana* concept of Pacific islanders. Mythology is simple and centers about tales of Sedna, the goddess of whales, seals, walrus, and everything that lives in the sea. Shamanism (medicine men) is prominent, but the only ritualistic ceremonies involving groups of people consist of yearly gatherings in which masked men impersonate the gods.

Culture Area 2—Northwest Coast

Although there is some variation from north to south within this region, the cultures are definitely maritime-oriented. The dominant subsistence activity is fishing, and during the time of the year when salmon swim upstream to spawn, great numbers of them are taken with weirs, nets, or spears, thus providing these tribes with literally a harvest of fish. Fish are preserved by smoking and sun-drying and constitute the year-round staple foodstuff. Additional items in the diet include the meat of sea mammals, deer, and rabbits, as well as wild plants, berries, and camass bulbs, which are collected by the women.

The Northwest Coast tribes have great wealth by American Indian standards. There is an emphasis on private property, and rival chiefs often compete for status and prestige by trying to outdo one another in the destruction of valued objects.

Since the climate in most of this area is mild but rainy, clothing for men consists merely of breech clouts, soft soled moccasins, fiber rain ponchos, and curious basket hats, not unlike those worn in certain parts of China. Women are attired in bark or skin skirts and sleeveless jackets in the north and skin aprons in the south of the region.

Planked rectangular houses, quartering several families, feature gabled roofs in the north, conical in the south. Typical household property includes wooden containers and baskets, but pottery is unknown. For purposes of travel and whaling, cedar dugout canoes are produced, some over one hundred feet in length.

The Northwest Coast family traces relationship through both sides of the family (bilateral descent),[2] and it is common for the newly married to take up residence in the village of the husband's kin. Clan organization is strong, and the head of the ranking clan serves as community chief. Villages are autonomous and warfare between these sovereign political units is common.

Secret societies dramatize myths concerning a host of deities including supernatural animals that can take human form. There is a belief in life after death and in spirits who serve as guardians.

Perhaps the most outstanding feature of the Northwest Coast culture pattern is its unusual art tradition. Highly stylized and symbolic animal motifs emphasizing bilateral symmetry are common decorative elements of totem poles, Chilkat blankets, and dance masks. Without doubt the artisans of the Northwest Coast are as fine woodworkers as may be found anywhere in the world.

Culture Area 3—California Basin

The California Basin has been referred to by one author as the "tower of Babel" because at least one hundred and four separate languages are known to exist in this area. A. L. Kroeber divided the

[2] See Chapter 9 for more precise definition of kinship terms.

area into four subdivisions, each representing a subculture, but for our purposes we will take the people of the central portion of the region as representative of the area. Although the tribes of this region hunt for certain varieties of small game that the land provides, the most important source of food is the acorn, which is collected and ground into meal for making bread. Men fish and hunt for small game with the bow and arrow, but it is mainly the women who provide food for these societies.

Living a nomadic existence, these people possess little in the way of material goods. Houses are brush structures, easily and quickly constructed, and clothing is scanty. Both sexes go barefooted and small aprons of shredded bark satisfy their modesty requirements. On certain occasions men wear headbands or crowns of brilliant feathers. While these people do not practice the potter's art, they are world renowned for their basketry. In spite of their material poverty, there is a definite concept of private and group property.

Families consist of a man, one wife, and their children, with kinship being reckoned through both sides of the family. Married couples have a tendency to settle down with the wife's family. Clan organization is non-existent and there is little in the way of class distinction. Tribes in this area are small and political organization informal.

A variety of shamans, each associated with the spirits of different animals or natural objects, are revered. Girls' puberty ceremonies and secret initiation ceremonies for men are common practices. The most important ritualistic activity, however, is the annual Kuksu ceremony wherein dancers, instead of wearing masks, drape and crown themselves with feathers. Among the northern tribes of the region there is a body of mythology that includes stories of a single creator deity.

Culture Area 4—The Plateau Area

Although this culture area has a number of distinct characteristics, it must be thought of as a zone of transition between the culture areas of the Northwest Coast and the Plains.

The inhabitants of the Plateau subsist primarily by hunting and fishing; the former being of greater importance in the east, the latter in the west. The hunting people, who are somewhat more nomadic than the fishermen, use bows and arrows, spears, and a variety of snares and deadfalls to take deer, elk, beaver, and mountain sheep. The fishermen of the west, however, subsist mainly on salmon and follow the lead of their Northwest Coast neighbors in the use of seines, dip nets, spears, and hooks. Gathering, an activity of the women, centers around the search for berries, bitterroot, and particularly camass bulbs.

In prehistoric times the people of this region wore rabbit-skin robes, or nothing at all. In historic times, however, they have adopted a pattern of dress where males wear shirts and thigh length leggings and soft moccasins while women wear belted and fringed tunics and leggings. Rabbit-skin robes and caps continue to be worn by both sexes in winter.

The typical Plateau house consists of a circular pit, four to five feet deep, over which is built a conical or pyramidal thatched roof covered with a layer of earth. A smokehole at the top serves as both exit and entrance for the several families occupying the house. Basketry is, in some places, a fine art, but there is little in the way of pottery.

The Plateau people have no clans, and descent is counted on both sides of the family. Some polygyny is found, particularly in the north. Village organization is loose and chiefs are chosen on the basis of their ability. In the west, there is a tendency toward hereditary offices and in the east, where Plains influence is felt, chieftainship often depends upon war exploits.

The most important religious ceremony is the Spirit Dance wherein frenzied dancers are possessed by their guardian spirits. However, most Plateau ceremonies are simple, featuring songs, prayers, and short dances in honor of the spirits of wild plants or the first salmon of the season. Purification rites for hunters and puberty ceremonies for both sexes are common. Mythology consists of little but a few simple explanatory and trickster tales. Shamans, often women, cure illness and even recover guardian spirits that have been lost or stolen.

Culture Area 5—Mackenzie—Yukon

In this vast wilderness area of Northwest Canada are to be found a group of nomadic caribou-hunting tribes that, except for certain minor features of their social organization and material culture, exhibit great cultural uniformity throughout the area. Men hunt and women gather, but agriculture is absent. It has been stated that the lives of these people are as dependent on caribou as Plains Indians' are on buffalo.

Clothing, tailored from caribou hide and decorated with quills, features shirts and leggings with moccasins attached. Conical skin tents and double lean-to huts suit their nomadic way of life, and household objects include baskets but not pottery. Encampments are commonly made along rivers or lakes and travel is facilitated by bark and skin canoes in summer and toboggans and snow shoes during the winter months.

Monogamous marriage is the pattern, but wife hospitality is common. The individual considers himself as closely related to his father's family as he is to his mother's. The location of marital residence, however, varies from region to region. In the south it is with the wife's family, with the husband's family in the north, and optional in the east. Clan organization is weak and the normal social grouping is the hunting band, chieftainship being an hereditary office.

Religion is not highly developed. Medicine men perform magic rites and healing rituals, but there is an absence of group ceremonies. These Indians have a concept of supernatural spirit guardians, which appear to them in dreams and to whom they make sacrifices.

Culture Area 6—The Plains

No Indian culture is better known to the average American than that of the Plains. Actually, most Americans erroneously believe that all American Indians lived like the people of this area. Prior to about 1700 the Plains inhabitants cultivated maize and hunted buffalo and other large game on foot, but by this date most tribes were in possession of horses and as a result became highly nomadic people living almost exclusively off the vast buffalo herds that roamed the western plains.

Since these people are constantly on the move, material goods have to be light and easily portable. Dwellings are buffalo skin tepees, which can be folded up and transported by travois (lodge poles with platforms, drawn by horses). Prior to the advent of the horse, dog-packing and dog travois were used. In place of pottery, these people utilize a hide envelope for various kinds of storage. Clothing, made exclusively of buffalo and deerskin, features shirts, hip-length leggings, breech clouts, and soft moccasins for men, and ankle-length T-shaped dresses with soft moccasins and short leggings for women. Famous articles of men's attire are the eagle feather war bonnet (the symbol of membership in a military society) and buffalo robes. Bows and arrows and lances are used in both hunting and warfare, but the most prized possessions of the men are their horses.

The hunting band is the significant social and political unit, although tribes do function as units on certain occasions. The majority of families are monogamous, although it is reported that about twenty per cent of the men have more than one wife. Since women play a rather insignificant part in the economy, they are married for their beauty rather than their industry. Kin relationship is traced through the mother's side of the family (matrilineal) among the Crow, Hidatsa, Pawnee, and Mandan, but through the father's side (patrilineal) among the Omaha, Ponca, Iowa, Kansa, and Osage. In most places (except the western edge of the Plains) marital residence is patrilocal (with the husband's family). Clans are exogamous (forbidding marriage to a fellow clan member) and most tribes place great emphasis on voluntary association groups, such as secret societies, age grades, or military or soldier societies. There are definite status differences; however, positions of prestige are not inherited but, rather, earned through war exploits or through amassing wealth (in the form of horses) by raiding other tribes. Great stress is placed on the individual in this society and competition for war honors is keen. Even the religion is highly individualistic. Every man has his own private guardian spirit, which appears to him in visions. Visions are induced through the ingestion of drugs or through self-torture. The Sun Dance is by far the most important of the religious ceremonies of these people. While the ceremony varies somewhat from tribe to tribe, generally it is a rite in which great numbers of men torture themselves so that they might establish communication with the spirits. War dances of various kinds, including the scalp dance, follow each encounter with the enemy.

Culture Area 7—The Northeast Woodlands

The Northeast Woodlands area is the largest of the culture areas and the one that presents a number of problems of classification. The Iroquois tribes, located at the very heart of the region, have a number of features—principally in the areas of social and political organization—that are not shared by other groups in the area. There has also been a tendency to set apart the Great Lakes, or Calumet, tribes becauses of unique cultural features.

Throughout most of the region, maize cultivation, a woman's occupation, is the dominant form of subsistence. Hunting is an important activity in the Great Lakes area, but shows decreased emphasis as one moves east. Whereas tribes like the Iroquois live a sedentary village life, the Great Lakes people live in villages during the summer but break up into nomadic hunting bands during the winter.

In the warmer months, Northeast Woodlands men commonly wear soft moccasins and a breech clout, but Iroquois frequently add a kilt and tunic, and tribes in the north wear thigh-length leggings with moccasins attached. Winter, of course, necessitates the addition of shirts and robes. Women throughout the area are outfitted with skirts and moccasins, but Iroquois women also wear a sleeveless shirt. Shirts and even leggings are worn by Great Lakes women during cold weather.

Birch Bark is a valuable resource throughout the whole area, and containers, canoes, and even houses are made of it. The Iroquois long house, constructed of bark over a pole framework, measures as much as three hundred feet in length, and houses a number of related families in separate apartments. The Great Lakes house is known as a wigwam. It is dome-shaped with a covering of bark, mats, or hides. In the northern parts of the culture area conical tepees are found.

Family organization varies in form. The Iroquois place great importance on the mother's line, while Great Lakes people trace kinship through the father's family. Northern tribes stress relationship with both sides of the family. Clans and groups of clans (moieties) are found among all tribes and in some, clan membership is a determining factor in the selection of leaders. The Iroquois elect their chiefs, but they are always members of a special clan. An outstanding phenomenon in this culture area is the League of the Iroquois, a confederation of six tribes for the purpose of maintaining peaceful coexistence among its members.

Shamanism (medicine men) and guardian spirits are common features of Northeastern Woodlands religion as are planting and harvest festivals. The Iroquois believe in a variety of deities, among them being gods of Thunder and Rain, Grains, Fruits, an Earth Mother, and the Three Sister spirits of maize, beans, and squash. Many of these deities are worshipped by members of secret societies, the most famous of which are the False Face and Bear Societies.

Culture Area 8—The Southeast Woodlands

The Southeast Woodlands is the home of the "Five Civilized Tribes" —the Creek, Chickasaw, Choctaw, Cherokee, and Seminole. If any group of North American Indians deserves the designation "civilized," it is certainly the people of this region. Greatly influenced by Mayan civilization, these Indians built earthen pyramids, developed complex religious, social, and political systems, and lived in what might be described as urban communities.

The Southeast Woodlands region is one where intensive agriculture is practiced. Corn, beans, and sunflowers, the principle crops, are cultivated on family plots by the women. A town plot is also worked in order to support the ruling chief (mico), who presides over the town council of chiefs and gives all of his time to civic responsibilities.

Some hunting for deer and small game is carried on by the men, but these activities are definitely secondary in importance to the work of the women. The major activity of the men is making war. Like the Aztec of Mexico these Southeast Woodland people built their culture around warfare. In these highly stratified tribes the highest honors and ranks are given to those most successful in battle. Great warriors are permitted to wear special costumes and tattoos and to be addressed with honorific titles.

Houses have thatched roofs and clay-daubed walls and, in the case of chiefs, are built on mounds. An exception is the Creek people, who live in semisubterranean dwellings. Household items include cane baskets and mats, coiled pottery, and wooden bowls, mortars, and stools. The bow and arrow is the sole weapon of the hunt, but warfare is carried on with bows and arrows, wooden clubs, shields, cane armor, and lances.

Summer clothing for men includes breech clouts and ankle-high moccasins. Winter temperatures, however, necessitate the addition of leggings and poncho-like shirts of buckskin. Women wear cloth or fiber wrap-around skirts and winter shawls of skin or fiber. Chiefs have the privilege of wearing feather robes and turbans of swan or eagle feathers.

Dugout canoes are the principal mode of transportation, and frequently they are used in making extended trading trips.

In spite of the relative wealth of the area, polygyny is rarely practiced. Families are mainly matrilineal and matrilocal—no doubt reflecting the importance of women in the economy.

The great emphasis on warfare is definitely reflected in the religious life of the people. No one can lead others in warfare unless he has first experienced a vision promising supernatural aid. Every village has its war bundle—a collection of bear claws, bird skins, and deer hooves—which through its magical properties makes warriors strong and brave. This bundle is so sacred that it is not allowed to touch the ground.

In thatched temples, built atop huge earthen mounds resembling pyramids, a special class of priests tend sacred fires and direct rituals to the Sun, Corn, and War gods that often include sacrifices of human lives. Like many other agricultural Indians, a first fruit celebration, known in this case as the Green Corn Ceremony, is an annual occasion of great importance.

Culture Area 9—The Southwest

Two major culture patterns may be distinguished in the American Southwest. One pattern, the Pueblo (Zuni, Hopi, and Rio Grande peoples), features maize agriculture and permanent village life, while the other, the Nomadic (Apache and Navaho), emphasizes hunting and herding.

The principal agricultural products of the Pueblos are maize, beans, squash, and cotton, and, contrary to the usual North American Indian pattern, these activities are in the hands of men. Other subsistence activities include some small game hunting with bows and arrows and a throwing stick, much like a boomerang, and gathering—primarily of piñon nuts. Maize, the staple food, is ground into meal and made into bread by the women.

Gathering and hunting play a much greater part in Apache economy than in Hopi, but even these people do some cultivating of corn, beans, and squash. The Navaho also farm, but since 1680 they have been primarily concerned with sheep-herding.

Pueblo villages are highly organized with elected governors and war chiefs, but, in spite of the existence of the latter, these people are far from being warlike. The Navaho and Apache, however, represent a constant threat to the peaceful Pueblos. The Apaches, because of their plundering habits, well deserve the name that was given them—"enemies of the cultivated fields." The Navaho were also a tribe of marauders until about 1868, when they were forced by the United States government to settle down to their herding and weaving and a more peaceful existence on the reservation.

A variety of housetypes can be found in the Southwest, but three major forms may be noted. Most Pueblos, as their name would indicate, reside in apartment house-style dwellings of adobe while the Navahos prefer the hogan. These homes are actually only a tripod frame of logs covered with sticks, bark, brush, and a six-inch layer of earth. The Apaches live in still another kind of house, a dome-shaped structure thatched with bear grass, known as a wikiup.

Quite characteristic of Pueblo dress modes are kilts of cotton, ankle high moccasins, and blankets of cotton or wool for men, and cotton or wool dresses with one shoulder bare and boot-type moccasins for women. Male Navahos typically dress in buckskin leggings and shirts, hard sole moccasins, and blankets, while their women wear dresses made from two small blankets sewn together at the shoulders and sides and belted. Buckskin, fashioned into shirts, leggings, and moccasins for the men and into skirts and poncho-type blouses for the women, represent the usual Apache apparel.

Although the Pueblos and Navahos utilize woven cloth, the art of weaving has never been an Apache accomplishment. In Pueblo societies, cotton and wool are made into cloth by men on an upright loom, but among the Navahos the women are the weavers. Using looms very similar to those of the Pueblos, they produce remarkably fine blankets in a variety of colors. Pottery and baskets are made by both nomads and village dwellers in this area, but no Indians in North America produce more superbly formed and decorated pottery than the Pueblo peoples.

In Pueblo society men go to live at the home of their bride where they serve as a friend to their children rather than a stern family head. The mother's brother is the disciplinarian. Maternal clans and matrilineal descent are universal. Monogamy is the rule among all Southwest peoples.

Western Apache and Navaho family systems are much alike. Both have mother clans, residence with the wife's family, and mother-in-law avoidance. Eastern Apaches (Jicarilla, Chiricahua, Mescalero), however, have no clans at all and descent is figured through both sides of the family rather than just through the women. Marriage residence is at the home of the wife.

For the Pueblos, religion is the most important thing in life. They have an advanced theology that includes ideas about a Mother Earth and a Father Sky and a special creation myth that tells of men emerging from the Womb of Earth with the assistance of two supernatural brothers, the War Gods. A special class of priests, as well as numerous secret societies, participate in a year-round calendar of ceremonies. One of the most famous Southwest dances, the Snake Dance, is performed by Hopis in the hope that the gods will send rain. Offerings of maize are made at special sand-painted altars located in underground ceremonial chambers called kivas. All Pueblo ceremonies are orderly and involve great ritual detail.

The religion of the Navaho differs greatly from that of the Pueblo peoples in that all ceremonies are carried on for the benefit of individuals rather than for the sake of the group as a whole. Most Navaho rituals are for the purposes of curing illness or of purification of those who have come in contact with outsiders. The Enemy Way ceremony is such a rite. No Southwest people have more magnificent ritual poetry (performed as chants) than the Navaho, and their sand-painting far excels that of the Pueblos.

Apache and Navaho religious systems have many things in common. Among these are sand-painting, curing rites and similar myths, but, in general, Apache religion is less elaborate in form, and the ceremonies are somewhat shorter.

THE ETHNOGRAPHIC PRESENT

In looking over the culture areas of the world and their unique forms of culture, the newcomer to anthropology will soon become aware of the fact that many of the characteristics mentioned as typical for a region can no longer be observed. Representations of the Central Andean region of South America, for example, describe the culture as it existed during the florescence of the Inca Empire. Although some remnants of this way of life may still be found in the area, the present picture is hardly characteristic of the civilization as it existed prior to Pizarro's conquest in 1533. The answer to why this is done in working out culture areas is that the characteristics of these regions of common culture are those that existed at the time of European contact, or at least at the time when the first adequate descriptions were made. Thus all cultures are placed on a common time plane that can be referred to as the ethnographic present. This type of procedure is necessary if cross-cultural comparisons are to be made, because it would be impossible to compare the Hawaiians, who live in Honolulu and are almost completely Westernized, with the natives of the Amazon Basin, who have had almost no contact with Europeans. All cultures must be rendered comparable and this means that we must analyze the culture as it was before coming under the influence of the industrial societies of the West. Thus, when the anthropologist uses the present tense in describing the culture of the Aztecs, he is fully aware that this culture no longer exists. He is merely using the "ethnographic present."

INSTITUTIONS

For many years it has been traditional in the social sciences to divide culture into units that are even more inclusive than the *complex*. These major divisions of culture are referred to either as *institutions* or *aspects* of culture. If the reader should pick up almost any general textbook in anthropology or sociology, he would find that there are separate chapters titled the Family, Government, or Political Organization, Economics, Education, and Religion. Thus, certain types of behavior are arbitrarily defined and set apart for purposes of study. The social scientist is very much aware, however, that institutions have no reality except in so far as he gives them reality. They are, in other words, abstract categories of norms, actions, and values extrapolated from the total configuration of culture. It is probably very unlikely that the representatives of any two cultural systems would ever make the same arbitrary divisions of culture. This is because culture is an interwoven fabric of elements and actions, in which family life has its economic and religious aspects; government cannot help but influence, and be influenced by, economics, education, religion, and so on. This problem of dividing up cultures into appropriate categories for study is somewhat less difficult for the sociologist than it is for the anthropologist. This is because the former is engaged to a greater extent in the study of Western industrialized society and in such society behavior tends to be much more compartmentalized than it does among primitives. By this we mean that the average American male is involved primarily in economic behavior between eight and five o'clock each day. He is involved in religious behavior from eleven to twelve o'clock on Sunday morning and on the first Tuesday after the first Monday in November he performs his political function. This, of course, is an extreme oversimplification of what happens in our lives, but for a moment let us compare our compartmentalized lives with those of primitives.

Suppose we were to approach an American Indian working in his fields. He is planting corn, but he is doing something rather unusual; he is placing a fish in each hillock. If we were to comment to him that he is engaged in an economic activity he might correct us by saying that he is really engaged in a religious activity. For the placing of fish in the hillock of corn might appear to us to be an act of fertilizing the plant but would be a religious act—an offering to the spirit of the maize—in his terms. The feast-giving phenomenon of the South Seas is another example of behavior that is hard to classify. A feast is a social event, but it is also a means of obtaining power and prestige for a chief and is therefore political. The fact that the event has involved the economic activities of an entire family or clan makes it still more difficult to decide whether a feast should be defined as a family, recreational, political, or economic activity. The same thing might be said of many of our own activities. Going to college may be at the same time (1) a way of getting a husband or wife, (2) a way of increasing one's earning potential, (3) a way of gaining social prestige, (4) a way of becoming educated, (5) a way of training one's self to become a religious specialist, (6) a way of having a good time, or (7) a way of meeting the right people (a political function in its broadest sense). If we were to study the phenomenon of higher learning, we would no doubt say that we were studying the institution or aspect of culture known as education, but we would also have to admit that attending college has many ramifications and extensions into other categorical areas of behavior.

While every social scientist approaches culture as a fabric of interwoven ideas and actions, it is nevertheless necessary to concentrate on separate categories of behavior, since it is obviously impossible to study everything at once. While the British functionalist Malinowski made a special point of stressing the interrelationship of institutions, his studies stressed one institution at a time and showed how various aspects of that institution related to other institutions. In his book, *Coral Gardens and Their Magic*, he concentrated primarily on the economic activities of gardening, but he also showed how gardening was related to family behavior, religion and magic, and political authority and prestige.

Aspects of Culture

Some anthropologists would prefer not to use the term institutions but instead apply the word *aspects* to the several categories of culture. This is because they think of institutions as being primarily a sociological term that stresses patterns of interrelationship of individuals—that is, hierarchies or structures of individuals such as church or political groups. The anthropologist, with his orientation toward the concept of culture rather than society, looks upon culture as a set of values and customs that necessitate in some cases interaction of individuals and organization of groups. Much of culture, he would point out, does not involve organizations of individuals at all. While one can hardly have a language by himself, the use of language does not necessitate a specific social organization. Although the artist must have public acceptance of his product, he does not necessarily have to interact with others in the creation of aesthetic products. In many societies religion is an entirely private matter. There is no elaborate theology, no class of priests, no religious equipment, but merely a tradition that, through a vision that a man seeks as an individual, he will encounter his own, unique guardian deity.

The Ambiguity of the Term "Institutions"

Institutions is for many sociologists and anthropologists a confusing term. An example of the problem social scientists face in the use of the word can be seen by analyzing the definitions given in one of our most widely read introductory sociology texts. In Ogburn and Nimkoff's *Sociology*, institutions are defined as "a constellation of socially significant customs collected around some function or set of functions, such as ruling, fighting, and worshipping, and important enough to be found in various places at different times" (1964:421). So far, this definition could apply to the most formal of religious systems or to the nonsocial function of an artist. However, the definition continues, "Social institutions are one of several types of social organization. Like all social organizations, they are social systems. Other types of social organizations are associations, crowds and publics" (*ibid.*). It would appear, therefore, that, on the one hand, social institutions are aspects of culture and, on the other, that they are also an arrangement of people. People and customs are not the same thing. The problem would seem to stem from a confusion of the abstract concepts of society and culture. Even the early sociologist Hobhouse points to the twofold aspect of all institutions as (1) "the recognized and established usages governing certain relations of men" and (2) "the organization (of men) supporting a complex of usages" (1924:48). Perhaps our problem would be solved if we were to think of *cultural institutions* as a set of values, customs, and principles handed down from generation to generation; and *social institutions* as those special areas of cultural and social behavior where group interaction and group organization are found.

At this point the student has a right to ask: Why is the term used at all, if it is so confusing? The answer seems to lie in historical reasons.

Institutional Origins

Interest in the "institutions" of man goes back to the very infancy of anthropology. The primary concern of early pioneers in anthropology, and even some of the social philosophers who came before them, was speculation on the origins of the family, religion, government, and so on. These categories of behavior were defined as "institutions" and designated as the proper and natural units for study.

Believing the European forms of these cultural entities represented the zenith in cultural development, they searched for institutional forms among primitives that they thought were furthest removed from those currently in operation. They believed that a simple belief in souls and spirits (*animism*), found among a number of technologically simple tribes, was probably closest to the belief system of primeval man. In time animism evolved into a belief in a variety of deities (polytheism). The final development, characteristic of civilized societies only, was a belief system that honored but a single all-powerful god (monotheism). While some scholars were manipulating the ethnographic data to prove their theory of the evolution of religion, others were concerned with theories for reconstructing the history of marriage and the family. Lewis Henry Morgan, John F. McLennan, and Sir John Lubbock maintained that the promiscuous horde was the first or earliest social unit, while Alexander Westermarck, a Finnish anthropologist, observing the male-dominated permanent families among even monkeys and apes, postulated a similar union or situation of mates and offspring among the earliest of men. Still other scholars proposed a matriarchal family preceded by a patriarchal form, and nearly all sociologists and anthropologists assumed that, since European families were monogamous, this must be a more advanced form than a polygamous family.

Modern anthropologists, while still interested in institutional behavior, have very different interests from their nineteenth century forerunners. The greater accumulation of ethnographic data, and the more objective approach to those facts that mark modern anthropology, has resulted in the position that there has been no universal uniform sequence of institutional forms. Furthermore, the futility of looking for institutional origins has long been a recognized fact.

Every modern anthropologist could probably venture an opinion of what the first form of family or religion might have been like, but such speculation is hardly conceived to be vital to the development of the science of man. The number one concern in modern anthropology is: What is the function of family, government, property, or religion in human society? Research today centers around studies of institutional behavior and how it satisfies social, biological, and psychological needs. Through an understanding of what family does in Masai society or Fiji Island society, it is believed that ultimately we will know more about the role of family among the human species in general. This is the goal of anthropological science and the reason for its cross-cultural and comparative approach.

SUGGESTED READINGS

BACON, E., and HUDSON, A. E. "Asia: Ethnology," *Encyclopaedia Britannica,* 1945. (Cultural characteristics of the six main culture areas of Asia.)

HILL, G. W. "Use of the Culture-area Concept in Social Research," *American Journal of Sociology,* 47:39, 1941. (Suggests how the culture-area concept may be adapted to sociological research of American society.)

LaFARGE, OLIVER. "Myths that Hide the American Indian," *American Heritage,* October, 1956. (Attempts to break down the stereotypes of American Indians by discussing their variability and cultural achievements.)

MOUNTFORD, CHARLES. "Earth's Most Primitive People," *National Geographic Magazine,* January, 1946. (The customs of the aborigines of Central Australia.)

OPLER, MORRIS E. "Themes as Dynamic Forces in Culture," *American Journal of Sociology,* 51:198, 1945–46. (Suggests the use of "theme"— dynamic affirmations of a culture that control and motivate behavior— in structural analysis and cultural dynamics research.)

SHAPIRO, H. L. "Peoples of the Pacific," *Natural History,* April, 1944. (A survey of culture and physical type in Polynesia, Micronesia, Melanesia, Indonesia, Australia, and Tasmania. Well illustrated.)

Paperbound Books

BOHANNAN, PAUL. *Africa and Africans*. Doubleday. (Varieties of race, language, and culture in Africa south of the Sahara.)

DRUCKER, PHILIP. *Indians of the Northwest Coast*. Doubleday. (Depth study of Northwest Coast culture area.)

LINTON, RALPH. *Tree of Culture*. Random House. (Cultural characteristics and historical development of all the culture areas of the world.)

LOWIE, ROBERT H. *Indians of the Plains*. Doubleday. (A comprehensive study of the cultures of the Blackfoot, Cheyenne, Crow, and Kiowa Indians.)

OLIVER, DOUGLAS. *The Pacific Islands*. Doubleday and Co. (The indigenous cultures of Oceania and their transformation.)

7

The American Culture Configuration

It is a common phenomenon for individuals who live in a culture to be the least aware of the characteristics of that culture. Much of life for the average individual consists of following certain customary routines, almost without thinking. Robot-like we rise at a prescribed hour, dress in the appropriate way, eat our usual breakfast, and guide our car along the regular route to the office. If there is a detour on one of the streets that we usually take, we often become upset and frustrated at having to work out an alternate solution in gaining our destination. Once at the office we participate in office routine, which might have been difficult to learn at first but after a time could be performed with a minimum of thought and effort. We are quite conscious, however, of the impression we are making on the boss because, after all, the important thing is to "get ahead." On weekends we pack the family up in the car and attend the church of our choice—probably the denomination we were raised in. The sermon reaffirms many of the beliefs that we have always ascribed to and the phrases of the minister are familiar and orthodox. About once every four years the average American exercises a cherished rite that is guaranteed him by the Constitution, but in most cases he scarcely takes notice of the issues at stake. If, for instance, our average American were raised in a Republican family, this is the way he will vote and he will tend to find the looks and personality of his candidate attractive and those of the opposition candidate offensive.

The point that we are trying to make is not that Mr. Average American is stupid or abnormal in any way. The point is that he is a product of culture and environment, and culture provides ready-made solutions to almost all problems. A man doesn't have to think about how and why he does things. It is easier and often more efficient for him to follow the regularly accepted procedure. This is what culture does for people.

Because most people are like this, they find it very interesting when an anthropologist describes how and why they behave in a certain way. After reading about themselves in a monograph on American culture by Margaret Mead or any number of other anthropologists, they might very well make the comment "She seems to have us pegged pretty well. I just never thought about it in that way." The real point is that Mr. Average American has never stopped to analyze his values and motivations at all. He has probably just never taken the time.

A CULTURE OF PARADOXES

The cultural pattern of the United States is one of numerous paradoxes and contradictions. This is probably the case in any complex civilization undergoing rapid change. We are a peace-loving people, but we have fought a war about every twenty years. We believe in rugged individualism, and yet we are known as a "nation of sheep." There is a basic belief in human equality and a lauding of the "common man" and yet there is great preoccupation with class differences. On the one hand, we express faith in the need for mass education and on the other we exhibit a general undercurrent of anti-intellectualism. Americans are great humanitarians, full of missionary spirit, but they are frequently hostile to welfare or foreign aid programs designed to relieve human suffering.

The interesting thing about these cultural contradictions is that the opposing attitudes just cited do not necessarily represent the views of different subgroups but are found simultaneously in the value system and behavior of the "average" American.

THE AVERAGE AMERICAN

Now we may rightly ask who the average American is and how it is possible to single out a set of cultural ideas and behavior patterns and maintain that it represents "the American Way." It is entirely true that America is a melting-pot nation with literally thousands of subcultures. There are class differences, ethnic differences, regional and even occupational differences, but social scientists have come to consider the relatively homogeneous values and customs of middle class America as being most representative of the American pattern of culture. It would seem that this is the image that is most frequently exported and the pattern that social scientists from foreign countries seem most impressed with in their visits to the United States.

Martin B. Loeb maintains that the real American way of life is that of the family in the little suburban row house, with the brood of well-scrubbed children, the picture window with its ribbon-trimmed lamp, and the hamburgers or other "bland foods" on the table. Such families, he believes, are quite puritanical about what they consider "proper," and this culture with its stress on cleanliness, respectability, and conformity is the same all over the United States. Geography or regional traditions affect this middle-class pattern very little, and in the South, for example, only the lower classes and the upper eat typical Southern food.

CONFORMITY

Any number of American and European observers have commented on the American compulsion to conform. This conformity is of a particular type, however. Riesman (1950) described our culture as other-directed—meaning that we are very much concerned with what our friends and neighbors think of us. We are concerned with what other people of our social position have and do, and, in order not to appear strange or peculiar, we tend to try to "keep up with the Joneses," carefully adhering to popular political trends and making sure that our houses, clothing, and cars are up to par. Capitalizing on this American characteristic, one clothing manufacturer has developed the phrase, "You can't afford not to dress right." Dressing "right" means, of course, having the right cut to one's pants, the proper width in the lapel, and the currently fashionable color. The tendency toward dressing "right" among one type of American businessman brought about the nickname "The man in the grey flannel suit." People of all cultures tend to conform, but not always in the ways found in America. Europeans conform also, but to the fashions and standards of the past. One need only recall the British coronation, with the ancient horse-drawn carriages and their footmen and military escorts in sixteenth century costume, to see how these people revere and conform to the past. Ancient castles, noble families, and coats of arms are vital elements of nearly all European cultures. Even peasants cling to ancient folk dances and customs and occasionally derive pleasure from donning the costumes of their ancestors. There is little of this type of thing in America. American centennial celebrations often feature beard-growing contests, but in most cases men neglect their razors not so much because their ancestors did, but because everyone else is doing it.

Perhaps the American pattern of conformity is different from that of Europe because the United States is still growing. It has not had time to establish its historic shrines and traditional customs. America is also a country on the move. Due to the high rate of mobility (approximately one American out of twelve moves from one city to another every year), few people have deep roots in any part of the country. The names and places of frontier or colonial days mean little to them. Of course, there is some interest in colonial furniture, civil war battlefields, and Independence Day celebrations, but Americans seldom feel constrained to do anything because "it has always been done that way."

Few Americans dare be different to any great degree and even the artist or intellectual who considers himself to be a "free thinker" deviates from the common culture pattern only on minor and insignificant points. The tendency to conform is reflected and reinforced on every hand. Housing developments feature row upon row of nearly identical houses with identical appliances. Mass education does little to foster or even tolerate individual differences. Dorothy Lee, an American anthropologist of Greek national background, tells of visiting her daughter's fourth-grade class and encountering a Thanksgiving Day frieze that the children had just completed. The teacher explained that there had been some problems involved in its production. She related that "it was hard to make all the heads alike. When the children first painted the pictures they all looked different, so we had to throw them away. And then I made an Indian profile and a Pilgrim profile; I wrote directions for coloring each part, and the children traced them and cut out their own. And now they make one frieze" (1959:17). The situation is quite similar to one encountered in an American college where the art teacher stated that she used only molds in her ceramic classes, since "hand modeled pieces sometimes didn't turn out right."

Not only is individual variation in behavior de-emphasized in our educational system but also in recreational activities. Such group-oriented organizations as Boy and Girl Scouts, Campfire Girls, and 4H Clubs offer regulated programs of recreational and educational activities designed to meet the needs of the "American boy and girl." The assumption is that all young people should enjoy camping, group games, summer camps, and handicrafts. The child who does not enjoy this kind of program is considered somewhat abnormal, if not even delinquent.

If Americans cannot make people conform to certain types of standards in any other way they will pass a law. "There ought to be a law" is a well-known American cry of anguish. A host of ordinances and laws regulates areas of life that most European cultures feel are personal matters. City and state laws regulating advertisement and sale of liquor, litter laws, Sunday closing laws, curfews, and movie and book censorship are but a few of the methods used to produce uniformity in thought and behavior. While, on the one hand, Americans savagely demand "liberty," on the other hand, they are constantly restricting liberty through their own law-making devices.

THE COMMON MAN

The tendency to conform is associated to a certain extent with the American "cult of the common man." While the majority of our citizens are motivated to "get ahead" socially and economically, it isn't nice to make too big a point of it. No one engenders greater enmity than the person who makes it known that he is better than other people. Some of the most admired of our public figures, millionaires like Bing Crosby and Perry Como, are highly respected because they have been extremely successful, but act as though "they didn't have a dime." While equal opportunity seldom is realized by racial minorities, the average American theoretically holds to the precept that all men are created equal. Americans have almost deified log cabin-born Abraham Lincoln, while the wealthy aristocrat George Washington runs far behind in national popularity even though he was the "father of our country."

Many a presidential candidate has learned that if he wishes to succeed in politics he must show the voters that he has something of the common man in him. It would appear that the role of farmer is highly representative of the common man, and President Franklin D. Roosevelt often gave his occupation as "farmer" although his estate on the Hudson was hardly what the common man would consider a farm. President Herbert Hoover had been an engineer and it wasn't difficult for the common man to take to a man who had spent several years wearing engineer's boots, khaki pants, and a flannel shirt. Franklin Roosevelt was quite aware that clothes (particularly old ones) can make a President. A common FDR symbol was his battered campaign hat. Wendell Willkie did not wear a hat but showed his lack of concern for fastidious grooming by letting his hair fly. John F. Kennedy also appeared to be an advocate of this particular campaign technique. President Roosevelt, however, had one urbane habit and this was a vulnerable point of attack. He used a cigarette holder. No cartoon of criticism ever left out the cigarette holder. Presidential candidate Adlai Stevenson, definitely an urban intellectual, found great difficulty relating to the common man. In spite of numerous pictures of Adlai perched atop a tractor on his Illinois farm, he never quite convinced the people that he really belonged there. President Johnson made a Texas ranch his "second White House" and further related to the common man by greeting tourists to Washington through the fence of the Presidential mansion.

While everyone makes a great point of being the common man (a recent study showed that eighty-eight per cent of the people in a random sample claimed middle class affiliation), we also seem motivated to move up the social scale and show that we are more than average, even if we do have the common touch. Our country abounds with "good Joes" trying to get into country clubs with exclusive memberships.

AUTHORITY

One aspect of the "common man" idea is that it makes the exercise of authority difficult when one's role demands it. Probably no army in the world has had greater difficulty in its officer-enlisted man relations than the American army. A not uncommon remark during World War II and the Korean War was "Why should that guy tell me what to do? All he ever was in civilian life was a shoe salesman." Enlisted men deeply resented the existence of Officers' Clubs and on some occasions were sustained in their hardships by the fact that the officers in the field didn't have things any better. Some scholars have conjured up some pretty mystical explanations for this resentment of authority in Americans. They maintain that in rejecting authority the American is symbolically rejecting the authoritarian European father. It would seem perfectly logical, however, to explain this phenomenon by the idea developed on the frontier and in the colonies that every man was his own master and no one had any right to exert his will over any other. In the New World, man had to earn his place in society; he couldn't inherit it. Sidney Hook (1950) maintains that an emphasis on personal autonomy and a distrust of authority are the basic requirements in a working democracy, and Americans think of themselves as devotedly democratic.

Not only did enlisted men find it hard to respect the authority of their officers, but officers felt somewhat uneasy giving orders. Frequently, they were rendered completely inadequate for their job because they worried too much about being a "good guy." Many solved their command problems by being "tough but fair." Officers in European armies seemed less concerned with creating the right image for themselves in the eyes of their men. A former student of the author, in relating his experiences in the British army and later in the American army, said that in England he had served an officer as an office clerk for over a year and had had but two informal phrases directed at him by his superior. These were "Good morning" and "Good evening." All other communication was by written memo. Compare this with the situation which prevailed in the average Flying Fortress crew during World War II. Officers and enlisted men lived together, fought together, drank and played together, and generally made as little of rank as was possible.

The problem of authority is also encountered in the world of business and industry. It is not unusual in our culture for the boss to take the office staff out for an evening and act like "one of the boys." Similarly, the factory picnic is a sort of day of atonement, when department heads, foremen, and even the boss himself take part in the interdepartmental baseball game in order to show that "bossing" is all part of getting the work done, but otherwise bosses are really people after all.

YOUTH AND CHANGE

America is a country where youth and change are valued. To the frequently asked question "What's new?" answers on any given day may include new dances, new child-raising techniques, new hairdos, new kitchen gadgets, new educational philosophies. In a civilization where each generation is exposed to a whole new set of technological facts and social conditions, elderly people are not respected for their greater experience but rather they are considered "old fogies," and out of date. The American accent is on youth because the future belongs to the youth of a nation and America is future-oriented. There is no people in the world that dotes more over baby pictures, concentrates as much on developing new and different (and often educational) toys for children, or stresses as highly that parents should devote great amounts of their time and energy to see that their children are amused and constantly attended to. In America, parents usually play the role of spectators while their children take the spotlight. In England and in

European countries in general, children are seen and heard as little as possible. When parents have guests, the small fry are relegated to the kitchen where they are expected to stay unless called by the parents.

In most primitive societies, customs have persisted over many generations; change takes place slowly and "youth" is synonymous with "inexperience." Government is frequently in the hands of village elders and the older citizens of primitive society serve as storehouses of tradition and are authorities on proper behavior. In such cultures individuals are secure in their knowledge of culture. There is no question about how children are raised and disciplined. Proper methods are those their mothers and grandmothers employed.

Such confidence is seldom found in American culture. Each generation lacks confidence in the methods of the former, but has no dependable solutions of its own. Since there is no faith in the old solutions, Americans turn to the "experts," but even they cannot agree on such things as how to raise, discipline, and educate children, or what the proper husband-wife relationship should be. There is no lack of advice, however. Every magazine for women has at least one article on one or all of these subjects. Self-styled experts on family problems write syndicated columns, and even a number of government agencies will furnish anxious wives and mothers with authoritative literature at nominal cost.

The desire to provide their children with better opportunities for success than they had heightens parents' anxieties in the area of child-rearing and education. This desire to see one's children have opportunities and advantages that were not available to oneself is part of the American faith in progress. Progress is the watchword not only for the individual but also for the nation. It has often been pointed out by students of American culture that the constant pursuit of material wealth is not so much a desire to have things for their own value but rather an attempt to provide evidence for one's friends and neighbors that one is succeeding and getting ahead. Therefore, the $60,000 home, or the Cadillac, is not valued because it represents, in the first case, additional living space or increased comfort, or in the case of the car, better engineering or better transportation. These material possessions are valued as symbols of hard work, ability, and achievement. It is inconceivable in this culture that a man should refuse to accept a better position even if it means taking on added responsibility, working longer hours, or even selling his home and moving to another community. The prospect of hard work is no obstacle to the average American if there is any opportunity at all to succeed. Hard work is, for Americans, not only a means to an end but to a great extent an end in itself. A survival of Puritan philosophy is the association of idleness with sin and industry with virtue. In commenting on this principle, Margaret Mead has stated, "Within traditional American culture, leisure is something that has to be earned and re-earned, except for the very old . . . Unearned leisure is something which will have to be paid for later" (1957:11).

Not only does the ideal type of American work hard, but he also plays hard. Successful vacations are often more exhausting than vocational activities.

Americans are prone to seek simple answers to complex questions and an example is the belief that there is a positive correlation between hard work and success. Although a commonly heard statement is "It isn't what you know, it's who you know," the behavior of most Americans would indicate that the real axiom that motivates their behavior is "It isn't who you know, it's how hard you work." The failure in business is an object of contempt rather than sympathy. Still another facet of this work-success belief is the idea of the "self-made man" and the idea of "pulling oneself up by the bootstraps." Fortunately, there aren't many self-made men around these days. The concept is, of course, ridiculous. The self-made man is really the egocentric one with the short memory in regard to all the people who have helped him along the way. Surveys show that most owners of big companies today are the sons of founders rather than the founders themselves. The bootstrap concept of self-help is still with us, however. The great popularity of charm schools and Dale Carnegie courses testifies to the strength of the belief that people can become more popular and more successful with just a minimum of direction and instruction. With a little know-how, they are prepared to take it from there.

THE PARADOX OF EDUCATION

One of the simple answers that Americans have singled out to solve complex problems is that almost any social problem may be solved through education; and most Americans value the type of education that most directly deals with practical problems. Parents often object to their children majoring in philosophy, history, or anthropology because, after all, "What can you do with that kind of an education?" Training in medicine, law, engineering, or business administration can clearly be seen as avenues leading to good jobs. There is less emphasis on what one learns in college than on what he can do professionally with a college diploma. There have even been those who were "smart" enough to short-cut the whole process by purchasing a sheepskin from a "diploma mill" and therefore not having to waste all that time being educated. Much is made also of the fact that the average college graduate will make $103,000 more during his lifetime than the high school graduate. Although there is great faith in the necessity for education in America, it can hardly be said that we have a nation of scholars. People in this country read book reviews and digests of articles rather than spending the time on the original. While every English and French hamlet has at least one book store, it is almost impossible to find such an establishment in most of the small towns of America. In 1957 a poll was run in various countries to discover how many people were currently reading a book. In England the figure was 55%; in West Germany, 34%; in Australia, 33%; in Canada, 31%; and in the United States the somewhat pathetic figure was 17%.

It is a much publicized fact in this country that intellectuals are "eggheads" and eccentrics. In one section of the country in recent years a common explanation for the fact that college professors often held quite different political and religious views from certain elements of the community was that they were "intellectually bound" and therefore could not understand the issues. Many states insist that educators at all levels take loyalty oaths while the same demands are not made on ministers, lawyers, or businessmen.

For many high school students good grades are a source of embarrassment rather than pride. A number of churches look upon colleges and college professors as corruptors of young people's faith and morality, and there is all too frequently the idea that working with the mind is somewhat less honorable and fatiguing than working with the hands. College professors are almost always pictured as absent-minded, cloistered, and terribly impractical.

Although there is faith in what education can do in increasing the prospects for success in our children, there is also a reticence to pay for education. In 1958 Americans spent $32.5 billion on automobiles and their operation, $8.4 billion on liquor, and only $10.3 billion on education for their children. Teachers as a group are the lowest paid professional people in America. While many citizens find no difficulty in purchasing a new car every year, they think that the cost of a college education for their son or daughter is nothing less than bankrupting.

TECHNOLOGY—OUR SACRED COW

America is a machine-age culture. It is a culture where machines think, talk, teach our children, put people out of work, inform on us when we are lying, and carry us through space at 18,000 miles an hour.

This is a country where it is almost a national holiday when the new model automobiles first appear in the dealer's showrooms. There are three times as many motor vehicles, radios, and television sets and twice as many telephones in use in America as in any single country of Europe, including England. If we were to erect a statue representing the essence of American youth, it would have to be a scene of a young man, wrench in hand, leaning over the hood of a hot rod drag racer.

Technology influences our motor behavior, our ideas of cleanliness and punctuality, and it generally influences our whole philosophy of life and our world view. Ours is a nation that places high value on energy, efficiency, orderliness, and precise measurement, and much of this can be directly attributed to the machines that we control and the machines that control us.

When the author was doing anthropological research in the Samoan islands, he became aware of two kinds of time—"Fa'asamoa time" and "white man's time." Fa'asamoa, or "the Samoan way" time, was far from being precise because it tended to be calculated by the position of the sun or the length of shadows. Whether a man's calculations were a half hour or so in error didn't make too much difference because the nature of the culture was such that there was little need for keeping appointments at a precise time. On Sunday morning, church services were supposed to start at eight o'clock, but no one really minded if the church bell rang at seven o'clock or at nine. There was not a single thing in their culture that had to be done exactly at an appointed hour. The same lack of precision was also found in lineal measurement. The length of a man's forearm or the length of man's outstretched arms (the fathom) were sufficient standards of measurement. Houses varied a bit in size because of the various sizes of carpenters' forearms, but no one got very upset over this. Measurement in the production of a finely balanced machine must be accurate to the thousandth of an inch, however. Mass production of complex products with interchangeable parts must include precision and accuracy. It is interesting to see how this necessity for precision has been transferred to American culture in general. The batting ability of baseball players is measured quantitatively down to the third place past the decimal point. Feeding schedules for babies must be precisely adhered to even if it means waking the baby at a definite time during the night. People do not sleep until they are rested; they attempt to get eight hours' sleep as though that were a magic number. In our schools a letter grading system is always backed up by a precise numerical evaluation. A's are worth four points, B's, three points, etc. Upon graduation a grade average such as 3.548 is recorded on the student's record. Far too often a student loses a valuable scholarship to graduate school because some other student surpasses him in his grade average by two or three thousandths of a point. The giving of grades is a most subjective task, to say the least, but once the grades are recorded and averaged, the result becomes an infallible, precise measurement of the student's academic and intellectual ability.

AMERICAN MATRIARCHIES

Most students of American culture appear to be in accord in their opinion that the American family is a female-dominated one, a characteristic that they claim stems in part from the males' evasion of their family responsibilities in order to spend more time at work, and in part from the males' inability to dominate his supposedly "weaker" mate.

In spite of the oft-voiced claims that "it's a man's world," most anthropologists would agree that the vital enculturation and socialization processes are largely controlled, in America, by females. This means that to a great extent the young learn their culture and social adjustment from the woman's viewpoint. The hospital nurse, the Sunday school teacher, the grade, intermediate, and high school teachers are predominately women and at home the greater amount of his development—in eating, toilet-training, walking, and talking—is under the close scrutiny and supervision of the mother. It is primarily the mother who decides what things the child must be disciplined for and it is she who often does the spanking. If she is not the dispenser of corporal punishment, it is done by the father at her order. While this female environment may not present any great problems for girls in our society, the male child finds great difficulty in establishing a male image of self in his petticoat world. More and more he finds himself in the company of girls. He is expected to compete with them in school, work, and play, but in most of these activities he finds that the girls have the edge in the competition. He finds that they want to enter more and more into his games but remind him that it's "ladies first" or "You don't hit girls." They wear his blue jeans and tee shirts, cut their hair short, and generally leave him very little that he can call his own. David Riesman has made the observation that boys can be boys only from six to ten. Beyond these years they are somewhat in doubt of their maleness. Perhaps the current interest in automobiles is in part an attempt by adolescent males to carve out an area of interest of their own in which girls have not as yet developed any great aptitude.

Even during the dating period, the right of the male to determine his own destiny has been overthrown. The former pattern of "playing the field" (primarily a male-dominated phenomenon) has given way to the institution of "going steady." As one writer has put it, this is "clearly a girl's scheme; taking advantage of our Puritan legacy, she is imposing 'monogamy' earlier and earlier" (Moskin 1958:77). A further extension of the girl's will over the boy's is to be found in the sexual aspects of dating and courtship. Gelolo McHugh maintains that the boy is expected to "get all he can" while the girl is expected to regulate him. Thus, during his adolescent years the male's attempts to exert masculinity, in one of the few ways clearly defined to him, is controlled, as much of his life has been, by feminine moral precepts. From this time on sexual relations are pretty much controlled by women. The male is constantly reminded by doctors and marriage counsellors that only a brute (and who wants to be that?) would impose his sexual demands on his wife. Furthermore, the responsibility of sexual compatibility in the marriage is placed squarely in the lap of the male. In a book titled *The Sexual Responsibility of Woman* Maxine Davis reminds the wife of her responsibility. It is "to make her husband realize . . . how important it is that she be satisfied" (1956:27).

The American matriarchy is hard to compete with, much less to overthrow. The biological role that the mother has played, plus her role as protector, comforter, and provider, makes the mother the dominant parent for most Americans. The value of the father's breadwinning role is more easily overlooked since most of his activities are carried on outside the home. In addition to his breadwinning activities, the father is responsible for establishing and maintaining the prestige of the family. The position of the wife is based to a large extent on the family head's success in business, as is a girl's prestige with her high school or college crowd. The success and position of the father is, all too often, a prime factor in whether or not a girl is accepted for membership in social clubs or sororities. For the young son the important thing is whether or not his father can compete with other fathers in the neighborhood in war experiences, ability in sports, or hunting and fishing skills. The father and his son do not have much in common other than their common sex and therefore this factor is highly stressed. It makes a good deal of difference whether or not one's father is bigger, stronger, and more masculine than other dads, but whether the mother is prettier or more feminine than other moms seems to be of secondary importance. If the son and father manage to develop a close relationship, it will be in sharing male activities. They may play ball together, boat together, hunt together, or attend athletic events together. They also represent a conspiracy against the women of the family. The father often secretly gives his son extra allowance, keeps to himself the knowledge of his son's indiscretions, and secretly takes pride in his son's attempts at flaunting authority (i.e., when he "cuts" school or swipes apples out of someone's orchard). Flaunting authority is often recognized as a sign that one is no "sissy" and therefore is masculine.

Not being a sissy is a great concern to males of all ages because the American male has never been completely grounded in what it means to be masculine. Due to the all-important quest for success, the father has not had the opportunity to spend much time with his son. There is even the question of whether this association would be of any help because the father may not be sure enough of his own masculinity to pass on masculine values and behavior to his son. Terms like "he-man" are used to differentiate the very masculine from the less so. One famous author of powerful war and adventure stories is reported to have knocked his publisher down when the latter referred to the author's lack of chest hair. The remark was taken as an insult to his masculinity. Perhaps the fact that the man "protests too much" is evidence of a basic insecurity in this matter. Some psychologists interpret repeated infidelity on the part of a husband as evidence of a constant unconscious need to be reassured of his maleness.

THE HAPPINESS MARRIAGE

Fifty years ago the American had a much greater sense of family than he does today. Many Americans have never even met all of their cousins and aren't particularly upset about the fact. The family reunions of yesterday are now rare and when they occur they are generally not a success. In the old days, families tended to be localized and reunions were occasions when relatives could get together and compare crop successes and failures. Today when such get-togethers occur, the various family members are so different in their interests and occupations that there is little to talk about.

Even the nature of the husband-wife relationship reflects the breakdown of the extended family structure in favor of the small nuclear or biological family. Francis Hsu points out in *Americans and Chinese* (1953) that the American family is definitely individual centered; individual happiness is stressed over family ties and family solidarity. Hsu feels that marriage in America—based on the principle of romantic love—is in effect a continuation of courtship. There is a constant need for the marriage partners to keep reassuring their spouses that they still care. One of the worse crimes in domestic life is to take one's husband or wife for granted. Wives become upset when their husbands forget anniversaries or birthdays, and husbands believe that their wives should "fix themselves up" in preparation for the husband's arrival home from work. Going out now and then to eat in a restaurant and perhaps to also take in a show is very much like their courtship and is considered vital to the happiness of the wife.

Thus, the members of the American family see the family as a source for obtaining personal happiness. The partners marry for happiness, have children for happiness, and have little concern for family tradition or continuity. The family is something to be exploited rather than perpetuated. Why are Americans like this? De Tocqueville once said that our zeal for democracy made us so. In *Democracy in America* he wrote:

Among democratic nations new families are constantly springing up, others are constantly falling away, and all that remain change their condition; the woof of time is every instant broken and the track of generations effaced . . . As social conditions become more equal, the number of persons increases who, although they are neither rich nor powerful enough to exercise any great influence over their fellows, have nevertheless acquired or retained sufficient education and fortune to satisfy their own wants. They owe nothing to any man, they expect nothing from any man; they acquire the habit of always considering themselves as standing alone, and they are apt to imagine that their whole destiny is in their own hands.

Thus not only does democracy make every man forget his ancestors, but it hides his descendants and separates his contemporaries from him; it throws him back forever upon himself alone and threatens in the end to confine him entirely within the solitude of his own heart. (1955, Vol. 2:105–106)

RELIGION IN AMERICA

America is primarily a Protestant nation. In a 1957 census 66.2 per cent claimed such religious affiliation. It took one hundred and eighty-four years for the people of this country to bring themselves to elect a Roman Catholic president. America has a very long history of Protestant domination because the value system of its people naturally finds Protestantism more acceptable than Roman Catholicism. Americans have never been much for ceremony or ritual, they tend to reject authority and rigid, absolute doctrine, and they could not tolerate an institution that is controlled in part by foreigners. There are in America more than two hundred and fifty distinct denominations. Free to interpret the Bible as they see fit, each of these groups has placed special attention on certain interpretations. Many represent splinter groups from the major denominations or, in some cases, entirely new denominations in themselves.

The independent spirit of Americans is seen in many other aspects of religion. There is complete separation of church and state, and a lack of an established church such as the Church of England in the British Isles, the Lutheran church in Sweden, or the Roman Catholic church in Spain. Furthermore, even among the major denominations it is seldom that there is any central authority or control. In nearly all American churches (including the Catholic) there is a great deal of district and church autonomy. Most churches are quite democratic and often give lay officials as much or more power than the minister. Still another aspect of the opposition toward authority is the tendency in many churches not to require theological training for religious leaders. It is not unusual for a man without any formal religious training to establish a church of his own or to declare himself an evangelist.

Being great advocates of tolerance and fair play, Americans generally believe in religious freedom. People tend to respect the rights of others to worship as they wish, although they may disagree violently with their beliefs. Whether or not they would want an individual of a certain denomination in a position of authority in business or government is another matter.

In spite of frequent references to America being a Christian nation and in spite of the high proportion (57%) of persons claiming church membership, students of American culture agree that it is not a particularly religious nation. With the exception of certain rural areas, where religion can truly be said to be a vital force in everyday life, religion tends to be a Sunday morning phenomenon. Religious precepts have little influence on business ethics or social issues. Religion stays aloof from political struggle and tends to support public opinion. Some of the basic principles of Christianity—the brotherhood of man and the renunciation of struggles for riches and worldly goods—are not popular causes in America and therefore very little is said about these things from the average pulpit. Many churches go out of their way to cultivate a wealthy membership and the number of pastors who have taken strong stands against segregation or other forms of social injustice are in the minority. Those who do find little support in their congregations.

There has been a trend toward secularization of beliefs with a strong emphasis on maintaining the status quo. There seems to be an insecurity in the ranks of religious leaders that prevents them from taking stands on certain issues for fear it will offend members of the congregation who will then sever their membership connections. It would seem that the culture has had a greater influence on religion than religion has had on the culture.

Another trend in American religious life is the great emphasis placed on social activities and group fellowship. Men's clubs, scout troops, bowling teams, young people's recreation groups, athletic programs, and fellowship dinners have come to be recognized as essential parts of any church program although they may be quite unrelated to the spiritual activities of the church. In regard to the fellowship aspect of American religion, Harry Golden has written, "The first part of a church they build nowadays is the kitchen. Five hundred years from now people will dig up these churches, find the steam tables and wonder what kind of sacrifices we performed" (1955).

Americans do not think deeply about religion. With the exception of a few outstanding professors and students of theology, there is little searching or questioning of religious beliefs. Most Americans are content to accept the interpretations and traditions of their denomination. It is like swallowing a capsule; no chewing is required. A great number of Americans are quite ignorant, however, of the doctrine of their own denomination, although they are quite sure that it is better than the others. Michael Argyle (1959) reports that although 95% of Americans claim church affiliation, only 35% are able to name the four gospels.

While most social scientists agree that Americans are not particularly religious, they also feel that they are not antireligious. Our country has never experienced any anticlerical movements. Our pastors and priests, although poorly paid, are usually treated with respect. Those who do not participate in the activities of a church do so out of indifference rather than opposition to religion.

RESOLVING THE PARADOXES

It would not be proper to conclude this chapter without attempting to reconcile some of the contradictions that seem to exist in our system of values. Although social scientists have often commented on our many paradoxes, few have provided any explanation as to how or why they exist. This very perplexing matter is the subject of an essay by Dr. Francis Hsu (1961), an anthropologist who in his many articles and books on American character has proved to be a very competent observer and theorist.

Hsu maintains that many of our cultural contradictions can be understood in terms of a single important core value, *self-reliance,* which is primarily manifested in a fear of dependency. Self-reliance is considered the key to all individual freedom and it is the ruler by which all mankind is judged. The self-reliant man considers himself his own master, controlling his own destiny through his own hard work and planning. Since the American seems to adhere to the "boot strap" theory, people who are forced to collect relief or the dependent aged are viewed with hostility and considered misfits. Absolute self-reliance denies the importance of others and explains the rather unique phenomenon of the "self-made man." This denial of the value of others has a tendency to produce instability in ascribed relationships within the family and in achieved relationships as between business partners or between husbands and wives.

American self-reliance prompts men to compete and value individualism on the one hand, but demands conformity on the other. In order to be deemed a success, a man must belong to the right status-conferring organizations but to do so he must conform to their standards and involves himself in their time- and energy-consuming organizational activities.

Self-reliance is also indirectly responsible for the coupling of such laudable values as Christian love, equality, and democracy with the less desirable values of religious bigotry and racism. This is because religious affiliation in the United States and in the West generally has become mostly a matter of associational affiliation. The successful man is drawn to the successful church where others of his social position attend. Hsu believes that the church is most frequently valued because of its social importance and this consideration greatly overshadows its doctrinal position or spiritual qualities.

The history of Western religion is believed to have always been marked by a search for original purity in both ritual and belief and this has led to the Reformation, the rise of multiple denominations, and even the Holy Inquisition. Dr. Hsu asserts that:

> This fervent search for and jealous guard over purity expresses itself in the racial scene as the fear of genetic mixing of races which feeds the segregationist power in the North as well as in the South . . . When religious affiliations have become largely social affiliations, this fear of impurity makes religious and racial prejudices undistinguishable. (1961:222–23)

In an open society like America there are no fixed or permanent places in the social structure. A man has an opportunity to climb, but so do others below him socially or economically. Thus the self-reliant man is afraid of being contaminated by those he considers his inferiors. He can accept them as long as their upward mobility is prevented, but when they have the opportunity to share desks in his child's school, live in his neighborhood, or share the pews in his church as equals, his insecurity mounts. Since discrimination against particular racial or socioeconomic groups runs contrary to both democracy and Christian theology, the self-reliant American must disguise his objections. In the South he evades the real issue by stressing states' rights and in the North by stressing property values.

The only security in a society stressing self-reliance is in personal success, superiority, and personal triumph, but unfortunately these achievements must of necessity be based upon failure or defeat of others, for there can be only one winner in every race. People are not valued for their mere participation.

In spite of its several shortcomings it must be pointed out that self-reliance is the key to progress. Because of this emphasis, the United States and the West generally has prospered and developed a great technological and industrial civilization. Leaders of developing nations are beginning to realize that if they wish to compete for recognition with Western nations, they will have to develop the value of self-reliance in their people also. Thus we have the final paradox—that the core value of American culture, self-reliance, is parent to both the best and the worst that is in us.

SUGGESTED READINGS

ARENSBERG, CONRAD. "American Communities," *American Anthropologist,* 57:1143, 1955. (Types of communities—New England town, southern county, cross-road hamlets, and main street towns—and how they reflect their region's culture.)

ATTWOOD, WILLIAM. "The American Male: Why Does He Work So Hard?" *Look,* March 4, 1958. (The cultural reasons why the average American goes in for more energy-consuming and tension-building activities than any other man in the world.)

BAIN, READ. "Our Schizoid Culture," *Sociology and Social Research,* 19:266, 1935. (Points up contradictions in values and behavior in American culture.)

COLEMAN, LEE. "What is American?" *Social Forces,* 19:492, 1941. (A list of traits believed to be characteristically American derived from a number of books dealing with "Americanism" or "the American Way".)

DuBOIS, CORA. "The Dominant Value Profile of American Culture," *American Anthropologist,* 57:1232, 1955. (Synthesizes and systematizes the relevant insights on American middle-class values advanced by a number of scholars.)

GILLIN, JOHN. "National and Regional Cultural Values in the United States," *Social Forces,* 34:107, 1955. (A list of seventeen values believed dominant in American culture; also comments on regional variations.)

GORER, GEOFFREY. "The American Character," *Life,* August 18, 1947. (Contains the basic ideas found in Gorer's book on national character, *The American People.*)

LEONARD, GEORGE B. "The American Male: Why Is He Afraid To Be Different?" *Look,* February 18, 1958. (Deals with pressures and pressure groups that make Americans conform.)

MILNER, HORACE. "Body Ritual Among the Nacirema," *American Anthropologist,* 58:503, 1956. (Satire on American culture.)

Moskin, J. Robert. "The American Male: Why Do Women Dominate Him?" *Look*, February 4, 1958. (Why American males accept petticoat rule.)

Paperbound Books

De Tocqueville, Alexis. *Democracy in America.* New American Library of World Literature, Inc. (This national character study of Americans recorded over one hundred years ago remains remarkably accurate even today.)

Klapp, Orrin. *Heroes, Villains and Fools: The Changing American Character.* Prentice-Hall. (American stereotypes reveal changing American values.)

Lerner, Max. *America as a Civilization.* Vol. I, The Basic Frame; Vol. II, Culture and Personality. Simon and Schuster. (The inner meaning of contemporary American civilization and its relation to the world of today.)

Seeley, J. R., Smith, R. A. and Loosley, E. W. *Crestwood Heights: A Study of the Culture of Suburban Life.* Science Editions, Inc. (The values and behavior patterns of middle class suburbia.)

8

Man and His Material Culture

Although man is basically an animal in his biological makeup, he has the special distinction of being a cultural animal. Therefore, he is able to interact with his natural environment in a way not open to those animals standing below him on the taxonomic pyramid. By this we mean that man does not have to grow a heavy pelt to live in a cold climate; he merely devises a garment of fiber or skins and builds himself a shelter. Man does not have to grow sharp teeth or long claws to hunt and protect himself from his enemies; he merely invents a weapon of the hunt or of defense. Nor does man have to have a special body structure to do certain kinds of work. Tasks beyond his physical abilities are accomplished through his genius for making tools or for utilizing leverage, gravity, or other natural principles. Because of culture, the solutions to technical problems become the heritage of subsequent generations who are then free to perfect and refine the techniques of their ancestors.

It will not be the purpose of this chapter to discuss all of man's material inventions and discoveries, but rather there will be an attempt to understand how man as a species responds to his needs for tools, shelter, and clothing. It will also be our purpose to see the extent to which man, even in primitive societies, is a scientist in solving his basic survival problems.

TOOLS

One of the outstanding characteristics about man is that he is a tool-maker. Although lower animals have proved themselves capable of utilizing natural objects to accomplish things that require something beyond their biological endowments, it is only man who managed to develop methods of developing and using tools. In recent years the subject of tools has taken over the anthropological spotlight. Some anthropologists have argued, and very convincingly, that the use of tools has made a great difference in determining the direction of human evolution. Man, the tool-making and -using animal, has protected and domesticated himself through his tools so that he does not face many of the environmental pressures of the lower animals. Of course, man has in his hands, in his stereoscopic vision, and in his complex brain a set of built-in tools that help him survive. His hands, for example, are very efficient tools. His prehensile fingers and opposable thumb give him a grip that is sure and powerful. At the same time he has an acute sense of touch and little treads or ridges (which produce fingerprints) to aid him in delicate manipulations. His flat nails allow him to pick up the smallest and flattest of objects. With these multipurpose tools attached to arms that rotate in an arc of 360° man can grip, strike, oppose motion, and accomplish a variety of complex manipulations that require cooperative movements. In spite of the great utility of man's hands as tools, they also have their limitations.

The skin that covers the palms and fingers is tender and the nails are frail. If one is to chop wood, skin animals, or cut flesh, it is obvious that something more than merely the hand is required. Originally, prehistoric man probably picked up objects of nature that suited his tool requirements.

Raymond Dart (1957) has pointed out that any number of natural objects can be quite efficient in accomplishing certain kinds of tasks. A piece of antelope mandible with the teeth intact can serve as an excellent knife or saw; the end of an antelope leg bone makes a good pounding tool or club, and, if ripping or slashing must be done, there is little better than a wild pig tusk or a hyena's lower jaw with its sharp canine teeth. Almost any stone makes an adequate missile for killing an animal; a broken pebble often has an edge sharp enough to sever an animal's tendon or separate a hide from the flesh. A length of wood is a good weapon of defense. Kenneth Oakley tells us that "some Australian tribes occasionally chop trees and fashion wooden implements with naturally shaped pieces of stone selected by virtue of their sharp cutting edges" (1957:10). There is nothing particularly extraordinary about being able to select natural objects to serve as useful tools. Even the great apes can do this. Oakley comments that

". . . apes of the present day are capable of perceiving the solution of a visible problem, and occasionally of improvising a tool to meet a given situation; but to conceive the idea of shaping a stone or stick for use in an

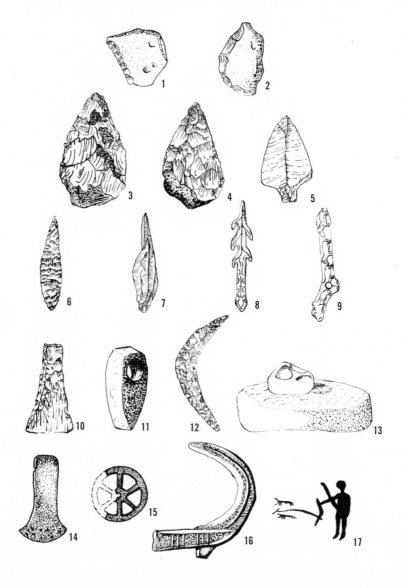

Fig 8–1. Tools of early man.

imagined future eventuality is beyond the mental capacity of any known apes. (1957:4)

Here we have arrrived at the problem that has separated the apes from the men: the ability to produce a tool of a given type to satisfy a tool requirement for some future work situation.

As man developed in his capacity for culture, there came a time when he realized that something more than natural objects would be required if he were to sustain life by converting natural resources. The problem he probably faced, however, was what kind of tools should he develop to satisfy his needs? Some of the earliest tools were simple, indeed, in that they were pebbles with a few flakes struck off to produce a sharp cutting or striking edge. For example, these earliest of tools, which date back better than a million years, have, because of their crudeness of manufacture, produced many an argument. Many claimed that these eoliths, or dawn stones, were not man-made at all. One man went so far as to throw a quantity of pebbles in a cement mixer in order to show that the tumbling action could produce stones of identical form as dawn stones. Another fact which added fuel to the argument was that there was no record of any kind of prehistoric man living at the time these tools were supposed to have been produced. However, on July 17, 1959, L. S. B. Leakey found four hundred bone fragments and a few tools of a variety of prehistoric man he called *Zinjanthropus*. These materials were later dated as being 1,750,000 years old. The tools were sharpened pebbles much like the eoliths that had been found earlier. It was therefore quite apparent that man had long been a tool-maker and that there was a tradition of tool manufacture, implying the existence of culture at a very early date.

About 500,000 years ago man developed a very efficient all-purpose tool, the hand or fist axe. With this tool he could saw, chop, scrape, drill, and slice. The implement must have proved to be very effective

---

Pliocene coliths
1. Knife (England)
2. Sidescraper (England)
   Lower Paleolithic Core Tool
3. Chellean handaxe (France)
   Tools of Neanderthal Man
4. Mousterian handaxe (France)
5. Mousterian point (N. Africa)
   Upper Paleolithic Tools of Cromagnon Man
6. Solutrean point of knife (France)
7. Aurignacian Burin—engraving tool (France)
8. Magdalenian harpoon point of antler (France)
9. Magdelanian arrow shaft straightener (France)
10. Flint axe (Denmark)
11. Stone axe-hammer (Denmark)
12. Flint sickle blade—notched for hafting (Denmark)
13. Mealing stones (France)
    Bronze Age Implements
14. Axe blade (Denmark)
15. Wheel for votive chariot (Switzerland)
16. Sickle blade (Hungary)
17. Petroglyph of man plowing with oxen (Sweden)

because varieties of this hand axe have been found in all parts of the world. This tool probably appealed to hunters and gatherers, who were always on the move and needed a single tool to do a number of tasks.

As culture developed and hunting techniques became more refined, there was a need for a greater variety of specialized tools. Thus we find a great florescence of tools, particularly in the Upper Paleolithic— i.e., the latter portion of the Old Stone Age. The basic hand axe shape was reproduced in smaller size and often hafted to a shaft, thus making a spear that could be thrown. Truly efficient axes were developed by Neanderthal men and it was probably these people who first attached a blade to a handle and thus increased its striking power. The old hand axe was not as efficient as it might have been in slicing or sawing operations, so the Aurignacian peoples, living in France, developed long flint knives and end scrapers to handle the removal of hides and the dressing of game. Among the Solutrean peoples, another European group, flakes actually were produced with serrations or teeth to facilitate sawing operations.

Upper Paleolithic developments in tool-making not only included refined methods of secondary chipping but new materials also were introduced. Bone and antler were used for needles, harpoon points, and shaft straighteners. The introduction of these new materials, in turn, required the development of specialized tools. Engraving tools called burins were developed, and flint drill points, often set in shafts and twirled between the hands or rotated as part of a bow drill, were invented to work bone and antler.

The Neolithic, or New Stone Age, brought new subsistence methods (agriculture and herding) and also new kinds of tools and new tool-making procedures. Flaking and chipping methods held on in many areas, but there was the addition of grinding and pecking techniques that produced smooth, even surfaces on the tools. The more reliable subsistence provided by agriculture and herding allowed for greater craft specialization and, as men began to work exclusively at special trades, they developed new specialized tools. An example of this would be the many varieties of wedges, axes, and adzes used in woodworking. Agriculture itself needed special kinds of tools and a whole variety of sickles and grinding stones have been found dating from the Neolithic period. The Bronze Age, which followed, introduced a new material for tools and many of the Neolithic tool types were merely reproduced in metal. This period also brought the plough, the potter's wheel, the wheeled vehicle, and lathe and, most important of all, introduced the concept of draft animal power. The new metal tools were stronger and more enduring; tasks could be performed more quickly and more efficiently.

The next great upheaval in tool-making did not occur until approximately one hundred and fifty years ago when the Industrial Revolution introduced mechanical and electrical energy. When one looks at the modern power lathe, drill press, planer or band saw, one realizes that man has come a long way from the days of the multipurpose hand axe. His ingenuity has brought him from a condition when every day was a struggle to keep alive as a species, to a point where his technology has made him master of all he surveys.

Fire

The story of man's tools would not be complete without mentioning man's servant and comforter—fire. We do not know when men first discovered the use of fire, but the first concrete evidence of its existence

Eskimos use a bow drill for piercing bone and ivory and for making fire. (Courtesy of Chicago Natural History Museum.)

is a fire-hardened hearth in a cave occupied by Pekin man some 300,000 years ago. This prehistoric man probably did not know how to produce fire but very likely borrowed and used it when a forest or field of dry grass was ignited by lightning or some other natural cause. The first method of actually making fire was perhaps a heat-through-friction method. Such methods are most widespread in the primitive world today. The Australian aborigines produce fire by making a sawing motion on a log of soft wood with a boomerang of hardwood. North and South American Indians use the bow or pump drill, and the people of the Pacific kindle a spark with fire graters or fire plows. This Pacific technique consists of rapidly rubbing a pointed hardwood stick back and forth in a grooved piece of soft wood until the resulting sawdust begins to smolder. Upper Paleolithic peoples used pyrites and flint to strike a spark, and the people of Borneo developed a fire pump or fire cylinder that compressed a column of air and thereby raised the temperature to a point sufficient to ignite tinder.

Fire has been such a valuable tool throughout human history that it has often been considered a sacred object. Many peoples have myths that associate fire with the gods. Greek myths relate that Prometheus stole the precious substance from Zeus, while the Polynesian peoples have a tradition that fire was given to man by the demigod Maui. Fire has been worshipped, anthropomorphized, and even considered private property. The Buryat, of the Steppes of Asia, feel that fire has a spirit that must not be offended by having refuse thrown upon it. These people also consider fire to be the property of the clan, and no stranger may take so much as a spark away from the family hearth.

It is not difficult to understand man's reverence toward fire, as it is perhaps man's most valuable tool. It has provided warmth, cheer, and light for untold numbers of men in habitations ranging from caves to castles. With fire brands, Polynesian peoples attract fish to the surface where they may be speared in night fishing. On the Northwest Coast of North America smoke was used to cure the annual harvest of fish so that the Indians could depend on a year-round supply. Every people in the world cook at least part of their food through boiling, baking, broiling, or steaming. Without fire, simple tropical forest peoples would find the clearing of land difficult or even impossible. In Ice Age times, fire was used to drive herds of animals into corrals or over cliffs, and many people today still rely on fire to flush game. The ancient Maori used fire to attract sea birds so that they could be caught in nets. Fire is used by primitive peoples to hollow out canoes, harden pottery, smelt ore, and consume the dead.

Hunting Tools

No group of technological inventions better reveals primitive man's scientific aptitude than his hunting traps, snares, and deadfalls. Concerning these various devices, Julius Lips comments:

Long before Archimedes [primitive man] invented, based upon the application of the laws of leverage, the important relay and release mechanisms whose analogous application in modern machinery can easily be observed by any layman, even if their construction has undergone considerable improvements. (1956:54)

Lips sees these hunting "machines," so widely used by hunting peoples even today, as falling into four basic categories. These he labels (1) the gravity trap, (2) the snare trap, (3) the spring-pole trap, and (4) the torsion trap.

THE GRAVITY TRAP. The gravity trap makes use either of the weight of the animal itself or the force of a falling object that when released

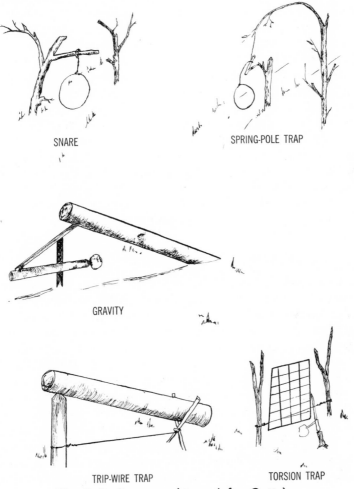

SNARE

SPRING-POLE TRAP

GRAVITY

TRIP-WIRE TRAP

TORSION TRAP

Fig. 8–2. Snares and traps (after Gatty).

will fall and hit the animal. This category of traps would therefore include camouflaged pits into which an animal might fall and be impaled upon pointed sticks set in the bottom, as well as a whole variety of log traps where the animal itself springs a release mechanism resulting in its being crushed by one or more falling timbers. A slightly different variety is the East African Lango elephant trap where a weighted spear falls on the elephant when he trips the release rope.

THE SNARE TRAP. This device depends on the forward motion of the animal to tighten a noose about its neck or one of its legs. Set either horizontally or vertically on frequently traveled game trails and partially hidden by grass or brush, the trap capitalizes on the animal's fear and effort to get away for its effectiveness. The greater the struggle, the tighter the noose is drawn, and if the neck is involved, the result is often death from strangulation.

THE SPRING-POLE TRAP. The spring-pole trap combines the features of the snare with the power of a bent tree or a branch that when released serves as a spring that will jerk the animal up into the air, killing it instantly and keeping the carcass out of the reach of other animals. This spring-pole principle also finds application in fishing, but, of course, in this case the snare is replaced with a hook or a basket.

THE TORSION TRAP. The torsion trap utilizes the power generated when a twisted sinew, root, or fiber is permitted to regain its original form. One variety of this trap uses a board twisted in a leather thong, which, when released, is forced down upon an animal. Another variation of this trap utilizes a net in place of the board and, instead of the animal being killed, the descending net merely captures it.

Weapons of the Chase

MAN-OPERATED HUNTING WEAPONS. The more conventional tools of the hunt—the spear, harpoon, bow and arrow, and so on—although often less ingenious than the traps and snares in their conception and construction, do nevertheless in their manufacture and use involve an acute awareness of scientific principles as well as a thorough knowledge of the habits of the game on which they will be used. The hand and missile tools of the hunt have served as the backbone of hunting economies since the beginning of culture and, although snares and traps have an important place in the activities of hunting, their utility has been of secondary importance when compared to the man-operated types of hunting weapons. The tools of the chase can, like snares and traps, be separated into several categories. One such system of classification is that of Daryll Forde (1954), who divides these weapons into (1) crushers—clubs, throwing-sticks, sling stones, (2) piercers—knives, spears, javelins, harpoons, arrows, blow gun darts, and (3) entanglers—lassos, bolas, and nets.

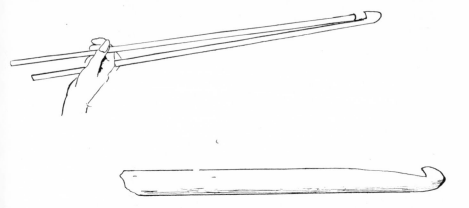

Fig. 8–3. Spear thrower (*atlatl*) (after Braidwood).

CRUSHERS. Of the several crusher-type weapons the club has perhaps the least effectiveness in the chase. It has great usefulness, however, in dispatching animals wounded or entangled by other weapons. The throwing stick, which increases its crushing effectiveness by virtue of its being a missile, has wide distribution throughout the world. The Hopi Indians and South African Bushmen use such devices for hunting birds and other small game, but the most outstanding example of native ingenuity is the Australian boomerang, which returns to the thrower if it has missed its mark.

Sling and missile stones have been more of a weapon of war than of the hunt, but their effectiveness is well known to anyone who has read the David and Goliath story. Such people as the Navaho and the Ona of Tierra del Fuego find that the sling-delivered missile makes an effective hunting weapon in that it represents an improvement in terms of speed, power, and range over the hand-thrown stone.

PIERCERS. The first piercing weapon developed by man was undoubtedly the knife or blade, since such implements made of flint date back to the Lower Paleolithic. Like the club, the knife is limited to close hand encounters with game. These are rarely possible in hunting unless the animal is either wounded or caught in a trap. Of the several piercer missiles the spear or lance has the greatest antiquity. The first spears were, very likely, stripped saplings with a sharpened point that might have been fire-hardened. There is evidence that Neanderthal man used stone spear heads lashed to wooden shafts for purposes of throwing and thrusting. Although this type of weapon was highly effective, the Magdalenian people of the Upper Paleolithic improved its utility by inventing a special launching device commonly known as the spear-thrower or atlatl. Usually made of wood or ivory, the spear-thrower has a grip, or handle, at one end and a peg, or notch, at the other to take the butt of the spear. These spear-throwers, which measure from one to three feet in length, act in the manner of a sling, thus increasing the force and effective range of the missile. The same leverage principle was used by the New Caledonians and Roman soldiers in their spear-throwing lanyards. The knotted end of the cord fit into a notch at the butt of the spear while a loop in the other end was attached to a finger. The lanyard had the effect of increasing the length of the arm and therefore allowed the weapon to be thrown with greater force.

Another significant invention of the Upper Paleolithic period was the harpoon. In many cases, an animal wounded by a spear could use the leverage provided by the weight of the shaft to dislodge the head of the spear, but the distinguishing feature of the harpoon is its detachable head. In many cases, the head is not only detachable but is supplied with a line that, like a fishing line, may be paid out or can be attached to a float as in the case of the Eskimo seal harpoon.

European cave painting, dating from approximately 13,000 B.C., includes scenes of hunters using bows and arrows. Although such weapons were probably widely used during the Upper Paleolithic, they became especially important in the Mesolithic when the retreating glaciers resulted in Europe changing from a tundra to a forested area. This change in climate and vegetation also brought a change in the animal life in central and western Europe. The great herds of reindeer had disappeared and in their place were elk, deer, and aurochs, the hunting of which required a good deal of skill. The bow and arrow, with its accuracy, powerful impact, and low trajectory at a range of several hundred feet, was the ideal hunting weapon. Many anthropologists believe that the concept of the bow was inspired by the spring-pole trap, since both utilize the power principle of the inertia of a flexible stick. The arrow also derives from earlier weapon forms. It is a miniature of the javelin. The bow may be made of either a single piece of elastic wood or, as in the case of the Siberian and New World Eskimo composite bow, it may be constructed of several pieces of wood or horn held together with glue and sinew.

The final type of piercing weapon with which we shall be concerned is the blow gun dart. The blow gun is found mainly in Southeast Asia and South America and, in spite of the wide separation of these two areas, the form and function of the weapon are remarkably similar. Whether this is the result of independent invention or diffusion has not as yet been settled. Wherever the weapon is found, its operation depends upon the propulsive force of the human thorax. Tylor points out that the blowgun principle is basically what was employed in the development of the musket or the cannon. He writes, "When . . . gunpowder was invented in China, its use was soon adapted to make the blow-tube an instrument of tremendous power, when instead of a puff of breath in a reed, the explosion of powder in an iron barrel drove out the missile" (1894:197). Although the blow gun is quite accurate up to about one hundred and fifty feet, the darts are relatively small to be a very effective weapon against large game. To correct this fault, most peoples arm the darts with poison.

ENTANGLERS. The most interesting of the entangling weapons is the bola. L. S. B. Leakey has discovered that weapons of this type were

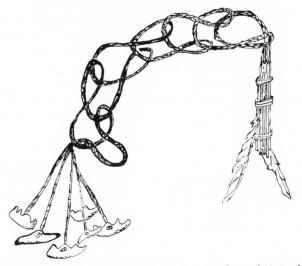

Fig. 8–4. Eskimo entangler (after Beals and Hoijer).

used in Kenya as early as Achulean times (450,000–250,000 B.C.). The bola stones that he discovered were three in number, about the size and shape of baseballs, and grooved. This type of device is still used by gauchos in Argentina. The South American variety consists of three stone or clay weights joined by thongs of leather. To operate the contraption, the Pampas cowboy holds one weight in his hand, whirls the other two about his head, and at the precise moment lets the whole thing fly at the animal he is pursuing. The whirling device entangles the animal's legs, trips it, and holds it securely. The bola as a hunting weapon is used today by the Tehuelche people of Patagonia and the Eskimos of North America. The Patagonians use a three-weight bola for hunting guanaco and rhea, while the Eskimo weapon is used for birds and has five ivory weights, shaped like birds, seals, or bears. The latter weapon has a handle with feathers that serve to guide its flight.

The line with a running noose at one end is used as a hunting weapon in every part of the world in one form or another. Polynesians catch sharks and moray eels by luring them into a noose, whereas Tierra del Fuegians use a long stick with a noose on the end for capturing birds. The lasso, truly a missile weapon, was employed by early Egyptians, Minoans, and New World pre-Columbian peoples in the hunting of large game.

While normally thought of as fishing devices, nets have been used widely in hunting. The fishing net was probably conceived during the Mesolithic period in Europe (7000 B.C.), but when it was first used for land animals is unknown. A relief decoration of a Grecian cup from 1600 B.C. depicts a bull caught in a net secured to two trees and an Assyrian bas-relief dating from 700 B.C. shows deer being hunted with nets. Contemporary Witotos, of the Amazon jungle, reportedly stretch great nets a thousand feet or more in length among the trees and then drive large animals into them. In Uganda the people use the same methods in hunting antelope. Vancouver, and other early explorers in the Puget Sound area of North America, recorded the existence of "flagpoles" in many of the Indian villages. Actually the forty-foot poles they discovered were used for stringing bird nets. Teal, mallard, and canvasback ducks have a habit of flying twenty to thirty feet above the ground, and early in the morning or at twilight when the light was poor they would unwittingly fly directly into the nets. Waiting men would then seize them and wring their necks.

HOUSING

Although a primitive man standing in front of a thatched hut with a stone-tipped spear in his hand hardly looks like a scientist, we have seen that he can do some remarkable things in adjusting to his environment. Scientific behavior involves observing certain regularities of the physical universe and utilizing this knowledge to solve life's problems. If we look at the problems primitives must overcome and the resources

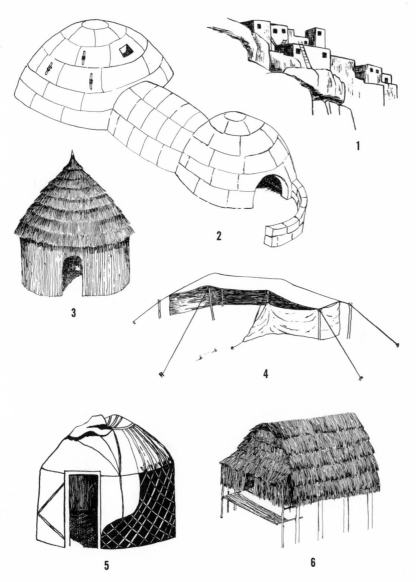

Fig. 8–5. Houses of primitive man.

1. Southwest Indian Pueblo
2. Eskimo igloo (after Fitch and Branch)
3. African thatched hut
4. Bedouin tent
5. Central Asian Kazak yurt
6. Melanesian stilt house (after Fitch and Branch)

they have at their disposal, we find that they can accomplish some remarkable things. There is perhaps no better example of this than in the area of native architecture. Fitch and Branch (1960:134–44) have made a thorough analysis of the architectural characteristics of the housing of contemporary primitives and find that these people, on the whole, show a greater awareness of climatic problems than the so-called "civilized" peoples who make such a point of their technical proficiency. They point out, for example, that far too often we have produced buildings that are beautiful to look at but are functionally very poor. Glass-walled skyscrapers are as modern as tomorrow, but unfortunately they often leak badly during rainstorms and in nearly every case they require special types of air conditioners and blinds to compensate for the excessive heat and glare produced by the glass.

Fitch and Branch describe the characteristics of native housing in all parts of the world, but for our discussion we shall focus attention on man's shelters in (1) arctic climates, (2) deserts, (3) equatorial zones, and (4) grassland areas.

The Arctic

Eskimos live in a variety of houses, but the snow igloo is architecturally the most fascinating. The hemispherical shape of the dwelling offers the maximum amount of resistance and the minimum obstruction to winter winds. At the same time it offers the largest volume with the smallest structure. An oil lamp, centrally placed, can, in a structure of this shape, effectively heat every cubic foot of the interior. When the house is first occupied, the combination of lamp and body heat causes the interior face of the snow blocks to melt slightly. In time a glaze of ice develops on this interior surface, thus insulating the house and serving as a radiant heat reflector. When the walls are covered with skins, the tiny house represents the maximum in comfort possible under these difficult climatic conditions. By digging the entrance tunnel at a level below that of the house floor the Eskimo shows that he understands that cold air is heavier than warm and thus keeps the unheated entrance tunnel from chilling the main house interior.

The Desert

Desert conditions such as those encountered in the African Sudan, in Iran and Iraq, or in the southwestern part of the United States also present serious house construction problems, but apparently none too great for the ingenuity of the native builders. While there is not a problem of protection from the rain, there are the problems of excessively hot and sunny days, rather cool nights, and a shortage of certain kinds of building materials. Fortunately there is a great abundance of clay and stone in such areas and there is no material any better for desert housing than these. The adobe houses found in all of these areas are so constructed that the roof and walls absorb the sun's heat during the day but tend to lose it slowly during the night. Thus the range of temperature for the occupants of the house is reduced. The mud con-

Hopi Indian housing. The thick walls of an adobe pueblo provide comfortable interiors in the hottest of weather. (Courtesy Chicago Natural History Museum.)

struction does not stand up well under heavy rains, but since rain is at a minimum in desert areas this is not a problem. In parts of West Africa where there are heavy seasonal downpours the mud walls of the houses must be protected by overhanging thatched roofs. Nomadic peoples in desert areas must of necessity utilize easily portable materials. The Bedouin tent, for example, is made of woven goat hair supported in the form of a canopy by half a dozen poles. The shelter serves primarily as a sunshade, but side walls may be attached to provide a shield against blowing sand.

Equatorial Zones

In equatorial zones houses must primarily keep out the rain and provide shade. The beehive-shaped roofs of Pacific island dwellings are very efficient in this respect. Frequently these houses are entirely open on the sides, thus allowing for a maximum of ventilation. In Melanesia, floors are often raised on stilts, partly for better exposure to the trade winds and partly for protection from rats, snakes, and crawling insects.

The overhanging thatched roof of the West African dwelling protects the mud walls from the torrential rain. (Courtesy of Chicago Natural History Museum.)

The Nigerian dwelling is an interesting example of adaptation to the environment. Here the natives have developed a double-roofed dwelling. An inner roof of clay has projecting pegs to receive an outer layer of thatch. The thatch sheds water and protects the clay. The clay dome conserves heat for cold nights, and the air space between the two serves as insulation from the heat of the afternoon sun.

Grasslands or Prairies

In many of the grassland or prairie regions of the world we find nomadic herders like the Kazaks of the Asian Steppes or nomadic hunters like the Plains Indians of North America. While the prairie environment poses certain architectural problems, the nomadic activities of the people further conplicate the housing situation. Most of the prairie or grassland regions have great seasonal differences in temperature, strong winds and a relative lack of trees for use as a building material. Furthermore, the nomadic economies of the inhabitants demand a type of house that is easily portable and simply and quickly erected. Both the Kazak yurt and the Plains Indian tepee appear to be quite adequate solutions to these problems.

The Kazak tent somewhat resembles a domed pillbox. The framework of the house has walls made up of crossed saplings tied together in such a way that they may be folded up like a child's safety gate. This feature allows the tent to be set up or dismantled in half an hour's time. Over the sapling framework is stretched a covering of felt that sheds water and insulates the interior. Ropes running in various direc-

Plains Indian tepee—made of buffalo hide and easily portable. (Courtesy of Chicago Natural History Museum.)

tions over the outer surface of the house hold the felt in place. In summer the felt wall panels may be rolled up, thus allowing the occupants a maximum of ventilation.

Similarly, the Great Plains tepee utilized saplings that could be taken from place to place thus solving the wood shortage problem. Instead of felt they used the hides of buffalo as a light but weather-resistant covering. The heavy winds of the plains bothered the structure little, as it was well anchored to the ground with pegs, and furthermore the conical shape provided a maximum of stability with a minimum of exposed surface. The hide covering could, with various adjustments, be closed up tight or opened to provide increased ventilation. When the house was dismantled, the lodge poles became part of a kind of trailer (travois), which was drawn by a horse, thus providing a means of transporting all of the material goods of the people.

CLOTHING

Why do people wear clothes? The most obvious answer, that clothing keeps them warm or protects them from the sun, wind, or rain, is but part of the explanation. It is also apparent, however, that we cannot go very far in explaining the variety of men's and women's costumes throughout the world in terms of an instinctive feeling of modesty. Modesty is not innate—it is learned cultural behavior—and Lowie has even suggested that it was the wearing of clothes that prompted the idea of modesty in the first place. To some people, it is indecent to show any part of the body other than the hands and face, whereas others settle for less. While women in Moslem countries are very particular about covering their faces, they often leave their breasts exposed. Samoan women are likewise not embarrassed about being nude above the waist but consider it quite improper to expose the knee. Among the Tuareg of the African Sudan, it is the men who believe they must cover their faces. In this society, it is considered very immodest for any male to expose his mouth, particularly while eating, and thus they have adopted a style of dress that has resulted in their being called "The People of the Veil." The story is told that an anthropologist traveling in the Amazon jungles encountered a group of people where the women wore nothing save lip ornaments. The anthropologist persuaded one of these women to sell him her labret. Upon removing this ornament, she ran away and hid because she was ashamed of her nude appearance.

With all these variations in the concept of modesty and with the fact that some people give no thought to wearing nothing at all, it is doubtful that man's widespread use of clothes is prompted to any great extent by moral considerations.

Clothing usually reflects the environmental conditions of the wearer, and it is the development of protective clothing and housing as well that has allowed man to inhabit all parts of the globe. The presence of the two basic types of clothing, tailored and loose-hanging, seem to show a definite relationship to the kind of climate to be coped with. Where retention of body heat is important, the former seem to be found, but where there is a need to facilitate heat loss or where special protection from the sun is important, we more frequently encounter loose-fitting garments.

There are, however, numerous examples of curious and even uncomfortable fashions that seem to relate little to the climatic problems or cultural activities of their wearers. The Ona people of Tierra del Fuego live in a region where the average temperature is forty-five degrees, and yet their normal dress includes a small otter or seal skin cape and a thin layer of grease and clay smeared over the body. The Tungus people of Siberia, who also live in a very cold climate, fashion their clothing out of fur, but seem to let style or tradition stand in the way of complete comfort. The Tungus fur coat greatly resembles a European morning coat. It could be a very warm garment, but it is always worn open, thus giving no protection to the chest, abdomen, or upper legs. One need not think that primitive peoples are the only ones who develop strange impractical fashions. The hobble skirt, the wasp waist, the high heel, the celluloid collar, and the powdered wig are European inventions that, in spite of their obvious impracticability, attracted millions of wearers for the sake of fashion.

Obviously clothes do more than satisfy modesty requirements and afford protection from the elements. They can represent objects of allure or they can serve as indicators of sex, age, occupation, wealth, caste, or class. Clothes can be used to indicate religious or political affiliations.

Perhaps the most important factor for determining particular kinds of clothing to be worn is the matter of prestige and position. There are few people who do not have some method of indicating who are the important people, either by special garments or by body decoration. The amount and the type of design of tattooing set apart the Polynesian nobleman from the commoner. The feather war bonnet told everyone that its wearer was a member of an honored Plains Indian soldier or military society. Nootka chiefs on the Northwest Coast of America showed their high status by wearing gaudier and more elaborate costumes than anyone else. They were the only ones who could wear dentails or abalone shells, and only their robes could be trimmed with sea otter fur.

Turning to our own culture we can see that clothing provides valuable status clues for us as well. We talk about "white-collar" workers and "blue-collar" workers as representing various levels in our class system. The college boy can, by his dress, be easily distinguished from shop or office workers of comparable age, and the college professor frequently sets himself apart by his "tweediness," from the banker, the salesman, or the minister. The latter, of course, is easily identified by one article of his clothing—the clerical collar.

In the area of ladies' apparel we find that the greatest status indicator is the coat. As a rule, it is a matter of how much fur and what kind of fur. There is the cloth coat, the fur-collared cloth coat, the fur coat, and then, most prestigeous of all, the mink coat. Mink coats are desired primarily because they indicate that the wearer is of the upper classes, or more important, the wife of a very successful member of the middle class. They are not necessarily more beautiful than other kinds of furs, nor are they any warmer, but merely more expensive because mink fur is rarer than other kinds. If the mink coat were worn for warmth, it would come equipped with buttons (which it usually is not) and it would have the fur on the inside. Viewing the situation very objectively, it would appear that mink will have to be assigned to the category of "conspicuous consumption." This was a term first used by the American sociologist and economist Thorstein Veblen (1899), who pointed out that tight-fitting knee breeches, powdered wigs, and lace cuffs served to identify certain colonial men as aristocrats or men of wealth who did not have to work for a living. Their impractical apparel was obviously not suited to any kind of physical exertion.

Clothing styles also seem to be influenced by factors of which people are not even aware. Anthropologists A. L. Kroeber and Jane Richardson once painstakingly analyzed three hundred years of European dress styles noting such features as length and width of skirts and position of neckline and waistline. They found that in spite of all the dress designer's and manufacturer's efforts, fashions follow a pattern of cyclic change. In times of peace and prosperity dresses featured a fitted bodice, a full skirt, and the waistline at the natural waist. In troubled times such as the Revolution, Napoleonic, and World War I and during the depression of the 1930's dress styles were extreme, featuring either ultra-high or ultra-low waistlines and skirts that were narrow or short or both. They concluded from their study that, "since the periods of dress-pattern instability were also periods of marked socio-political instability and churning, there is presumably a connection" (Kroeber 1948:334).

1789   1813   1839   1859

1879   1899   1916   1935

Fig. 8–6. Style variations in women's fashions (after Kroeber and Richardson). (From *Anthropology* by A. L. Kroeber. © 1923, 1948, by Harcourt, Brace and World, Inc., and reproduced with their permission.)

PRIMITIVE MAN AS SCIENTIST

We have learned from a brief cross-cultural inventory of man's tools and technical methods that all men, whether primitive or civilized, have the ability to work out solutions to quite complex problems by using a type of scientific behavior involving observation, experimentation, and generalization. Where irrational types of behavior occur, such as in the quirks of clothing styles, "civilized" men seem to be as guilty of these follies as are the primitives. It is fair to ask, however, why primitive people who have shown such great ingenuity and ability in many areas of culture have been so overshadowed by the technical accomplishments of the West. This is a fair question because it was not always the case. When Northern Europeans were still chipping stone for their weapons, the West Africans were smelting iron. In the twelfth century, a Negro university in Timbuktu was equal to or better than, any in Europe at that date. When the conquistadors conquered the Mayan territory of Yucatan, Guatemala, and Southern Mexico in 1562, they found that these Indians had developed a scientific body of knowledge, at least in the area of astronomy, that surpassed that of Europeans at that time. Approximately one hundred years before the peak of the Italian Renaissance, Inca craftsmen in Peru were weaving priceless tapestries of gold and silver cloth and producing unbelievable objects of sculpture. One Spanish account describes a great golden garden on the grounds of the Inca emperor's palace where llamas and their herders, flowers, and birds were wrought life size out of gold. The garden was complete even to tiny golden butterflies with filigree wings, which fluttered like tiny kites over the flowers.

Why have these outstanding primitive technicians not gone beyond a certain point in their development? The answer is to be found in a single factor—isolation. Through some quirk of fate, Europe has been a great mixing bowl of peoples and ideas. Armies of every nationality have surged across the continent like waves on the sea. They have often brought destruction, but they have also brought new ways of doing things and making things. Trade routes criss-crossed the area bringing goods from afar. Europeans have not had the opportunity to isolate themselves from new ideas, even if they wanted to.

Compare this situation with that of the Australian aborigines who entered the continent of Australia about twenty-five thousand years ago and remained almost completely cut off from contact with other people until the first European contacts about 1788.

The remoteness of the islands of Polynesia and Micronesia made difficult contact with other Pacific peoples, let alone contact with peoples with foreign cultures. Although there was always some inter-tribal contact and trade in Africa, this continent remained a rather remote and isolated area until its coasts were explored by the Portuguese in 1415. Even today, movement from one part of Africa to another is difficult without air transportation.

Complex technological inventions do not grow out of thin air; every new idea rests on a base of accumulated knowledge. The invention of television, for example, could not have taken place until the way was paved by the discoveries of electricity, metallurgy, glass manufacture, sound and light wave theory, and hundreds of other innovations, which we forget about because they are so much a part of our daily lives. Inventions breed inventions, and the larger the technological base of knowledge the more likely it is that still newer and more ingenious inventions will appear. While history books estimate that the really significant technological inventions and discoveries between the years 1000 A.D. and 1400 A.D. were about ten in number, these same references set the figure at twenty-one hundred for the years 1800–1899.

It is also true that cultures that have been forced to develop in a world continually exposed to new ideas will be more responsive to change than those who have not had this experience. In most European cultures, the fact that father and grandfather did it that way is no reason at all for continuing, if a better method is available. Primitive people, however, who have worked out their technology painfully, through the process of trial and error, tend to find an acceptable method and stick to it for generations. Change takes place slowly and deliberately. The new and different holds no fascination for them. Life is difficult, and if they have found effective methods of hunting, fishing, or farming, they tend to hold fast to them rather than take a chance with a new untried method.

SUGGESTED READINGS

BARNETT, L. "Man Invents Tools," *Life*, November 7, 1955. (The tool industries of Stone Age man.)

BORDES, F. "Mousterian Cultures in France," *Science*, 134:803, 1961. (New tool discoveries give a clearer picture of the way of life of Neanderthal man.)

BUTTERFIELD, HERBERT. "The Scientific Revolution," *Scientific American*, September, 1960. (The cultural circumstances associated with the development of a new scientific outlook in the Renaissance.)

EISELEY, LOREN. "Man the Fire-Maker," *Scientific American*, September, 1954. (How man has used fire to better his condition since the early Pleistocene.)

FITCH, JAMES M., and BRANCH, DANIEL P. "Primitive Architecture and Climate," *Scientific American*, December, 1960. (How primitive man has produced housetypes in tune with the weather.)

GUGGENHEIM, HANS. "Smiths of the Sudan," *Natural History*, May, 1961. (Prehistoric development of iron smelting in Africa.)

HEINZELIN, JEAN DE. "Ishango," *Scientific American*, June, 1962. (African inventors in the New Stone Age.)

SHAPIRO, HARRY. "Be It Ever So Humble There's No Place Like Home" (in two parts), *Natural History*, December, 1944, and January, 1945. (Primitive man's housing around the world.)

STRUIK, D. J. "Stone Age Mathematics," *Scientific American*, December,

1948. (Presents evidence that the beginnings of arithmetic and geometry were in the Stone Age civilizations.)

WASHBURN, SHERWOOD L. "Tools and Human Evolution," *Scientific American,* September, 1960. (How the use of tools figured in the physiological development of modern man.)

WISSLER, CLARK. "Man and his Baggage," *Natural History,* September, 1946. (Methods used by primitive man in transporting his material wealth.)

Paperbound Books

LIPS, JULIUS E. *The Origin of Things.* Fawcett Publications. (Very readable book dealing with primitive man as inventor.)

OAKLEY, KENNETH P. *Man the Tool-Maker.* University of Chicago Press. (The tool industries of the Pleistocene.)

9

The Economic
Aspect of Society

The basic economy of a people is an integral part of their way of life
and cannot easily be separated from their patterns of family, government, and, to a certain extent, religion. Patterns of subsistence correlate
with certain kinds of movement and settlement, and the relative
amount of wealth made possible by the use of certain subsistence
methods supports varying degrees of specialization and facilitates
trade.

The problem of studying economics cross-culturally is not an easy
job as there are literally hundreds of separate combinations of methods
of getting a living. For purposes of study it will be convenient to utilize
a scheme of classification of economic types or models. Such a scheme
has been developed by J. H. G. Lebon, a British human geographer.
Although the following eight categories perhaps do not embrace every
single society in the world, they do represent significant types of
economies and they help us to see the influence of economic activities
on the nature of culture.

ECONOMIC TYPES

Lebon (1952) divides the economies of the world into the following
categories: (1) hunters, fishers, and gatherers, (2) specialized hunters,
(3) pastoralists, (4) simple cultivators, (5) advanced cultivators, (6)

sedentary highland cultivators of the New World, (7) Oriental agrarian civilizations, and (8) Occidental economies.

Hunters, Fishers, and Gatherers

The nonliterates who are identified with this type of simple economy include such peoples as the Andaman Islanders, the Semang and Sakai of the Malay Peninsula, the African Bushmen of the Kalahari desert, and the Australian aborigines. Although these peoples live in a variety of climates and their cultural histories vary greatly, there is a general similarity in their lives that derives from the nature of their economic activities.

Generally, these people make intensive use of the environment. Everything that is edible, except traditionally taboo foods, makes up the diet. This may include such things as a wide range of fruits, nuts, eggs, rodents, reptiles, and even insects. The weapons of the hunt are manufactured mainly of wood and stone and fishing is done with spears, hooks, or traps. Pottery, weaving, and metal-working are unknown arts and there is little specialization of labor other than sex or age differentiations. Every man is a hunter and every woman and child a gatherer of wild plants. The only systems of trade known to these peoples are irregular barter or silent trade activities carried on with neighboring sedentary peoples.

Since hunting and gathering activities can seldom provide more than a meager and unreliable living, hunters and gatherers must limit their numbers. Often a single extended family makes up the hunting band. With autonomous bands of only a dozen or two people, it is not surprising that government is informal. In a manner of speaking, family structure and political structure are one.

Hunting and gathering peoples are commonly nomadic. They must constantly move from one place to another in search of new supplies of game. These movements seem to be patterned. No hunting people ever wanders aimlessly from place to place. Hunting is a difficult activity at best, but it would take on added difficulty if carried on in unfamiliar terrain.

Because of this mobility, these bands seldom live in more than temporary shelters constructed of brush, bushwood, or leaves. All hunting and gathering people seem to have well-established ideas of territoriality. Boundaries of hunting and gathering areas are recognized by the groups that occupy them and are jealously guarded against trespass from outsiders.

Specialized Hunters and Fishermen

As examples of this kind of economic life we might point to the Indians of the Pacific Northwest, Alaska, and northern Canada; a number of hill and forest peoples of India and Southeast Asia; and the fishermen of Malaya and the East Indies. A specialized hunting and fishing economy differs from the former category in that subsistence comes from a few abundant species. Pacific Northwest Indians depend upon salmon and sea mammals; Northern Canadian Indians utilize caribou as the main food source; and the "Sea Gypsies" of Indonesia completely eschew agriculture and subsist entirely on fish.

With a dependable source of subsistence and with efficient methods of exploiting it, these cultures have a relatively high standard of living as hunting and fishing cultures go. Weapons, clothing, houses, and their furnishings are quite elaborate, since a certain degree of specialization in arts, crafts, and industries can usually be supported by the dependable and stable economy. In modern times many of these cultures have become involved in commercial hunting or fishing enterprises for European entrepreneurs and therefore acculturation and acquisition of European goods have been accelerated.

Settlements often include assemblages of as many as fifty families, and tribal groupings are even found among some of these peoples. The Northwest Coast Indian societies occupied permanent villages and Canadian Eskimos and Indians utilized sizable winter camps. Where mobility is found, movements tend to be seasonal and traditionally patterned. Hunting and fishing areas are considered group or community property and are jealously guarded against trespass by other groups.

Pastoral Economies

Although pastoral economies are found in a great variety of environments, and the animals domesticated differ greatly from place to place, the very nature of this kind of economy imposes a certain pattern of culture that is roughly similar in all of these areas. In Africa, the Masai and Fulani keep cattle, the Siberian Tungus tend reindeer, the Bedouins of Syria and Arabia herd camels, and the Siberian Kazaks live mainly off their herds of horses, sheep, and goats. In most of these societies the cultural patterns may generally be described as follows:

Movements of societies, dictated by the needs of animals for fresh pasture or water, are basically seasonal ones. All these cultures have concepts of either summer and winter pasture or wet and dry season areas of grazing. Aside from the seasonal migrations there are constant movements from place to place, and material goods are consequently limited. Housing takes the form of tents in many of these cultures—materials ranging from felt to skins, or cloth of wool or cotton. Frequently, herding peoples are able to establish trade relationships with sedentary agricultural peoples, thereby enriching their diet and material wealth. Herding peoples do little themselves, however, in the way of developing craft specialization.

The significant social unit among pastoralists is typically the clan or group of related families with patriarchal rule. Permanent settlements are seldom found and it is difficult for them to maintain social or political units larger than the clan. Loosely organized tribal units have been known, however, and in the case of nomads of the Asiatic steppe lands, "hordes" and even nations were formed under the Khans.

Simple Cultivators

This rather rudimentary type of economy, which greatly resembles that of Neolithic man, is represented by the cultures of peoples living in the hill regions of India, Indonesia, and Central America as well as any number of Amazon river societies. The societies practicing this way of life occupy warm forest regions where they cut away and burn the underbrush in order to clear small plots of land for the cultivation of root crops and grains. The hoe and the digging stick (dibble) are the principal tools of subsistence, but weapons of the hunt are also present, as both gathering and small game-hunting activities appear in combination with farming.

Life is simple, and textiles, pottery, and housing are rudimentary. Settlements, which include from five to twenty families, tend to be impermanent, as soils are often infertile and erosion caused by the simple cultivation methods forces these people to move periodically to new locations with virgin soil. In some areas a pattern of weak tribal organization exists, but the usual pattern is village autonomy. Trade relationships between villages are seldom of a regular nature and most economic exchanges take the form of simple barter.

Advanced Cultivators

Somewhat more advanced agricultural methods characterize the cultures of the people of the Southwest Pacific, and the agricultural regions of Negro Africa. While most of these people utilize hand cultivation methods, there is a greater dependence upon crops than is found among the cultures in the simple cultivator category. Forests are permanently cleared and there is a regular pattern of resting land after a few seasons' cultivation. Agriculture is often combined with stock-raising, but there is little hunting or gathering. Tribal government is often well developed, and some villages are very large, with populations numbering in some cases into the hundreds and even thousands. Land tends to be clan or village property, but individuals or families are given land-use rights. In some areas, particularly West or Central Africa, an elaborate system of markets and trade relationships may be found. These agricultural methods support a good deal of specialization in the areas of government, religion, and the arts and crafts.

Sedentary Highland Cultivators of the New World

The Aztecs, Incas, Chibchas, and Quechuas prior to Spanish conquest represented a type of economy that, although limited to one area of the world, is significant enough to warrant a special category. These cultures, specializing in maize, potatoes, beans, and other subsidiary crops, irrigated dry lands and terraced fields located on hilly slopes. Land was permanently cleared, and intensive agrarian methods supported substantial permanent towns as well as organized political states. Hand cultivation was a universal characteristic with domesticated animals being found only in the Peruvian area, where llamas were raised for their wool and as pack animals.

A well-established system of trade, made possible in part by a network of permanent roads, enhanced the standard of living. Specialization in the areas of arts and crafts, religion, science, and government reached a zenith with the substantial support made possible by maize agriculture.

Oriental Agrarian Civilization

For examples of this type of economy the reader's attention might be directed to the civilizations of India, Burma, Java, Siam, Cambodia, China, and Japan. In most of the Oriental cultures, the greater bulk of the population is supported by irrigated rice cultivation, but in a few cooler and drier regions millet or other Western cereals take on major importance. In addition to the cereal staples, fruits, vegetables, spices, oil-producing seeds, and fibrous plants bolster the economy. Plough cultivation is characteristic in all of these cultures, but there is not a great deal of emphasis placed upon domestication of animals. Arts and crafts are elaborate, and local and regional trade is highly developed.

In most of these areas there is evidence of an early development of this rather advanced economic complex, with the result that well-organized political states have existed for hundreds of years.

Rice-growing areas have, under this form of subsistence, been able to support as many as fifteen hundred people per square mile. In most of these cultures the permanent village is the significant settlement unit and land is usually privately owned, either by peasant farmers or by a land-owning class that controls large estates. In all of these Oriental countries, towns or cities developed as centers of craft specialization, trade, and government.

Occidental Economies

Although anthropology to a great extent concentrates on cultures outside the Western tradition, it has been our purpose throughout this book to study man cross-culturally, and therefore some note must be taken of the industrial economies of Europe, Brazil, Argentina, the United States, South Africa, Australia, New Zealand, and other areas of the world that have been influenced in their economy by the presence of European emigrants.

Basic in this type of economy is nonirrigated plough cultivation of Western cereal crops with mechanized equipment and the large-scale raising of domesticated animals. The most characteristic feature of this kind of economy, however, is the widespread use of mechanical power in mass production industry. Still another support of the Occidental economy is the exploitation of oil, natural gas, mineral, water, and timber resources. Efficient production and management techniques in all facets of agriculture and industry make for abundance, a high standard of living and adequate support of well-organized states with world economic interests. Because of mechanization and advanced scientific knowledge in the areas of plant and animal production, it has been possible in most Occidental cultures for a small percentage of agriculturalists to support large urban populations who engage in highly specialized occupations in industry, commerce, the arts, and sciences. Such economies as these must for purposes of product distribution feature networks of roads and railways, and transoceanic commerce is a vital aspect of the economy.

ECONOMIC ORGANIZATION

Morton Fried has remarked that "from the point of view of anthropology, economic studies have three primary facets: the description of the tools and techniques of production, the designation of the particular means and level of subsistence, and the analysis of the social relationships which involve the movement of goods and services" (1959:114). Having already dealt with the first two facets in this chapter and Chapter 8, we shall now consider how individuals interact to facilitate the economic production and distribution of goods in a society. Our discussion of the eight model types of economy has shown us that economies in various parts of the world can vary greatly in detail, but a second look will reveal that all economic systems have a great number of things in common. These things are called *universals* and they arise out of man's human needs and the nature of society. The term universal does not imply identical features in all societies but rather similarities in classification of economic behavior. Requesting the reader to keep this fact in mind we may move on to a statement of what these worldwide economic features are. No economic system in the world is without (1) an organized system of production, (2) an economic value system, (3) methods of product distribution, (4) common monetary symbols, and (5) a concept of property.

ECONOMIC UNIVERSALS

An Organized System of Production

No society can long exist without a traditional formula for what kind of work will be engaged in for its support and who is going to do that work. In a society where there is great surplus, people may pretty much choose what they want to do, but where precise organization and utilization of talent may mean the difference between life and death by starvation the culture carefully prescribes who shall work at what.

The most basic organization of productive labor, found even among hunting and gathering people, is a sex division. This represents an attempt at least to produce specialists in jobs they are capable of doing and at the same time it has the effect of reducing duplication of activities and needless competition between the sexes.

SEX DIVISION OF LABOR. An inventory of sex divisions of labor among the world's peoples would reveal that there is no great uniformity in what should be the jobs of men or the jobs of women but that there is a tendency for women to be given those jobs that keep them relatively close to the home (a necessity while nursing and caring for small children) and require less physical strength. Men, on the other hand, not being biologically tied to small children, often engage in activities that might require an absence from home of several days or even weeks and require great endurance and physical strength and often a measure of danger thrown in as well. It will be noted in the analysis of 224 cultures made by Murdock (Table 3) that while men may cook and women may trap, it is more common for men to hunt, fish, and trap and for women to gather, preserve food, and cook. Wherever the pat-

Table 3. Sex division of labor in 224 societies
(from Murdock 1937:551).

Activity	Males only	Males mostly	Males or Females	Females mostly	Females only
	Number of societies in which activity is performed by:				
Pursuit of sea mammals	34	1	0	0	0
Hunting	166	13	0	0	0
Trapping	128	13	4	1	2
Fishing	98	34	19	3	4
Gathering shellfish	9	4	8	7	25
Gathering fruits and nuts	12	3	15	13	63
Preserving meat and fish	8	2	10	14	74
Gathering herbs, roots, and seeds	8	1	11	7	74
Cooking	5	1	9	28	158

tern runs contrary to this, it is usually possible to find special cultural reasons. In Samoa, for example, men do the major part of the cooking, but food is often involved in matters of high ceremony. Many of the foods are considered too sacred to be handled by anyone other than titled or especially authorized untitled men. Not only are men the cooks in this society, but often the serving people as well.

AGE DIVISION OF LABOR. In addition to dividing the jobs between men and women, most societies also do so according to age. To a certain extent this organization reflects the relative strength, experience, and temperament of people at various ages. In most societies children are given light tasks like baby-sitting, running errands, and collecting firewood, while postadolescents and adults handle the heavy work—the hunting, cultivating, or house-building. As a man advances toward middle age, his experience is of great value to his society, but his strength is beginning to wane. In many societies it is at this time that a man enters the village council of elders and helps deliberate vital issues concerning the welfare of his community. The aged are often recognized as storehouses of tradition and knowledge and as people who have experienced much of life. Thus, they are often the educators of the young and the advisors of the village political leaders. The elderly are often given light tasks so that they might keep themselves busy, but in most societies (excepting those to be found in difficult

environments where everyone must do his share or be abandoned) the
aged are felt to have earned their rest.

Among the Dyaks of Borneo lighter tasks such as drying rice are
assigned to the children. (Courtesy of W. R. Geddes.)

OTHER DIVISIONS. Still another way of dividing labor duties is
according to family, caste, or class. In parts of Africa, working in iron
or manufacturing salt is the special prerogative of certain families or
clans, a concept also held in Europe until comparatively recently. Craft
specialization was handed down from father to son in particular
families. A survival of this period is to be seen in such family names as
Carpenter, Mason, Hostler, Miller, etc.

A Temne weaver busy at his trade. (Courtesy of V. Dorjahn.)

Among the East African Bikitara people, class completely determines occupation. Nobles are pastoralists and peasants are agriculturalists. In India one of the most striking aspects of the *jati*, or caste, is its labor specialization. In the Southern Indian village of Gopalpur, Alan R. Beals lists the various *jati* as priest, farmer, carpenter, blacksmith, saltmaker, shepherd, barber, butcher, weaver, stoneworker, basket weaver, and leatherworker (1962:36).

As we move from primitive societies to peasant and industrial ones, we find that labor specialization becomes more diverse. As Redfield has put it:

With the development of tools and techniques, with increase in population, and with the advancement of communications and transportation, the division of labor has become far more complete and complex. In the Guatemalan village of San Pedro de la Laguna, fifty-nine different kinds of specialists are to be recognized in a population of less than two thousand. A classified telephone directory suggests but by no means completely lists the thousands and thousands of kinds of specialists that make up a modern city. (1956:346)

COOPERATIVE WORK. The organization of labor extends beyond a mere designation of who should do what job. In some societies labor is organized around an individualistic and competitive pattern whereas the members of some others could not imagine working under anything but a cooperative group situation. In Dobu, farmers work alone and in competition with everyone else, even the members of their own lineage. Harvesting is done in strictest secrecy so that no one can see how prosperous a man might be, for a "good crop is a confession of theft" (Benedict 1959:135). If a man has harvested many yams, it is because he has used powerful charms to attract his neighbors' yams into his own garden.

Eskimos are quite individualistic in their work patterns. Most men hunt separately in their own kayaks while their wives stay at home working alone at cooking, tailoring, and processing hides. The family, however, tends to work in a joint cooperative effort, and several families on occasion can work together successfully in communal caribou drives or in spring seal hunts. Plains Indians often went out alone to hunt deer or antelope but the society insisted that buffalo hunting be done communally. Police societies enforced this regulation and imposed penalties upon private hunting.

The West Africans are almost completely cooperative in their labor patterns. Agricultural work is done by groups who help each other in turn, and even in the village, women often like to pound grain, cook, and wash clothes in groups. Although there may be no special advantage to working in groups, the people say that the social aspect makes the work seem lighter. There is, however, some reason to believe that more work is accomplished with group cooperation. While this proposition has never been tested, it is logical that in group work there is great pressure to work up to the standard of one's coworkers. A much quoted statement by Hogbin gives us the impression that cooperative work has its advantages in increased productivity. He writes,

A man who toils by himself feels like having a smoke . . . But when two men work together each tries to do the most. One man thinks to himself, "My back aches and I feel like resting, but my friend there is going on: I must go on too, or I shall feel ashamed." The other man thinks to himself, "My

In West Africa cooperative work seems easier when accompanied by drum rhythms. (Courtesy of V. Dorjahn.)

arms are tired and my back is breaking, but I must not be the first to pause." Each man strives to do the most, and the garden is finished quickly. (1938:296)

While America prides itself on its competitive spirit, there is and has been a good deal of cooperative work found in this society as well. The rural barn-raising, quilting bees, and threshing parties were not unlike the communal activities of many West African peoples, and our modern contractors really control what, in effect, are cooperative work groups. While each man operates in terms of his specialty—carpentry, plumbing, plastering—the work is coordinated and complementary and results in the final product, a house.

An Economic Value System

Every society, in addition to having an established system of organizing the productive efforts of its members, has a traditional set of economic values. Every people must decide how best to direct their efforts and where to invest their scarce means in order to derive the maximum satisfaction. All men are somewhat like the school boy standing in front of the candy counter trying to decide how to get the most for his lone penny. Maximizing one's satisfactions thus involves making choices, and choices are made in terms of one's set of values. In attempting to understand any people's economic system the place to begin is at the level of learning what things they deem most valuable.

THE IRRATIONAL PRIMITIVE. From the European point of view the actions of primitive people often seem quite irrational and often this leads to the conclusion that primitives do not have standards of economic value. Actually, primitive people have quite adequate reasons for what they do, but it is based on their own value system. Samoan islanders have often been criticized for what has been called their "church-building mania" while their water supplies and sanitation systems go neglected. But apparently having a beautiful place to worship is more important to them than having good water and sanitary villages. The Indians who sold Manhattan Island for twenty-four dollars, a few trinkets, and a barrel of rum did so, not out of ignorance, but rather because of their different concept of land tenure, their valuation of the few acres involved (they still had hundreds of square miles for their own use), and the attraction of the novel, foreign goods that could be purchased with the money.

It is the common practice for Eskimo hunters to refrain from killing animals considered sacred by their family, even if it means that they must go hungry for days. Faced with the choice of filling the belly or respecting the spirit of their totemic animal, they will choose the latter every time.

WHY MEN WORK. Still another phase of the system of economic values concerns why men work and also the amount of effort they will expend. The fact that American men work so hard that they get coronaries and ulcers is, from an objective point of view, rather irrational. Few men, regardless of culture, really enjoy the physical exertion involved in work, but all normal individuals do it. Why? Aside from the rather obvious reason that most men work to eat, the follow-ing reasons have been given:

American—"To be counted a success you have to have money. That means work . . . It's habit, I suppose. We don't like to be seen on the streets or around home doing nothing be-cause we think people will talk about us." (Keesing 1958:229)

Hopi Indian—"Work provides pleasure through group activity marked by joking and laughter, gossip, singing and perhaps recital by the old people of folk tales." (Keesing 1958:228)

Maori—"Successful completion of a certain piece of work will raise a man in the esteem of his fellows and give him a feeling that he has done his duty in the community." (Firth 1929:156–59)

Omaha Indian—"If a man is not industrious he will not be able to entertain other people. A lazy man will be envious when he sees men of meaner birth invited to feasts because of their thrift and their ability to entertain other people." (Fletcher and LaFleche 1911:331–33)

Samoan Islander—"I get satisfaction out of seeing things grow which I have planted with my own hands. People work because it is something that people admire and respect. It brings them prestige."

Almost anybody—"One works because one must; because every-one else works; because it is one's tradition to work." (Herskovits 1952:122)

In every society goals are different and the means of attaining goals are different. We cannot expect someone of another culture to exert himself equally to achieve the goals important to us. Franz Boas (1938) has pointed out that while the primitive often appears unreliable and disinterested in his work habits, the only fair way to compare primitive and civilized man's work incentive is to observe them both in undertak-ings that are equally important to each. In such cases, it has been seen that the native can proceed with just as much purpose as the white man.

Some people work because it gives them enjoyment, self-respect, and prestige, or they work because it is the thing to do. We have noted in the several statements from men of various cultures that the prestige motivation greatly overshadows the profit one. In the Northwest Coast of North America, Kwakiutl chiefs used to work and save all year so they could compete successfully with other chiefs in the destruction and distribution of property at the annual potlatch ceremony. The chief who could destroy and give away the most property and thereby embarrass the other competing chiefs had very little material to show for his year's work but he had a giant measure of prestige to glory in. Prestige is often of greater importance than profit in our society also. While white-collar jobs are considered prestigeful and are sought after by the majority of high school and college graduates, salaries are notoriously poor when compared with blue-collar jobs. The old joke about the boss not being able to give his clerk a raise but only a bigger title expresses a basic value principle in ours as well as many other societies.

Not only is incentive to work tied in with status but so is the distribution of economic products in many primitive societies. As a matter of fact, Robert Redfield categorizes economies as being based either on a status system or on a market system. He states,

In primitive societies most of the production . . . is brought about not because somebody sees a chance to make a profit in some market, but because it is part of the traditional status of that man or woman to hunt or farm or make baskets. And what is made is shared with others according to status. (1956:353)

Methods of Product Distribution

Every economic system must of necessity include methods or means of product distribution. This distribution, as Redfield points out, may be based on status considerations or it may involve markets and money. A man may, because of his status as mother's brother in a matrilineal society, be required to provide food for his sister's children while his own are fed by his wife's brother.

In Samoan society individual chiefs gain great prestige by giving food to the village council of elders. Each council member is the head of a village family and the food he is given will be taken home and distributed among the members of the family. Gifts to the council serve to feed the whole village, but the food presentation itself in the council-meeting is formal, ceremonial, and status-rewarding. Tradition has established a voluminous set of distribution regulations, and pigs and fish are carefully divided by the village talking chief according to an age-old system. (See Fig. 9–1.)

GIFT EXCHANGE. Distributions of products within a society or between different societies often take the form of reciprocal gift exchanges. At marriages, funerals, or title installations of a new chief, Samoans are required to give gifts to the families involved. After much ado about thanking the guests for the gifts, each guest is given a gift to take away with him which is roughly equal in value to but different from what he brought. In the case of weddings, the family of the bride and

1. THE SHARE OF THE VILLAGE ORGANIZATION OF UNTITLED MEN (AUMAGA)
2. THE SHARE OF THE VILLAGE PRINCE (MANAIA)
3. THE SHARE OF THE VILLAGE ORGANIZATION OF UNTITLED MEN
4. THE SHARE OF THE HIGH TALKING CHIEFS
5. THE SHARE OF CHIEFS OF LOWER RANK
6. THE SHARE OF CHIEFS OF LOWER RANK
7. THE SHARE OF THE PARAMOUNT CHIEF
8. THE SHARE OF THE FAMILY OF THE PARAMOUNT CHIEF
9. THE SHARE OF THE VILLAGE CEREMONIAL HOSTESS (TAUPOU)
10. THE SHARE OF THE CHIEFS OF LOWER RANK
11. THE SHARE OF THE CHIEFS OF LOWER RANK

Fig. 9–1. Ceremonial food distribution in the Manu'a Islands of American Samoa.

the family of the groom are required to exchange goods. The bride's family must bring finely woven hibiscus fiber mats and tapa cloth and present them to the groom's family. In return they will be given pigs and other kinds of food. The exchange is reciprocal, but the important thing is that goods are circulated throughout a certain segment of the society and a number of people have had an opportunity to gain prestige through their generous giving.

The gift exchange phenomenon of Samoa has the effect of rescuing the society from economic stagnation. Since each family is actually economically independent of every other, there is normally no need for trade and no need for producing beyond the family's daily requirements. The exchange system stimulates economic interaction within the society and provides a strong motivation for individual family initiative.

Gift exchange can operate on an intersociety basis also. Not only does this type of transaction serve as a means of trade, but it is often an effective means of maintaining peaceful relations between a number of villages.

THE KULA RING. Often gift exchange is only one ceremonial aspect of a greater complex involving barter. Such is the case with the Trobriand Island kula ring. Malinowski describes this now famous trade complex as follows:

> The Kula is a form of exchange, of extensive, inter-tribal character; it is carried on by communities inhabiting a wide ring of islands, which form a closed circuit . . . On every island and in every village, a more or less limited number of men take part in the Kula—that is to say, receive the goods, hold them for a short time, and then pass them on. Therefore every man who is in the Kula, periodically though not regularly, receives one or several *mwali* (arm-shells), or a *soulava* (necklace of red shell discs), and then has to hand it on to one of his partners, from whom he receives the opposite commodity in exchange . . . The ceremonial exchange of the two articles is the main, the fundamental aspect of the Kula . . . Side by side with the ritual exchange of arm-shells and necklaces, the natives carry on ordinary trade, bartering from one island to another a great number of utilities, often unprocurable in the district to which they are imported, and indispensable there. (1961:81–83)

There are several intermediate stages between reciprocal gift exchange and true market distribution of products where money and prices are present. We do not imply, however, that a given society will evolve through these various stages. The trade continuum presented here is merely a means of classifying data and is not meant to represent an evolutionary sequence.

BARTER. We have already made passing reference to barter, the exchange of goods for goods. In this kind of transaction members of different families or villages or even different societies come together and through much haggling and bargaining effect an exchange of, say, pottery for spearpoints or yams for fish. Such exchange often takes place between coastal and inland people where each has a special kind of commodity which the other wants but does not produce itself. Barter may also include trading services for services.

Barter has been known to take place even where the trading parties are feuding or at war. If a symbiotic relationship exists between two societies but warfare prevents their meeting face to face, a procedure known as *dumb* or *silent* barter may be brought into play. In this kind of transaction one society places their trade objects in an agreed upon spot and then departs so that their trading partners can take the products they want and leave objects of equivalent value in their place. Such transactions are reported as occurring between the Veddas and the Sinhalese of Ceylon where exchanges of meat for arrow points take place during the night, among the Bantu and the pygmies of Africa, and among the Christian tribes of Northern Luzon and their Negrito neighbors.

Still a further step in the direction of a market distribution economy is the phenomenon of *money barter*, where a useful consumption commodity serves as a standard value for all goods exchanged. In Nicobar the commodity is coconuts; in Kenya, cattle and goats; in China, bricks of rice; and most unusual of all, in Easter Island, rats (eaten raw).

While barter may prove quite sufficient for a small isolated society, it is quite likely that an expanding society can arrive at a place where it has outgrown a simple exchange of goods through barter. As craft specialization becomes more diverse, something more efficient must be developed. In his book *Principles of Political Economy* J. S. Mill wrote, "A tailor who has nothing but coats might starve before he could find any person having bread to sell who wanted a coat; besides he would not want as much bread at a time as would be worth a coat, and the coat could not be divided" (1898:287).

The statement is, of course, a gross exaggeration of the problem. Even the simplest of minds could work out some arrangement where bread would be provided over an extended period in payment for the coat. The statement does, however, emphasize the fact that something more than simple barter is required when an economy expands and a high degree of labor specialization exists.

THE MARKET. True market exchange seems to be found mainly among agricultural and industrial people. In describing its characteristics, Redfield writes,

> In larger communities, where people do not know each other personally, and more and more kinds of goods appear, the market may be more fully a matter of an effort to sell at the highest price and buy at the lowest; then buyer and seller alike "shop around", and who the man is who buys or sells does not matter as compared with the opportunity to get the best price." (1956:354)

Thus we may see that compared with gift and ceremonial exchange, market transactions tend to be impersonal and often hostile. The sense in which such transactions can be considered hostile may be seen in the following quote from a series of articles about salesmen which appeared in *Fortune Magazine* (Whyte 1952). A veteran salesman is reported as advising an unsuccessful novice—"Fella," he finally said in exasperation, "you're not going to sell a damn thing until you realize one simple fact: The man on the other side of the counter is THE ENEMY" (*Consumer Reports* 1958:546).

". . . A market," writes Redfield, "can to some degree operate by the exchange of one sort of goods for another, but money, as a universal measure of value, is an enormous help in facilitation of market exchanges" (1956:354).

Common Monetary Symbols

We may be quite certain that Redfield would have maintained that the use of money, however, is not restricted to market economies. Actually, many forms of currency that we shall discuss facilitate economic transactions where there is no concept whatsoever of an organized market.

Although some economists insist that true money must have the qualities of portability, durability, homogeneity, divisibility, and stability of value, we find that any number of monetary symbols used in the market and informal trade transactions of primitive peoples fall far short of the criteria listed. These incomplete monies have been labeled "primitive money" as opposed to "modern money" by Paul Einzig: and in regard to their utility, Einzig states as follows, "An object may function as a primitive money, in spite of its defects, if a sufficiently large proportion of the community is prepared, for no matter what reason, to accept it in payment for goods and services and in settlements of debts" (1951:335). A study of the function of some of these monies in particular societies reveals many parallels in our own economic system.

MELANESIAN DIWARA—BANKS AND TEN PER CENT INTEREST. One of the most efficient forms of currency used among primitive peoples is Diwara shell money of New Britain. The standard unit is the fathom-long string of half-inch-long shells, but prices are also quoted in fractions of units. A fathom is sufficient to purchase sixty to eighty taro roots, but chickens cost only one fourth of a unit. Even individual shells may be taken off the string to make small purchases such as a handful of betel nuts. While the people of New Britain carry on a great deal of barter with neighboring villages and islands, transactions involving Diwara are definitely considered purchases.

Diwara is stored in special money houses in coils of fifty to two hundred fathoms. This capital is rarely drawn upon but instead provides its owner with prestige when it is frequently exhibited. Not only are there large shell fortunes but there are also bankers in each of the villages with whom wealthy men place money to be loaned at a ten per cent interest. Money is loaned without security, but the man who fails to repay his debt pays a heavy price in loss of prestige. He is considered an embezzler and never will be able to secure another loan. As in the case of American installment buying, the wealthy men of these

Melanesian villages make it easy for villagers to have the things they want. Rich men often distribute food, weapons, and ornaments among the members of the community. Then, on a given day, a festival is held and those who have accepted the goods have to make payment by laying strings of Diwara at the feet of the village banker.

WAMPUM—MULTIPURPOSE MONEY. When the New England colonists arrived in America, they found that the Indians were using beads as Europeans "use gold and silver" (Einzig 1951:178). While the clam shell beads known as wampum were an effective medium of exchange and were used even by the colonists in their transactions, they also had many other uses. At the same time, wampum served as a measure of wealth, as ornaments, as a method of conveying important messages and recording historical events, as tokens of friendship, and as a pledge of honor in treaties.

The value of a wampum string was determined partly by the number of beads it contained and partly by the color of the beads —purple and white having different values. Since the production of wampum involved great amounts of time, skill, and patience, it tended to maintain a high value and did not experience inflation until faked porcelain beads were introduced by fur traders in the nineteenth century.

The utility of wampum lay in the fact that its value was highly standardized throughout eastern North America, it was to a great extent imperishable, and it was small in bulk, light in weight, and easily divisable. The standard unit of monetary value was the fathom-length string, but for small transactions wampum beads were measured in wooden spoons.

KWAKIUTL COPPERS—BIG BANK NOTES OF THE NORTHWEST COAST INDIANS. In the United States no one carries around a $10,000 bill, but they are necessary units in our complex monetary system. The same was true of copper shields among the Kwakiutl Indians of British Columbia. The actual unit of exchange in this area was a cheap white woolen blanket with a value of about fifty cents. Everything was valued in blankets, and loans made at 100 per cent interest were repaid in blankets. Most important, blankets served as one form of wealth to be given away or destroyed when chiefs vied for prestige in the pot-latch ceremonies. The really big operators at these ceremonies bothered less with blankets than they did with copper shields. These "coppers" were worth thousands of blankets and the higher the rank of the purchaser the greater their price in blankets. The sole function of these copper shields was ceremonial exchange. Each had its own name and separate history. After a wealthy chief had succeeded in crushing his rivals by giving away several of these "big bank notes," he basked in the glory of his conspicuous consumption and planned for his next "battle of wealth."

SUDANESE COWRIES—DISCOUNT ON A CAR LOAD. Shell money was also important in Africa and white cowries served as standard monetary symbols in much of West Africa and the Congo. In the Sudan there never have been enough cowrie shells in circulation to meet trade requirements. But even though other currencies are used, the value of everything is quoted in cowries. One of the most peculiar characteristics of Sudanese cowrie transactions was the method of counting out shells for large purchases. Einzig describes the procedure as follows:

> Nominally the decimal system was in operation. Nevertheless 8×10 was reckoned as 100; 10×80 (nominally 100) was reckoned as 1,000; 10×800 (nominally 1,000) was reckoned as 10,000 and $8 \times 8,000$ (nominally 10,000) was reckoned as 100,000, so that what they called 100,000 was really only 64,000. (1951:142)

While this system may seem a little strange to us, it was merely a means of selling wholesale. If a trader made a big purchase of, say, five large bars of salt for 100,000 cowries, he actually only had to lay out 64,000. However, in his retail sales small quantities of salt were sold for five or ten cowries. When all the salt was sold, the trader had 100,000 cowries, which meant a profit of at least 36,000 shells.

One of the great difficulties in using cowries was that in big transactions counting was a major chore and then transporting the currency was even more of a problem. C. H. Robinson describes in his book *Hausaland* the problem he ran into in Nigeria when one of the horses used in his expedition became ill and could not go on. He writes, "The trouble is that we cannot sell it, as its value in cowries would require fifteen extra porters to carry, to whom we should have to pay all the money they carried and a great deal more besides" (1896:46).

YAP MONEY WHEELS—MICRONESIAN BANK ACCOUNTS SUBJECT TO INFLATION. One of the most peculiar monetary standards ever devised by man is the "stone money" of Yap. Although this "money" is neither portable nor divisible, it certainly is durable and its function on this Micronesian island is not unlike that of a European bank account. This currency was produced in various sizes (silver-dollar size to twelve feet in diameter) from aragonite, a calcite rock quarried on the islands of Guam and Palau. A hole in the center for the insertion of a carrying pole facilitates their transport. The value of the money depends upon three factors: (1) scarcity, (2) cost of production, and (3) risk.

One could hardly expect these money wheels to be very abundant since the material had to be quarried at least three hundred miles away (five hundred and fifty miles in the case of Guam stone) and then transported by frail outrigger canoes. Not only did production crews have to be paid in food but gifts had to be given to the island sovereigns for permission to quarry. Once the stones were in the boats the chances of getting them home were not the best. Often whole crews were lost along with their hard cash cargoes. Naturally, the larger the wheel the more it was worth and Guam money was worth more than Palau money.

When the newly quarried money arrived on Yap, it was rolled or carried to a special place where it could be admired by the island populace. While silver-dollar- and plate-sized stones circulate, the larger stones are not moved. They serve mainly as stores of wealth and sources of prestige for their owners. The owners of the stones change but the stones remain in place. A twelve- to fourteen-inch diameter stone of good quality will purchase fifty baskets of taro, yams, and bananas or a pig weighing approximately eighty to one hundred pounds. Owning a large money wheel is very much like having a large bank account. When an American businessman makes a large purchase he merely writes a check on his account and the money is credited to the account of the seller, but neither man actually handles the money. The same thing happens with Yap money. In the event that a man wants to buy another's plantation, the purchase is made with the large money wheel. The stone money is not moved from its usual location beside the village path; only its title is transferred from one man to another.

In the 1880's an Irish trading schooner captain by the name of O'Keefe called at Yap and got the idea that with enough stone money he could become its king. He immediately set sail for Palau and Guam and returned with a whole boat load of large money wheels. While the natives of Yap were quite impressed with his cargo, his money was immediately labeled "O'Keefe money" and he found that it would buy very little. The problem was that his methods of obtaining the money had inflated it. The cost of production and the risk of transport were, through his methods, greatly reduced and so was the money's value. Just as United States currency has to be backed by gold, Yap money has to be backed up by considerable expense, labor, and risk.

PROPERTY

One cannot talk about the economic organization of any people without taking into consideration their concepts of property. In our analysis of the "common understandings . . . which attach to things that may be used, enjoyed, or disposed of" (Redfield 1956:356) we

immediately are involved in a consideration of the rights and obligations of individuals in regard to one another and to their society. It is
easy to be guilty of oversimplification however in the analysis of particular societies' attitudes toward property ownership. As *Notes and
Queries* states:

> Ideas concerning property may vary, not only in different societies, but
> even within a single society according to the nature of the property and
> the type of ownership right involved. A full understanding of these ideas
> calls for careful analysis; simply to label a system as "individualistic" or
> "communistic" is never adequate and often misleading. (1951:149)

There is probably no society in the world that makes more of individual ownership of property than that of the United States but even
here there is much communal property. Visitors to every National
Park, for instance, are reminded "This is your park. Keep it clean."
People also talk about "our town," "our postal system," and "our
church."

On the other hand, no naturally evolved society is totally communistic, not even the Soviet Union. There is always the recognition of
some private ownership of tools, weapons, clothing, or ornaments.
Linton has pointed out that "the only exceptions are a few completely
communistic societies established by sophisticated individuals as a part
of religious movements and no society of this sort has ever had a long
duration" (1952:657).

It is true that primitive people generally are more communal in their
property concepts than industrialized ones. Many primitive people
faced with rigorous environments where hunger and danger are always
present have found that they cannot afford the luxury of private
property. One cannot be selfish when the very existence of the group is
at stake. Sahlins suggests, "It is a demand of group survival that the
successful hunter be prepared to share his spoils with the unsuccessful.
'The hunter kills, other people have,' say the Yukaghir of Siberia"
(1960:86). Even in the less rigorous climate of Southeast Asia, the same
kind of awareness of group needs prevails. Of the Semang, Lisitzky
writes:

> The common principle seems to be that the catch is the private property
> of the successful hunter, but the food is expected to be shared among those
> who have less than himself. The reason is, of course, everywhere the same:
> No man is always fortunate, and he who lets his neighbor starve while he
> has plenty will have no one to help him survive in future times of need.
> But the generosity of the Semang does not come from a cool calculation of
> this principle. He shares as naturally and spontaneously among his kinsmen
> as do the members of our own smaller families among themselves. (1960:49)

What actually operates in many primitive societies is what Sahlins calls "kinship-friendship" economics or what Redfield labels "status" economics. In this kind of system there is a set of obligations arising from one's position in society or one's kinship relationship. After these obligations have been met, then and only then can one consider oneself. In Western culture the conditions concommitant with industrialization have broken the kinship structure and have produced an atmosphere of anonymity that has reduced one's sense of obligation to his fellows.

Although we have pointed out that some private property exists in all societies, the exact interpretation of what private property means varies greatly. The man of Western culture emphatically states that "what is his is his!" and he has a title, a deed, or a no trespassing sign to prove it. In many primitive societies, however, a man may refer to an article as "his" because he made it and has the sole right of disposal, but if a kinsman should ask to use the object he is obligated to loan it. In the Samoan islands there is communal family land and also private land that a man has carved out of the virgin bush for the support of his immediate family; but since such private lands are left to all of one's heirs, in time they also become communal.

Many primitive people must consider Western concepts of ownership a personification of the "dog in the manger" parable, for to them ownership is validated primarily through use. A man owns a piece of land if he clears it and plants a crop, but if, after the harvest, he allows the bush to take over again, he has lost his claim to that land.

In many parts of the world property consists of things that we ordinarily do not think of as property at all. Weaving or pottery designs are often owned by individual craftsmen or their families. In Samoa every chief has a special name for the location of his guest house and that name is the exclusive property of his family. Bush doctors in a variety of societies "own" their power to heal. In many areas of Polynesia family heads own their family legends and genealogies and have the exclusive right to their recitation.

Property and Prestige

It would seem that a common human desire is for recognition—to be singled out by members of society as someone worthwhile, someone important. A number of people throughout the world see property as an avenue through which this recognition may be obtained. But how property is used for this purpose is an interesting story when considered cross-culturally.

Having a $40,000 home, two cars, and a multifigure bank account is a major goal for many an American but, as we have seen earlier, for the Kwakiutl Indian, prestige and recognition come from giving property away rather than hording it.

Many times men are far less concerned with the products of their labors than with the applause they receive for a job well done. Eskimos consider the kill the private property of the succesful hunter but the animal must be divided equally among the whole party. The fact that the slayer of the animal gets to choose his portion first is of little consequence compared to the prestige he derives from being the skillful hunter. Merely being designated as the owner of the kill is more important than the meat.

In still other societies prestige comes through holding no property at all. Asceticism places great value on turning one's back on wealth. This was an important principle in early and medieval Christianity and is found today to some extent among Roman Catholic clergy and monks. Scorn of worldly wealth is also an important principle followed by Buddhist and Brahman priests whose practices of self-denial gain for them the maximum of respect and prestige among the laity. Having, giving, or doing without property can bring to peoples of various cultures the acclaim of their fellow men and represent a portion of the panorama of values that motivate man and determine for him solutions to problems that demand his decision.

SUGGESTED READINGS

BARNETT, H. G. "The Nature of the Potlatch," *American Anthropologist*, **40**:349, 1938. (Corrects a number of misunderstandings concerning the potlatch of the Northwest Coast Indians.)

BARNETT, L. "Man Shapes his Environment," *Life*, April 16, 1956. (How the domestication of plants and animals changed man's life and brought victory in his battle against nature.)

BRAIDWOOD, ROBERT J. "The Agricultural Revolution," *Scientific American*, September, 1960. (The cultural ramifications of domestication of plants and animals in the Middle East.)

DALTON, GEORGE. "Economic Theory and Primitive Society," *American Anthropologist*, **63**:1, 1961. (Reasons why economic theory cannot be fruitfully applied to the study of primitive communities. Suggest an alternative approach to the study of primitive economics.)

GRATTON, C. H. "The Things the World Wants," *Harpers*, November, 1956. (Variations in people's values in different developing countries.)

HSU, FRANCIS L. K. "Incentives to Work in Primitive Communities," *American Sociological Review*, **8**:638, 1943. ("Self-interest" as a motivation for labor in all societies.)

MALINOWSKI, BRONISLAW. "The Primitive Economics of the Trobriand

Islanders," *Economic Journal,* 31:1, 1921. (How economic considerations enter into all aspects of tribal life.)

THOMAS, ELIZABETH MARSHALL. "The Herdsmen," *New Yorker,* May 1, 8, 15, 22, 1965. (A four-part article describing the pastoral life of the Nilo-Hamitic people of northern Uganda.)

WISSLER, CLARK. "Corn and Early American Civilization," *Natural History,* February, 1945. (The mystery surrounding the origin of corn and how it came to dominate the economy of prehistoric civilization in the New World.)

Paperbound Books

FORDE, C. DARYLL. *Habitat, Economy and Society.* Dutton & Co. (A classic study of the relationship between geography and culture.)

MALINOWSKI, BRONISLAW. *Argonauts of the Western Pacific.* Dutton & Co. (Comprehensive study of the Melanesian kula trading ring.)

MEAD, MARGARET (ed.) *Cooperation and Competition Among Primitive Peoples.* Beacon Press. (Contains information on the economic activities of such people as the Eskimos, Iroquois, Maori, Bathonga, and Samoans.)

RICHARDS, AUDREY I. *Hunger and Work in a Savage Tribe.* World Publishing Company. (Struggle for survival in an East African society.)

10

The Family and Kinship

Anthropologists know of no people in the world who do not have some form of family. It would actually be inconceivable to imagine man, even in prehistoric times, being able to exist without this vital social group. Although the family is a universal phenomenon, it exists in an almost unbelievable number of forms. One of the many varieties is the American family, which is (1) *monogamous*—uniting one husband and one wife, (2) *conjugal*—placing greatest importance on the marital bond rather than the blood relationship, and (3) *nuclear*—consisting only of the biological parents and their offspring. Since this is the form of family that Americans are reared in, there is a tendency for them to think of it as natural and "right." However, people in other societies, reared in quite different kinds of families, also think of their familial situation as natural and "right."

For example, many a Tibetan child has grown up in a family that is made up of a single mother and a number of fathers, all of whom are brothers. The child will look to the eldest of these brothers as his "real" father, but any one of them might actually have been his biological father. This system involving a woman married to more than one husband is called *polyandry*.

The West African child has had quite a different experience. There is a very good chance that he may live in a family practicing *polygyny*. This is still another form of *polygamy*—i.e. plural marriage. His father has several wives; he lives with his own mother in a hut in a large family compound, but he rarely has any contact with his father. While he must share his mother with two or three siblings, he may have to share his father with dozens of half-brothers and -sisters. His own mother feeds him and cares for him, but he also has additional "mothers," the other wives of his father, who may discipline him or send him on errands.

191

Typical of still another family type is the traditional Chinese family. Here the child has but one mother and one father, but he lives in an *extended family*, where he and his parents share the house with grandparents, uncles, aunts, cousins, and perhaps a few nieces and nephews. Another characteristic feature of this family is that it is *consanguine*, that is to say, the important ties and obligations are not to one's spouse but to one's blood relatives. The father-son relationship, for example, is considered vitally more important than the husband-wife relationship. Marriages are usually arranged by the parents and the choice of a wife for a son is determined by whether or not the girl will be compatible and industrious in the total family situation. The bride will have nothing to say about the running of the household and must be a "dutiful daughter" until the time of her mother-in-law's death when she will take over the domestic responsibilities.

DESCENT PATTERNS

Families also vary greatly throughout the world in the manner in which they determine kin relationships. Americans are so accustomed to reckoning kinship through both the mother's and the father's family that other kinship systems seem very strange and often are not understood. The American system is known as a *bilineal* or *bilateral* one. It is a common form among Western people but is found only sporadically among primitives. A child who grows up in such a system has two sets of grandparents—a maternal and a paternal pair—and he regards both as being equally related to him. He might, as in the case of Europeans and Americans, inherit his family name from his father's side of the family, but this does not alter his feeling of affinity to his mother's people.

With very few exceptions, primitive people recognize dual biological descent but often stress a single line of social inheritance. If these unilineal systems emphasize the father's side of the family, they are known as *patrilineal* systems, and if they stress the mother's side of the family they are *matrilineal*. In the latter system, for example, a man inherits his name, property, and occasionally family secrets from his mother or his mother's brother. In such a system a man does not ignore his biological relationship to his father and his father's relatives but recognizes that his major social obligations are to his relatives on his mother's side.

Many societies that feature matrilineal descent also feature *matrilocal* residence. This means that when a man marries he is expected to go to live with his wife's family. In this group he is, of course, a guest, owning no property, but he is expected to fit in with the family's work activities and social routine. In such a family, leadership will often be in the hands of the mother's brother.

Patrilocal residence, on the other hand, involves an arrangement where the bride moves in with her husband's people. Other commonly found residence patterns are those labeled *bilocal* and *neolocal*. The former implies a choice of residence or alternate residence with both families, whereas the latter involves setting up an independent household.

Since it is often difficult for us to comprehend the peculiarities of a single-line kinship system, anthropologists have developed diagramming techniques that greatly simplify our problems of analysis and understanding. The following are examples of two such diagrams involving three generations. The first describes a matrilineal system and the second a patrilineal one.

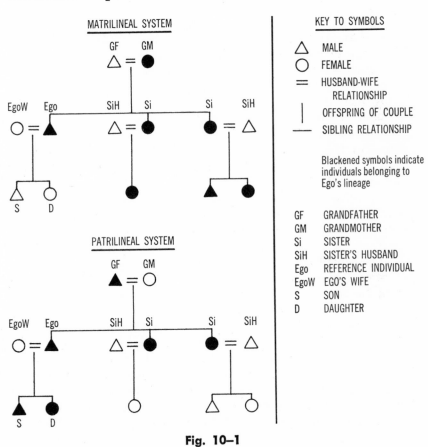

Fig. 10–1

THE MINIMAL FUNCTIONS OF FAMILY

We can see that there are many forms of family that can and do satisfy man's need. The important thing to note is that all of these families perform a number of functions that are essential to the survival and perpetuation of the human species. The minimum functions that family must perform in this respect are seen by anthropologists to be the following:

1. The family must make provision for legitimate sexual outlets for adults.
2. The family must perpetuate the species through controlled reproduction.
3. The family must educate and socialize the children.
4. The family must serve as a unit of economic cooperation.

The Sexual Function of Family

One of the most basic and necessary functions of the family is providing sexual outlets for the adults of a society. While man's need for such outlets is not as demanding as his need for food, water, or shelter, it is nevertheless a strong motivating force in his behavior and, if we are to explore the reasons for the universal existence of family, we must not forget the nature of human sexuality.

Among humans and higher primates in general, sex activity is continuous. It is not limited to mating seasons, rutting periods, or heat cycles as it is in nearly all lower animals. This ever-present attraction between sexes makes for continual association, and in part explains the existence of a permanent union of males and females in all human societies. Among many lower animals there is only seasonal association of the sexes for the purpose of breeding, but after the female has conceived, the male departs since there is no promise of continued sexual activity. Among such animals as wolves or lions, the association will often continue until the young are suckled. During the nursing period the males will hunt for the females, but in the case of deer or buffalo and domesticated dogs and cats, the female can get her own food and the union is immediately ended when the mating is over.

We must not, however, be lured into explaining too much in terms of sexual behavior, particularly in the case of man. Humans are far from being dominated by their sexual feelings. In human society the sex act cannot be engaged in irresponsibly, because there is always the possibility of conception. In such an event the resulting child must be carefully nurtured for a prolonged period until he is capable of caring for himself. Thus, sex behavior is considered serious business, and there is no society in the world that does not impose some kind of controls on such activity. These controls stipulate whether or not the couple must be married or they may define what constitutes incest, but there are always clear statements concerning what is sanctioned and what is taboo. There is a time and a place and a certain kind of partner for sex behavior in all societies. While it is often felt to be a natural human function, sexual behavior tends to be learned behavior and its forms vary greatly from culture to culture.

There are also other reasons for the existence of a permanent family among humans. In nearly all cultures there is a high valuation placed upon offspring and particularly sons, by their fathers. Whether this is a matter of passing on a name, property, or family traditions, or whether it is a matter of the father's considering the child his property, or perhaps even an image of himself, a feeling of special attachment is usually present. The situation varies from society to society, of course, but human males generally take pride in their offspring, cherish them, and want to watch them grow and develop. There are few societies where a father would not lay down his life to protect his children. These ideals and emotional feelings that tie the father to the children no doubt account in great measure for the maintenance of a compact family unit.

The attachment between mother and her children is the result of somewhat different factors. There is no evidence to support claims of a special motherly instinct in women, but there is some evidence that there is a biological basis for a mother's love and concern for her child. Niles Newton, for example, points out that "research . . . indicates that motherly behavior is related to menstrual flow, breast feeding, hormonal changes and some other physical and social factors" (1955: 70–71).

Of course, cultural ideas can always overrule biological pressures of this kind. There are societies, the Marquesas, for example, where children are nursed but are shown little affection. Mothers merely provide the nutritional necessities but then leave the children to others to care for their other needs. On the other hand, many modern European mothers do not nurse their babies and the mutual satisfaction of both mother and child is not experienced, but their behavior is highly influenced by cultural attitudes that make it mandatory that they consider their babies to be "cute," "lovable," and "dear." The family relationship can be considered as a triangle of affection and dependency. The mother is drawn to the child through physical satisfactions and cultural ideals, the father through pride and identity of blood. The parents are drawn together through sexual satisfaction, economic necessity, and a shared sense of responsibility for the welfare of the child. There are always those who do not feel their responsibilities, those who deviate from the societal norms, or those who never develop an emotional feeling for their wives or their children, but these are exceptions; and while such behavior should be considered, it hardly alters our explanation of the nature of universal family cohesion.

Nurture of the Young

It is more important for man than for any other type of animal to have a permanent and intimate family orgaization. This is because of the nature of the offspring that man produces. The human infant is born completely helpless, without instincts and without the ability to effectively use his body. For many years the child must be protected and cared for while he learns to obtain his own living and while he learns his culture's system of customs, ideals, values, and attitudes. This takes time and it takes intimate association with the members of a permanent group who have a special concern for the child. Aristotle once stated that "What is everybody's business is nobody's business." This was, of course, a criticism of Plato's idea of a communal group that would have resulted in a de-emphasis of parent-child ties. We find, however, that the adults who care for and educate the children need not be the biological parents. In many societies "sociological" or surrogate parents actually have more to do with the rearing of children than do the actual parents. As long as someone shoulders the responsibilities, it doesn't really matter what their true relationship is.

Sociological "Parents"

In societies that trace kinship through the mother's family only, there is often a phenomenon present known as the *avunculate*. In this situation the most important adult male in the lives of the children is not the biological father but the mother's brother, or maternal uncle. Such an arrangement can be found among the Trobriand Islanders of the Southwest Pacific. Concerning this system Malinowski writes as follows:

As he (the child) grows up . . . the mother's brother assumes a gradually increasing authority over him, requiring his services, helping him in some things, granting or withholding his permission to carry out certain actions; while the father's authority and counsel becomes less and less important. (1929:7)

Still a different surrogate situation is that labeled the *amitate*. Here we find a counterpart to the mother's brother's position. The amitate refers to a special relationship which prevails between the father's sister and his children. Lowie describes this family feature among the Haida as follows:

The paternal aunt of a Haida appears in every critical phase of life, ful-filling some obligation, but also receiving compensation therefor. Thus, when a girl comes of age, this aunt cares for her, and at a youth's wedding she conducts the bride to him. (1948:74)

Among the Canella of Brazil "a little girl spends much time at her aunt's and the sentimental tie between the two is likely to grow stronger than that between the nephew and uncle" (*ibid.*).

In the Samoan Islands a variety of "parents" provide for the needs of the children. Margaret Mead describes this arrangement as one where children are "reared in households where there are a half dozen adult women to care for them and dry their tears, and a half dozen adult males, all of whom represent constituted authority" (1959:123). The Samoan household is actually an extended family unit wherein all adult relatives feel a certain responsibility for and exert a certain amount of control over all the children. It doesn't matter how many "mothers" and "fathers" there are, so long as they definitely feel and attend to their responsibilities toward the children.

Parents and Socialization

Aside from the love and care that the parents give to the child, the mere association of these adults with the children is important in their personality development and in their learning to get along with others. The desirability of having a father and mother in close association with the child is well pointed up in the family situation in American culture. The American nuclear family represents the maximum extent to which the size of family can be reduced without adversely affecting the personality development and socialization of the child. With this bare nucleus of family, a common problem is the "broken home." The family may be broken in a number of ways—by death, divorce, separa-tion, or desertion. How the family is broken is not as important as the fact that it is an incomplete family unit.

Statistics show that most American "broken" homes are homes without a father. Although the father exerts less influence over his children today than in generations past, the family in which the mother must be both mother and father to her children is less than satisfactory. Sociologists generally agree that young people from "broken" homes in America are more likely to engage in deviant behavior than those who come from complete families. Barker (1940) found the rather high correlation of .79 between broken homes and delinquency. Other studies have shown that deviant behavior is also more frequent in complete families where there is hostility on the part of the parent toward the children or where one or both of the parents refuse to accept their responsibilities in raising and educating the children. In either of these cases, the situation is roughly the same: The family either is incomplete or is functioning as an incomplete unit and therefore the enculturation and socialization of the children is impaired.

Why is it that problems sometimes arise where one of the parents is missing? Since "broken" home situations more frequently involve a missing father than an absent mother, let us consider for a moment the importance of the male parent in the family. Not only is the father important as a provider but his mere presence and interest in the children are valuable for their development. The father represents for them a model of adult male behavior. Sons learn what is expected of them as men, husbands, and fathers by observing the behavior of their fathers.

Sociologists have found that sons raised in families where there was a happy relationship between the father and mother will themselves be quite likely to develop a satisfactory marriage relationship. Many a modern father in America takes an interest in the activities of his sons because his own father took an interest in him. The father also establishes for the son a pattern of masculine behavior and aids the child in understanding his own sexuality. Green and Money, in a study of effeminacy, have observed that "many men do not realize how important it is for a boy to identify with his father and impersonate him, which is made easier when the two participate in activities and recreation together. In the absence of a father, a grandfather, uncle, stepfather, brother or other male may serve as a father substitute" (1961: 289).

A number of psychological studies have shown that homosexuality in males is often associated with mother dominance or with situations where the father-son relationship is a hostile one and therefore only a minimum of association and identification is possible.

The presence of a father in the family is almost as important for the daughter as for the son. The daughter needs this association so that she may have some insight into male behavior, particularly that associated with the role of husband and father. In this way she gets some idea of what to expect from her husband in her own future marriage. Furthermore, a father represents an example of men in general. He has a man's point of view and although a girl may consider her father terribly old fashioned, his opinions about a new hairdo or dress are often more valuable to her than her mother's. She doesn't expect dad's point of view to correspond exactly with that of her young man, but at least it is a male opinion.

THE NAYARS—A FAMILY WITHOUT A FATHER. While we have made the generalization that in order to adequately raise children the family unit should be a complete one involving both male and female parents (either biological or sociological), it is only fair to state that there are one or two notable exceptions. The most interesting example of a well-functioning but incomplete family is that of the Nayar of India. The Nayar are a warrior caste that prior to 1792 served the local feudal rulers. Since the men were engaged in this extremely dangerous occupation, and since they were often away from home for extended periods of time, a form of family develped wherein men played a very insignificant role in family life. The significant social unit in Nayar society is the matrilineal lineage, or as it is sometimes expressed, the uterine family. This is a group of related women, their children, and occasionally a few men—the brothers of the women. No relatives by marriage are included in the Nayar households—not even husbands. The eldest woman in the lineage is its head and administrators of its house, lands, and other property. Every twelve to fifteen years there is a ritual marriage ceremony for all the adolescent girls. On this occasion ritual husbands give the girls gold ornaments, called *tali,* and this legitimizes the marriage. Following this ritual marriage ceremony the couples separate, but from this time on the girls are considered mature and therefore ready to engage in a series of casual unions, called *sambandham* "marriages," with men of her own subcaste or with those of higher castes. *Sambandham* relationships are hardly marriages in that they actually involve *sambandham* "husbands" giving their "wives" gifts of cloth and then being entitled to share the girl's room for the night. The men leave their weapons outside so that other "husbands" will know enough to stay away. The men do not support the women in any way, nor are they obligated to aid in the rearing of any children that might result from their meetings. Nayar children often do not know their fathers and even if they do, there is no sense of a relationship between them.

While this family apparently represents an exception to all we have said about the importance of a family with both a father and mother, it represents a unique situation. This form of family was developed to cope with the rather serious problem of the absence or even loss of adult males as a result of their activities as soldiers. The system solves the usual economic problems by placing all property and wealth in the hands of the mother's lineage, and the fact that the lands are cultivated by an inferior caste, subservient to the Nayar, ensures that the needs of all will be satisfied. Since the female lineage does include the brothers of the women, something of the role of surrogate father is undoubtedly assumed by these men for the many children residing within a given household.

The Family as an Economic Unit

It has been pointed out that one of the more important functions of the family is its activities as an economic unit. The family is a unit of both production and consumption. In some societies every family member has a share in the production, but in others only certain members shoulder the responsibilities of production for the entire group. Production may mean actually growing the food that the family will eat or it may mean earning a wage so that the goods that the family consumes

The family as an economic unit. Among the Kung Bushmen of the Kalahari desert region of South West Africa men hunt and make weapons and their wives gather wild plants and care for the home and the children. (Courtesy of L. K. Marshall Expedition, Peabody Museum of Harvard University—Smithsonian Institution.)

can be purchased. Whatever the economic problems, the family seems to find a way of organizing itself so that satisfactory adjustments may be made. An example of the influence of economic matters on family form and function may be seen by contrasting the urban American family with that of the rural areas. Traditionally the farm family has been one where all its members contributed to the family welfare. Mother kept chickens and sold eggs; the children had their chores and often had a calf, the raising of which was their responsibility alone:

Samoan wedding party.

and father was the main laborer and director of economic activities. The more children there were, the easier it was to run the farm; thus, farm families were traditionally large. In the city, however, we find that the structure and organization and even the size of the family are very different. In the city, people are involved in an industrial or commercial way of life, and more often than not, there is but one wage earner per family. While the mother has an important role to play as homemaker, she and the children are actually economic liabilities in that they consume but do not participate in the production, or wage-earning activities. In the city therefore the size of the family is limited by the earning power of the single wage earner and the fact that the cost of living is higher in the city. The cramped living conditions which usually prevail in urban areas also tend to restrict the number of children a man will want.

MATE SELECTION. The influence of economics on family life may also be seen in the matter of mate selection. In contrasting European with primitive society, Marshall Sahlins writes, "Marriage and family are institutions too important in primitive life to be built on the fragile, shifting foundations of 'love.' The family is the decisive economic institution of society. It is to the hunter and gatherer what the manor was to feudal Europe, or the corporate factory system is to capitalism: it is the productive organization" (1960:82). "The economic aspect of primitive marriage," he continues, "is responsible for many of its specific characteristics. For one thing, it is the normal adult state; one cannot economically afford to remain single . . . The number of spouses is, however, limited by economic considerations among primitives" (1960: 83).

POLYGYNY. While polygyny is allowed in almost all societies except Western, only in economies of surplus can men mass enough wealth to afford more than one wife. In many agricultural societies women do much of the cultivating and actually can increase the wealth of a man, but in most societies where polygyny is practiced the main problem is having enough money to obtain extra wives in the first place. There is often the matter of *bride price,* the counterpart of the European *dowry.* Since a man must save enough money to "purchase" a wife and since the price is usually high, most men in polygamous societies practice monogamy as a matter of economic necessity. Plural marriage is seldom prompted by sexual desire; in most cases a man wants extra wives because of the increased status and prestige they will bring. In West African society, for example, no man who really wants to be somebody would ever be content with having but a single wife. In many families it is the wife who urges her husband to acquire extra wives because her own work will then be lighter and she will be known around the village as one of the wives of a very important man. The situation may be compared with the American wife who wants to keep up with the Joneses by having her husband buy a second car.

While polygyny is found much more frequently in surplus rather than subsistence economies, it would not be correct to say that wealth is the only factor involved. Of all the societies of the world the one with the highest standard of living and the greatest amount of wealth is undoubtedly the United States and yet we have laws to prevent polygyny. Bengt Danielsson, the anthropologist who accompanied the Kon Tiki expedition, in his book *Love in the South Seas* suggests, in a tongue-in-cheek manner, that we are making a mistake in limiting our number of spouses to one. He explains his position as follows:

In the first place, there are great individual variations in the strength of the sexual impulse, so that for many people one partner is simply not enough. In the second place, certain people, for example, captains of industry, politicians, large landowners, etc., have very heavy social and economic duties which are often too overwhelming for one unfortunate wife. (1957:275)

Such an idea would be quite shocking to most Americans, because their Judeo-Christian tradition labels any form of polygamy immoral. Danielsson considers such a reaction as rather inconsistent, however, and reminds us that "from the moral standpoint . . . there can be no difference between being married to several wives in rapid succession and being married to them at the same time" (*ibid.*). Regardless of the inconsistencies involved, the fact remains that cultural norms, often based on religious ideals, can overshadow the influence of the basic economy on the form and function of family.

RESIDENCE. There is also some evidence that economic factors play a part in influencing the location of marital residence and the way kinship is reckoned. In a study carried out by William I. Thomas it was found that temporary matrilocal residence tends to be found in hunting and gathering societies. In other words, it is a common pattern for hunters and gatherers to live with and serve their parents-in-law for a time before taking their brides to their own family group. It is believed that this practice occurs where bride wealth is paid in installments. Once having paid for his bride, the husband moves to the community of his own people.

It has also been found in an examination of many primitive societies that permanent matrilocal residence, and matrilineal descent as well, is to a great extent associated with large sedentary groups that subsist primarily from the agricultural activities of women. A typical example of this kind of situation is to be found in Iroquois society. Underhill describes the role of women as follows:

Women were important people in an Iroquois village. They owned the fields, an arrangement which is often found in agricultural tribes where women do the field work. Since property went down in the female line, descent also was counted in that way . . . Iroquois women also owned the houses. A matron with her daughters, her younger sisters, and the husbands of all of them often occupied a longhouse, while the brothers and sons moved away to live with their wives. (1953:90)

In herding societies and in those where plough agriculture is present, married couples tend to reside with the husband's people and kinship is generally traced through the male line. Where cattle are kept or where the plough has been introduced, the men's subsistence contribution

tends to be greater than that of women and there is a desire to keep
the control of the property in the hands of the father and his sons.
Furthermore, since the main source of family support is with the
father's family, it is only natural that a bride would go to live with the
family of her husband. The Nilotic people of East Africa illustrate this
relationship between herding and male inheritance very well. As Ralph
Linton points out, "Cattle were the emotional and cultural center of
native life. All work with them was pre-empted by the men, and all
cultures having this economy were strongly patriarchal and patrilineal"
(1955:432).

LEVIRATE AND SORORATE. In studying the economic ordering of
family some mention should be made of two widely found customs
known as the *levirate* and the *sororate*. The levirate is an arrangement
where at the death of a husband the wife is expected to marry a
brother of her deceased husband. In the case of the sororate, on the
other hand, a man who has lost his wife will be expected to marry one
of her sisters. There are undoubtedly many plausible reasons for such
customs, but one of the better explanations can be made in terms of
economics. Let us imagine a matrilineal, matrilocal situation where
throughout a man's entire married life he has been living with his
wife's family and through his labor has been contributing to that
family's welfare. The family has effectively worked him into its labor
force and he has become a valuable asset to the family. He works well
with his wife's brothers and they have come to accept him as one of
them. At the death of the man's wife, however, the whole situation
might be changed. With his wife gone there is little to hold him in the
family. If he leaves to go home to his own family group where he has
some property, he might insist on taking his children, and perhaps they
too have developed into real economic assets for the family. In order to
remove the possibility of such a disorganizing occurrence, the society
has developed a way of retaining the individual and his children within
the group, thus ensuring the economic and social continuity of the
family. While we shall not make an analysis of the reasons for the
levirate, it conceivably works in much the same way, only in this case
there is pressure to retain the wife of the deceased and her children
within the group.

THE FAMILY AS A UNIT OF SOCIETY

The role of the family in the total society might be likened to that of
a brick in a great masonry structure. The whole is dependent upon the
strength and durability of its component parts, which fit together in a

particular way to produce the desired total configuration. Just as the characteristics of the individual bricks influence the color and style of the total structure so the individual families influence and reflect the tone and quality of the total society.

In general we can say that the values learned within the family represent the values of the society as a whole. The child who learns to interact successfully with the members of his family and learns to regulate his behavior in terms of family concepts of what is right and wrong, what is important and unimportant, will have little trouble making a successful adjustment to society as a whole. In our culture, only-children are listed as poor marriage risks by sociologists who specialize in family studies. There is no doubt that such children find it difficult to adjust to a marriage partner because they have never experienced the give-and-take situations that characterize larger families. They have never had to share with others or work out compromises with their siblings.

A good example of how the nature of family is reflected by the society and vice versa may be seen in an analysis of traditional Chinese social organization. Lin Yutang tells us that in pre-Communist China:

. . . the family system is the root of Chinese society, from which all Chinese social characteristics derive. The family system and the village system, which is the family raised to a higher exponent, account for all there is to explain in the Chinese social life. Face, favor, privilege, gratitude, courtesy, official corruption, public institutions, the school, the guild, philanthropy, hospitality, justice and finally the whole government of China—all spring from the family and village system, all borrow from it their peculiar tenor and complexion, and all find in it enlightening explanations for their peculiar characteristics. (1938:175–76)

It is doubtful if as strong a statement as Lin Yutang's could be made about the relationship between the American family and American society, but certainly there are resemblances between family values and the cultural values of our nation. For example, the democratic nature of our total culture is reflected to a very great extent in our patterns of family behavior. While the father is nominally the head of the American family, it is seldom that he can exert autocratic rule. He controls the family through persuasion and gives reasons for the demands he makes on family members. Geoffrey Gorer carries this concept of the democratic family even further. He says:

To a certain extent the pattern of authority in the state is reproduced in the family: it is as if the father represented the Executive, the mother the Legislative, and the neighbors, headed by the school teacher, the Judiciary authority. The child is in the position of the public, playing off one authority against another, invoking the system of checks and balances to maintain his independence. Although this is a somewhat far fetched comparison, it more nearly represents the structure of the ordinary American family than does the patriarchal picture derived from Europe, or the mirror image of that picture, with the father's authority transferred wholesale and unaltered to the mother. (1948:44–45)[1]

Carrying our family-building block analogy further, we must point out that building blocks or bricks are not just piled one on top of the other with nothing holding them together. They require mortar if the structure is to last. The mortar holding the individual family units of society together is kinship and marriage. We have already discussed how kin relationship traced matrilineally, patrilineally, or bilineally can tie families and generations together and promote mutual aid and cooperation. The part that kinship plays can further be seen in a commonly found phenomenon known as the *classificatory system*. A common form of this is the generation system where the majority of relatives of one's own age and lineage are referred to as "brother" or "sister," while relatives of one's parents' generation are collectively known as either "mother" or "father." Relatives of the generation of one's offspring are referred to as "son" or "daughter." Since specific kinship terms require appropriate corresponding behavior, this system tends to pull the group together and promote cooperation and respect. Under such a rule one's uncle and aunt have equivalent status with one's parents and expect to be treated accordingly.

Occidental societies, on the other hand, tend more toward *descriptive* kinship terminology. This kind of system uses separate terms for designating particular degrees of relationship. Instead of referring to all relatives of one's own generation as "brother" or "sister," relatives are singled out as "brother," "cousin," and "second cousin." By thus designating inner circle relatives from those further removed, civilized societies display their lack of concern for family and the reduced function of kinship as a force for social solidarity. Where specialists perform the functions of social control and where formal agencies control economic cooperation, kinship assumes a less important role in the organization of society. In many primitive societies, however, kinship is everything. It determines all social, economic, and religious interaction within the group. It has been said that many primitive groups consider a stranger an enemy unless they can establish some kinship relationship

[1] From *The American People* by Geoffrey Gorer. Copyright 1948 by Geoffrey Gorer. Revised Edition Copyright © 1964 by Geoffrey Gorer. W. W. Norton & Company, Inc. Reprinted by permission.

between him and the group. The practice of adopting individuals into a group as "blood" brothers derives from this concept.

The Incest Taboo

Stressing the importance of marriage bonds in the organization of society, John Layard states, "The whole structure of human society, in whatever form it may be found or wherever it may be . . . is based on something extremely concrete; namely, the incest taboo" (1961:51).

The incest taboo is the prohibition of marrying or mating with someone within one's own circle of kin. It is a universally prevalent taboo that has interested anthropologists for years. Westermarck, one of the first to investigate the phenomenon, maintained that inbreeding is biologically bad and man is therefore instinctively repulsed by the idea of marrying a relative. The main problem with this theory is that inbreeding does not necessarily produce harmful effects. A great deal of inbreeding has occurred in isolated Swiss villages and on Pitcairn Island, without any noticeable ill effects. Hawaiian, Egyptian, and Incan monarchs even married their sisters, and yet these royal lines were remarkably sound biologically. We might also ask Westermarck why a taboo must be installed to restrain men from doing what they instinctively abhor. Another criticism that might be leveled against the Westermarck theory is that among many primitives, individuals are often permitted and even encouraged to marry partners no farther removed genetically than those they are forbidden to marry. To understand how this can occur in primitive society it will be profitable to analyze the concepts of "cross" and "parallel" cousins.

CROSS AND PARALLEL COUSINS. *Cross cousins* are defined in anthropology as offspring of siblings of the opposite sex—i.e., the children of the families of a brother and a sister. Parallel cousins, on the other hand, are offspring of siblings of the same sex—i.e., the children of the families of two sisters. In many societies where kinship is traced either matrilineally or patrilineally, parallel cousins are considered siblings, and therefore, cannot marry; but cross cousins in such societies are allowed to marry because they belong to different lineages or clans and are therefore considered less closely related than parallel cousins. It is not unusual to find cross cousins considered ideal marriage partners because when such a marriage takes place every generation it permanently links two kin groups. The diagram in Fig. 10–2 will help to explain the different kinship status of the two varieties of cousins but will also provide evidence of their biological affinity.

Another theory of incest holds that familiarity breeds contempt or at

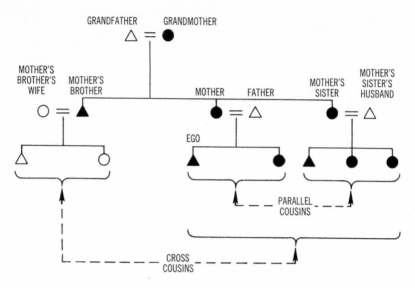

GRANDFATHER   GRANDMOTHER

MOTHER'S
BROTHER'S   MOTHER'S   MOTHER'S   MOTHER'S
WIFE   BROTHER   MOTHER   FATHER   SISTER   SISTER'S
                                                                           HUSBAND

EGO

PARALLEL
COUSINS

CROSS
COUSINS

Note: Blackened symbols indicate all individuals
      who consider themselves related through
      the grandmother's lineage.

Fig. 10–2.

least a lack of sexual interest. Bentham insisted that siblings raised in the same home would find it impossible to want a brother or a sister as a marriage partner. Perhaps the most extraordinary theory of incest is that of Sigmund Freud. He postulated a mythical human horde existing in a primeval era that was led by a jealous and powerful father (the "old man"). In keeping all the females for himself he incurred the hatred of his sons and they in turn banded together and slew and ate him. Each of the sons would have liked to have taken over the role of the "old man," but none was strong enough to seize control and expel the others. In order to survive as a group they removed the source of their temptation by establishing an incest prohibition on all the women of the group. This prohibition has in some mysterious way been handed down through hundreds of generations so that today men instinctively have a horror of incest.

Moving to more logical explanations of the universality of the incest taboo we read that Edward Tylor believed that by forcing men to seek brides outside their own group they established ties with other groups. This, of course, has the effect of reducing intergroup hostilities and at the same time creates larger social and economic groupings. Supporting evidence for Tylor's theory comes from the account of the anthropologist who asked a primitive why the men of his tribe didn't marry their sisters. After an initial shock reaction the native replied, "If we married our sisters, what would we do for brothers-in-law?" For this man, and for primitives all over the world, brothers-in-law mean additional strength in cooperative labor enterprises and aid in time of trouble or warfare.

The cultural consequences of marrying one's sister can be much more serious than just being without brothers-in-law. Nadel describes the extent to which certain groups might be disorganized by such a move. He writes:

> If any man married in disregard of the [incest] rule, the others would fail to work also. The bride-price would have to be paid within the same descent group, while in the people's conception it is a payment suitable only between such groups, being meant (among other things) to indemnify the bride's group for the loss of her prospective progeny. The offspring of such an irregular union would forfeit the double assistance from two kin groups since the father's and mother's kin now coincide, and would be less advantageously placed than the offspring of customary marriages. And there would be various other, minor but no less confusing, complications; for example, rules of avoidance (obligatory towards in-laws) and intimacy (towards blood relations) would now apply to the same people. (1953:269)

Thus we can see that Layard's idea that the concept of incest has the concrete result of building a structure of society is a profound insight into the understanding of social organization. Leslie White concurs with Layard's position that forcing people to marry outside the group tends to "increase the size, and therefore the strength of the group." He feels, however, that exogamy (marrying out) is more important "in preliterate societies than in literate cultures, whereas the reverse is the case with endogamy (marrying in)."

The latter arrangement has the effect of "fostering solidarity and integrity." Endogamy tends to be found in more advanced types of society "based upon property relations, ones having occupational groups, the political state, and a police force, than in a society based upon kinship" (1959:116). Hindu society, with its emphasis on caste endogamy, or our own with emphasis on marriage within religious, racial, or class divisions is an example of the situation in question.

IS ONE FORM OF FAMILY BETTER THAN ANOTHER?

We have seeen that all known family types perform the minimal functions required for the survival of man and society, but it is only fair to ask "Is one form of family better than others?" The answer to this is that the various forms each have their own distinctive strengths and their own weaknesses. Let us compare for example two major categories of family organization—the *conjugal* and the *consanguine*—in order to illuminate this problem.

The Conjugal Family

The *conjugal* form of family, found so frequently in Western society, provides its members with the greatest amount of personal freedom. There is usually freedom of choice of mates, and the power to control the family activities and destiny lies in the hands of those directly involved: a married couple and their offspring. There is little concern for the larger extended family or with family lines of descent and kinship, and it is rare when any great emphasis is placed on family lands or property.

While this form of family organization offers its members maximum freedom and minimum concern for distant relatives or extended family affairs, those who participate in this kind of social organization must pay for that freedom at the cost of reduced family stability and lack of family continuity. The conjugal family is formed when a married couple have produced their first children and it exists as a complete unit for a period of only sixteen to twenty-five years. Since there is little stress placed on the parent-child relationship, children are expected to develop an independence from their parents and upon marrying to set up their own homes and maintain only minimum contacts with parents. When all the children have married and moved out of the home, the parents are left alone and the life cycle of the conjugal family is completed. The conjugal family not only lacks continuity but also efficiency. Each generation must start anew to obtain its own property and experience and to expect little or nothing from their relatives.

The American form of conjugal family places great emphasis on severing the parental ties, and it is seldom that a man and his bride will want to move in with their parents. They will instead be eager to start their own home and make their own way. The major problem, however, is that these young people have no experience in running a home. In addition to this, the earning power of the young father is at a minimum as he and his wife raise their children. He is too proud to ask his parents for help at this time when expenses are great and income is small. Independence from parental authority also carries the responsibility of self-support.

By the time the children start to move out of the home, the father, by virtue of his experience, has in many cases reached his maximum earning capacity, but now he does not need the money. His children, in turn, want their chance at making their own way. Thus the cycle begins anew.

The Consanguine Family

The *consanguine* family, characteristic of many Oriental cultures, presents a very different picture. A typical consanguine situation involves a family consisting of several generations living together in a common household on family land that has supported the family for dozens of generations. This family unit shares both the work and the resources. The eldest male may very likely direct the family activities and serve generally as the family patriarch. As the sons marry they will tend to remain at home. As long as the family head lives, the sons must obey him and work the land according to his wishes. When the

The Dyak longhouse is actually a series of individual houses with a common veranda. Such a structure often houses half of the families in the village. (Courtesy of W. R. Geddes.)

patriarch dies, however, the eldest son will take over the authority of his father as well as the control of the family property. Since the son is often middle-aged by this time, he has long observed the manner in which the household must be run and he merely takes over the management of its material and human resources. Neither the efficiency nor the continuity of the family has been disturbed. In such families, however, individual action is discouraged. Personal considerations must be subordinated to family considerations, and men must often take directions from their older relatives when they themselves are mature adults.

Who is to say which of these families is *better*. One offers maximum freedom and the other offers maximum stability. Those who grow up in each prefer their own system and are anxious to have it perpetuated. Both kinds of families satisfy man's needs, but each places emphasis on different areas of satisfaction.

SUGGESTED READINGS

FORTES, M. "Primitive Kinship," *Scientific American*, June, 1959. (Comparison of structure and function of family in Africa and the United States.)

LEWIS, OSCAR. "Anthropological Approach to Family Studies," *American Journal of Sociology*, 55:468, 1950. (Demonstration of the method of studying families as functioning wholes.)

MEAD, MARGARET. "The Contemporary American Family as the Anthropologist Sees It," *American Journal of Sociology*, 53:453, 1948. (A picture of the urban American family and suggestions for solving its problems.)

————. "What's Happening to the American Family." *U.S. News and World Report*, May 20, 1963. (Dr. Mead analyzes the effect of early marriage, working mothers, and idle grandparents in American culture.)

NIMKOFF, M. F., and MIDDLETON, RUSSELL. "Types of Family and Types of Economy," *American Journal of Sociology*, 66:215, 1960. (Subsistence patterns associated with immediate and extended family systems.)

OPLER, M. K. "Woman's Social Status and the Forms of Family," *American Journal of Sociology*, 49:130, 1943. (Woman's social status and sexual role are related to rules and attitudes governing marital and extramarital relations.)

SAHLINS, MARSHALL. "The Origin of Society," *Scientific American*, September, 1960. (The sexual basis of social organization.)

Paperbound Books

FORD, CLELLAN S., and BEACH, FRANK A. *Patterns of Sexual Behavior*. Ace Books. (Best book available on comparative sexual behavior.)

LOWIE, ROBERT. *Primitive Society*. Harper & Row. (Chapters on marriage, family, and clan organization.)

MALINOWSKI, BRONISLAW. *Family Among the Australian Aborigines*. Schocken Books. (Analysis of one of the most complex kinship systems known to anthropologists.)

QUEEN, S. A., ADAMS, JOHN B., and HABENSTEIN, R. W. *The Family in Various Cultures*. J. B. Lippincott Co. (Contains chapters on Toda, Hopi, Baganda, Chinese, and Kibbutz families.)

SERVICE, ELMAN R. *Primitive Social Organization*. Random House. (An evolutionary approach to the study of social organization.)

11

Government

Many anthropologists believe that a categorical term like "government" is not sufficient to describe the many kinds of political systems found throughout the world. For example, Walter Goldschmidt uses the term "governance" to delineate political systems where "authority is a kind of extension of kinship roles and familial decision-making processes" (1960:366). He reserves the word "government" for societies that have "a set of political institutions, separate and distinct from other elements in the society" (1960:367). Meyer Fortes and E. E. Evans-Pritchard (1940) would agree that not all people have government and they prefer to use a less controversial term, "political system," to encompass the total range of political activity.

Schapera (1956), on the other hand, feels that any society has "government" which recognizes that certain of its members have the authority to make communal decisions. He would maintain that even Kalahari Bushman bands have a system of government although the kinship and political structures are nearly one and the same. This chapter will take the broader view and will refer to any political system as "government" if it maintains order, originates decisions that affect the entire group, and provides leadership in communal enterprises.

THE ORIGIN OF GOVERNMENT

Observing that every society in the world has some formal or informal governmental system, social scientists and social philosophers alike have long pondered the source of the concept of government. Although modern anthropology is less concerned with origins than it is

213

with the role of government in human society, it is interesting to look
at some of the more popular theories of genesis which have been put
forward.

Aristotle claimed that man is by nature a political animal, implying
that it is instinctive for men to live under some system of societal
control. The origin of man and the origin of government could not be
separated in time. Other scholars have maintained that government
was merely a man-conceived idea through which the selfish and

Among the Kung Bushmen of South West Africa kinship and political
structures are nearly one and the same. Here the father and headman
of the band (hand to face) discusses plans with his three sons-in-law.
(Courtesy of L. K. Marshall Expedition, Peabody Museum of Harvard
University—Smithsonian Institution.)

cunning were able to impose their will upon their fellow men. The
"contract theory" advanced by Hobbs and Locke postulated a deliberate agreement, in some primeval period, between the dominant and
subordinate members of society which established mutual respect for
one another's rights. Each had responsibilities as well as privileges.

The idea that government was given to man by the gods is a concept
that has appeared time and time again in human history. It explains
the "divine right of kings" and serves as a sanction to theocratic

systems in Mesopotamia, Egypt, Japan, and numerous primitive societies where rulers are looked upon as the descendants of deities.

Most social scientists today would explain government as being a
natural outgrowth of group living. They would maintain that the larger
and more complex the group the greater the need for satisfactory
controls over behavior. In all societies, primitive or civilized, some
means must be provided to enforce rules, punish wrong doers, settle
disputes, and protect private and group property. Political organization
facilitates the growth of society by mobilizing its resources, providing a
sense of unity, and serving as a source of decisions designed to promote
the general welfare of the group. As Redfield puts it, "Formal political
institutions not only keep societies going in the good old ways; they
also provoke a challenge of those ways" (1956:361).

AUTHORITY AND SOCIAL CONTROL

Whether government decisions are in the hands of a paramount
chief, a council of elders or an elected legislature, there cannot be
government without authority. Authority may be seized, inherited, or
accorded, but if it is to be effective it must be backed up by force or
the threat of force. Goldschmidt (1960) refers to authority as the *power*
to govern and Mair maintains that "there is no society where rules are
automatically obeyed, and . . . every society has some means of securing obedience as well as of dealing with offenders" (1962:18). In every
society there are various levels of rules and regulations and various
degrees of punishment for their infraction. Not all rules that control
behavior, however, are enforced by political authorities. Many of the
controls are built into the culture. Many societies have neither formal
law nor a police force, but in their absence public opinion serves as a
powerful deterrent to unruly citizens.

The least obvious forces of social control are folkways, or manners.
Only the force of tradition backs up these customs, but it is a very thick-
skinned person who can ignore them. If a person is expected to attend
a party or dance in a dinner jacket and black bow tie, an uninformed
guest can suffer untold agonies in a business suit and four-in-hand
tie.

Even more powerful instruments of social control than manners are
mores, or morals. As in the case of manners, they are a product of a
cultural tradition although associated with only a certain aspect of that
culture. An example would be the strong stand taken against divorce
and interfaith marriage by some churches in the United States. Infrac-

tions of these taboos are not considered a crime against the society but only against the church.

Laws are the most formal and obvious instruments of social control. They are rules enforced by the authority of the state and they are often supracommunity and suprainstitution. This may best be seen in the case of United States Supreme Court and Federal law pronouncements concerning integration. Although these legal orders run contrary to the sentiments of the people of many communities and contradict *mores*, they nevertheless have precedence. Law often overrules the systems of folkways or *mores* developed within certain institutions. When a number of religious sects advised their young men to ignore the draft, the offenders were prosecuted under Federal law. In Utah, state law overruled Mormon church canons by forbidding the practice of polygamy.

CHECKS AND BALANCES

Societies must have leaders, and leaders must be granted authority. A society that withholds the power to govern from its leaders robs itself of effective government. On the other hand, the leader who is given too much authority can in some cases further his own selfish interests and ignore the rights of those under his authority. The answer to this, of course, is the creation of a set of checks and balances whereby authority can be given but where it can also be controlled. Leaders must not only have rights but responsibilities as well.

The reader is no doubt well aware of the system of checks and balances that operates in the government of the United States. The executive branch may curb the legislative through the power of the veto, but the executive authority is in turn held in check by the legislature's power to override a veto and in extreme cases, to remove the executive officer through impeachment. The judicial branch has the power to declare legislation unconstitutional, but the legislature has the right to pass on judicial appointments. Still another factor, the voting franchise of the people, directly or indirectly serves as a control over all three branches of government. Most modern governments have a system that employs devices of a similar nature to ensure human rights and maximum participation of citizens in their government. It must not be concluded, however, that a system of checks and balances is a characteristic of civilized societies alone. A large number of primitive societies have very effective systems of controlling authority; indeed, it seems to be a natural requirement of stable and just government.

The Samoan islanders of the southwest Pacific have lived under a very ingenious system of governmental checks and balances for centuries. Instead of the Samoans' having three separate branches of government, the executive, judicial, and legislative functions are carried out by a single body, the village council. Each of the members of

Conch shell trumpet calls Samoan chiefs to the village council meeting.

the council is the head of a separate extended family group and is known as a *matai*. Mataiship carries with it the rank of either Chief or Talking Chief depending upon the traditional status of the family. Actually, these chiefs are arranged in a hierarchy and their power and authority in the village vary with their status—a matter to a great extent determined by tradition. The paramount chief of the village is a

High Chief, and it is he who presides over the village council meetings (*fono*) and to a great extent influences its decisions.

The checks and balances in this system work as follows: Each Chief or Talking Chief is elected to his position of family head (*matai*) and council representative by the members of his extended family. Unlike many societies of Polynesia, primogeniture plays little or no part in his selection. More important is his leadership ability, general intelligence, knowledge of Samoan lore, and his past service to the family. Just as a *matai* may be elected to his position of family leadership, he can be removed from it by his family if he proves to be an autocratic or an ineffective leader. The chief's role in the village council is not unlike that of the elected congressman who goes to Washington to represent his district or state.

Even if a man holds the paramount chief title in the village, he will not have free rein to do as he pleases. While he has great authority and will receive great respect, his actions are to a great extent regulated by the rest of the council. To begin with, in most villages his authority is balanced by the only slightly lesser power of the village High Talking Chief. These orator chiefs are known for their power to persuade and are frequently referred to as the "hard" or "difficult" people. It is not a bit unusual for a political question to be completely deadlocked when a paramount High Chief and a High Talking Chief are on opposite sides of the issue. Since all village council decisions must be unanimous the High Chief is careful to nurture the Talking Chief's support.

If a paramount chief should prove to be an autocrat, the village council merely votes to remove him and informs the surrounding villages that they no longer look to him as their village leader. Once such drastic action has been carried out, the family of the former paramount chief will begin to exert pressure on their deposed representative. Since they do not want to be robbed of their powerful voice in the council and since their prestige has been impaired by his high-handed actions, they will in many cases threaten him with title removal unless he manages to reestablish himself in the good graces of the council. This is usually enough to make the chief go to the village council, ask their forgiveness, and mend his ways in future interaction with his fellow council members. The governmental system that has evolved in Samoa is ingenious in that it represents the ultimate in representative government and provides for effective leadership although holding in the background the threat of removal of authority if that authority is misused.

In some societies it appears that a leader has tremendous unchecked authority because all of his decrees are immediately and unquestioningly obeyed. This is often deceiving and the leader may have less

Samoan Talking Chief with orator's staff.

power than it appears. It is a universal principle of successful leadership that one should never give an order that one knows will not be obeyed. The shrewd leader knows just how far he can go in making demands on his followers. It is also true that even in the most autocratic of governments there are always methods that can be resorted to to bring the most despotic of leaders to terms. An example of this is cited by Vernon Dorjahn in his writings on the Temne of Sierra Leone. In precolonial days, when a paramount chief used his tremendous power to oppress the people, or as the Temne put it to "eat his chiefdom," a common defense was recourse to supernatural means. Dorjahn records that:

The use of swearing medicines was usually secret, for if word of it reached the chief he would take steps to protect himself, by supernatural means, and employ a counter-medicine . . . Nevertheless, the belief was strong that swearing medicines employed by a man who had been wronged were especially powerful, and fear of such was said to have been a powerful deterrent on a chief's behavior. (1960:136)

Another method of bringing pressure on an errant chief was to appeal to the officials of the powerful Poro or Ragbenle secret societies or to subchiefs who were the paramount chief's confidants and advisors. If all this failed, there was always the threat of withdrawal of military support by the war chiefs, or even threats of assassination.

LEVELS OF GOVERNMENT

To obtain an understanding of the universal features of government as well as those that become necessary as societies grow in population and in complexity of culture, it will be necessary to survey its forms in various geographical and cultural regions of the world. Of the various levels of political complexity known to man the kinship-based government is perhaps the simplest. In such a system it is difficult to see where family leaves off and government begins. This type of political organization is found in many parts of the world—primarily among hunters and gatherers—but we shall look to the Bushmen of the Kalahari desert of South Africa as being somewhat typical of this form.

Bushman Government—A Kin-Based System

The Bushmen follow a hunting and gathering way of life in one of the most difficult physical environments in the world. They are organized into bands of twenty-five to fifty individuals who in many cases are the members of a single extended family. Their leader is usually the head man of the dominant extended family, a position that he inherits in the male line. His actual authority over the group is slight, and anthropologists who have worked among these people describe his role as that of a leader rather than a ruler. While this man is in a sense the "executive officer" of the group, his main functions are those of directing the band's movements, officiating at certain ceremonies, and providing leadership in time of warfare. There is some variation in the authority of these headmen from band to band, but this is largely dependent upon the man's personality and leadership ability. He is expected to hunt like everyone else, as this kind of society cannot afford specialists of any variety. He has no judicial functions and even his "executive" proclamations are subject to veto by the other adult males of the band. The Bushmen may be described as having a completely classless and democratic society. There is great freedom of action within the group and individuals are free to do much as they please as long as it does not work a hardship on the group or infringe upon some traditionally honored law or custom. The enculturation and socialization processes place major stress on conformity to the norms and regulations of the group and there is little need for law enforcement among adults. The head of each nuclear family is responsible for the behavior of his wife and children. Since there is no recognized judiciary authority, disputes between families tend to be settled through feud.

It has often been stated that a major distinction between primitive and civilized governmental systems is to be found in the emphasis they place on territoriality. It is true that the territorial boundaries of modern nations are extremely important in determining citizenship and in defining their jurisdiction of authority and sovereignty, but ideas of territoriality are far from lacking among the Bushmen. Each band has a clearly defined territory of approximately two hundred square miles which they fiercely defend against encroachment by neighboring bands. While bands may be allowed to cross the territorial boundaries of one another, settlement or hunting would mean war.

The Hottentots—Multiple-Kin Government

To the south of the Bushmen lives a group known as the Hottentots. While these people are racially related to the Bushmen, their economy and political organization are different. The Hottentots are a pastoral people who primarily herd cattle and sheep but carry on some hunting and gathering activities. The government of these people is somewhat more complex than that of their Bushmen neighbors and might be described as being of the *multiple-kin* variety.

The Hottentots are organized into tribes of roughly five hundred to twenty-five hundred people. Each tribe is autonomous and composed of a number of clans. All the members of a particular clan claim a common ancestor and think of themselves as being related through the male line. One of these clans is considered senior and paramount and it is from this clan that the chief of the entire tribe is drawn. The office of tribal chief is an hereditary one, handed down from father to son. Although the status of chief commands great respect, his executive authority is subject to the advice and rulings of a tribal council. Council members are "elected" at a mass meeting of all the married males, but they actually are the normal heads of the several clans making up the tribe. It is from this body of clan heads that senior officials, such as subchief, magistrate, and war chief, are appointed. While this council has been described as the tribal executive, its votes on specific issues are frequently influenced by the chief's desires, particularly if he is an individual of strong character. The main functions of the council are those of making wars and treaties, and formulating rules and regulations for intra- as well as intertribal relations. Judiciary matters are handled primarily by the magistrate or the subchief, but the total council often serves as a court of appeal.

It will be noted that at this level of government the council is a formal body of officials with tribally sanctioned powers and responsibilities. While the adult males in Bushman society no doubt serve as a type of council, it is not recognized as an official governmental body to which one might be elected.

Even at this somewhat more advanced level of government we still do not find full-time political specialists. Apart from the fact that the Hottentot chief is generally the wealthiest man in the tribe, he is not distinguished in dress or size of house and household from his subjects. He and the other tribal officials have to tend their own animals the same as anyone else.

Tribal boundaries are not as clearly defined for these people as they are for the Bushmen, but there is a concept of use rights of water holes. If one tribe were to enter the area of another, application for rights to use grasslands and water holes has to be made to the resident chief. If friendly relations exist between the two groups, permission will be freely given; otherwise a tribute might be demanded for using the land and the water. Thus we can see that something in the way of intergroup diplomacy takes the place of feud where there is a conflict of interests.

The Tribe

Multiple-kin units are often referred to as "tribes," but tribes need not have a kinship principle of organization. It is also true that the word "tribe" does not necessarily imply a centralized form of government. Often it is hard to lay one's finger on why a group of relatively self-governing bands is collectively referred to by this term. Some would maintain that a tribe is merely a group of individuals who share a common language, culture, or territory. Mandelbaum feels that

The important basis for the existence of a tribe is not any one of these factors, but the combination of them that gives every person in the tribe a feeling of belonging with the other men and women of the tribe. The real bonds which hold any group together, whether it be tribe, clan, or state, are the attitudes which the individuals in that group have toward each other, and the behavior patterns of reciprocal help, of cooperation, which are the tangible demonstrations of those attitudes. (1956:296)

The word "tribe" does not imply any specific form of government but instead singles out a group of people who work together for the common good. Tribes may be headed by an hereditary chief of a senior clan or leadership may be entirely independent of kinship.

Associational Tribes

Many Plains Indian tribes, for example, elected the chiefs for their council from the bravest and most reputable men of their communities. In addition to this decision-making body, there were political units that actually held greater authority in controlling the society than did the council chiefs. These were the soldier or military societies. Of the Cheyenne, Llewellyn and Hoebel write:

There were six military societies . . . the Fox Soldiers, Elk Soldiers, Shield Soldiers, Bowstring Soldiers, Dog Men and Northern Crazy Dogs. These were free associations in which membership was voluntary and at the discretion of the individuals. Open to all men of all ages, they were of the ungraded type.[1] (1941:99)

The leaders of these military societies were generally appointed by the chief's council and given almost supreme authority to maintain law and order. Any order issued by them had to be obeyed—frequently on pain of death. While the main function of these societies was to police tribal buffalo hunts and make sure that no one would spoil the hunt, their duties often extended to matters of everyday village contol as well. Typical of the functions of military societies was the adjusting of quarrels between village members, forbidding gathering parties from going out when enemies were near, preserving order when villages moved to another campsite, and restraining war parties from going out on inopportune raids. Often they served as judge, jury, and penal authority over thieves and murderers.

Age-Grade Tribes

Still another type of tribal organization involves a system of government based upon various age categories. Among the Nandi, Masai, and Kikuyu tribes of East Africa, political roles are not allocated according to lineage or clan units but according to age grades. An age grade is a

[1] From *The Cheyenne Way* by Karl N. Llewellyn and E. Adamson Hoebel. Copyright 1941 by the University of Oklahoma Press.

group composed of all those men who passed through manhood initiation ceremonies together. The members of these groups share a common status and this status changes as they grow older. After their initiation they share a common lot as warriors, and then, after they marry and raise their families, they pass on to elder status. In the tribes where this kind of organization is found, the many segments of the tribes are widely scattered and nothing in the way of centralized authority was ever developed. The territorial groupings that cross-cut family and clan organization look to their elders to settle disputes, direct the group in ritual matters, mobilize the warrior grades in time of war, and generally serve as decision-making authorities in local and territorial matters.

Tribal Confederations

Sometimes independent tribes with similar cultures are drawn together for purposes of their mutual welfare. Although the groups might have strong pride in their own sovereignty, it is a rather common phenomenon that when people are threatened by external forces they tend to forget their minor differences for the sake of their common defense. This was the case with the League of Five Fires, a multitribal grouping of Plains Indians organized for the purpose of driving off the ever encroaching white man. Although this defense organization was shortlived and not very effective, the League of the Iroquois represents a classic example of a primitive confederation of sovereign nations.

LEAGUE OF THE IROQUOIS. The League of the Iroquois represented a federation of northeast woodland tribes—the Onondaga, Mohawk, Oneida, Seneca, Cayuga—in the area that is now upstate New York. A sixth tribe, the Tuscarora, was added after the initial charter was formed. While the League is sometimes referred to as the first United Nations, its actual operation was more like that of the North Atlantic Treaty Organization (NATO). These six Iroquois-speaking tribes were interested in maintaining peace only among themselves and they often took the war path as a group against their neighboring tribes.

The political structure of the League greatly resembled our own Federation of States, and it has been suggested that the authors of the United States Constitution might very well have borrowed certain features from the League, since they had knowledge of its organization. Each of the tribes was autonomous in local affairs, but matters that concerned the League as a whole, such as declarations of war, were under the jurisdiction of a council of fifty representatives, or *sachems*. Some tribes sent as many as fourteen *sachems*, while others sent as few as eight; but since all council decisions had to be unanimous the unequal representation was not a drawback. In each of the tribes there were eight matrilineal clans—the Wolf, Bear, Beaver, Turtle, Deer, Snipe, Heron, and Hawk—of which the *sachems* were representatives. Although the legislators were always men, they owed their appointments to the clan matriarchs. It was the kinship bond between a man and the representatives of his clan in other tribes that helped stabilize the confederation. The traditional capital of the League was in Onondaga territory and it was here that the representatives assembled to settle disputes and thus maintain peace within the group, make treaties, send and receive ambassadors, regulate the affairs of subjugated tribes and decide on matters pertaining to the general welfare.

Monarchy

As in the case of the tribe, it is difficult to generalize on the nature of monarchy for it may exist in very primitive societies with fairly small populations or in complex industrial states. In most cases, however, it represents a form of kin-based government in that the ruling monarch usually derives from a royal family or clan. A king may receive his position by virtue of primogeniture or, as in the case of Samoan kings, be chosen from a special group of candidates by a traditional body of "king-makers." In a number of Bantu societies where ruling monarchs have numerous sons because they have many wives, succession is decided by fighting.

In a monarchy, government is centralized, with decisions originating with the king, whose authority usually has both sacred and secular sanctions. We are all familiar with the concept of "divine right" of kings, which was so emphasized by the Stuart kings of England. In Egypt the king was himself a god, and in a number of primitive societies myths can be called upon to prove that the royal line extends back to a time when its members were supernatural. The Shilluk of the African Sudan believe that their king, the Reth, is a living representative of the partly divine culture hero Nyikang, who is credited with leading them to their present home. It is believed that the spirit of Nyikang enters the body of each new king at the time of his installation and from this time on he exhibits some of the supernatural characteristics of the mythical founder. Because he embodies these qualities he is considered incapable of poor judgment. Should bad decisions be made, the blame is always placed on his advisors who gave him bad counsel.

The secular power of a king is acquired through a system of clientage that Mair describes as the process of "building up a body of

A faithful subject bows before his king in the Cameroons. (Courtesy
of Chicago Natural History Museum.)

persons who depend upon their leader in such a way that their first
loyalty is to him" (1962:166). This may be done by giving people
economic advantages or by rewarding them for special service. Samoan
kings rewarded their chiefs for outstanding service with lands, honorific titles, and special privileges. The talking-chief title Lolo, of Sili
village, for example, carries the special privilege of wearing a turban in
the village—a prerogative withheld from all other chiefs regardless of
their rank.

The power of kings varies a great deal. In some cultures they hold
life and death power over their subjects while in others they are merely
figureheads or ceremonial leaders—e.g., modern European sovereigns.
Monarchy is almost always associated with pomp, ceremony, and
symbolism, all of which serve as a method of drawing upon sentiments
of national pride, thus creating a more unified nation.

The State

"The state" is a designation indicating complex government. While it
is possible to enumerate several characteristics of "state" political structure, not every complex government incorporates all of them in its

organization. Generally, most of these features are essential to the operation of political systems in densely populated areas with urban communities.

Characteristics of the Political Structure of the State

CENTRALIZED GOVERNMENT WITH DELEGATED AUTHORITY. In attempting a definition of a state, Lucy Mair writes,

> If we were to try to put in a single sentence the essence of the state system we might say that it consists in the delegation of power by the ruler who holds final authority, in such a way that he can expect his orders or decisions to be carried out throughout the land which he claims to rule (1962:138)

Complex governments must of necessity delegate authority in order to tend to the many problems that develop at all levels. Since no single man can carry the whole burden of authority, hierarchies of officials are created who are directly responsible for certain portions of the population and for various areas of activity. Often these lesser authorities are appointed by the central ruler, elected by the people, or in some rare cases these positions are hereditary. At this level of government, kinship almost ceases to enter into the political structure.

There is perhaps no more clear-cut picture of the delegation of authority in a state system than that which existed among the Incas, a government that employed literally hundreds of officials with graduated spheres of authority. Chapple and Coon describe the Inca bureaucratic system as follows:

> The administrative hierarchy consisted of nine ranks of officials beginning with the Inca. The empire was divided into four quarters, and each of these had a ruler who was directly responsible to the Inca. In each quarter were officials who ruled an area containing 40,000 households, and under them were officials who ruled 10,000, 1000, 500, 100, 50, and 10. Each rank of official was appointed by those immediately above him in the scale (1942:352)

POLITICAL SPECIALIZATION. As has been noted in other areas of culture, advanced societies tend to be characterized by specialization of occupation. It is true in religion, in the arts and crafts and also in government. In simpler societies the political leader earns his own living by hunting, herding, agriculture, or whatever the prevailing economy might be. His political activities take little of his time and he is well paid for them in prestige and in the respect accorded him by his followers. In more complex societies the political leader is called upon more frequently to settle disputes, coordinate group activities, and maintain order and he finds less and less time for tending to the support of his own family. As the demands on the paramount ruler become more oppressive, there is a delegation of power to specialists such as war leaders, judges, advisors, diplomats, and ambassadors whose full-time activities must be supported by the citizens they serve.

TAXATION. One of the consequences of complex government is that someone must pay the bill. Taxation, which provides a nation's fiscal power, is the natural outgrowth of bureaucracy and political specialization. If leaders are expected to devote themselves full-time to the affairs of government, they expect to be rewarded. Support for state projects and state officials is not always in money but may very likely be in the form of goods or services. In many societies the first fruits of the harvest go to political and religious leaders, and among the East African Ganda it is common practice for the more important families to give tribute in the form of young women who become the wives of the king. In Egypt every able-bodied man was expected to donate a few months' labor each year to the building of royal monuments. In the Inca empire, taxes in the form of food were required of the people, but the value of labor performed for the state was deducted. A similar phenomenon is still found in the laws of the state of New Hampshire where it is possible to work on public roads in lieu of paying taxes.

In a number of Copper Age civilizations of the Middle East, such discoveries as writing and mathematics are believed to have developed out of the necessity of keeping records of royal tribute. In Mesopotamia tax records were incised in wet clay and then baked into permanent documents.

The Athenians had a unique tax system that had the effect of making the burden somewhat less objectionable. While the rich were heavily taxed, the system was not as impersonal as modern income tax procedures. It was not uncommon for a man of wealth to be charged with the operation of a particular naval vessel for a year. If he chose, he could even serve as its captain. Greeks with theatrical interests were given the opportunity to serve as patrons of the state-supported plays. In this fashion, government enterprises took on the nature of private hobbies for affluent citizens.

TERRITORIALITY. At one time it was believed that this factor set apart simple and complex political systems. We find, however, that even a simple hunting band like the Bushmen were territorial in the sense that they claimed a certain territory as their own and drove all trespassers from it. Gearing points out that "almost all groups which act politically . . . possess or control territory; but gypsies and Shoshonis do not" (1962:71).

The aspect of territoriality that we can invariably associate with complex government is something quite different. Fortes and E. E. Evans-Pritchard explain that in more complex societies "the administrative unit is a territorial unit; political rights and obligations are territorially delimited" (1940:10). The political machinery, whatever its form, has total administrative and judicial authority within a certain set of geographical boundaries; everyone living in the defined area is subject or citizen and owes loyalty and economic and military support to the territorial government. The Greek city-state, or *polis*, had this concept of a centralized government with jurisdiction over a fixed territory. The Athenian people occupied a territory technically known as Attica consisting of many villages. A citizen of any of these villages was known as a citizen of the state of Athens and subject to its laws. This concept of citizenship is much the same as that which prevails in the United States or any modern complex nation.

PROFESSIONAL MILITARY. A characteristic feature of the state is its ability to engage in total war. One aspect of this capacity is the necessity of maintaining a professional body of full-time soldiers. Among American Indians the only society of sufficient complexity to support such a force was the Inca, who had a standing army of about 10,000, which essentially served as bodyguards to the emperor. A few African societies, such as Dahomey, had a standing army and it is to be found in several of the more complex societies of Asia. Japan, for instance, had a special class of professional soldiers, the samurai. In many European countries where a standing army was a common phenomenon, military leaders were drawn from the prominent families in which it was traditional for one son in each family to enter the army as a career.

While the Spartans maintained a society that was almost a military camp, the Athenians represent an exception to our generalization. Warfare for Athenians was a civilian enterprise and mobilization meant that everyone went home and got his shield, spear, and rations. The citizen assembly formulated war plans and directed the military. While the Athenian fighting man was both brave and intelligent, campaigns were anything but efficiently planned and executed. An example is the decision of the Athenian assembly to invade Sicily during the Peloponnesian War, when most of the legislators knew neither the size of the Sicilian army nor the location of the island. Warfare was so much of a civilian enterprise that campaigns were planned to be short in duration so that the soldiers (mostly farmers) could return to attend to their harvesting activities.

A COURT SYSTEM. Whereas in simple kin-based political systems headmen or chiefs settle disputes and punish offenders, complex governments extend their services to include specially established courts with professional judges. In Inca society, officials that governed the various sized political units included as part of their regular duties the function of magistrate, but in Aztec society an extremely elaborate system of courts existed. The least important of these was the merchants' court, which regulated the business of the market. It consisted of a body of twelve men who sat each day in the market and settled disputes between the various vendors of merchandise. The courts hearing civil suits of all types, which were located in the four quarters of the city, were more formal. Each district had its court presided over by a body of judges who derived their support from the products grown on special sections of government land. If there were need to appeal a decision, this could be done in a special appellate court located in the emperor's palace. Appeals of noblemen were channeled to a still higher court, the supreme court of the land. Its presiding officers were the Aztec war leader and a body of thirteen elders.

In England under the Norman conquerors special courts had to be established to relieve the king of an increasingly time-consuming task. When originated, these courts remained under the king's supervision, but in time they became separate specialized organs of government with their own administration.

INTERNATIONAL RELATIONS

In addition to providing methods of controlling the behavior of the members of a society, the political authority must also work out ways of dealing with the sovereign nations with which it comes in contact. In some cases satisfactory peaceful relations cannot be established and a continual state of war or feud exists. The Willigiman-Wallalua people of the highlands of New Guinea wage war almost weekly with their neighboring tribe, the Wittaia. Although the two tribes practice the same culture and speak the same language, each thinks of the other as a subhuman form of man. Their weekly battles last only a day but they go on month after month, year after year, as there is always a death on one side or the other that must be avenged.

In many other societies the people have managed to escape the constant threat of aggression from their neighbors by establishing with them diplomatic relations of some variety. These methods of maintaining the peace may in some cases be strictly political arrangements (e.g., the League of the Iroquois) worked out by the authorities of the groups, but in other cases amiable relations may grow out of trade interaction, intermarriage, or common membership in ritual associations.

Economic and Social Ties

People who have developed an economic dependency with adjacent tribes will often go to great lengths to work out treaties so that war will not leave each without sorely needed commodities. In the case of the Trobriand Islanders, although two communities might be engaged in hostilities, kula partners do not take up arms against one another.

It is always a difficult matter for any sovereign group to yield to a greater authority, but it is often done when some material advantage is envisioned. So it was at the annual buffalo hunts of Plains Indians. At this time ordinarily independent hunting bands came together and submitted to the paramount authority of soldier societies who regulated and policed the hunt. Since it had often been proved that a carefully coordinated operation would result in more game than when each band hunted on its own, even these fiercely independent people worked out a system of intergroup cooperation.

European dynasties, as well as the royalty of the Maori and others, have long utilized international marriages as a method of establishing goodwill and cooperation. There are any number of cases in the anthropological literature of adjacent villages with separate political authorities becoming a single entity through the intermarriage of not only chiefly families but commoners as well.

Religious Ties

Just as an American college student can find sanctuary on a rival campus in the house of the fraternity to which he belongs, so members of ritual associations or secret societies in primitive groups can expect friendship from members of a common cult when they are traveling through foreign territory. In Sierra Leone a Temne tribesman who is a member of the secret association known as the Poro Society has something in common with Poro members in distant parts of his own tribal territory and even with members in the adjacent Mende country. In Western culture an example of the power of religion to produce political allies is to be seen in the Crusades, when the nations of western Europe combined to free the Holy Land from Moslem control. Chapple and Coon add that "in Morocco at the time of the Riffian War, the Spanish deserters would be spared if they approached their captors shouting, 'There is no god but Allah, and Mohammed is the messenger of Allah!'" (1942:343).

Conquest

One system of establishing workable relations with a hostile group is by conquering them. Conquest is almost always undertaken for economic reasons—to obtain either natural resources or additional tribute —and it is not unusual for the conquerors to interfere in the internal affairs of a subjugated nation only to the extent necessary to keep the peace and to collect the desired tribute. Often the conquerors impose an oligarchical rule and establish themselves as a sort of landed gentry, living off the fruits of the vanquished population. This situation was common in medieval Europe and can be found even yet in East Africa in the relations between the aristocratic Tusi and the Hutu commoners.

Conquest empires are rarely able to establish serene administrations. In a United Nations building in Geneva, Switzerland, there is a mural bearing the title *The Burden of Conquest* that depicts an inevitable result—that the vanquished will plot revenge. One of the most successful conquest empires was that of the Incas, who ruled an area about the size of most of western Europe (380,000 square miles) and attempted to allay any possible resistance by systematically breaking down conquered cultures through a juxtaposition of population. Even in this extremely efficient totalitarian state, internal dissension was not eliminated and the empire had already begun to disintegrate when Pizarro dealt it a deathblow in 1531.

DEMOCRACY

One method of delegating authority in government is by means of a representative democratic system. Democratic government may be differentiated from other forms by the fact that those in positions of political power acquire them through election rather than inheritance or appointment. Although representative government is common to a large number of complex governmental systems, it is found at other levels as well. It is present among the Samoans, the Yakut of Siberia, and the Cheyenne of North America.

The democratic system, of which the United States is justifiably proud, has been heralded as the most stable and effective of governmental forms. While the democratic process at times appears agonizingly slow and inefficient, its strength lies in the fact that there is a maximum of interaction between the governors and the governed. This interaction and the concomitant communication allow for constant adjustment in the system to meet current needs. Chapple and Coon see democracy as having greater staying power than either autocratic or totalitarian forms. They state:

The democratic governments . . . are so constituted that they can weather adversities of warfare or technological changes which would destroy the equilibrium of others. (1942:363)

As scholarly as any evaluation of the democratic system are the remarks delivered by Adlai Stevenson in January, 1963, before the Center for the Study of Democratic Institutions in New York City. A portion of his speech reads as follows:

There is precious little dignity or equality in our natural state. Most human beings have to spend their lives in utter vulnerability. All are born unequal in terms of capacity or strength . . . and survive only through the restraint shown by more powerful neighbors. For nearly three thousand years "Western man" has struggled to create a social order in which weak, fallible, obstinate, silly, magnificent man can exercise his free and responsible choice.

Whether democracy can prevail in the great upheaval of our time is a valid question. We have good reason to know how clumsy, slow, inefficient and costly it is compared to the celerity, certainty and secrecy of absolutism. But the important thing is that even the absolutists masquerade as democrats; even the military and quasi-military dictatorships strive in the name of democracy to manage the public business. And all of them say that authoritarianism is only a necessary transition to democracy . . . The enemies of freedom, whatever the magnificent ends they propose—the brotherhood of man, the kingdom of saints, "from each according to his ability, to each according to his needs"—miss just the essential point: that man is greater than the social purposes to which he can be put. He must not be kicked about even with the most high-minded objectives. He is not a means or an instrument. He is an end in himself.

This is the essence of what we mean by democracy—not so much voting systems or parliamentary systems or economic or legal systems (though they all enter in), as an irrevocable and final dedication to the dignity of man. In this sense, democracy is perhaps mankind's most audacious experiment.

SUGGESTED READINGS

ALMOND, GABRIEL A. "Anthropology, Political Behavior and International Relations," *World Politics*, 2:277, 1950. (Evaluation of the applicability of the anthropological views of Kluckhohn and Leighton to the study of international relations.)

BASCOM, WILLIAM R. "Ponape: The Cycle of Empire," *Scientific Monthly*, March, 1950. (How the Ponapeans have adjusted to a variety of imposed governmental forms.)

HART, H., and D. L. TAYLOR. "Was there a Prehistoric Trend from Smaller to Larger Political Views?" *American Journal of Sociology*, 49:289, 1944. (How technological level and political development correlate in 46 representative modern preliterate societies.)

HOEBEL, E. ADAMSON. "Law and Anthropology," *Virginia Law Review*,

32:836, 1946. (Points out equivalent features of our legal system in primitive societies.)

Lowie, Robert. "Primitive Social Organization," *Encyclopedia of the Social Sciences*, 1944. (Gives examples of kinship and association organization in a variety of primitive societies.)

Malinowski, Bronislaw. "Anthropological Analysis of War," *American Journal of Sociology*, 46:521, 1941. (The effects, negative and positive, that warfare has on culture and society.)

Radcliffe-Brown, A. R. "Primitive Law," *Encyclopedia of the Social Sciences*. 1944. (The role of family, custom, and courts in maintaining social control in various preliterate societies.)

Tannenbaum, F. "Balance of Power in Society," *Political Science Quarterly*, 61:481, 1946. (Deals with the interrelationship of cultural institutions; how political behavior relates to other aspects of culture.)

Paperbound Books

Mair, Lucy. *Primitive Government*. Penguin Books. (Concepts of law and systems of government in indigenous African cultures.)

Malinowski, Bronislaw. *Crime and Custom in Savage Society*. Little-field, Adams and Co. (Law and order, crime and punishment in a Melanesian society.)

Wilson, Monica. *Good Company*. Beacon Press. (A study of villages in southern Tanganyika, where the social organization is based strictly on age and generation.)

12

Religion

Religion is many things to many people. While it has been referred to by anthropologists as a universal aspect of human behavior, its forms are so varied that it is impossible to define it in other than the most general terms. Religion must be seen in context to be understood; it might be said that it is easier to write a whole book about forms of religious behavior than to develop a definition that will encompass its multiplicity of forms.

How religion is defined depends to a great extent on one's background and point of view. It has been said that in many primitive societies missionaries cannot see religion anywhere but anthropologists see it everywhere. To some, religion is Christianity, Judaism, Islam, Buddhism—i.e., the major historic religions—and everything else is idolatry and superstition.

While the anthropologist sometimes uses the term superstition, he does not apply it to men's meaningful sacred beliefs. To him superstitions are survivals of an earlier age that people no longer believe in but observe anyway (like our fear of the number 13). When applied to religion, superstition is a derogatory and unscientific term. Many Americans have no qualms about calling a West African's beliefs superstition but are greatly upset when they hear Soviet Marxists refer to Christianity as such. People who insist on dwelling upon the "primitive" and "irrational" religious behavior of primitives should think seriously about the following item found in a newspaper "chuckle" column. "Natives who beat drums to drive away evil spirits are considered stupid (and heathen) by Europeans who honk horns to break up traffic jams."

Religion has been defined as "a set of earnest policies," "a philosophy," "a special mode of behavior," "a pragmatic attitude," but in all cases it has to do with the realm of the supernatural. It has been argued, however, that Confucianism regarded the supernatural aspects of religion as unimportant and felt that religion was a device for unifying society and supporting its values. Generally, however, we shall follow the view of Finegan, who has written, "Religion . . . has to do with something more than the obvious surface of things . . . In religion . . . there is an attempt to relate life to a dimension of existence other than that with which common sense and science are concerned" (1952:6). What this "something more" is may be defined differently in different cultures, and the attitudes and acts judged appropriate in relation to it may likewise vary widely. One thing is certain: This "something more" is of vital importance. Lessa defines religion as a "system of beliefs and practices directed toward the ultimate concern" of a society (1958:1) and Redfield concurs by relating that religion is "about what most matters" (1956:362).

Thus, we find that almost all people in the world have a supernatural belief system and a category of behavior which we might call religious but each and every religious system is unique, satisfying that particular culture's needs. When any religion moves from one cultural setting to another, it becomes something quite different than what it was in the parent culture.

Since religion reflects culture it is not easily transferable and thus can only be completely understood in context. An example is the understanding of the Twenty-Third Psalm by the Khmus tribe of Laos. Literally translated it would read something like this:

> The Great Boss is the one who takes care of my sheep
> I don't want to own anything.
> The Great Boss wants me to lie down in the field.
> He wants me to go to the lake.
> He makes my good spirit come back.
> Even though I walk through something the missionary
> calls the valley of the shadow of death, I do
> not care.
> You are with me.
> You use a stick and a club to make me comfortable.
> You manufacture a piece of furniture right in
> front of my eyes while my enemies watch.
> You pour car grease on my head.
> My cup has too much water in it and therefore
> overflows.
> Goodness and kindness will walk single file be-
> hind me all my life.

And I will live in the hut of the Great Boss
until I die and am forgotten by the tribe.

(From an interview with Dr. William Smalley. *Wichita Eagle,* January 7, 1960.)

WHY PEOPLE HAVE RELIGION

As we look about the world and see that all men are drawn to a belief in something greater than everyday reality, we find justification for asking why religion of some variety is found everywhere. Religion, after all, is not a response to any biological need and, as far as simply living out one's three score and ten, man *can* live by bread alone. And yet, religion must satisfy some basic psychological need. It appears that all religious behavior represents a response to the wonder and the fear of the uncontrollable forces of nature. Awed by the overwhelming power of the wind, waves, lightning, and thunder, man perhaps develops an idea of a supernatural deity on which he can call in order to deal with these forces that he fears and that mystify him.

Religion supplies answers to things that man does not understand—such things as creation, ill fortune, illness, and especially death. When the Australian aborigine asks "How did men come into being?" the sacred myths of his society tell him that the Numbakulla spirits created them out of animals and plants. When the Samoan child asks "Where did the islands come from?" his mother draws upon mythological traditions and answers that they were created as resting places by the god Tagaloa. When the Hopi Indian wonders what will become of him after death, he recalls the teachings of his tribe, which maintain that his "breath body" will journey to the underworld where it will live as a Hopi but never have to worry about a lack of water. In time it may return to the village as a kachina to reward or punish Hopi children or bring needed rain to their parents.

Religion provides solace when one faces important crises of life. The well-known statement that there are no atheists in foxholes backs up this point as does the fact that in many primitive societies dangerous activities, such as going to war, were always surrounded by numerous ceremonies and supernatural taboos (religion-derived restraints) applied to the warriors.

Other scholars have explained the universality of religion by the fact that man turns to the supernatural to get those things that he cannot get himself. Still another explanation is that religion develops in order to satisfy a need for moral and ethical order. Customs and value systems that have supernatural support are always more powerful than those with social sanction alone. These important values are maintained through the ceremonies and rituals of the society, which bring them ever closer to the individual.

The French sociologist Durkheim believed that religion is an outgrowth of crowd excitement and the thrill that people feel when large tribal gatherings take place. Religion, according to this definition, is actually nothing more than man symbolically worshiping his own group unity and *esprit de corps.*

Culture and personality specialist Francis Hsu explains the universality of religion in terms of the parent-child relationship. The infant, helpless to do things for himself, calls upon a greater power, the parents, who tower above him and who care for all his needs. As the child grows older, he exchanges his parents for a supernatural deity or force when strength greater than that of mortals is required.

Speculations about the *raison d'etre* of the many world religions are interesting but offer no concrete answers in our study of religion. The more important question—one which can be observed and documented—is, what part does religion play in men's lives and in the functioning of human society? What forms does it take in satisfying human needs?

HUMAN AND CULTURAL FACTORS

Wherever religion is found, it is always related to human experience. This is certainly not a new conclusion since around 500 B.C. Xenophanes wrote,

Yes, and if oxen and horses or lions had hands, and could paint with their hands, and could produce works of art as men do, horses would paint the forms of their gods like horses, and oxen like oxen, and make their bodies in the image of their several kinds . . . The Ethiopians make their gods black and snub-nosed; the Thracians say theirs have blue eyes and red hair.

Concerning the total variety of religious practices today, we can say, with all due respect to its Biblical counterpart, that *man creates his gods in his own image.* This, of course, is not surprising as man's finite mind can only think in terms of his own cultural experience. The authors of the several books of the Bible, unable to catch a meaning greater than that provided by their own experience, paved the streets of heaven with gold and saw heavenly rewards in terms of jewels in a crown. Many a Sunday School lesson pictures God as a man with a long white beard very much like great grandfather, only more stern, more knowing, and more enduring.

Gods often have human emotions and human behavior patterns. Norbeck has called attention to this tendency to humanize the supernatural in Judaism, Christianity, and Islam and he points out that the important deity in each

> . . . is often conceived as having human form, and is consistently regarded as being sentient, as having a will, wishing, watching, judging, feeling anger and joy, and meting out punishments and beneficences in accordance with individual and group morality—in short, acting as men act. (1961:45)

While the deity in these religions embodies those characteristics that are considered good and proper, a number of religions present their gods as having human weaknesses and failings. Greek and Roman gods caroused, seduced, lied, and often stole and generally were no more virtuous (perhaps a little less) than the mortals they dominated. The Yoruba explain that the god Obatala missed the honor of being the creator of the world because he got drunk and fell asleep. His brother, Odudua, finding him, took the creation articles—a chicken and a chain—and created the world himself by lowering the fowl to the surface of the sea where it scratched up earth and formed the major continents.

In Chinese society, as well as others with polytheistic religions, hierarchies of gods reflect family and political structures. In China there are gods of varying degrees of authority and jurisdiction not unlike the bureaucratic hierarchy of the ancient dynasties. Gods are conceived of as having kinship ties and they observe patterns of respect which have parallel in the mortal Chinese family.

All people, however, do not conceive of the supernatural in entirely anthropomorphic terms. Some look to supernatural power totally divorced from human characteristics and believe it to be in an impersonal force or spirit such as *mana* or *manitou*. Still other cultures seize upon natural phenomena—rain, thunder, the sun, or winds—and give them human attributes although not human forms.

MANA

The concept of *mana* was first brought to the attention of the scholarly world in a book entitled *The Melanesians* (1891) by a missionary, R. H. Codrington. Codrington found that in certain Melanesian religions there was a belief in an impersonal supernatural force that could reside in human beings, animals, or places. Viewed as an invisible mysterious force like electricity, it can flow from place to place, be stored up, and even be inherited, and through the use of magical acts gained and controlled.

Although this concept was first observed in Melanesia, it is perhaps more typical of Polynesia. Here, kings and high chiefs (frequently believed to be descendants of the gods) were often regarded as having so much mana that it was dangerous for commoners to approach, much less touch, such an individual. In the Manu'a Islands of Samoa, the king could only be served his meals by his wife, as it would have been dangerous for those of low rank to touch his food. In Tahiti, chiefs were not allowed to walk where commoners might tread on their footprints and thus such nobility had to be carried on litters when they went out in public in order to protect the lives of their subjects.

Much of the cannibalism reported in Polynesia and Melanesia was directly tied in with mana. A warrior ceremonially ate certain parts of a valiant enemy so that he might add his victim's mana to his own. Actually, success in almost any venture—war, fishing, house or boat building—was believed to be an evidence of mana. All societies believing in mana also have personal deities or spirits as well, but often it is felt that these supernatural beings also have varying amounts of mana depending upon their position in the pantheon. It is also quite possible to be given mana by a personal deity. There is no society where impersonal force constitutes the total religious belief of a people.

ANIMATISM

Intermediate between the concept of a personal god and a completely impersonal supernatural force like mana is the concept of animatism. This term, developed by Marrett, describes those situations where primitive man endows inanimate objects with life. The South African shouts at the hurricane, the Crow Indians attribute power to reproduce to a stone and the Australians revere a piece of wood (*churinga*) and perhaps even, in many cases, endow it with a spirit.

ANIMISM

The essence of religion is supernaturalism and a universal aspect of this is belief in spirits, souls, and life after death. The cultural evolutionist E. B. Tylor felt that belief in a spirit in man, animals, and even inanimate objects represented the earliest form of religion. It developed, he believed, from dream and trance experiences. When early man slept, he often dreamt that he went places and did things. Upon discovering that his body had not left the house during his slumber, he hit upon the idea that his soul or spirit had had the experiences he recalled from his dream.

TOTEMISM

One of the curious and little understood manifestations of religion is the concept of totemism. This is the recognition of some special spiritual relationship between a clan or other social group and some animate or inanimate object of nature. We are all familiar with the totem poles of the Northwest Coast Indians. These are, in effect, coats of arms of the various clans, symbolizing (or commemorating) supernatural experiences that remote ancestors had with animals or objects of nature.

There is often the tendency to explain totemism in terms of economics—i.e., it reflects the concern with animals, which would be natural in a hunting society. The only problem is that totemism is found more frequently in agricultural societies than in hunting or gathering ones. There is even evidence that something of the nature of this category of religious behavior is present in industrialized societies. What seems to be involved is a tendency to associate the group with some natural object or phenomenon that typifies the *elan* or the goals of the social group. Thus, we find athletic teams proudly bearing such names as Wildcats, Wolverines, or Lions, but never Kittens, Mice, or Lambs.

One of the most interesting developments of totemistic-like behavior emerged during World War I in connection with the 42nd, or Rainbow, division. It reveals that in times of stress, American soldiers adopted the rainbow as almost a protective deity or guardian spirit. Linton describes the developing totemistic attitude as follows:

A feeling of connection between the organization and its namesake was first noted in February, 1918, five to six months after the assignment of the name. At this time it was first suggested and then believed that the appearance of a rainbow was a good omen for the division. Three months later it had become an article of faith in the organization that there was always a rainbow in the sky when the division went into action. A rainbow over the enemy's lines was considered especially auspicious, and after a victory men would often insist that they had seen one in this position even when the weather conditions or direction of advance made it impossible. (1924:296)

Linton feels that this rainbow totem and the manifestations of totemic beliefs among many primitive peoples represent a common social and supernatural phenomenon. In all cases, the prevailing characteristics are: (1) a distinct grouping conscious of their identity; (2) an exclusively possessed object of veneration derived from nature; (3) a reverent attitude toward, and a faith in, the object to function as a guardian spirit capable of giving omens.

It would be unfair to say that religion is a response only to man's insecurities and fears. If religion amounted only to solace, we would be hard pressed to explain the elaborate ceremony that usually accompanies appeals to the supernatural.

Even societies without a basic defined theology have a set of shared beliefs about the nature of the universe and man's relation to it. More than the mental activity required in holding such beliefs, all religions seem to require action—participation in the manner of prayer, praise, adoration, or sacrificing.

Both existence of belief systems and the ubiquitous ceremonials have been explained by many as giving support to the existing social structure of a society and to its configuration of culture—its moral and ethical system as well as its social institutions. Most religions stress group participation perhaps because group ritual gives "psychological assurance and promotes societal unity through joint action and common aims" (Norbeck 1961:132).

ROLE IN ECONOMICS

Not only do the behavior and activities of the gods reflect the structure and values of society, but the nature of its deities, to a great extent, also reflects the economic level of a society. Radin has remarked that "no correlation is more definite or more consistent than that between a given economic level of society and the nature of supernatural beings postulated by the tribe at large or by the religious individual in particular" (1957:192).

On the walls of the caves frequented by Paleolithic hunters we find paintings of bison, deer, and mammoth. Not infrequently these animals appear with spears protruding from their sides and some of the paintings have holes in them made by actual spears. While these sketches might only record the events that took place on memorable hunts, the more common interpretation is that they represent examples of contagious magic—i.e., it was believed that a symbolic wound on the drawing would become a real one on the next hunt.

One cave painting from southern France often called the "sorcerer" depicts a man in reindeer costume. Very likely this is the kind of religious practitioner who officiated in ceremonies designed to ensure a successful hunt. It is plain that some of the earliest forms of religion centered around the worship of animal spirits. One of the oldest altars of sacrifice thus far discovered dates to Neanderthal times. It is an altar on which the skulls of cave bears are neatly arranged on slabs of rock.

It is possible that this altar formed a part of a religious complex something like that of the Eskimo. These arctic hunters believe that the soul of the polar bear is sacred and that it is necessary to apologize to this spirit when the animal is killed. After the animal is skinned, the skull is painted red or black, offerings are made to it, and the bones of the animal have to be put into the fire in a specific order.

The hunters of the Aurignacian period called upon the supernatural power of magical charms to ensure an abundant supply of game. These charms are described by Childe as being:

. . . small figurines of women, carved out of stone or ivory. Normally the bodies are excessively fat and the sexual features exaggerated, but the face is almost blank. It is assumed that such were fertility charms. The generative powers of women would inhere in them, and through them be canalized to provide food for the tribe by ensuring the fertility of game and vegetation. (1957:56)

As far as religious personnal are concerned, we almost universally find that hunting and gathering societies are served by part-time religious practitioners known as shamans. Benedict describes this kind of an individual as follows:

The shaman is the religious practitioner who, by whatever kind of personal experience is recognized as supernatural in his tribe, gets his power directly from the gods. He is often, like Cassandra and others of those who spoke with tongues, a person whose instability has marked him out for his profession. In North America shamans are characteristically those who have the experience of the vision. The priest, on the other hand, is the depository of ritual and the administrator of cult activities. The Pueblos have no shamans; they have only priests. (1959:93)

Radin (1957) feels that the existence of true deities and theology as opposed to indistinct spirits and ghosts is associated with societies that have enough economic surplus to support a priest class. Such specialists are, of course, seldom found in societies that do not have an agricultural base for their economy. Priests find it both necessary and profitable to develop elaborate theology and ritual.

Since religion is seldom separated from the daily lives of primitive people, the form of economy is often directly or indirectly connected with kinds of deities and ceremonies that comprise the religious complex. Let us look, for example, at what is sacred to the predominantly agricultural Hopi Indians.

Their ceremonial calendar reads something like this: The first important ceremony of the year is at the winter solstice—a ceremony to ensure the return of the sun. Then, in February comes the Powamu ceremony of germination and early growth. This is climaxed by the

A Dyak priest makes supplicatory food offerings to the spirits to ensure a successful harvest. From the roof hangs an offering to the omen birds to induce them not to give evil omens. (Courtesy of W. R. Geddes.)

return of the spirits of the rain, the *kachinas,* from their winter retreat in the San Francisco Mountains bearing bean sprouts and ears of corn. In July the Home Dance marks the departure of the *kachinas* to their winter homes. At this time the dancers impersonating the spirits distribute the first green ears of corn and melons fresh from the fields. Then they leave carrying the Hopi prayers for rain and good health to their cloud parents.

In August the most spectacular of the Hopi ceremonials is held. It is the Snake Dance, designed to bring the rain that is so essential to the growth of their last crop of corn. The final major ceremony of the year is the Wuwuchim, which serves as an occasion for the initiation of young men into adult status and also ensures, through the kindling of New Fires, the advent of the winter solstice and the rebirth of the sun.

Even in Christianity, a religion that grew up in an agrarian economy, the important ceremonies in the church calendar tend to be synchronized with the annual agricultural cycle of the Middle East. Many of the New Testament parables depend for their proper impact upon an understanding of agricultural terms—e.g., shepherds, lost sheep, mustard seed, sowing, reaping, vineyard, flock, rocky ground, wineskins, etc.

Although economic level is invariably reflected in the religious activities of a people, it would be folly to carry it to its logical conclusion that industrial societies literally worship the machine or the dollar. However, German sociologist Max Weber, in describing what he refers to as the Protestant ethic, maintains that there is a connection between the fundamental religious ideas of Protestantism and the ideal of behavior compatible with industrial capitalism. He asserts that stress has come to be placed on such conduct as frugality, honesty, industry, respectability. Far too often these are seen not so much as virtues in themselves as for their utility in attaining economic goals. Typical of the Protestant ethic emphasis is the verse "Seeth thou a man diligent in his business: He shall stand before kings" (Proverbs 22:29).

As insecurities of life disappear, so their reference tends to disappear from the religion. There is good cause to state, however, that our economic insecurities have been replaced by other kinds that are equally reflected in religion. Many a day of prayer for peace has been proclaimed and religion becomes more and more the only solace against the possibility of annihilation by hydrogen blast.

We must not go overboard in our correlations of specific forms of religion with specific economies. As Lowie has written:

Nothing is more proper than to stress primitive man's insecurity, but that is only in part the result of a specifically economic situation. The very fact that shamans are almost everywhere primarily curers shows that man's physiological risks are at least as significant in this context as his dread of an inadequate food supply or an insufficient accumulation of pelf in any form. (1952:334)

MORALITY

For those raised in the Christian tradition religion is apt to be thought of as a keeper of the morals of society; and one of the basic tenets of Christianity and its parent, Judaism, is the struggle between good and evil in the hearts of men. This feature is not found, however, in all religions; many leave moral and ethical matters to society and individuals to work out. This was certainly true of the old Samoan religion. This South Sea religion explained such mysteries as how the world was created, who controls the universe, and what happens to a man after he dies, but it left definitions and judgments of proper behavior to the village council and to individual families to work out. Adulterers were not punished by the gods but by the injured family or by the village counsel of chiefs. There are some religions, on the other hand, like Buddhism and Confucianism that deal so much with conduct and spiritual qualities of man that they do not even center about a god at all.

We can say that in nearly every society religion embodies an expression and reaffirmation of its central values. It "contributes to the operation of society through the power and authority and sacred meaning which it provides to the support of man's conduct and to his understanding of his place in the universe" (Redfield 1956:363).

Although religion may not deal with matters of morality as we define the term, every society has its set of sanctions (actions it approves) and taboos (actions it forbids), which are made more powerful by the threat of supernatural punishment. These acts are considered so important that some power greater than man must enforce them. Francis Hsu points out that:

Although taboos have a tremendous variety, they pertain to a few basic matters: food, sex, life's crises (such as birth, initiation, marriage and death), sacred persons and potent things. What is common to these categories?— Danger. These are objects or occasions of danger to the individual and danger to the society of which the individual is a member. (1958:13)

He explains that food can give life but the wrong food can bring death. Although sex is the origin of life, sexual jealousy is a source of tragedy the world over. Life's crises involve a rearrangement and realignment of individuals and events that can disorganize individuals or groups if not properly managed. Sacred persons have a great power over the destinies of their fellow men, whereas potent objects may affect one's life or fortune.

"All of these matters," writes Hsu, "are of greatest concern to every individual and his society. Each society, in order to safeguard the individual and the group, has a particular set of symbols with which to express its corporate concern in the problems of existence. This concern has two facets: the solidarity of the group at any moment; the survival of the group through time" (ibid.: 14).

W. W. Howells, in his book The Heathens, included as part of his definition of religion that "religion is a set of earnest policies which a group of peoples adopts . . . in order to tidy up their distraught relationships with one another and with the universe . . ." (1948:22).

Certainly the taboos and sanctions that Hsu writes about are part of these "earnest policies." Many religions seem to have these policies, which comment day to day on social relationships as well as relationships to the deity or whatever form the supernatural assumes. The Ten Commandments are, to a certain extent, a statement of taboos and sanctions that comment on man's proper behavior toward God and man. Not only do they instruct man as to his proper relationship to his deity, but they represent as good a formula as can be found for maintaining a well-organized social system.

THE POWER STRUGGLE

Religion is not only closely tied to the social and economic dimensions of a society, but it also has a part in its struggles for power. It is seldom when any coup, revolution, or war is carried out without claims that its actions, motives, and goals are god-directed or -inspired. Thomas Jefferson, in penning the Declaration of Independence, justified dissolution of political bonds with Great Britain on the grounds that all men are "endowed by their Creator with certain inalienable rights, that among these are life, liberty, and the pursuit of happiness."

Also claiming supernatural support for their position, Confederacy Vice-President Alexander Stephens stated in a discussion of the South's constitution that "this, our new government, is the first in the history of the world based upon this great physical, philosophical, and moral truth [that the Negro is not the equal of the white]. The great objects of humanity are best attained when there is conformity to the Creator's laws and decrees."

It would also appear that deities often play a rather significant role in warfare either by portending omens or by sanctioning the action. In old Samoa, for example, *Le Sa,* the Forbidden One, was a war god incarnate in the lizard. Before an impending battle the actions of a lizard were carefully watched. If it ran around the outside of a bundle of spears, it was a favorable sign; but if it worked its way into the center, a victory could not be expected.

Not only did the chief god of the Aztecs sanction their warlike behavior, but hostilities were actually made necessary by his demands for human blood. Believing this god had to be nourished with human hearts, as many as 20,000 war captives were put to death at a single ceremony. "A martial success," writes Vaillant, "could be achieved only through the exercise of divine favor. Thus, sacrifice led to war, and war back to sacrifice, in an unending series of expanding cycles" (1962: 169).

Even in modern times nations involve their deity in power struggles. During World War II the popular song *Praise the Lord and Pass the Ammunition* indirectly implicated God in a gun-crew action. The

Germans, also claiming supernatural support provided uniforms with belt buckles inscribed with the words *Gott mit Uns* (God is with us).

MAGIC AND RELIGION

One of the oldest controversies in anthropology has been the relationship of magic to religion. Magic has been defined by Redfield as

. . . That activity directed toward accomplishing some special limited end and one in a form which is determined not by the real effectiveness of the act to bring about the result but by the desires and fears and general thinking and feeling of the man who performs them. (1956:365)

Magic is the manipulation of symbolic material objects or words in order to achieve desired practical results. The assumption in magic is that, if a rite is performed correctly, the expected results will be automatic.

"Magic is characteristically colorful, even dramatic. Magical rites are little pictures of what one wants" (*ibid.*). A well-known form of this magic is imitative magic, found in West Africa and the Caribbean, where the image of one's enemy is formed out of wax and pins are stuck into it in the belief that supernaturally caused illness and even death will overtake the intended victim. The idea behind this is that the magician can produce any effect he desires merely by imitating it. Imitative magic is not always carried out with malevolent goals. Among the Bering Strait Eskimos, barren women often consult a practitioner of magic (a shaman) to obtain a doll-like image imbued with magical properties, which is placed beneath the woman's pillow so that in time she may produce a baby of her own. Imitative magic not only pays attention to form but also to color. In Germany, folk remedies prescribe yellow turnips, gold coins, gold rings, saffron, and a variety of other yellow things as remedies for jaundice.

Still another category of magic, contagious magic, operates on the principle that things that were once associated will remain so even when they are separated. One of the most widespread fears among primitive peoples is that an enemy will be able to obtain nail clippings, excrement, or hair cuttings and utilize them against him in witchcraft magic. Even in comparatively recent times, varieties of contagious magic could be found in England. Frazier tells us that "if a horse wounds its foot by treading on a nail, a Suffolk groom will invariably preserve the nail, clean it, and grease it every day, to prevent the foot from festering" (1958:48).

In comparing the many forms of magic with the characteristics of religion, many scholars have considered magic as psychologically simpler, more specific, and more impersonal than religion. Since magic lacks a church and a communion of the faithful, it has been proposed by some that it represents an early form of religion. Other students of religious behavior recognize magic as a part of religion and feel that too much has been made of minor differences. Goode (1951), for example, points out that both magic and religion (1) are symbolic, (2) have a ritual system, (3) are concerned with non-empirical phenomena and thus stand in the same relationship to Western science, and (4) call forth similar psychological responses in those who participate.

Almost all religions, including Christianity, have magical aspects woven into their institutional fabric in that they combine both praise and propitiation of their deity or conception of the supernatural with a means of harnessing supernatural power for the solution of human practical problems. If we look at Christianity very objectively we must admit that it includes many practices that would qualify under our definition of magic. In all Christian denominations some rote prayers are repeated which are said with the belief that the repetition of such set formula will result in God providing for daily needs. Christian prayers are more frequently requests than they are statements of adoration, faith, or praise. Often, as Finegan puts it,

A prayer may be uttered with a belief in the automatic efficacy of the pronouncement of certain syllables or in the compulsive effect of a sufficient number of repetitions, and thus the line of demarcation often remains indistinct between magic and religion. (1952:7)

It was not uncommon for frontier families to use the Bible for divining (another form of magic). The Bible was opened at random and the finger placed on the first verse that caught the eye. It was believed that the contents of the verse provided direction for making decisions on difficult problems.

The Christopher medal is interpreted by many as affording absolute protection from danger while traveling, and during World War II a New Testament (often with a steel cover) was frequently carried as a sort of charm to protect its bearer against death or injury.

In the folklore of Eastern Europe we find that the cross was an effective device for warding off evil spirits and the "evil eye," providing protection against witches, vampires, and werewolves and as a means of neutralizing the activities of sorcerers.

Although every religion has these magical aspects, there is great variation in the importance placed upon a set formula and symbolically potent objects in the world's religions. The historical or major religions have tended to throw off much of their magical content. While we can dwell upon the manifest differences in behavior called forth by the two aspects of supernatural belief, it is almost impossible to separate them in the thoughts and actions of the believers. Finegan stresses this point when he observes that "magic and religion are coexistent and even more inextricably interwoven in too many instances to make it possible to believe that the one was the predecessor and the root of the other" (1952:6).

MAGIC AND SCIENCE

Whereas religion has often been considered in conflict with science, magic has sometimes been called pseudoscience. Some would contend that at a certain level magic takes the place of science. The Hopi Indians, for example, explain the coming of rain as the result of their dancing with snakes rather than as the result of certain winds and barometric pressure systems. The Arunta say "Our magic rites are just as necessary and efficacious in keeping up the supply of emus and grubs, as the digging and weeding done by wretched cultivators."

Childe points out that magic involves:

. . . an act of faith, and that is what distinguishes a magical operation from a scientific experiment. In judging its results, negative instances, i.e. failures, are simply ignored. Or rather objective judgment gives place to hope and fear . . . Feeling very helpless, he just dare not let that hope go. And just in so far as Nature seems alien and unknown is man afraid to omit anything that might help him in that menacing environment. (1957:50–51)

In the Hopi snake dance, the performers believe beyond question that if the ceremony is performed correctly it will surely rain. Hopis have certainly seen much evidence of the power of the ceremony to produce rain. Some years it has rained so hard that visitors were stranded for days by muddy impassable roads. From the scientist's point of view, however, the Hopi does not subject his religious beliefs to the same rigorous tests required in science. He does not count how many times he has danced and how many times it has rained. He does not question the causal connection between the two events. He does not ask if there could possibly be some other factor (such as proper weather conditions) that brought the rain. He merely has faith in the power of his ceremony and if it doesn't bring the desired result he will explain that the fault was his because there was something improper about his performance. One failure, or even many, is not sufficient for him to reject his religious beliefs. The important fact is that for the Hopi, and for anyone else, science and religion represent quite different categories of behavior. It is impossible to disprove religious phenomena to the same extent as it is possible to test and reject scientific data.

The primitive in his approach to the supernatural forces that control his universe behaves very much like the average American in his approach to the scientific explanations of his surroundings. Both men lack understanding of the nature of the phenomenon, but both have taken on good faith the teachings of their sacred tradition and thus both believe. Let us say, for example, that a man returns to his apartment and upon opening the door throws the light switch. Although he has performed the correct action, the light does not come on. In most cases, this man does not understand the nature of electricity or how his electric circuit works, but he believes that there is a causal relationship between switch-throwing and illumination. When the light does not come on, he does not reject the presence of this causal relationship or his belief in it, he merely says that there is something wrong in the circuit—a short, a blown fuse, a faulty switch, or a burned-out bulb.

This is the same kind of faith that the primitive has in his magic and religion and is the reason that it is not easy for him to drop his magical concepts in favor of more scientific ones. In our own culture, there have been many religious explanations replaced by scientific ones, but the transition has always been a difficult one. When we look at the religious and magical behavior of primitives, untenable from a scientific point of view, we must identify with the primitive and realize that scientific and religious behavior are sometimes quite indistinguishable. An example of this may be seen in the following exchange between a medical doctor and an African rain doctor as described in Livingstone's *Missionary Travels:*

Medical Doctor: So you really believe you can command the clouds? I think that can be done by God alone.

Rain-Doctor: We both believe the very same thing. It is God that makes the rain, but I pray to him by means of these medicines, and, the rain coming, of course it is then mine. . . . If we had no rain, the cattle would have no pastures, the cows give no milk, our children become lean and die, our wives run away to other tribes who do make rain . . . and the whole tribe become dispersed and lost; our fire would go out.

Medical Doctor: . . . you cannot charm the clouds by medicines. You wait till you see the clouds come, then use your medicines, and take the credit which belongs to God only.

Rain-Doctor: I use my medicines, and you employ yours; we are both doctors, and doctors are not deceivers. You give the patient medicine. Sometimes God is pleased to heal him by means of your medicine; sometimes not—he dies. When he is cured, you take the credit of what God does. I do the same. Sometimes God grants us rain, sometimes not. When he does, we take the credit of the charm. When a patient dies you don't give up trust in your medicine, neither do I when rain fails. If you wish me to leave off my medicines, why continue your own? (Livingstone 1857:25–27)

SUGGESTED READINGS

BARNETT, L. "Dawn of Religion," *Life*, December 12, 1955. (Part II in Epic of Man series. Religion in paleolithic times and among modern Australian aborigines.)

BENEDICT, RUTH. "Magic," *Encyclopedia of the Social Sciences*, 1931. (The nature of magical belief and the role it has played in human history.)

COZE, P. "Kachinas: Masked Dancers of the Southwest," *National Geographic Magazine*, August, 1957. (Varieties and functions of ceremonial dancers in Pueblo society; also discusses Hopi snake-dancing.)

GOLDENWEISER, A. A. "Totemism," *Encyclopedia of the Social Sciences*, 1931. (The social, religious, and psychological function of the totem object.)

LOWIE, ROBERT. "Religion in Human Life," *American Anthropologist*, 65:532, 1963. (Comment on the universal importance of religion.)

McNICKLE, D. "Peyote and the Indian," *Scientific Monthly*, September, 1943. (Physiological and psychological aspects of peyote use in modern American Indian religious life.)

NEWMAN, PHILIP. "Sorcery, Religion and the Man," *Natural History*, February, 1962. (How traditional forms of magic are solving modern-day problems confronting the people of New Guinea.)

WORSLEY, PETER M. "Cargo Cults," *Scientific American*, May, 1959. (Describes the religious cults of Melanesia which await a black Messiah who will bring them a great cargo of European goods.)

Paperbound Books

GOODE, WILLIAM J. *Religion Among the Primitives*. Free Press of Glencoe. (Religion as a unifying and motivating force in five primitive societies.)

HOWELLS, W. W. *The Heathens: Primitive Man and His Religions*. Doubleday. (Excellent summary of the varieties of primitive religious experience.)

JAMES, EDWIN O. *Prehistoric Religion*. Barnes and Noble. (Religious forms in ancient stone age cultures.)

LESLIE, CHARLES. *Anthropology of Folk Religion*. Random House. (Essays on primitive religion based on field research in Africa, India, Oceania, and the New World.)

LEVI-STRAUSS, CLAUDE. *Totemism*. Beacon Press. (A consideration of all the theories concerning totemism.)

LOWIE, ROBERT. *Primitive Religion*. Grosset & Dunlap. (Probes the psychological basis common to all primitive religious practices.)

MALINOWSKI, BRONISLAW. *Magic, Science and Religion*. Anchor Books. (Discussion of the theories of religion held by Tylor, Frazer, Marett, and Durkheim.)

RADIN, PAUL. *Primitive Religion*. Dover Publishing Co. (Economic and social influences which have shaped primitive religions.)

TYLOR, EDWARD B. *Religion in Primitive Culture*. (Part II of *Primitive Culture*) Harper & Row. (Discusses animism, totemism, magic, and other common features of primitive religion.)

13

Art

In his artistic works man creates a monument to his own uniqueness, to his own human capacities, and to his spirit. Whatever it is that motivates man to create and beautify, it is distinctly human. While lower animals have shown themselves capable of altering their environments to suit their needs, only man does so to suit his tastes. It would seem that man's need for expression carries him beyond the activities of his practical day-to-day existence, and no matter how hard he must struggle to merely survive there is still a desire to express himself in prose, poetry, song, the dance, or the graphic and plastic arts.

For a working definition of art we may say that it is the production or expression of what is considered beautiful or what appeals to the canons of taste. While art is universal, concepts of beauty and taste vary from culture to culture and within cultures. They are the products of those cultures. Culture even defines what is and what is not art. There are any number of primitive art forms that would motivate a comment like "Do you call that art?" from the average American.

Art, being a cultural product, cannot be influenced by race. The art of African Negroes, South Sea islanders, or Western Europeans is different not because it was created by representatives of different races but because the historical art traditions are different in each of these areas. People tend to reproduce objects familiar to them and people of different areas are sometimes limited or influenced by the materials they have available, but ideas of how best to handle line, form, and color are a matter of learning and experience within a given art tradition. Living in different parts of the world, primitive peoples have had different life experiences and therefore their ideas of what is beautiful, what is aesthetically satisfying, and what is in good taste are infinitely varied.

Art is more than mere expression: It is expression with skill and with some measure of originality. Our culture, as well as others, recognizes the difference between a mere paint dauber and a real artist. In one of America's major literary arts, the production of novels, the distinction has facetiously been made between "typing" and writing.

Although the idea of beauty is usually included in any definition of art, it is not possible to say that art expresses but one feeling or searches for but one result. An artist may find as great a pleasure in creating something that he considers grotesque and horrifying as in creating something which his culture defines as beautiful. Ivan Albright's *Picture of Dorian Grey* and many of his other works fascinate audiences because of their superbly created ugliness.

ANTHROPOLOGICAL APPROACH TO ART

Many people are surprised to find that the study of art is an integral part of anthropology. Art is not commonly an area of study for a scientific discipline, but since anthropology is the science of culture it cannot ignore any cultural activity. The anthropological approach to art is somewhat different from that of the artist or the art critic. Whereas the major concern of the art critic is the art product itself and how it was produced, the anthropologist considers the function of art in the total cultural configuration more important. Since function often affects form, he realizes that a complete understanding of an art object may only be obtained by probing into the reason for its production. No less important is the study of the role and status of the artist in society.

The art critic is also interested in the psychological process of creativity and in the artist's expression and communication of emotion and experience as well as in an evaluation of the quality of a work according to certain traditional or current standards of aesthetics. It is very difficult to extend these interests cross-culturally, and some of the most sophisticated art specialists in anthropology have confessed their inadequacy in this respect. E. R. Leach states:

> When you or I first encounter a carving from New Guinea or West Africa or British Columbia we automatically see it as if it were a work of European art. One may like it or dislike it, but in either case judgment is based on an assumption that the primitive artist is trying to "say" the same sort of thing as European artists try to say. (1961:26)

Although the problem is admittedly difficult, anthropologists feel that by concentrating on the role of art and the function of the artist and by seeking standards by which to evaluate art works from the people themselves, they can attempt to translate for the viewer of primitive art just what the primitive artist is trying to "say" and how well he has said it.

THE PRINCIPAL ARTS

Any creative activity performed with some measure of excellence which serves as an emotional outlet for its author and as a source of pleasure or satisfaction for the observer is art. The activities that may be covered by this definition are so many and varied that it will be convenient to arrange them in some categorical system. For purposes of analysis the following divisions might be considered: (1) the graphic and plastic arts, (2) the verbal arts, and (3) the performing arts.

The Graphic and Plastic Arts

This broad category is used to designate those activities connected with the production or decoration of cultural artifacts that are considered aesthetically pleasing. Varying from Aurignacian Venuses to totem poles to Henry Moore productions, sculpture is probably the most universally practiced art in this category. Painting follows, a close second in world importance. Some of the most famous varieties are Bushman rock paintings from the Kalihari, Polynesian tapa cloth decoration, exterior wall designs among the Mangbetu of the Congo, or the frescoes of ancient Mayan ceremonial centers.

Weaving, a plastic art, dates back at least to the Neolithic and includes, in various parts of the contemporary world, basketry, matting, and production of textiles from various vegetable and animal fibers through the use of the loom. In the Andes, gold and silver threads were utilized for tapestry production.

Although architecture, when applied to the construction of ceremonial structures or monuments, has been considered a fine art in both primitive and Western culture, it is only in the latter that the artistry has been carried over into the design of dwellings. In most primitive societies house structures are more the work of the artisan than the artist. Houses may be beautifully and intricately constructed, but originality is not an important factor. House types are usually traditional and are more in tune with temperature than with taste.

Of the many wonders of megalithic architecture throughout the world none are more astounding than those produced by the isolated and primitive people on the island of Nias in Indonesia. Nias villages often contain stone-paved plazas with bathing pools and altars, great walls, majestic staircases, and superbly sculptured statuary of enormous size which are truly marvels of architectural and stone-cutting art.

Although pottery is often thought of as confined to strictly useful objects, the treatment of the surfaces and even the form of the pots have afforded much opportunity for artistic expression. Each tribal group in the American Southwest has its distinct tradition of form and surface decoration and in South America ceramics approached sculpture in the form of effigy vessels. In Mexico it is possible to date a number of Pre-Aztec cultures by small modeled ceramic figures which still may be found around ceremonial sites. Ceramics were also used in making toys

Nias warrior in full regalia awaits ceremony at the plaza altar. (Courtesy of Chicago Natural History Museum.)

in this area and the only example of the use of the wheel in Pre-Columbian America is found in a little toy horse that might have served as a pull toy.

Artistic work in metals appeared somewhat later in the history of culture than most of the arts previously described, but it is nevertheless widespread today among the peoples of the world. Most frequently the production of art objects in brass, bronze, or precious metals has utilized the "lost wax" process similar to that employed by modern dentists in casting inlays or bridges. Not all art metal work employs casting, however. The Pueblo and Navaho silversmiths have long produced belts, bracelets, and necklaces from silver pellets by using a hammer and cold chisel, and in many parts of Mexico and Asia today, primitive people produce from precious metals delicate filigree ornaments in wire form.

Also classed as a form of graphic and plastic art is body decoration. Serving as a source of beauty, as a symbol of rank, or as an indicator of family or tribal membership, tattooing and scarification are widespread. The decoration of the body is nearly always the job of a specialist. His duties do not always call for originality or creativity, but they always demand skill. Hairdressing also attains the status of a fine art in some areas—notably in the Congo, in the American Southwest, and, of course, in Japan and in much of the Western world.

The Verbal Arts

The verbal arts, which might also be referred to as folklore, are often less apparent to the average American than the graphic and plastic arts. Aside from a group of Old English and Early American folksongs that have enjoyed recent popularity, literature in America has largely been restricted to the printed page. Primitive cultures, with their lack of writing, have quite naturally been the main exponents of oral or verbal literature, which maintains its immortality by being passed down by word of mouth from generation to generation.

From the standpoint of the people, *myths* are often the most important variety of verbal art. Essentially, these are narratives that deal with the remote past before the world was in its present condition. The principal characters are usually gods or culture heroes and their activities and personality characteristics represent—sometimes symbolically —an exposition of the basic value system of the society.

Legends are sagas of individual humans or societies and are considered to be true historical accounts. *Folktales,* on the other hand, are stories of anthropomorphic animals or exceptional humans which are told for entertainment and frequently for educational purposes since they often contain a moral. Sometimes coupled with a narrative but more frequently used independently, *proverbs* are brief epigrammatic statements suggesting a course of action consistent with a society's system of values. Since statements like "A stitch in time saves nine" or "Honesty is the best policy" represent consensuses of opinion about what is culturally acceptable behavior in a society, they are sometimes used in court litigation as precedents for judgment of conduct. Mankind reveals its capacity for humor in the universal existence of the *riddle*. Riddles are, of course, cryptically phrased questions or statements that demand an answer based on association, comparison, and perception of likeness and difference in natural or cultural phenomena.

Closely approximating music in its rhythm and choice of word tones is poetry. Many societies consider the poem the most dramatic form of narrative and assign their most sacred lore to the realm of the rhyme and the meter.

A Samoan *taupou* is the village ceremonial hostess and dance leader.

The Performing Arts

The division between folklore and the performing arts is an arbitrary one, for certainly many a story teller is essentially a performing artist. The performing arts, however, in our classification are represented by such artistic genre as oratory, music, the dance, and drama. In each of these activities the performer draws heavily on the forms of the other categories. The dance, for example, may utilize masks or brilliantly designed costumes, and drama usually draws upon the significant mythology of a society. In the Samoan islands oratory tends to be mainly political in nature, but every orator liberally utilizes proverbs, poetry, and allusions to myths and legends to sway his audience. To a certain extent every artist must please his audience, but the performing artists are more directly subject to their demands. Although there are many cases, particularly in the area of the dance, in which total participation by the group is present, most often performing artists are involved in a performer-spectator situation in the practice of their art. The performer and his audience are frequently psychologically very close, since the dance often expresses the emotional state of the group; the songs may represent songs of anguish or joy and dramatic performances play out the desires, anxieties, and satisfactions of a whole society.

STYLE

Each artist in every culture tends to maintain a continuity in the form and quality of his art. There also seems to be a tendency, at least in non-Western culture, for artists to work within a traditional framework of form, quality, and mode of expression. This consistency, called *style*, allows us to identify the work of a certain artist and also to place his work in a specific cultural context. In analyzing style traditions of the world we shall begin by establishing three categories of art: (1) representative; (2) stylized, and; (3) abstract art.

Representative Art

Representative art is often described as "photographic" or "naturalistic," i.e., closely approximating nature. Good examples of this kind of art are to be found in magazine illustrations and to a large extent in portrait-painting. This is the kind of absolute reproduction that many artists disdain, maintaining that it can better be done with a camera.

Actually, the term "representative art" is not a very objective one because not even a photograph is a true copy of nature. Anthropologists have reported that primitives, upon being photographed and given the print of the picture, turn it one way and another without being able to recognize themselves. The problem is that they cannot reduce their three-dimensional world to the two-dimensional one of the camera.

Many examples of art forms are naturalistic or realistic to the artist but might appear very abstract to a viewer from another culture. A good example of this is the X-ray-like bark paintings of the Australian aborigines. These paintings, usually of fish or kangaroos, show not only the outer form of the animal but the skeleton as well. To the eyes of a European the painting looks abstract but to the Australian it represents an accurate representation of nature.

A similar concept of representative form is found in the art work of the Indians of Northern British Columbia. Their subjects, usually animals, are portrayed as though one were viewing their hides stretched out to dry. This kind of treatment was considered very realistic by the artists and their reasoning is described by Boas as follows:

> It is easily intelligible that a profile view of an animal in which only one eye is seen and in which one whole side disappears may not satisfy as a realistic representation. The animal *has two* eyes and *two* sides. When it turns I see the other side; it exists and should be part of a satisfying picture. (1955:72)

Stylized Art

By stylized art we merely refer to those art traditions following a general pattern of deviation from what is commonly recognized as naturalistic within the culture. This deviation may in some cases consist of such techniques as simplification of forms such as the bird and deer forms found on Zuni pottery or the abbreviated drawings characteristic of modern American advertising and cartoon art. Still another variety of stylization is distortion—i.e., emphasizing certain significant aspects of an object by purposely altering form or perspective. An example of this kind of stylization is found in a special kind of little wooden figurines carved by Yoruba artists in West Africa. Each of these depicts a different occupational status and features size distortion of the characteristic tools of each trade; the missionary carries a huge Bible, the magistrate wears a gigantic wig, and the anthropologist comes complete with an oversize pencil and notebook.

Northwest Coast Indian art utilizes the stylistic principle of distorting the normal arrangement or location of anatomical parts of an animal in order to achieve a desired design. While the eyes, mouth, ears, paws, and other parts of the body are realistically drawn, they are set into the design without regard for their normal arrangement in life.

Abstract Art

Among primitive peoples abstract art almost always carries one into the realm of symbolism. Although there are undoubtedly numerous examples of primitive artists merely getting satisfaction from experimenting with line, form, and color, in most cases art products that are not

Northwest coast totem poles represent family coats of arms. (Courtesy of National Museum of Canada.)

recognizable as representations of objects from nature are produced for their symbolic quality. On occasion, as in Arapaho beadwork symbols, we are not sure whether the abstract designs such as a diamond for "man" or a cross for "star" were created to symbolize objects or whether the designs were created first and meaning read into them secondarily. The Arapaho Indians utilized color symbolism as well. Red stood for "blood," "man," "earth," and "sunset"; blue represented "sky," "smoke," "distant mountains," or "night"; and white carried the meaning of "snow," "sand," or "water."

Symbolism is one of the most important aspects of Navaho sand-painting. Concerning this form of Southwest ritual art Bunzel records,

The figures of masked gods are greatly elongated; male gods are symbolized by round masks, females by square masks . . . There is a fixed color symbolism associated with the four cardinal points: white for east, blue for south, yellow for west, black for north. The clothing of the Gods and the corn plants which are conventionally represented are of the colors appropriate to the directions with which they are associated . . . The same system of symbolism which appears in the sand paintings is even more fully developed in myth and song. (1938:580–81)

In Samoa, young men obtain tattoos that extend from the knee to the small of the back. The designs consist of a series of straight and curved lines interspersed with sections of solid color. There is little variation in the traditional pattern from individual to individual and nearly every design element is symbolic. A solid section extending across the small of the back is called the "boat" or "canoe," while other aspects of the design symbolize "the head of a bird," a "centipede," and important beams and ribs of the traditional Samoan house framework.

Art symbolism also carries over into the area of Samoan architecture, for various components of the Samoan house with its beehive-shaped roof have symbolic references. The ridge beam is referred to as "a sleeping barracuda," the curved, parallel beams of the eaves as "the rainbow," and the numerous house posts that support the roof are referred to as a "school of fish in shallow water." Symbolic representation, however, has found its way into few other Samoan arts. Contrary to the situation encountered in the Hawaiian *hula*, the Samoan *siva* does not attempt to tell a story. Tapa cloth designs likewise have neither symbolic color nor design.

STYLE IN MUSIC AND DANCE

It is difficult to categorize music in the same manner as we have the graphic and plastic arts, as the category "representative" is not meaningful. The closest approach to this, however, is to be found in the structure of the Chinese and Hindu musical scales, which mythology relates were first developed by imitating the sounds of nature—mostly bird and animal calls. The important consideration in this area is conventional style, which involves differences in scales, rhythm, tone quality, relative importance of harmony and melody, and so on.

In the area of singing alone, the styles of the world's cultures are so diverse that it would be impossible to decide which was most naturalistic. A few characterizations of vocal styles by Lomax will give us some idea of the variety to be found.

American Indian: The solo singer uses a chesty voice, wide rather than narrow, yet with strong characterizers of nasal resonance and throaty burr and with forceful accent.

Oriental: He (the solo voice) performs highly complex strophes composed of many long phrases, with maximum ornamentation . . . in a voice that is usually high and falsetto, narrow and squeezed—with maximum nasality, raspy, and often characterized by forcefully precise articulation.

Polynesian: One of the most notable traits of old Polynesian music is the choral performance (rather than solo performances) in perfect tonal and rhythmic unison of long and complex texts, where every syllable is clearly enunciated. In some areas, a rudimentary form of polyphony occurs: one of the voice parts rises in pitch and maintains this level while the chorus continues to sing at the original pitch, thus creating a simple drone harmony. (1962:*passim*)

Ceremonial Symbolism

Among the performing arts none is more replete with symbolism than dramatic ritual and the dance. Whereas the Western world has long been accustomed to idea plays with symbolic plots and characters and there is a well-established pattern of interpretive dancing, we are often surprised to learn the extent to which primitive people rely on dramatic ceremonies and dances to perpetuate the basic values of their culture.

THE SUN DANCE. Of the many colorful ceremonies performed by primitive peoples none is more symbolic and dramatic than the Sun Dance of the Sioux Indians. The Sun Dance is essentially a ceremony of self-torture in which dancers offered their bodies and souls to the Sun (Wakan Tanka) in order that the people of the Sioux nation might be revitalized. The ritual also ensures an abundance of buffalo as well as success in hunting them.

Every action, every word, every bit of paraphernalia associated with the dance carries religious and social symbolism. The lodge in which the Sun Dance is performed is constructed of twenty-eight poles (the number of days in each moon). At the very center (symbolic of the center of the earth) is planted the most sacred object of all—a cottonwood tree to which a buckskin bag filled with fat is attached. The cottonwood, selected because its leaves resemble the outline of a tepee, is said to unite the earth and the sky, and the fat-filled bag serves as a petition to the sun deity to make the earth fat and plentiful. The tree,

A Plains Indian chief holds the sacred Sun Dance Calumet. (Courtesy of Chicago Natural History Museum.)

referred to in the chants as the "standing person," is "captured" and cut down by a Sioux war party. Just as in actual battle, the four warriors and the war chief who fell the tree receive war honors (coup). As the tree is carried into camp, the warriors howl like coyotes—the Sioux symbol of victory. After reverently planting the tree in the dance lodge, the men proceed with the detailed preparations for the dance itself.

Rawhide is cut into circles, one colored red symbolizing the sun; another blue, representing the moon; and still others are produced and decorated to stand for mother and grandmother earth, and for the buffalo—the source of Plains Indian subsistence. A five-pointed star-shaped piece is produced symbolizing the desire that the people might receive knowledge as they received light, from the Morning Star. These and other sacred objects such as buffalo skulls, a calumet, leather thongs, and skewers are taken to a sweat lodge where they are purified by tobacco smoke and prayed over. It is at this time that the dancers volunteer to endure suffering and give their flesh so that their people might flourish.

The actual ceremony begins at dawn with a procession of dancers led by a woman, the White Buffalo Cow Maiden, who carries the sacred calumet. The dancers repeat a simple chant requesting Wakan Tanka to reward their suffering with longevity for their people. Soon the spectators also take up the chant. As the drums begin to add their rhythm to the chant, special attendants seize the dancers, pierce the skin of their chests and insert pegs that are fastened by long thongs to the top of the cottonwood tree. With faces raised to the sun the dancers circle the sacred tree tugging at the thongs until the pegs tear out the flesh of the chest leaving bloody wounds. When all the dancers have pulled free of the thongs, they return to the sweat lodge where they are commended for their courage and promised that their sacrifices will not readily be forgotten.

ART FOR ART'S SAKE

It is not possible to make the flat statement that in primitive society there is no "art for art's sake," but it is true that the major part of it is utilitarian and is produced for religious, economic, social, or other purposes. Art always has utility even when it is produced with no purpose in mind but enjoyment. Anyone who has worked with the mentally ill will attest to the therapeutic value of creative activities. The psychological factor in art has been summed up by John Lewis as follows: "Art releases tensions by enabling the artist to externalize some of his emotions and ideas in an objectice way; and this makes him the emotional leader and representative of his tribe" (1961:115).

The artist's sheer pleasure in creating beautiful forms is witnessed in the decoration of a particular kind of rawhide box or wallet produced by the Sauk and Fox Indians. The artists of this tribe took great pains in laying out a beautifully balanced and symmetrical design on a rectangular piece of rawhide. The colors were chosen to give a harmonious, pleasing effect. However, the design was laid down with no thought to the folding of the box. When the proper folds were made, the original effect of the design was destroyed. To the artist the *parfleche* (as the box was called) was a work of beauty, but to its owner and user it was merely a useful object made more valuable because effort had been spent in its decoration.

A similar situation is encountered in the legging decorations made by the Thompson Indians of British Columbia. In that culture, beads of various kinds are strung on legging fringe in such a way that they give a rhythmic design. While the artist may gain a good deal of pleasure from her creation, the beauty of the leggings is not actually enhanced, for when they are worn, the fringe hangs down in such a way that the elaborate design is destroyed.

There are many cases of apparent art for art's sake in which the tendency to create a thing of beauty actually detracts from the usefulness of the decorated object. This mystic psychological phenomenon can be seen in the manner of producing stone hand axes in the Lower Paleolithic. In an attempt to achieve symmetry, these tools were flaked on both faces all around. While this produced an aesthetically appealing form, it also reduced the implement's utility, for its user undoubtedly had to use a piece of hide or some other form of protection to keep his hand from being cut by the sharp butt edge.

While doing research among the Bush Negroes of Surinam in Dutch Guinea, Melville Herskovits discovered that the people had in their possession "rice-winnowing trays" that their artists had rendered useless by carving designs completely through the wood. Since they obviously would not even hold grain, they represented only a Surinam decorative object.

In the Cook Islands of Polynesia "art for art's sake" is represented in the ceremonial adzes, which feature a wooden handle so delicately carved that they have an appearance of filigree work. While the stone head of the adze is exactly like those used in house or boat construction, the artist's treatment of the handle has relegated the implement to the ceremonial sphere.

It may be argued, however, that the artistic embellishment of this tool has merely removed its utility in one aspect of culture and has created a useful object in another—in this case, in the area of religion. This is one of the problems involved in making flat statements about the existence or lack of existence of an "art for art's sake" concept. Even in our own culture it is possible for a given work of fine art to be (1) a thing of beauty to be enjoyed in a museum, (2) a symbol of affluence to a private collector, or (3) an aid to retailing when used in a magazine advertisement.

Although artists in all cultures produce works of art to gratify a creative impulse, it is safe to say that in most primitive societies art is usually produced for a particular purpose. Art objects must often be more useful than ornamental. Ruth Bunzel tells of a Pueblo potter who rejected a piece of pottery with the statement "It is beautiful but not strong" (1938:538). A wooden figurine carved by a West African may be aesthetically satisfying, but its major function is an abode for a spirit. A Navaho sand-painting is an appealing creation even to the Western eye, but its main purpose is healing. A dance may thrill dancers and spectators alike with its grace and beauty, but the first thought of the choreographer is its function in the worship of the gods. In primitive society it is difficult to view art as an isolated activity. It is always an integral part of the total cultural configuration. Art may be an adjunct to economics, social organization, religion, communication, education, and any number of cultural aspects.

ECONOMICS

The quantity and quality of art as well as the role of its authors is often related to the form of subsistence of a society and the amount of its surplus. Boas explains the dearth of art in some societies by the fact that a hunter's life is so taken up with obtaining life's bare necessities that there is little time or energy left for the luxury of artistic expression. Even if the required leisure could somehow be found, hunting peoples must constantly be on the move and they cannot be burdened with unnecessary or unfinished art products. Thus, art activities often take the form, in these societies, of decoration of clothing or weapons or occasionally small carved objects such as Eskimo needlecases which can easily be transported (1938:589).

An apparent contradiction to this generalization is to be found in the hunting and fishing peoples of the Northwest Coast of North America, who were prolific and proficient carvers and weavers. While primarily hunting and fishing peoples, their dependable supply of salmon and sea mammals provided the surplus leisure necessary for a full concentration on their art activities. Their heavy wood sculpture—totem poles, mortuary posts, and house posts—was made possible because of their sedentary village life.

Specialization

The great art traditions of Mesopotamia, Egyptian, Mayan, and Incan civilizations were made possible only by economic systems where there was sufficient surplus to support specialized craftsmen and artists in the full-time pursuit of their activities. Each of these societies not only supported great numbers of artists but actually trained them through art apprenticeships or in government-supported schools of fine art.

In some cases economic security leads not to art specialization but to a general raising of art interest and production in a population as a whole. This has been the case in Bali. According to Covarrubias:

> Everybody in Bali seems to be an artist. Coolies and princes, priests and peasants, men and women alike, can dance, play musical instruments, paint, or carve in wood and stone . . . The effervescence of artistic activity and the highly developed esthetic sense of the population can perhaps be explained by a natural urge to express themselves, combined with the important factor of leisure resulting from well-organized agricultural co-operatism. However, the most important element for the development of a popular culture, with primitive as well as refined characteristics, was the fact that the Balinese did not permit the centralization of the artistic knowledge in a special intellectual class. (1937:160–62)

Economics and art are related in still other ways. For example, it is not unusual for art products to serve as repositories of wealth or even as units of exchange. The delicately woven hibiscus-fiber fine mats of Samoa, North American Indian beadwork in the form of wampum belts, and Banks Islands crimson-dyed feather ornaments are examples of aesthetic currency. Undoubtedly, trade relationships have been closely tied in with the development of the arts in many areas. In ancient Crete the development of fine pottery vessels as well as their decoration with floral and marine designs is directly traceable to trade relationships with Greece and Egypt. The pottery served to package Crete's principal export—olive oil.

Oral art has its economic tie-in also. In parts of Melanesia it is believed that there is a direct relationship between the nightly telling of folktales during certain seasons and the success of the garden harvest. Further to the West, in Indonesia, one Celebes tribe believes that riddles may be asked only during the period when the rice crop is developing. At this time the farmers sit in the fields and ask each other riddles. When a correct answer is given, the assembled group chants, "Let the rice grow." It is believed that a man's success in riddling has a very definite effect on his success as a rice farmer.

SOCIAL ORGANIZATION

Art in its various forms contributes materially to the maintenance of the social organization of any society. One reason for this is that art can represent a strong unifying force. Consider for a moment emblems of family, clan, and national solidarity that have come from the hand of the artistic craftsman.

For the European, family unity is often symbolized by a coat of arms, while Northwest Coast Indians expressed pride in their clan and family traditions and heritage by raising a totem pole. Nations have also utilized graphic symbols (the French Fleur-de-lis and cockade or the German swastika or Maltese cross), national anthems, and traditional folk or fatherland songs to arouse patriotic feelings in their citizens. No country is without its flag, pregnant with symbolism, or its emotion-stirring paintings and sculpture—e.g., *Washington Crossing the Delaware*, the Flag Raising on Iwo Jima statue, the seated Lincoln in the Lincoln Memorial.

In the case of music, and particularly folk music, Lomax believes that this form of art is a great source of personal and cultural security. He believes that:

> The primary effect of music is to give the listener a feeling of security, for it symbolizes the place where he was born, his earliest childhood satisfactions, his religious experience, his pleasure in community doings, his courtship and his work . . . (1959:929)

Art has been used not only to symbolize *esprit de corps*, but it has also fortified prevailing social structures by serving as a designator of role and status. In the New Hebrides, men purchased their way up the social ladder with payments to the village elders of a special breed of pigs. Each social grade carried the privilege of wearing a special mask made of cane and clay and decorated with the colors appropriate to his rank.

In the Samoan islands, tapa cloth is considered the ceremonial clothing of the chiefs only, and the exalted village *taupou* (ceremonial hostess) is easily distinguished by her garments of the most finely woven hibiscus bast. On her head she wears an artfully constructed head ornament of human hair, sticks, and small pieces of mirror. Of the Aztecs Vaillant writes:

> The warriors frankly gloried in their costumes. Rich mantles and ornate feather head-dresses were not enough for some, who carried on their shoulders a harness of wicker supporting an elaborate structure in feather mosaic. Others wore costumes modelled on the appearance of an ocelot or an eagle. (1950:140)

RELIGION

Art has ever been the handmaiden of religion. Without artists there can be no idolatry. Whether it be the earliest cave art of Lascaux or Altamira, the chants of Gregory, the murals of Michaelangelo, or the Sallman *Head of Christ*, art has served a common function in religion—to express awe and adoration of the supernatural. Man has exhibited a pronounced tendency to require something material upon which to focus his worship. Whether man looks to a stained-glass window, a six-branched candlestick, or a Polynesian *tiki*, art serves man as symbolic of faith and unity in a given religious system.

Navaho sandpainter. (Courtesy of Arizona State Museum.)

Frequently art shades into religion to such an extent that the two are inseparable. Such is the case with the Navaho. Lee describes this fusion as follows:

The sand-paintings are no more art than they are ritual, myth, medical practice or religious belief. They are created as an integral aspect of a ceremony which brings into harmony with the universal order one who finds himself in discord with it; or which intensifies and ensures the continuation of a harmony which is already present. Every line and shape and color, every interrelationship of form, is the visible manifestation of myth, ritual and religious belief. (1959:167)

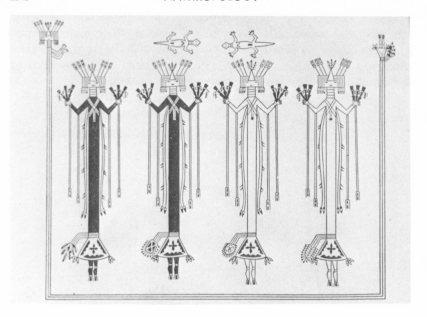

Navaho sandpainting.

COMMUNICATION

Before men recorded their thoughts and experiences in words, they did it in pictures. Many peoples, known only through the findings of archeologists, would remain inarticulate except through their art.

In North America, Ojibwa Indians drew quite recognizable pictures of gods, birds, and animals on bits of birchbark in order to remember the sequence of songs in ceremonies. One of the most interesting bits of early American art is the wampum belt given to William Penn by the Leni-Lenape Indian chiefs at the Treaty of 1682. This belt, made predominantly of white shells (the color of peace), depicts Penn and an Indian with joined hands and represents a record of the agreement between Whites and Indians to live in peace. In the West, Plains Indians covered the outsides of their tepees with story pictures of memorable hunts or victorious battles using symbolic colors and figures to spell out the accurate details. The Sioux Indians even developed a way of keeping historical records of the tribe over a period of years. By looking at their chronological picture record, it was possible for them to recall years in which specific births, deaths, wars, and epidemics took place.

In a great number of civilizations it is possible to trace an evolution of writing from a pictograph stage to one in which abstract characters were used. Of Aztec civilization Vaillant states:

The priesthood . . . instructed youth in the mysteries of writing and keeping records . . . There was no alphabet, but a picture of an animal or thing could be combined with the picture or another animal or thing to give a third meaning in terms of its sound value . . . The Aztecs wrote the name of their capital by drawing stone *tena* from which sprouted a napal cactus, *nochtli,* or the town Pantepec, by drawing a flag, *pantli,* on a conventionalized hill, *tepec.* Color, position, puns and abbreviations all contributed to recording sounds by this means. Conventionalized signs, like footprints to show travel or movement, a shield and club for war, a bundled corpse for death, gave simple connotations of action. (1950:201)

The Aztec numerical system also depended upon art work. The number 1 was indicated by a dot or a finger; 20 by a flag; 400 (20×20) by a fir tree, 8,000 ($2 \times 20 \times 20$) by a bag commonly used for carrying cacao beans.

EDUCATION

As some form of communication is essential in socializing and enculturating the young people of any society, it is difficult to separate the communicative and educational functions of art. Audiovisual aids are hardly new to mankind, and the concept of a "picture being worth a thousand words" probably emerged during the Stone Age.

The Micronesians used as their principal aid in teaching navigation delicately fashioned frameworks of bamboo and shells. These were supposed to instruct novices concerning prevailing winds and currents. While some do not consider these bamboo charts works of art, they do feature in many cases bilateral symmetry and artistic arrangements of sticks and shells often at the expense of accurate scale.

In Pueblo cultures one of the more significant forms of art is the Kachina dolls, which are carved by the men with great concern for accurate detail. These dolls, often given to children as gifts, are faithful models of Kachina dancers. When the men teach their children to carve these dolls, dress, color, and posture have to be correct or the spirits will be offended. Thus, the children learn through the creation of these playthings the important elements of their religious heritage.

Turning to other forms of art, we find that among the Lamba of Africa there is one class of proverbs that is used especially for the training of children. And Reichard records:

Almost every tribe has stories which they consider children's tales, or moralizing stories for the main purpose of inculcating virtue . . . The fact that the very rehearsal of the tales by adults with the children present, as well

Elements of artistic design may be observed in the Micronesian sailing chart. (Courtesy of Chicago Natural History Museum.)

as frequent reference to the tales in various situations of daily life, exerts a potent influence in the teaching and learning process. Children learn the right and wrong of a matter by implication and inference and by repetition, and it would be difficult, if not impossible for them to tell how they know many things. (1938:478)

Myths serve as repositories of values in every society including our own. Just prior to the turn of the century fifty million young people were reading about the life and times of a number of American culture heroes created by the novelist Horatio Alger. Sociologist R. Richard Wohl, who has made a study of the impact of Alger's works, points out that the myth usually went something like this: A respectable country boy goes to the city to make good in order to assist in the support of his recently widowed mother, who is being threatened by mortgage fore-

Pueblo kachina dolls. (Courtesy of Chicago History Natural Museum.)

closure. Through clean living, thrift, honesty, and hard work he is victorious over bullies, thieves, and economic difficulties.

In trying to understand Alger's great popularity Wohl suggests that (1) Alger's novels appeared at a time of great mobility from farm to city; (2) Alger helped define the aspirations of a nation of farm boys—to make money, to get ahead, to make good; (3) the principles of proper conduct found in the novels were reinforced from the pulpit, in the press, and in the advice of the average American to his children; and (4) the stories have universal appeal for every age who would like to believe that "push" and not "pull" is the secret to success. The Horatio Alger stories represent a primer for success for millions of Americans and incorporated the basic principles of the "great American dream."

ROLE IN SCIENCE

It is doubtful if scholars will ever develop a very satisfactory science of art. The value of art lies in its relatively unpredictable nature. Art objects and art processes have, however, provided important data in developing a science of man. In the study of New World archeology, for example, ceramic analysis has been one of the major methods of recognizing and dating prehistoric cultures and civilizations. In Mexico and Central America frescoes and books of polychrome pictures (known as codices) have given us a glimpse into Mayan and Aztec life as it existed prior to the destruction or abandonment of many of the ceremonial centers.

Analysis of folklore motifs appearing in a variety of cultures has been utilized to study cultural diffusion, and ethnomusicological studies have provided evidence of cultural contact where historical records are missing. When cultural evolutionists were claiming that art progresses from the representational to the abstract, Franz Boas demonstrated that at least in Eskimo needle-cases this had not been the case. He found that originally the cases carried only geometric incised designs but "the various parts of the needle-case excite the imagination of the artist" (1908:337) and in time certain portions were decorated with realistic animal forms.

Ackerknecht (1953) has pointed out that art works have served the physical anthropologist well in his studies of paleopathology. Egyptian paintings and statues provide evidence (corroborated by mummies) of the presence of congenital clubfoot and both achondroplastic and cretinistic dwarfism. Art objects from both hemispheres indicate the presence in prehistoric populations of poliomyelitis and Pott's disease (tuberculosis of the spine). Aztec codex pictures accurately depict both dwarfs and hunchbacks, and pottery and clay sculpture from the Peruvian Andes throws light upon the antiquity of certain skin diseases in that area.

In the study of contemporary peoples analysis of works of art has been utilized in studying personality structure in primitive as well as industrialized cultures. Honigmann describes the theory behind such analysis as follows:

> Professional works of imagination do not only reveal the character structure of their creators, as might be thought. Successful stories, plays, films, and similar creative products contain themes that appeal to existing needs and aspirations of the community. Popularity indicates that the expressive product satisfies audience needs and suggests a relationship between that product and character structure. (1954:129)

Still other studies have revealed how basic value systems may be investigated by analyzing the peculiarities of a culture's art works. It has been noted, for example, that in China, where rank and station were of paramount importance, the costumes and other emblems of rank of Emperors were painted in detail by portrait artists, but little attention was paid to the distinct facial characteristics of individuals (Hsu 1953). In colonial America, however, where the "rugged individual" was extolled, itinerant portrait painters used to paint clothing in advance leaving only the accurate representation of the face of the customer to be painted in at the time of the sitting.

Frankfort (1948) has called attention to the fact that in Egyptian paintings of battle scenes the Pharaoh was always the dominant figure, being represented in much larger size than fellow warriors. In Mesopotamian art, however, the king is not easily distinguishable from his subjects. This difference is significant because Egyptian kings were regarded as gods while those of Mesopotamia were merely highly honored mortals.

SUGGESTED READINGS

BENEDICT, RUTH. "Myth," Encyclopedia of the Social Sciences, 1931. (The relationship between folklore and religion.)

CARPENTER, E. "Artists of the North," Natural History, February, 1962. (Realism and style in Eskimo art.)

EISELEY, LOREN. "Island of Great Stone Faces," Holiday, March, 1962. (The giant statues of Easter Island presented as the Pacific's most provocative riddle.)

ERNST, A. H. "Northwest Coast Animal Dances," Theatre Arts, September, 1939. (Totemic nature of Northwest Coast Indian dances.)

————. "Thunderbird Dance," Theatre Arts, February, 1945. (Mythology and ritual dance on the Northwest Coast of North America.)

HERSKOVITS, M. J. "African Literature," Encyclopedia of Literature (ed. J. T. SHIPLEY), 1946. (Deals with both African and New World forms of Negro oral art; form and function of trickster tales, explanatory tales, historical narratives, proverbs, and riddles.)

JORGENSEN, B., and JORGENSEN, V. "Ancient Bushman Brushwork," Natural History, February, 1949. (Bushman rock paintings, a link with the past in South Africa.)

KROEBER, A. L. "Art: Primitive," Encyclopedia of the Social Sciences, 1931. (Explores the nature of the artistic impulse in primitive man.)

LUOMALA, KATHERINE. "Polynesian Literature," Encyclopedia of Literature (ed. J. T. SHIPLEY), 1946. (Excellent survey of forms and subjects (gods and culture heroes) of Polynesian folklore.)

MERRIAM, ALAN. "Ethnomusicology in Our Time," American Music Teacher, January–February, 1959. (Defines interests of cultural anthropologists who study music cross-culturally. Good bibliography of ethnomusicological sources.)

METRAUX, A. "South American Indian Literature," Encyclopedia of Literature (ed. J. T. SHIPLEY), 1946. (Culture hero myths, trickster tales, drama, proverbs, and riddles of South American Indians.)

MOVIUS, H. L., Jr. "Archaeology and the Earliest Art: Cave Art of Southern France and Northern Spain," Scientific American, August, 1953. (Prehistoric man attempts to control his universe through the magic of art.)

NELSON, E. W. "Metal Arts of the Indians," Natural History, February, 1947. (The artistry of prehistoric Indians in working with precious and semi-precious metals.)

ROBERTS, H. H. "Music: Primitive," Encyclopedia of the Social Sciences, 1933. (Varieties and functions of music among non-Western peoples.)

TURNBULL, C. "Men and their Music round the World," *Natural History*, June, 1961. (Discusses the field of ethnomusicology and suggests records that may be obtained as examples of the music of several primitive societies.)

VOEGELIN, ERMINIE. "North American Native Literature," *Encyclopedia of Literature* (ed. J. T. SHIPLEY), 1946. (Basic forms of Indian folklore discussed by culture area.)

Paperbound books

BEARDSLEY, R. K. *Art and Anthropology*. Random House. (The function of art in primitive society.)

BOAS, FRANZ. *Primitive Art*. Dover Publications. (Discusses representative art, symbolism, and style with examples drawn from various Indian art traditions.)

BOWRA, C. M. *Primitive Song*. The New American Library of World Literature, Inc. (Form and function of song in Australian, Eskimo, Andaman Island, and Bushman culture.)

KOLINSKI, M. (ed.). *Studies in Ethnomusicology*. Vol. I, Oak Publications and Folkway Records. (Essays dealing with characteristics of Hindu, Dutch, Latin American, African, and American jazz music.)

14

Cultural Change

An anthropological description depicting the way of life of a particular society freezes the action, so to speak, at a given point in time. Thus, no anthropological work is a completely accurate account of a contemporary culture, for that culture today is not quite the same as it was when it was visited and studied by the ethnographer. Although primitive societies are undoubtedly more conservative than civilized ones, there is no culture in the world that remains completely static, year in and year out. We might also add that some primitive societies are more conservative than others and in every culture some aspects or institutions tend to change more rapidly than others. In discussing this phenomenon of human society Raymond Firth (1958:149) maintains that the "bony structure," i.e., the basic underlying principles that give a culture form and meaning, is not easily altered, but the "flesh and blood," the traits and complexes that fill out the cultural configuration, can and do change quite rapidly.

The validity of this principle can readily be seen by looking at our own American cultural system. There are certain moral, religious, social, and political principles that are nearly as strong today as they were when our country was founded. The Puritan morality of early New England survives in various parts of the country in the form of Blue Laws, Prohibition, and anti-evolution movements and parties, Sunday closing laws, movie and book censorship, and dozens of other restrictions.

Although these underlying principles remain recognizable, there have been alterations and realignments of the associated cultural elements. The church remains a dominant force in our culture as far as morality is concerned, but there have been changes in its role. While the church continues to minister to the spiritual needs of its members, it also provides recreation, education, and even social and psychological counseling. It is often the sponsor of Boy Scout troops, drama clubs, and athletic teams.

Our ideal of what the American family should be socially and morally has prevailed over a great period of time, but the family itself has certainly changed from colonial and frontier days—in size, in function, and in structure.

Lower animals are born to behave in a given way and the behavior of their species is subject to change only if subsequent generations experience a change in physical type. Man, however, is a cultural animal and one of the most characteristic things about his manners and mores is that unique circumstances within the culture or exposure to the ideas of another culture can cause him to arbitrarily drop old ideas and adopt new ones.

INTERNAL CHANGE

Changes that spring from within a society may be either of a technological or a social nature. In other words, they may involve new kinds of gadgets like helicopters or electronic ovens or they may involve new and different values, ideologies, or social procedures. The "sit-in" is a social invention just as were the ideas of laissez faire, universal suffrage, and social security. These things may be termed inventions because like artifacts they represent new cultural ideas that did not previously exist in the society. Sometimes inventions, social and technological, represent an entirely new principle or they may merely involve a special or novel application of a known principle to a new situation. An example of the latter is the military prep school, where the principles of military training and discipline have been borrowed from the armed forces and applied to the area of elementary and secondary education.

Causes of Internal Change

What are the reasons for a society altering an institution that has perhaps remained quite stable for many generations? Here are a few of them.

POPULATION PRESSURE. Population pressure may force a change in social structure or in residence or subsistence patterns. One of the most striking examples of the effect of population growth on culture occurred in Europe during the nineteenth century. For hundreds of years

Europe had remained stable in its population and mode of life, but during the last century:

> . . . a combination of factors, no one of which can be completely isolated from the whole and weighed independently, began to disturb the balance. One factor of outstanding significance was clearly the growing pressure of the population itself. It was that as much as anything which was responsible for the breakdown of the old established order. For a succession of crises was thereby created, necessitating new forms of economic, political, and community organization, new institutional and technical developments, new ideologies and programs of reform. Much of Europe was in fact remade as a result. The old bounds of community and cultural life were literally burst asunder. European society could not reorder and readjust itself rapidly enough to meet conditions and at the same time contain itself; it therefore overflowed. Tens of millions of people began to migrate to the new world. In this movement appeared the evidence that profound change was sweeping through the whole social structure. (Sims 1939:247–48)

CHANGE IN CLIMATE. A change in climate may cause a society to adopt new subsistence methods, clothing styles, and diet. For an example of this we may take what happened at the end of the great Ice Age period. V. Gordon Childe describes the situation as follows:

> . . . Ice Age Europe . . . produced a dazzling culture . . . made possible by the food supply bounteously provided by glacial conditions . . . With the end of the ice age these conditions passed away. As the glaciers melted, forest invaded tundras and steppes, and the herds of mammoths, reindeer, bison and horse migrated or died out. With their disappearance the culture of societies which preyed upon them also withered away . . .
> By contrast to what had passed away, the mesolithic societies leave an impression of extreme poverty. (1948:43)

The most important aspect of the Mesolithic changes in climate was the growth of forests. In place of the great herds of game that had been characteristic of the Upper Paleolithic, Mesolithic species consisted of the stag deer, aurochs (wild cattle), wild boars, and hares. The majority of these animals had to be hunted individually rather than in herds. No doubt this circumstance brought about the domestication of the dog as an aid in hunting. The people of Mesolithic Europe, many of them no doubt the descendants of the Paleolithic hunters, also came to depend upon shellfish, fish, and waterfowl. During this time habitation sites were first located along beaches, at river mouths, and on the shores of lakes. We must not suppose that these changes in culture took place overnight or even within one man's lifetime. Those people who remained in Europe gradually altered their culture to meet the problems of their environment over a period of a thousand years or more.

An example of a slightly different type involves the Maori of New Zealand. This is a case of changes required of people who migrated to a new climate. Changes had to be made more rapidly than in the case of the people of the Mesolithic and greater adjustment was required on the part of the individual South Sea islander.

The Maoris migrated in a great flotilla from Central Polynesia, probably Tahiti, in about the year 1350 A.D. When they arrived at their destination, New Zealand, they found that the temperate climate of this area would require changes in their basic pattern of living that would be nothing less than revolutionary. Maori carpenters trained in the construction of airy thatched houses were forced to build insulated planked longhouses of heavy construction in order to keep out the cold. In the new climate, tapa cloth garments had to be abandoned, first because the paper mulberry plant from which tapa is made would not grow and, secondly, warmer clothing was required. The latter requirement was met by the development of a process of weaving flax into suitable garments. Perhaps the most drastic change concerned their basic diet. Breadfruit, bananas, and coconuts would not grow in New Zealand. Taro and yams could be raised, but only with great difficulty and only in certain regions. The people adjusted by developing the fern root as a vegetable staple and preyed upon sea birds and the giant ostrich-like moa for their protein.

While the temperate climate of New Zealand forced drastic changes in Maori living habits, certain areas of the culture continued in the traditional central Polynesian form. The institutions of family and government changed but little. Religion and mythology remained stable elements and language changed so little that even today it can easily be recognized as a central Polynesian dialect.

INNOVATORS AND REFORMERS. Especially gifted individuals may be born into a society, and their inquiring minds, searching for new and better ways of doing things, may conceive programs of reform or technological experimentation. It must be pointed out that such individuals are rare in primitive society, for the pressure is to conform, not to innovate. Progress and reform are to a great extent Western inventions. Robert Redfield has remarked that in "primitive societies uninfluenced by civilization the future is seen as a reproduction of the immediate past" (1958:120).

However, innovators and reformers have lived in every century and in every society. Legend tells us that Hiawatha one day conceived of an idea whereby all the warlike Iroquois tribes could live at peace with one another. He foresaw a time when they would come together in a great league or confederacy whereby they might work together rather than fight among themselves. Fired by this idea, he is supposed to have spent years traveling from tribe to tribe until he finally succeeded in persuading the tribal chiefs to try his unique idea. The League of the Iroquois, once established, lasted for more than four hundred years.

Whereas there is little chance of verifying the above legend, an incident concerning another reformer is a matter of recorded history. In the journals of the James and Bell expedition to Nebraska in 1818 there appears the story of a rather unusual young man, Petalesharoo, the son of Knife Chief of the Loup band of the Pawnee. The issue on which this young man broke with tradition and truly established himself as a reformer is described as follows by Redfield:

By ancient custom, this group of Pawnee each year sacrificed a captive to Venus, Morning Star, to ensure abundant crops. The victim, fattened and kept uninformed of the fate ahead, was on the proper day bound to a cross or scaffold, tomahawked, and shot with arrows. For several years Knife Chief "had regarded this sacrifice as an unnecessary and cruel exhibition of power, exercised upon unfortunate and defenseless individuals whom they were bound to protect; and he vainly endeavored to abolish it by philanthropic admonitions."

A young girl from another tribe was brought captive to the Pawnee village . . . She was bound to the cross when Knife Chief's son stepped forward "and in a hurried but firm manner, declared that it was his father's wish to abolish this sacrifice; that for himself, he had presented himself before them, for the purpose of laying down his life upon the spot, or of releasing his victim." He then cut the victim's cords, put her on a horse, mounted another and carried her to safety. (1958:130–31)[1]

CULTURE FATIGUE. Still another reason for internal change is suggested by A. L. Kroeber, who maintains that people may merely tire of a certain institution. A prime example of this kind of "cultural fatigue" concerns the sudden decision of the Hawaiians in 1819 (premissionary days) to abolish their ancient taboo system and repudiate their Polynesian gods. Of this incident Kroeber writes:

Strangely enough, the high priest of the islands was also active in the coterie, and in fact subsequently took the lead in extending the movement from mere abolition of the taboo (system) to the overthrow of the gods whose representative he was. This man seemingly had everything to lose by the change, and it is difficult to imagine what he could have had to gain . . . He evidently represented, therefore, an element in the population that was psychologically ready for a breach with established religion, from internal reasons. (1948:403)

Kroeber further suggests that this kind of "cultural fatigue" or disillusionment finds parallels in the defeatist attitude in France in 1940, the attitude toward the 1929 depression in America, which brought on

---

[1] Copyright, 1953, by Cornell University. Used by permission of Cornell University Press.

the New Deal, or the Japanese Emperor's renunciation of divinity at the end of World War II.

While we have pointed out a number of ways in which the members of a culture themselves may be prompted to find new solutions for old problems, it must be remarked that most societies, if left entirely to themselves, will remain quite stable. Once primitive people have found workable solutions to the challenges of everyday living, they show little interest in inventiveness or experimentation. However, Nadel reminds us that such people show "little hesitation in copying (or borrowing) novel methods, that is, in adopting them when they can be seen *in use*. The pull of tradition, then, means in fact reluctance to abandon a safe routine for risks that go with untried methods" (1953:267).

EXTERNAL CHANGE

Acculturation and Diffusion

The borrowing of ideas from a neighboring society has been referred to in anthropology as *diffusion* or *acculturation*. There has been some disagreement as to the proper definition of these terms, but we will make the following distinction: Acculturation represents a situation where borrowing and lending of cultural traits takes place between two societies living in continuous first-hand contact. Notable examples are White-Indian relations as they existed for some four hundred years of American history, the Maori and English contacts in New Zealand, or those of Arabs and Jews in the Middle East.

Diffusion, on the other hand, is also a borrowing phenomenon, but, as Winick defines it in his *Dictionary of Anthropology*, it may involve only "a part of a culture (spreading) to other areas" (1958:167). What might be spread may be only a single institution, invention, trait, or complex. A major distinguishing factor is that "although it is found in every example of acculturation, it can take place without the contact necessary in that process" (1958:168).

Herskovits, however, makes still another distinction between diffusion and acculturation. "Diffusion," he maintains "is the study of achieved cultural transmission" (1949:525). He reminds us that frequently such questions as how, when, where, and by whom the change was brought about are only matters of conjecture in diffusion studies. Having relegated diffusion to the past tense, Herskovits defines acculturation as "cultural transmission in process" (*ibid.*). In other words, acculturation is, in most cases, a contemporary phenomenon and the historical facts of contact are either known or obtainable.

Studies of acculturation and diffusion have become a major pursuit of anthropologists today. While an interest in culture change and culture transmission is as old as anthropology itself, never before have so many people come under the influence of Western culture and never before have people had such easy access to the ideas of others. The days are over when an ethnographer can settle down among an isolated untouched people and study their age-old traditions. In the course of his field study, every anthropologist today will find that if he wants to record truly indigenous customs and beliefs, they are to be found—if at all—only in the minds and memories of the old men and women. All too often the young people care little for the "old ways" and are more interested in dressing, behaving, and making money like the "white man." Thus, an accurate study of almost any primitive people today must of necessity take into consideration the influence of foreign (usually Western) cultures on the way of life.

Most anthropologists feel that they can make their greatest contribution in studying the processes of culture change. Change is certain, but the results of change cannot always be foreseen. Anthropology may never formulate *laws* of cultural change but, as Gillin puts it:

> If we know the conditions under which culture operates and lines of its internal integration and coordination, we are able to predict within certain limits what form and direction cultural change will take. . . . As prediction becomes possible, so control and manipulation of changes are possible. (1948:568–69)

Principles of Cultural Dynamics

Although anthropology has just scratched the surface in its understanding of cultural dynamics, the following are well-agreed upon principles.

SELECTIVE BORROWING. Borrowing is always selective. If a trait or a trait complex is to find acceptance in another culture, it must have utility, compatibility, and meaning in the adopting culture. What is more, it must lie within the area of culture where change is acceptable. We in America are exposed to all sorts of foreign ideas, but we incorporate only some of them into our cultural system. We accept Schiaparelli gowns from the French but not national socialism from the Swedes or hari-kari from the Japanese. The fashion world, like the world of mechanical gadgets in America, is one where the new and the novel have high prestige. But even here there is the matter of compatibility and meaning to be considered. The Schiaparelli dress has features that are definitely Western and in harmony with many American accessories. It is doubtful if a Siamese or Japanese fashion house utilizing traditional style features of those countries in their dresses could ever become as sought after as this famous French house. The Oriental dress with the slit skirt or the Indian sari may have brief fad acceptance in America, but it is unlikely that their influence would be lasting.

National socialism, on the other hand, appears, to the majority of Americans who value rugged individualism and a Jeffersonian variety of democracy, to be a direct threat to personal freedom and individual initiative.

Not only is hari-kari or any form of sanctioned suicide in direct opposition to the very foundation of American religious principles, but its practice is completely inconceivable to Americans. It involves a concept of "face" that has never become institutionalized in Western culture.

A new element coming into a culture has a tough gauntlet to run. It faces the vested interests, the difficulty of finding a congruous slot in an integrated cultural configuration, and also the temporal factor—it may be introduced before its time is ripe.

RATES OF TRANSMISSION. Cultural transmission takes place at different rates of speed. This point is closely tied to our earlier one concerning the selectivity of borrowing. The rate of adoption also depends upon the resistance it will meet in the various areas of the cultural configuration. A thing that is immediately seen to be more useful than an existing trait stands a good chance of gaining quick adoption, provided it can easily be integrated into the system and provided that it does not encounter the force of vested interests. The anthropological literature would tend to support the fact that simplicity in a cultural element facilitates transfer. Also, a trait of a nonsymbolic nature can be digested more rapidly by a culture than a symbolic one. It is also apparent that form transfers with greater speed than function. This fact is known all too well to missionaries in various parts of the world who have been very encouraged by the speed with which church attendance, hymn singing, and Bible reading have been accepted by a native people, but have then found that the outward forms of Christianity are much more quickly acquired than the regenerating influence it is meant to have in their lives. Furnas recalls a number of incidents in Oceania where this phenomenon was present. He writes:

The newly-converted natives of Anaa (Tuamotu) seized and plundered a ship suspected of pearling without a license, and then trooped in a body to church to give thanks for their loot. (1948:277)

On Tubuai (Australs) natives converted by L. M. S. teachers from Raiatea fought bloodily with natives converted by L. M. S. teachers from Tahiti over whether hymns should be sung standing or sitting, a matter which the L. M. S. had neglected to standardize. (1948:279)

Melville J. Herskovits has called attention to the concept of *cultural focus* as being a major consideration in the rate of cultural transmission. Herskovits believes that:

. . . the greatest variation in form is to be found in the aspect of a culture that is focal to the interests of a people. This variation, by implication suggests that the focal aspect has undergone greater changes than other elements . . . We find that where cultures are in free contact, the focal aspect will be likely to be the one where new elements are most hospitably received. (1949:549–50)

In a work entitled *Cultural Dynamics and Administration* (1953b) the late Felix Keesing analyzed a number of acculturation situations and generalized that the areas of culture that tend to be resistant to change are those pertaining to basic survival, security, integrity, value, and problem-solving. Specifically, he found the more conservative aspects to be those having to do with (1) psychosomatic conditioning, (2) communication, (3) primary group relations, (4) prestige status maintenance, (5) territorial security, and (6) religious security. He found that not only were these areas resistant to change but if change should be forced it would be with maximum disturbance and tension.

On the other hand, he found that areas of culture responsive to change are those concerned with (1) tools, (2) etiquette, (3) military tactics, (4) voluntary elements of taste and self-expression, (5) achieved status systems, (6) competitive types of behavior, and (7) mass social structure.

From the writings in Personality and Culture comes still further light on the problem of conservativism and the lack of it. There is a good deal of evidence to support the theory that those aspects of a culture learned through conditioning as a child will tend to be more resistant to change than those things acquired as an adult. Examples of stable elements are language, facial expression, moral and ethical standards, and basic food preferences.

An interesting example of how things learned as an adult can be more easily changed than those things learned as a child, is to be found in Margaret Mead's writings about cultural change in the Manus Islands. In 1928 Mead found the Manus people plagued with a variety of taboos and avoidances, a great inequality between the sexes, and a puritanical sex code that equated the sex act with excretion. She also found that most of these unpleasant and restricting aspects were part of the adult world only. One might say that the young were exposed to the better side of the value system. From mere babies they were trained to be independent, alert, and resourceful. Children did not play at adult activities and therefore the adult world of ritual, taboo, and fear was little known to them. Thus, when change came crashing down on these Melanesian people through the medium of World War II, the personality traits gained in childhood aided them in accepting new ideas and techniques. The later-acquired values of the adult world were replaced by a European value system, which proved to be more satisfying.

INVOLUNTARY CHANGE

The relative difference in rate of adoption of culture items also depends to a great extent on whether change is voluntary or involuntary. As Keesing states:

> The fieldworker . . . is likely . . . to encounter numerous case examples of arbitrary manipulation in terms of governmental, missionary, or other outsiders or by internal elites or other authorities: the process is doubtless as old as human history." (1953:81)

Examples of such change are easily found. If it had not been for the insistence of Hiram Bingham and his Yankee missionaries, the Hawaiian women would probably have taken considerable time in exchanging tapa cloth wrap-arounds for Mother Hubbards. And many a South American Indian has given up headhunting prematurely at the request of government officials. However, Herskovits maintains that there are certain areas of culture which are resistant to any amount of manipulation. While it has been pointed out that the *focus* aspects of a culture are often areas where there is great interest in new ideas, Herskovits also observes that "in situations where one people is dominated by another, and pressure is brought against customs lying in the focal aspect, retention will be achieved by devious ways . . ." (1949: 550). What is meant by "devious ways" is that the customs will either go underground or they will be reinterpreted so that they will appear less objectionable to the dominant culture.

REINTERPRETATION

Because no two cultural configurations are exactly the same, and because a cultural configuration is an integrated and compatible bundle of meaningful traits, complexes, and patterns, a borrowed item will often have to be reinterpreted to have meaning and utility in the borrower's culture. Reinterpretation may be defined as the process whereby either the form or the function of a trait is altered to enhance its meaning or compatibility in the borrowing culture. An example of this principle first at the level of material culture is the case of the New Guinea canoe paddle that moved inland. It is a common pattern in parts of this island for new ideas (perhaps obtained through voyages to other islands) to originate in the coastal villages. As members of the inland tribes come to the coast to trade, they also observe the new

Reinterpretation—A Samoan *fale* of traditional design is "thatched" with galvanized iron rather than sugar cane leaves.

artifacts, ceremonies, and ideas of their more sophisticated seagoing neighbors and often carry home a few new ideas to try out themselves. On one of these visits an inland native became enamoured with a canoe paddle he observed in one of the coast villages. The laurel leaf shape of the blade pleased him greatly so he purchased it and eagerly bore it home with him. The main problem was that in his area there were no navigable rivers or lakes, thus no canoes to propel. If the paddle were to catch on in this new setting, its function would have to be changed. In this particular case our story has a happy ending, for a few weeks later when a large ceremony was held several of the men appeared twirling dance batons shaped very much like laurel leaf-bladed canoe paddles.

It is possible to point up a number of cultural traits that have undergone reinterpretation before they could be adopted into American culture. A fascinating example is the form of Italian pizza pie in the Middle West. Pizza probably diffused to the United States in the twenties or thirties but remained a localized delicacy in certain eastern seaboard states until the end of World War II. At this time it rapidly spread to every part of the country. Originally, this Italian pie was made with mozarella or scamorza cheese, tomatoes, highly spiced sausage, oregano spice, and a crust made of flour, water, olive oil, and yeast. Although this type of pizza is still found in most eastern cities, and in midwestern ones as well, in many cases the dish has been reinterpreted to meet midwestern taste preferences for bland food. Authentic Italian pizza in such states as Kansas, Missouri, Iowa, Nebraska, or the Dakotas is often considered too spicy; therefore, it is possible to purchase in restaurants or in supermarkets pizzas that are topped with American process cheese, have no oregano at all, and, in place of spiced sausage, hamburger or even tuna fish rounds out the Americanized version. In many home recipes, the crust is made of biscuit mix. Although the Italians would hardly recognize it, it still carries the name pizza and has become extremely popular.

A final example of reinterpretation in American culture concerns the Maori greenstone fertility pendants, which are known as *hei tiki*. This borrowing situation is described by the Maori anthropologist Sir Peter Buck as follows:

The Red Cross in Auckland brought joy to the hearts of numbers of convalescent American soldiers during World War II by giving each one a small nephite *tiki* as a good luck talisman. As a result a new myth was born, for in the United States the *tiki* is regarded not as a fructifying symbol for women but as a protective war amulet for men. (1958:301)

BORROWING AND FUSION OF CULTURES

Whenever two societies live in continuous first-hand contact, borrowing is a two-way process. For a long time it was believed that prolonged contact between a "civilized" and a "primitive" culture resulted in the latter's soaking up all of the ideas and traits of the former but having none of its own borrowed. This, of course, was built on the idea that a "superior" culture had nothing to learn or take from an "inferior" one. No anthropologist today would venture such a statement for they know that advanced technology does not necessarily make a culture superior. We know that when members of different cultures meet day after day, both give and take cultural traits. We may be certain that the New England colonists considered themselves vastly superior to the American aborigines with whom they lived side by side, yet we know that three hundred or more years of contact have resulted in a great deal of cultural borrowing in both directions. The white man brought the horse but borrowed the canoe; while many American Indians today live in European style houses, many Americans spend at least their two weeks' vacation living in a tent. American Indian Jim Thorpe was a nationally known All-American college and pro-football player, while many an Ivy League college student plays on a varsity lacrosse team. In the area of foodstuffs, the white man got somewhat the better of the deal. He borrowed corn, beans, squash, hominy, popcorn, wild rice, melons, cocoa, tomatoes, pumpkins, potatoes, and turkeys. Probably no other American product has experienced such mass consumption or created such wealth for its producers as tobacco—also a gift from the American Indian. One often wonders what the names of scores of towns, rivers, counties, and states might have been if it had not been for their Indian namesakes, and one even wonders if our constitution might not have been somewhat different if it had not been for its prototype in the League of the Iroquois. Shifting our focus from North American to South American acculturation and considering Negro-white as well as Indian-white contacts, we find in the writing of Melville J. Herskovits that the same type of mutual borrowing existed there. He writes:

Negroes who were brought to Brazil influenced the culture of the dominant Portuguese, themselves migrants, and subject to Indian influence as well. These varied influences are to be seen merged in such widely differing aspects of modern Brazilian life as the cuisine, the social structure, beliefs of various sorts, current musical forms and linguistic usages, to say nothing of the extensive retentions of African belief and behavior that were maintained by the Africans themselves. (1949:533)

BORROWING AND FUSION OF CULTURES

Where there is continuous first hand contact between groups with different cultures we might expect, although it is not inevitable, that the two will eventually fuse their cultural systems. Just because two people live side by side does not mean that they will accept one another's ideas. History records that the Hakka and Punti people lived side by side in a valley of Southern China for nearly a thousand years without exchanging any cultural traits whatsoever.

More typically, however, two peoples living in such circumstances would be involved in much mutual borrowing that would lead ultimately to a fusion of culture known as *assimilation*. Assimilation represents a situation not where one society abandons its culture in favor of its neighbors but rather where the two will fuse to form a new society and culture. When this happens, the final product will be a culture having elements of the two contact societies represented in varying proportions. There will also be some new traits that were found in neither of the parent cultures. An example of assimilation in America is cited by Linton as follows:

> Thus the Italians in America usually lose their identity as a distinct society by the third or fourth generation and accept the culture in which they then find themselves. At the same time this culture is not the same which their ancestors encountered on arrival. It has been enriched by the American acceptance of such originally Italian elements as a popular interest in grand opera, spaghetti dinners,. . . (1936:335)

and we might add art movies and Ferrari sports cars.

And of Europe, Kroeber writes:

> The Norman and Saxon fusion after 1066 is a familiar instance. Within three centuries these two strains were assimilated in culture, speech, and mainly in blood. English civilization was greatly enriched by the infusion of the large Norman-French element into the Anglo-Saxon, so that by say 1400 it had come to approximate more nearly French culture in its level; but of course it remained definitely distinct from French. (1948:429)

Pitcairn Island Assimilation

One of the most controlled scientific studies of cultures in contact was that carried out by Harry Shapiro on Pitcairn Island. The reader will perhaps recall that in the year 1789 a mutiny occurred on H.M.S. *Bounty* while it was under the command of Lt. William Bligh. Immediately after casting Bligh and several loyal crew members adrift in the *Bounty*'s cutter, the twenty-five mutineers led by Fletcher Christian sailed to nearby Tahiti where they took aboard twelve Tahitian women and six Tahitian men. Selecting Pitcairn Island as their retreat from justice, the fugitives founded a society that would exist in complete isolation for nearly seventy years. The Pitcairn culture that emerged had, as might be expected, traits that were partly Tahitian, partly English, and partly original. Shapiro, who studied the society and culture in 1934, describes the strange blend of traits in the construction of their houses. He writes,

> We find them . . . building houses ingeniously put together, the frame mortised, the walls ingeniously constructed of roughly hewn planks fitted into slotted uprights, the interiors provided with bunks as in a ship's cabin. The roof, however, was thatched in the Tahitian manner. (1953:41)

Table 4 describes the kaleidoscopic nature of the assimilation.

Table 4. Origin of elements of culture in Pitcairn
(Shapiro 1953:42).

	Tahitian	English	Original
The household arts:			
Underground oven	+		
Food preparation	+		
Tapa-making	+		
Use of calabash	+		
Dress style	+		
Hats	+		
Houses:			
Building materials		+	
Structure		+	+
Roof thatch	+		
Arrangement			+
Household equipment:			
Furniture		+	
"Linens"	+		
Lighting	+		
Fishing:			
Gear		+	
Methods	+	+	
Boats	+		+
Agriculture:			
Tools		+	
Methods	+	+	
Family life			+
Social life:			
Social organization			+
Separation of sexes at meals	+		
Position of women			+
Dance	+		
Music	+	+	
Surf-riding	+		
Kite-flying	+	+	
Private ownership of land		+	
Common fund			+
Education		+	
Religion		+	+

DIFFUSION AND CULTURE COMPLEXITY

In a previous chapter it was pointed out that the more complex societies of the world have been those most exposed to the cultures of others, for the cross-fertilization of ideas enriches any culture by providing it with innovations it may not develop itself. All too frequently differences in the level of cultural accomplishments have been explained in terms of superior or inferior intelligence. Ralph Linton has pointed out the embarrassing fact that even the most sophisticated of societies have invented only a small percentage of the cultural traits they utilize. To get some idea of the amount of borrowing that has been necessary in order to produce our complex American culture let us look at the day of an average American as humorously described by Linton:

Our solid American citizen awakens in a bed built on a pattern which originated in the Near East but which was modified in Northern Europe before it was transmitted to America. He throws back covers made from cotton, domesticated in India, or linen, domesticated in the Near East, or wool from sheep, also domesticated in the Near East, or silk, the use of which was discovered in China. All of these materials have been spun and woven by processes invented in the Near East. He slips into his moccasins, invented by the Indians of the Eastern woodlands, and goes to the bathroom, whose fixtures are a mixture of European and American inventions, both of recent date. He takes off his pajamas, a garment invented in India, and washes with soap invented by the ancient Gauls. He then shaves, a masochistic rite which seems to have been derived from either Sumer or ancient Egypt.

Returning to the bedroom, he removes his clothes from a chair of southern European type and proceeds to dress. He puts on garments whose form originally derived from the skin clothing of the nomads of the Asiatic steppes, puts on shoes made from skins tanned by a process invented in ancient Egypt and cut to a pattern derived from the classical civilizations of the Mediterranean, and ties around his neck a strip of bright-colored cloth which is a vestigial survival of the shoulder shawls worn by the seventeenth-century Croatians. Before going out for breakfast he glances through the window, made of glass invented in Egypt, and if it is raining puts on overshoes made of rubber, discovered by the Central American Indians and takes an umbrella, invented in Southeastern Asia. Upon his head he puts a hat made of felt, a material invented in the Asiatic steppes.

On his way to breakfast he stops to buy a paper, paying for it with coins, an ancient Lydian invention. At the restaurant a whole new series of borrowed elements confronts him. His plate is made of a form of pottery invented in China. His knife is of steel, an alloy first made in southern India, his fork a medieval Italian invention, and his spoon a derivation of a Roman original. He begins breakfast with an orange, from the eastern Mediterranean, a canteloupe from Persia, or perhaps a piece of African watermelon. With this he has coffee, an Abyssinian plant, with cream and sugar. Both the domestication of cows and the idea of milking them originated in the Near East, while sugar was first made in India. After his fruit and first coffee he goes on to waffles, cakes made by a Scandinavian technique from wheat domesticated in Asia Minor. Over these he pours maple syrup, invented by the Indians of the Eastern woodlands. As a side dish he may have the egg of a species of bird domesticated in Indo-China, or thin strips of the flesh of an animal domesticated in Eastern Asia which have been salted and smoked by a process developed in northern Europe.

When our friend has finished eating he settles back to smoke, an American Indian habit, consuming a plant domesticated in Brazil in either a pipe, derived from the Indians of Virginia, or a cigarette, derived from Mexico. If he is hardy enough he may even attempt a cigar, transmitted to us from the Antilles by way of Spain. While smoking he reads the news of the day, imprinted in characters invented by the ancient Semites upon a material invented in China by a process invented in Germany. As he absorbs the accounts of foreign troubles he will, if he is a good conservative citizen, thank a Hebrew deity in an Indo-European language that he is 100 per cent American. (1936:326–27)

RAMIFICATIONS OF CHANGE

Before closing our discussion of cultural change, it will be worth-while to comment on the ramifications of change in terms of social integration, emotional stability of the individual, and group morale. In situations of change, people and cultures must adjust and the problem is to achieve the least amount of personal and group disorganization with the amount of change that is inevitable in our modern industrial world. There are anthropologists who might favor a "keep primitives primitive" policy believing that they will be better off in the long run. While this is probably true, it is a most artificial and unworkable solution that most primitives would oppose themselves. The answer is not to stop change but to channel it, or at least attain some measure of success in predicting what will happen under certain conditions of change, as for example if the wrong kind of change is forced upon a people or if it comes too rapidly. We know that it is possible for societies to become so disorganized through revolutionary change that they can completely lose their cultural identity. The Inca made it a policy to destroy the cultures they conquered. By moving out great numbers of the population and replacing them with peoples from foreign cultures they were successful in dividing peoples and imposing both their rule and their culture on them.

A similar but perhaps less studied result occurred in much of Mela-nesia. Here, colonial administration coupled with blackbirding, eco-nomic exploitation, and mission ardor succeeded in breaking down the culture to such an extent that many of the people lost their will to live. Rivers reported in 1922 that some peoples were unwilling to bear or care for children and they took no interest in educating or socializing them. Thus, they existed as a people without hope and without faith in their old culture or an understanding of the new.

Steel Axes in Australia

The effects of what might be considered a very minor change are often unpredictable and may be demoralizing to a highly integrated cultural and social system. Such was the case among the Yir Yoront group of northeastern Australia. One would hardly think that a change in axe blades could precipitate a chain of events that would undermine the foundations of the whole society but that is exactly what happened.

Lauriston Sharp, who studied these Australian aborigines in 1933–35, tells us that prior to the introduction of steel axe blades, the blades were made of stone. They were produced and owned only by the men but used to a great extent by the women and children and there was a pattern of borrowing axes from specific male relatives. This helped maintain a system of superordination-subordination. During the dry season fiesta-like tribal gatherings were held which featured exchanges between traditional trading partners. These occasions were anxiously awaited as it was sometimes possible to acquire a whole year's supply of stone axe heads from one's trading partner.

When steel axes began to appear in the area, the local mission purchased a supply of them and began to dispense them to worthy parishioners. "By winning the favor of the mission staff," Sharp writes, "a woman might be given a steel axe. This was clearly intended to be hers. The situation was quite different from that involved in borrowing an axe from a male relative, with the result that a woman called such an axe 'my' steel axe, a possessive form she never used for a stone axe" (1952:83–84). Not only were the steel axes introducing new linguistic forms but also a more serious social situation "in which a wife or young son . . . need no longer bow to the husband or father, who was left confused and insecure as he asked to borrow a steel axe from them" (*Ibid.*:86).

The whole concept of ownership became confused and stealing and trespassing began to occur. The annual festivals, so anticipated by trading partners, declined because a single steel axe might last several years. As this festival waned, so did interest in the religious and social events that were associated with it.

Thus, we see that a steel axe blade introduced by people who conscientiously wanted to help the Yir Yoront produced a situation that is summed up by Sharp as follows:

> The most disturbing effects of the steel axe, operating in conjunction with other elements also being introduced from the white man's several sub-cultures, developed in the realm of traditional ideas, sentiments and values. These were undermined at a rapidly mounting rate, without new conceptions being defined to replace them. The result was a mental and moral void which foreshadowed the collapse and destruction of all Yir Yoront culture, if not, indeed, the extinction of the biological group itself. (*Ibid.*:85)

Profiting from the experience of what happened to the Yir Yoront and other broken cultures, students of change such as Felix Keesing have drafted generalizations about cultural change and disorganization such as the following, which prove very valuable rules of thumb. He writes:

So far as groups and individuals in a dynamic situation have their self-esteem little impaired, retain confidence that they are keeping in touch with the best sources of security, power and prestige, and so maintain a high level of morale, they will tend to remain "well integrated"; cultural fundamentals are likely to be highly persistent, and voluntary cultural change may occur with a minimum of tension and disorganization. So far as they feel superior, in relation to groups and individuals with whom they are in contact, their culture may be held to the more firmly, or change may go further with little tension. By contrast, to the extent that groups and individuals come to feel themselves inferior, lose confidence in their basic sources of security, power and prestige, and so lapse in morale, the way is opened for extensive and even drastic change. Unless reasonably satisfying cultural substitutes can be found, extreme disorganization and emotional stress will occur. (1953:89)

In ancient Samoa there was a sport for high chiefs known as *seuga lupe* (pigeon-netting). The platforms on which the chiefs stood while trying to snare the birds were often set up out on the reef. On rough days there was always the possibility of being washed off the platform. This explains the meaning of the Samoan proverbial saying *Seu le manu ae taga'i le galu* (Catch the pigeon but look out for the waves) or in modern terms as the motto of American Samoa "Progress with Caution." Many a trusteeship or colonial or newly independent government would do well to bear this proverb in mind, for every culture, no matter how unimportant in world affairs, that fades away and dies is a loss to mankind as a whole.

SUGGESTED READINGS

ADAMS, ROBERT M. "The Origin of Cities," *Scientific American,* September, 1960. (The urban revolution in Mesopotamia.)

BENEDICT, RUTH. "Anthropology and Cultural Change," *American Scholar,* 11:243, 1941–42. (How anthropology's breadth of interests has been an asset to the study of cultural change.)

COLLIER, JOHN, and COLLIER, MARY. "An Experiment in Applied Anthropology," *Scientific American,* January, 1957. (Social and cultural changes are brought about by working within the existing structure of a Peruvian village.)

DOZIER, EDWARD P. "The Hopi and the Tewa," *Scientific American,* June, 1957. (How the encroachment of Western culture has brought together two Indian cultures that have remained distinct for centuries.)

ERASMUS, CHARLES J. "An Anthropologist Looks at Technical Assistance," *Scientific Monthly,* March, 1954. (Personal observations of attempts to direct or accelerate culture change in Latin American countries.)

HEINE-GELDERN, R. "Vanishing Cultures," *Scientific American*, May, 1957. (Stresses the importance of studying rapidly disappearing cultures.)

MALINOWSKI, BRONISLAW. "The Pan-African Problem of Culture Contact," *American Journal of Sociology*, 48:649, 1943. (The problem of cultural identity faced by acculturated Africans.)

TURNBULL, COLIN. "The Lesson of the Pygmies," *Scientific American*, January, 1963. (How the pygmies of the Congo have maintained their cultural integrity in changing times.)

WHITE, LESLIE. "Man's Control over Civilization: An Anthropocentric Illusion," *Scientific Monthly*, March, 1948. (Takes the position that man has very little control over his changing culture.)

Paperbound books

BARNETT, H. G. *Innovation: The Basis of Cultural Change*. McGraw-Hill. (The conditions under which innovation has occurred in six different cultures.)

BASCOM, W. R., and HERSKOVITS, M. J. (eds.). *Continuity and Change in African Cultures*. University of Chicago Press. (Essays dealing with the study of cultural dynamics in Africa by Herskovits' students.)

HERSKOVITS, M. J. *Cultural Dynamics*. Knopf. (Reprint of sections of Herskovits' *Cultural Anthropology* that deal with problems of cultural change.)

MALINOWSKI, BRONISLAW. *Dynamics of Culture Change*. Yale University Press. (Consideration of the acculturation process in African cultures.)

MEAD, MARGARET (ed.). *Culture Patterns and Technical Change*. New American Library of World Literature, Inc. (The impact of modern technical advances on traditional life in five societies.)

————. *New Lives for Old*. New American Library of World Literature, Inc. (Radical revision of a South Sea island culture resulting from contact with American culture during World War II.)

REDFIELD, ROBERT. *The Primitive World and its Transformations*. Cornell University Press. (The impact of urbanization and civilization on the minds and manners of primitives.)

————. *Village That Chose Progress*. University of Chicago Press. (A society chooses technological advance but suffers a decline in religious faith and traditional values.)

15

Anthropological Perspective in the Study of Personality

It is commonly thought that the study of personality is the preroga-tive of the psychologists but for some thirty or forty years, anthropolo-gists have been interested in the development of personality, particu-larly from the point of view of how it is influenced by the forces of culture. More than any other scientist, the anthropologist has been struck by the many directions that personality development can take throughout the world. Observing that behavior and temperament can be radically different from one place to another, the anthropologist has become very wary of such popular statements as "It's just human nature to want to get ahead," or "Human nature being what it is, what can you expect." While the layman glibly makes such pronouncements, students of anthropology, who have been able to view many cultures, would doubt that when it comes to temperament and behavior, there is any such thing as a common "human nature" shared by all men. The person who assumes that "human nature" is the same everywhere is so involved in his own way of life that he begins to feel that everything he does is natural for the species. Perhaps a much more valid term to refer to the way men typically think and act and feel in a given culture would be "cultural nature." Depending upon how a man's culture shapes him and rewards him, he may be selfish, generous, mild, pugnacious, cooperative, modest, or boastful. Margaret Mead found that culture can even influence the behavior and personality which are considered masculine or feminine in a society.

Because the term "human nature" has been erroneously used does not mean that it is a bad concept; on the contrary, it is a useful concept if used correctly. In order to understand the relationship between human nature and cultural nature let us look at the following statement by Kluckhohn and Murray:

> Every man is in certain respects
> a. like all other men,
> b. like some other men,
> c. like no other man. (1949:35)

LIKE ALL OTHER MEN

Men are in certain respects like all other men in that they *do* have a human nature. This is the nature of the human animal arising out of the fact that man is one species and shares the same kind of basic physiology. It is the nature of man to experience live birth, feel pain, meet with hunger, respond to feelings of sexual excitement, weaken with age, and finally die. Man walks upright on the earth, he does not burrow in the ground, live in the trees or under the sea, or fly through the air under his own power like the birds. Men have a certain set of needs that must be met, certain physical and mental limitations, and certain abilities. At the moment of birth, every child of every race and culture shares these things in common, it is his heritage as a human, his human nature. From that moment on, however, this bundle of raw material will be shaped by its group and its culture. The processes of developing a human being might be compared to the process of a sculptor carving a statue out of wood. The sculptor knows the limitations and strengths of his material, and he must work in terms of the nature of it. As long as he observes certain precautions, he knows that he can develop a finished product. Two sculptors, however, both working in terms of the nature of the same raw material, might fashion quite different products, one producing a heavy and strong figure, the other a delicate, fragile, and beautiful one. The two figures will be alike in some respects—in their material, with its color and grain, but they will also differ greatly in their appearance due to the different approaches of the two artists. For human beings, this development of a finished product from a raw material amounts to growing up in a culture with its own unique material artifacts, ideologies, system of family, and configuration of values.

LIKE SOME OTHER MEN

Since all people in a given society share much the same culture, they will have had similar experiences and therefore can be expected to demonstrate similarities in personality. In even the most heterogeneous of cultures fellow members share a common language with its inherent values and a similar ideological orientation. In less heterogeneous cultures they will have experienced a similar childhood training experience. Although we must keep in mind that culture is but one of many forces helping to mold personality, let us look at the experiences of the Alorese child as he learns his culture and see how it helps in shaping his adult behavior.

Alorese Culture and Personality

Alor is an island in Indonesia but its inhabitants are Oceanic Negroes. The village of Atimelang, lying high on a volcanic ridge, was the site of one of the first detailed studies of culture and personality carried out by a cultural anthropologist. The investigator, Cora Du-Bois, reports that these people are agriculturalists, deriving their daily food requirements primarily from corn, peas, rice, and squash and occasionally from chickens, pigs, and dogs. The women are the principal cultivators and the men concern themselves mainly with the raising of pigs. The village is largely self-sufficient, but food is a source of much anxiety. The people might be described as highly materialistic, and every trading transaction within the society involves the expectation of profit. There is very little hospitality. Wealth determines status, and marriage is accompanied by financial exchanges of dowry and bride price.

The child growing up in this society experiences many frustrations, the most severe being connected with food. Since the women are the tillers of the soil, and thus frequently away from the village, small children are placed in the care of older siblings, who are often careless about providing them with nourishment. Weaning is described as being done "gradually and simply by pushing the child gently away from the breast" (1961:40).[1] The overly insistent child however is likely to get slapped. Should these measures not prove sufficient, the child is taken to live in the household of a relative for a few nights.

Toilet-training is also described as a gradual and easy process. An

[1] From: *The People of Alor: A Social-Psychological Study of an East Indian Island* by Cora DuBois. The University of Minnesota Press, Minneapolis. Copyright 1944 by the University of Minnesota.

occasional child may get a rap on the head with the mother's knuckles for his lack of control, but generally this aspect of training is rather smooth and without incident. Alorese parents appear to be little concerned about whether or not their offspring get sufficient rest. Lack of proper bedtimes and numerous sleep-disturbing activities in the average household result in children learning to sleep whenever and wherever they can.

Discipline often involves shaming, ridiculing, and even frightening children by brandishing knives and threatening to cut off ears or hands. While children are not, in general, treated harshly, the kind of discipline is so inconsistent that they are never able to "establish a clear image of punishment for 'being bad' or reward for 'being good.' They are just as likely as not to be rewarded for the 'badness' of excessive crying" (1961:51). There is little in the way of rewards for being good and on such occasions when children are promised a reward for good behavior, the promise is rarely kept.

Rages and tantrums are commonplace among the children of this society, a common cause being desertion by the mother when she leaves to work in the fields. Like discipline in general, her reaction to the wailing child is one of inconsistency. Concerning the mother's responses DuBois writes, "On successive days I have noted her ignore him, return to comfort him, return to slap him, and return pretending to stay for the day, only to slip away when he had been diverted" (*Ibid.*).

Later childhood is a period when some of the child's earlier anxieties are reinforced. Food still remains a problem. Children are fed at 7 A.M. and 7 P.M. but between these hours they have to learn to forage for themselves. In time, they learn any number of ingenious ways, including theft, of getting midday nourishment. Parents are not above appropriating the property of their children, who must stand helplessly by without any source of redress. Another cause of frustration among prepuberty children is the continuation of teasing, ridicule, and deception as a form of both discipline and amusement.

DuBois records, "I have seen youths in their late teens and early twenties send boys on fool's errands and deceive them with false promises of rewards for services, and then guffaw with laughter when the crestfallen child returned" (1961:65).

The consequence of such behavior is that lying is taken as a matter of course and to call a person a liar is not an insult or a reproach but merely a statement of fact. While children in late childhood no longer are deceived by bogeymen stories or threats of amputating ears or hands, they respond to suggestions that they will be sold into slavery. There is little in this period of their development that would allow them to develop feelings of trust or loyalty toward others and "the lack of training and praise, as well as the presence of teasing, ridicule, and fear, combined with lack of privileges and esteem, must create in the child an essential distrust of itself" (1961:79).

As the child approaches adulthood, it is possible to see the effect of childhood cultural experiences on his attitudes and behavior toward marriage partners. As young men begin their search for a wife, they unconsciously, or consciously in some cases, seek a mother image. As her chief interpreter related to Cora DuBois, "Wives are like our mothers. When we were small our mothers fed us. When we are grown our wives cook for us" (1961:96). Since women do most of the farming, they tend also to be the backbone of the economy.

One of the many problems in Alor relationships, however, is that the male tends to be somewhat ambivalent toward his "mother image," for childhood recollections of the mother are not altogether pleasant ones. Mother was a somewhat unreliable and uncertain provider. Women, on the other hand, are somewhat reticent to accept the role of provider with its greater economic responsibilities, especially where this added burden brings little increase in status. In order to obtain a wife, a young man must produce a rather substantial bride price, which is paid to her kinsmen, and frequently a new bride will refuse her husband sexual privileges if his financial arrangements with her family have not been satisfactorily settled. Wealth is of great importance both in obtaining a good provider and in establishing self-esteem, through freedom from dependency on the woman. Thus, DuBois concludes that "the culture fosters a linkage of food, sex, and wealth. All three of these are associated with many avenues of possible frustrations and prepare the ground for instability and distrust in the marital relationship" (1961:115).

In keeping the cultural experiences of the Alorese childhood, adolescence, and young adulthood in mind it is interesting to note some of the more commonly found personality characteristics of adults. Abram Kardiner, a psychiatrist who analyzed much of DuBois' data, finds the following traits to be typical: (1) anxiety, (2) suspicion, (3) mistrustfulness, (4) lack of self confidence, (5) lack of strong parental fixations, (6) overvaluation of sex and food, (7) lack of enterprise, and (8) repressed hatred.

The DuBois study did not take into consideration only the very early years of the child's life—the period of toilet-training and weaning—but instead considered how personality was built through an interaction of an individual with his culture and with his fellows over a period of some twenty years.

Childhood Experiences

There has been a tendency in studies of culture and personality in past years to rely heavily on the theories of Sigmund Freud that personality formation is almost entirely determined by the child's early experience in weaning, toilet-training, and discipline. Geoffrey Gorer, for example, maintains that behavioral patterns established early in life influence subsequent learning. Thus Gorer feels that experiences of early childhood must be carefully documented. Attitudes of a child toward his father and mother and his siblings will greatly influence his attitudes toward others met later in life. In one study of the personality characteristics of the peasants of Great Russia Gorer postulated that many adult personality traits could be related to the fact that as infants the average peasant was swaddled with long strips of cloth that restricted the movement of the limbs.

The rationale behind this approach is that these early years are the ones in which a human organism experiences its first contacts with its environment. It is believed that during this period the child's sensitive and highly impressionable nervous system is most vulnerable to trauma. Furthermore, it is a time when both pleasant and unpleasant experiences become associated with people, objects, and situations.

In recent years there has been much less emphasis placed upon the deterministic character of the early years of a child's life. Infant experiences are thought of as providing certain potentialities, but whether such potentialities are realized depends to a great extent on the individual's subsequent life experiences.

Although experiences of early childhood are undoubtedly of great importance in shaping personality, there are any number of influences, such as ideological environment and material culture, that the individual is not likely to be exposed to or at least be greatly influenced by until later in his life.

Ideological Environment

The influence of varying ideologies upon the personality structure is well illustrated in the comparative value systems of Athens and Sparta. Every society has an idea of what an ideal man is and all the training and teaching in these societies were dedicated to what each held up as the proper way to behave.

While the people of Sparta and Athens were rival city states over a period of years, they developed quite different philosophies of life, although each society attempted to instill in its individuals a sense of patriotism and a high valuation of bravery. Sparta placed maximum emphasis on military virtues while Athens stressed the acquisition of knowledge, appreciation of beauty, and development of the body through physical exercise and sports. Since the Spartans glorified the courageous and ingenious warrior, the training of youth centered about military tactics, resourcefulness, and endurance of hardships. It is reported that after eating at the public mess in Sparta one visitor remarked, "Now I understand why Spartans do not fear death." Spartan boys were often required to steal their food in order to develop their ingenuity and one of the favorite Spartan folktales, told and retold to boys, was about the boy who stole a fox and hid it under his coat. While making off with his prize, he was stopped by a man who engaged him in conversation. Giving no indication of his theft, the boy stood and talked with the man until he fell dead as the result of being repeatedly bitten by the pilfered animal. The Spartan boy received no intellectual education but was impressed with the desirability of modesty, obedience, and courage.

Sparta, with a constitution but very little democracy, stood in strong ideological contrast to her neighbor Athens. Pericles in a famous funeral oration pointed up many of the differences that shaped the minds and manners of Athenians and Spartans. He said:

We admit anyone to our city, and do not expel foreigners from fear that they should see too much, because in war we trust to our own bravery and daring rather than to stratagems and preparations. Our enemies prepare for war by a laborious training from boyhood; we live at our ease, but are no less confident in facing danger . . . We love the arts, but without lavish display, and things of the mind, but without becoming soft.

Material Environment

In American culture children grow up in a world of rapid transportation, congested urban centers, overstuffed furniture, porcelain plumbing, and clocks with accuracy ensured by Western Union. Since a majority of Americans are reared, or at least feel at home, in such an environment, there is basis for seeing in these influences a factor in our personality configuration. Although this factor is often overlooked in studies of dominant personality, Malinowski has recognized it as a vital influence. He states:

The secondary environment, the outfit of material culture, is a laboratory in which the reflexes, the impulses, the emotional tendencies of the organism are formed. The hands, arms, legs and eyes are adjusted by the use of implements to the proper technical skill necessary in a culture. The nervous processes are modified so as to yield the whole range of intellectual concepts, emotional types and sentiments which form the body of science, religion and morals prevalent in a community. (1931:622)

Variation Within Culture

Although common cultural experiences tend to standardize personality and make "every man in certain respects like some other men," we cannot carry the influence of uniform cultural experience too far. Culture is not a mold that turns out its participants as exact facsimiles. There is always a great variety and range of personalities even in the simplest of cultures. This fact has been well documented by C. W. M. Hart in a character analysis of five brothers of the Tiwi tribe of Bathurst Island, Australia. Although the younger two of the five brothers had a different father, all had the same mother, a common family conditioning, and an almost identical cultural environment. According to Hart's very detailed accounts of their personalities, each was drastically different from his siblings. Antonio, the eldest, was "insecure" and "uneasy." As heir to his father's social position, he was "a man pushed into a position rather too big for him to fill. He was not by nature, particularly aggressive or domineering."

Mariano, the second brother, was a great contrast to the first. He was a "forceful, domineering, self-important, introverted man" whose gloomy and hostile behavior resulted in his having no intimates or close friends. Equally lonely was Louis, who wanted no friends and sought only to be left alone. He was "completely devoid of humor" but a man of great intelligence and dedication. Louis was dedicated to but one cause—the seduction of other men's wives.

Brothers Tipperary and Bob were slightly younger (late twenties) than the other three and vastly different in personality. Tipperary was "gay, completely relaxed, and unselfconscious," always looking on the brighter side of things and always surrounded with friends; while Bob, the youngest, was completely lacking in color—a "born follower" and a complete conformist.

Hart concludes that "we should expect to find, in any culture in the world, a pretty similar range of variation in what must roughly be called 'types of people.' The anthropologist on the other hand who is looking for 'stereotyped personalities' in even the simplest culture must expect to be disappointed" (1954:261).

Unfortunately, statements of the variety of personality types have all too often been neglected in the writings of culture and personality researchers, and often the factor of variation has been disguised by the very method of presentation. For example, in Ruth Benedict's description of the personality of Siamese men she states:

Thai men are cheerful, easy-going, jolly, gay, indolent. They accept subordination to higher rank or power without either resentment or servility; they do not cringe. They respect and obey authority without demanding return or assistance from it. They are self reliant in a quiet, careless way—without much sense of responsibility for others. (1943)

In reading such a description the student is tempted to think that *all* Thais behave in exactly the same way, as there is no statement of variation or range of personality. Certainly there must be personality subtypes that could logically develop from various roles or statuses that can be found within the society.

MODAL PERSONALITY. The term *modal personality* has been useful in the proper understanding of personality variation. Modal personality may best be understood by calling attention to the concept of the *mode* in statistical measurement. The mode is a type of average that is derived by ascertaining the value appearing most frequently in a series of numbers. Let us say that we are interested in the average size of family in a suburban area and as we go from house to house making inquiry we receive the following responses: 5, 6, 5, 4, 3, 2, 5, 2, 4, 9, 5, 7, 5, 3, 4. One way of figuring the average size of family would be to find the number that appears most frequently—in this case, 5. Transferring the concept of mode to the area of personality we would say that modal personality is that personality that is found most commonly among a variety of personality types. There may be a whole range of personalities just as there were many other numbers in our series. Those enjoying the modal personality might very well represent a small percentage of the total number of personalities represented.

A study of modal personality of Tuscarora Indians by Wallace (1952), utilizing Rorschach ink blot tests, illuminates the concept of modal personality and gives greater understanding of the extent to which personality is shared within a society. In Wallace's study, the personality traits of seventy adults were ascertained from their performances on twenty-one scoring categories normally used in Rorschach interpretation. Although some traits, such as their ability to make use of the entire blot (index W), were shared to the extent of 86%, when all twenty-one trait indices were considered cumulatively, only twenty-six people were calculated as making up the modal class.

NATIONAL CHARACTER. Modal personality when applied to the people of complex industrialized societies is often referred to as *national character*. Studies of this phenomenon, as explained by Margaret Mead, are "like all culture and personality studies, . . . focused on the way human beings embody the culture they have been reared in or to which they have immigrated" (1953:642). Just as all members of a given nation tend to share certain cultural traits (e.g., the American heritage), this approach assumes that being exposed to somewhat similar cultural experiences they will also tend to share certain personality traits, even though they come from numerous subcultures. Some investigators tend to think of these national character descriptions as "scientifically drawn stereotypes" of personality. We must remember, however, that although culture is a powerful determinant of personality, it is but one of many influencing factors—among them body structure and constitution, family situation, class, caste, and employment status.

LIKE NO OTHER MAN

In stating that man is in certain respects like no other man, Kluckhohn and Murray are commenting on the uniqueness of every individual personality. This uniqueness might be accounted for partially by constitutional determinants—that is, the state of the human organism at a particular time with regard for general body build, sex, age, and the health and well being of the body. The possibilities for variation in each of these several factors are enormous when a total population is considered and thus the possibilities for personality variation as influenced by these factors are great.

Roger Williams, who has sometimes been referred to as a "chemical anthropologist," has pointed out the great variation in physiological factors that definitely affect personality in a given population. Glands, for example, do not control but certainly influence our behavior. In normal individuals the size of thyroid glands may vary from eight to fifty grams and the amount of thyroid hormone in the blood may vary in perfectly healthy individuals over a fivefold range. Pituitary gland secretions vary in normal individuals over a forty-fold range. Taking such factors as sensitivity to pain, nutritional requirements, size and performance of the heart, and gland secretion into consideration, Williams tells us that there is one chance in 6,500 of being average.

While Sheldon's findings (page 7) on the effect of somatotype on personality are far from conclusive, we can certainly assume that body type, at least in extreme cases, has some influence on personality. We may be sure that a seven-foot Watusi has a very different world view than a four-foot six-inch Pygmy. One's height, strength, and how close one's body approaches what is considered beautiful by a society greatly influences how the world and one's fellow men are viewed. The constitutional factor includes considerations of age and health, and all of us know that our personalities are quite different depending on whether we are ill or healthy. It is also possible to observe changes in personality in a given person as he advances in age.

Family Environment

There are probably no two people in our society who have been exposed to exactly the same combinations of personalities in the family. The overprotective mother, the domineering father, the happy-go-lucky, the neurotic, or even the psychotic parent can all be found in family groups in our culture. There is also the factor of sibling order; the eldest child in a family is quite likely to have had different training and treatment from the youngest and both have probably had different life experiences than an only child. The social status of the home also provides a special environment for personality development.

TWINS REARED APART. In a study of identical twins reared apart, carried out by Newman, Freeman, and Holzinger, there is a case of sisters separated at the age of three months and raised for fifteen years in two vastly different socioeconomic environments. Mildred grew up in the home of a bank president and former mayor of a town of five thousand population, while her twin, Ruth, was reared in a large city where her foster father was a foreman of day laborers. While Mildred was encouraged to make friends and play with groups of older children, Ruth was overly sheltered by her foster mother, who discouraged any contacts with other children. Mildred's home environment was intellectually stimulating, and she had an opportunity to read widely, take music lessons, and come into contact with highly educated people. Although Ruth had as much formal education as her sister, her home was depressing, with nothing in the way of good books, good music, or stimulating companions. When examined at the age of fifteen, the girls differed little in their health records, and there were "no marked contrasts in physical characters." In regard to personality differences, however, they were quite dissimilar. The investigators describe the two as follows:

Observation of the sisters revealed a marked difference in their overt behavior. Mildred was sociable and relatively easy in her manner and conversed freely. While not at all bold, she seemed to show no signs of timidity or embarrassment. Her diction was good and her enunciation clear. Ruth, on the contrary, was excessively timid, would not converse, never spoke except when questioned, and then spoke with a pronounced lisp. (1937:225)

Still other factors may produce variation in personality and explain why in some respects every man is like no other man. Even in primitive societies we cannot expect every individual to have had exactly the same set of life experiences in terms of successes and failures, injuries and harrowing experiences. In modern nations the situational aspect is magnified in terms of class, region, and occupational differences in experience. Taking all these into account it is understandable why the anthropologist feels that personality may be dealt with in terms of general national or cultural tendencies but not without recognizing a wide range of variation.

NORMAL AND ABNORMAL PERSONALITIES

The fact that early studies of culture and personality were highly influenced by Freudian and other psychiatric theory has led many to believe that anthropologists are more interested in abnormal than normal personality. This is not true. By far the greatest number of psychological studies done by anthropologists have merely been concerned with documentation of representative or modal personality types in the cultures of the world. In a normally functioning society one could hardly expect the representative personality to be abnormal. Since anthropologists felt that their studies tended to be "vague, impressionistic, subjective, and not amenable to check or transubjective verification" (Spiro and Henry 1953:418), they turned to the instruments utilized by psychologists and psychiatrists for measuring personality in an attempt to be more scientific and objective. In most cases these instruments had been used more in diagnostic tests of mental illness than as ways of studying normal personality.

Anthropologists believed, however, that certain tests used in clinical psychology could be used as originally developed or altered slightly so that they could be used cross-culturally to challenge the indivudual to reveal his inner thoughts, feelings, emotions, and fears. Those tests that have been selected and used most extensively for this purpose have been (1) the Rorschach test, (2) the Thematic Apperception test (usually modified), (3) free drawings, and (4) doll play.

The Rorschach Test

The Rorschach test consists of a series of ten cards on which ink blots of varying form and color have been reproduced. Developed by Swiss psychiatrist Hermann Rorschach, it is essentially a test wherein the subject reveals his personality by his verbal responses to the amorphous blots. This form of projective test has been used widely by anthropologists in foreign cultures because the equipment is simple, does not require literacy, can be used on either adults or children, and does not have rigid administrative standards. Spiro and Henry maintain that the test:

. . . elicits material covering a wide range of personality characteristics. Among these are: sensitivity to inner promptings as contrasted with responsiveness to outer stimuli; degree of control over emotions; capacity to relate affectively to other people; capacity to see total situations as contrasted with absorption in petty details; tendencies to submit as contrasted with tendencies to react vigorously to the environment; various aspects of sexuality; degree of hostility; degree of imagination, conformity, originality; tendencies to psychopathy. (1950:419)

The Thematic Apperception Test

The TAT, as it is commonly called, consists of thirty thought-provoking pictures and a blank card, to which the subject is to respond by telling a story of what each picture represents. The theory behind the test is that every author reveals himself in his work, and the pictures are used merely as a stimulous to the less imaginative person. Since the set of TAT pictures used in clinical diagnostic situations shows people in European dress and Western settings, many anthropologists have modified the pictures to match the circumstances of their native subjects. The drawings on pages 312–13 show how William Lessa altered the TAT for use on the Micronesian island of Ulithi.

One of the most extensive uses of the modified TAT was a study of 1,000 children in six different American Indian cultures conducted by the U. S. Office of Indian Affairs and the University of Chicago in 1947. Using a series of twelve pictures representing varying social situations within the everyday experience of Indian children, the test studied such things as emotional orientation to the physical world; characteristics of interpersonal relations, particularly those of family members; the extent to which individual spontaneity was encouraged or restricted by the group; the influence of white contact on personality; and the influence of culture training at various periods of a child's life.

Free Drawings

This test of personality simply involves giving children an opportunity to draw anything they desire. By analyzing content as well as the characteristics of rendition, it is believed that much can be learned

Modified TAT developed by William Lessa for use on Ulithi.

about self-image, sibling and parental relations, the fantasy life of the child, as well as his conceptions of the physical universe and of his society.

Doll Play

In this test situation a child or group of children are given dolls, usually representing members of a family. The children are free to do anything they want with the dolls, but the manipulations of the dolls and the children's comments are closely observed and recorded. It is believed that the manner in which the children play with the dolls will reveal their attitudes toward their own parents and siblings, their conceptions of sexual behavior, and their tendencies toward aggressive behavior.

Cross-Cultural Validity

In European culture, norms have been developed so that the above devices for studying personality may be used to identify psychotic and neurotic individuals, but these criteria are seldom, if ever, valid when testing in foreign cultures. Although Cora DuBois feels that the Rorschach can be used cross-culturally if properly handled and interpreted

Modified TAT (*Continued.*)

(1961:xx), many anthropologists insist that responses considered abnormal in one society may be considered perfectly normal and desirable in another. A good example of how a different set of values can
greatly affect a subject's test responses is the case of a Quaker girl in
our own culture, who made an error on a test where she was to tell
what was wrong with a picture in which a frontiersman was shooting
distant Indians while those close to him were about to take his scalp.
Instead of writing that one should always shoot the closest Indians
first, the girl answered "One shouldn't shoot Indians." This was not the
expected answer, but in terms of the girl's pacifistic ideological background it was her natural and normal response.

ABNORMALITY

One of the most difficult problems in psychology today is how to
define what is abnormal in our own culture let alone in foreign or non-
Western cultures. Something of the dilemma may be seen in Yehudi
Cohen's discussion, which reads:

We generally tend to think of psychotics as people who are confined to a
psychiatric ward or hospital. This is a misconception, since psychiatrists generally hospitalize a psychotic only when he is in danger of hurting himself or
others or when he is incapable of functioning by himself. There are many
people labeled by psychiatrists as psychotic who are perfectly capable of
performing everyday functions, including earning a living, and for whom

hospitalization is not required. Because there is no definition of psychosis which is universally applicable, we must have an operational criterion of psychosis which is meaningful in the context of the data which social scientists are capable of gathering. Hence, we shall say that a person is psychotic when, because of personality or psychological factors, he is unable to perform his roles as a member of the society or group of which he is a member. (1961:469)

With this definition in mind we must recognize that in many societies certain mental states that are by our definitions abnormal may allow or even specially qualify a person to perform his role as a member of society. Among certain California Indian groups as well as among Siberian Eskimos, the individual who has hallucinations and cataleptic seizures is not pitied but rather regarded as a very important religious practitioner. Since it is believed that the spirits possess and speak through him during seizures, he enjoys a great amount of authority over his fellow society members.

Another example of behavior that would be termed psychotic or at least abnormal by European standards but in no way hinders a man in the performance of his social roles is cited by Herskovits, who relates that:

In West Africa and Brazil the gods come only to those who have been designated in advance by the priest of their group, who lays his hands on their heads . . . The terminology of psychopathology has been readily applied to these states of possession. Such designations as hysteria, auto-hypnosis, compulsion, have come to rest easily on the tongue . . . (but) . . . in these Negro societies the interpretation given behavior under possession—the meaning this experience holds for the people—falls entirely in the realm of understandable, predictable, normal behavior. (1949:67)

Opposing this view is that of Derek Freeman, who feels that Herskovits' relativistic approach is an erroneous doctrine that seriously hinders the proper understanding of human culture. It is Freeman's position that:

. . . to assert . . . that behavior is normal because it is set in a cultural mold, is to say no more than it is shared and accepted by the members of the culture concerned, but dereistic thinking and irrational behavior are not one whit the less dereistic because they happen to be shared and accepted. (1962:273)

A middle ground position in this controversy is that of Yehudi Cohen, who writes,

There can be little doubt that the hallucinary experiences of a Plains Indian young man in quest of personal supernatural power is as much a "clinical" manifestation or entity as are the hallucinations of a hospitalized psychotic. Somehow or other, however, the Indian's membership within a bounded societal group keeps this hallucination encapsulated so that it remains within its proper cultural place and does not intrude upon or flood the rest of the personality. (1961:469)

Much of this trance and hallucinary behavior, which appears abnormal in European terms, is quite normal in the eyes of the members of a particular society if it remains in the proper context. If we define normal behavior as that which is expected and predicted, then possession in African cult ceremonies and hallucinations in the Plains Indians' vision quest are normal. If Africans have seizures or trances in areas of behavior where they are not expected or if Plains Indians have hallucinations about things other than guardian spirits, then even their fellow society members would consider them psychotic. Every society does recognize certain kinds of behavior as being abnormal and considers those who exhibit these traits as being psychotic. While mental illness might generally be thought of as a matter of losing touch either temporarily or permanently with reality and behaving in unpredictable ways, this concept is not entirely valid; for it would appear that the mentally ill have enough of a grasp upon reality that they follow culturally prescribed patterns of psychosis.

In Latin America "magical fright" is the common mental malady and its symptoms are "depression, withdrawal from normal social activity and responsibility, and signs of temporary collapse of the ego organization" (Gillin 1948:387).

In Ulithi one who is mentally ill swims about in the lagoon for hours with an old rotten log under his arm. An Ojibwa Indian suffering with *Windigo* shows signs of "melancholia, violence and obsessive cannibalism" (Landes 1960:24). The mental disturbance known as *Pibloktoq* among Greenland Eskimos produces such symptoms as singing until one becomes unconscious, imitating the calls of birds, throwing things about, tearing off one's clothing, and sometimes running out of the house into the snow. In Samoa anyone can easily recognize one afflicted with *ma'i aitu* (spirit sickness) for they talk in their sleep, run aimlessly about, yawn repeatedly, compulsively count their fingers, and frequently pick flowers and sing.

Causes of Psychosis

An even more difficult problem to tackle than defining "normal" and "abnormal" behavior is the task of isolating cultural or environmental factors that seem to precipitate mental illness. Studying the problem cross-culturally, anthropologists have come up with a series of factors that they believe may contribute to psychological disorganization. They are (1) the presence of conflicting values, (2) heterogeneity of culture, (3) discontinuity in life experiences, and (4) too rapid cultural change accompanied by a loss of norms.

CONFLICTING VALUES. Modern America, which psychiatrists claim has an alarming rate of one out of ten persons with some degree of mental illness, is a perfect example of a society with conflicting values and ideologies combined with rapid cultural change. The United States is a country that advocates brotherly love, yet fights at least one war every generation; sanctions ruthless business competition and tacitly sanctions racial segregation. It holds up monogamy and chastity as ideals and yet has one of the highest divorce rates in the world and is obsessed with sex in its literature, motion pictures, and advertising.

In comparison with Samoa, Margaret Mead finds America an exceedingly difficult place in which to come of age. She describes our society as one:

. . . which is clamouring for choice, which is filled with many articulate groups, each urging its own brand of salvation, its own variety of economic philosophy, will give each new generation no peace until all have chosen or gone under, unable to bear the conditions of choice. The stress is in our civilization, not in the physical changes through which our children pass, but it is none the less real or less inevitable in twentieth-century America. (1959:138)

CULTURAL DISCONTINUITY. Closely associated with the phenomenon of conflicting values is the discontinuity of cultural conditioning, which is found in ours and other societies and represents a source of great emotional stress. Ruth Benedict has dealt with this problem at some length (1938) and points out that in our society as a child advances from childhood to adulthood very different demands are placed on him—many of which he has not been prepared for by his culture. In our society childhood is considered a time for play and the child is asked to assume very little responsibility. High school students are often discouraged by their parents from seeking part-time work on the grounds that they should go to all the high school dances, sporting events, and other social events they can because they have the rest of their lives to work. On the other hand, the moment a young person completes his schooling he is expected to know how to work hard, efficiently, and responsibly. Concommitant with this change in roles is also a change in submission-dominance behavior. Many societies, including our own, require or at least expect perfect obedience and submission from children. If this is not forthcoming, the child is punished. In our society this pattern continues as long as the child lives under the same roof with his parents. When he manages to leave the nest, however, he is supposed to be able to "stand on his own two feet," stick up for his rights, and show signs of dominance and leadership. Becoming an adult also involves developing a sexual role. In our society especially, children are shielded from knowledge of sexual functions and yet young people are expected to establish normal and satisfactory marital sex relationships.

Each of these changes in role represents an almost complete reversal of attitude and behavior from earlier conditioning and, although it is true that the majority of individuals take these major hurdles without great difficulty, there are many others who for one reason or another never adjust. Sometimes this inability results in our branding individuals as immature, but in other cases these adjustments can be a real source of psychic disturbance.

HOMOGENEITY AND HETEROGENEITY. Ordinarily it is assumed that the more homogeneous a culture and the fewer its discrepancies and discontinuities, the lower its incidence of mental illness. In such a society people tend to be in pretty much "the same boat." There is little class distinction, little difference in economic position, little disparity of values, little mobility or change, and childhood experiences tend to be supported and reinforced as the individual grows older.

Although we are not sure whether heterogeneous societies attract or produce abnormal individuals, the fact remains that in cities like New York, Chicago, and Detroit approximately 10% of all hospital admissions involve severe or moderate personality disturbances (Weinberg 1952:362–67) and approximately one person out of five in the United States visits a doctor every year for some nervous disturbance.

No attempt to assess the many causes for this phenomenon will be made here, but they surely lie in the anonymity, the diversity of value in its many subcultures, in whirlwind change, in the tension and demand for efficiency and production, and in the breakdown of family ties that prevails in our urban and industrial areas.

Although a number of studies have shown that the lot of the primitive or rural community member is somewhat better as far as maintaining mental balance, homogeneous societies are not always free from the shadow of psychosis just because life is simpler and more uniform. It has shown, for example, that the nature of the values held is also an important factor.

THE HUTTERITES. The Hutterites, an Anabaptist religious group who inhabit sections of the Dakotas, Montana, and the prairie provinces of Canada, live a simple communal life in some ninety-eight small agricultural communities. As a group they believe in pacificism, adult baptism, and communal ownership of property. They reject jewelry, art, comfortable household furnishings, radios, and movies. Although they see no need for education beyond the primary grades, they read newspapers, utilize outside medical and legal services, and engage in highly mechanized agriculture. In regard to their cultural homogeneity, Eaton and Weil write:

> In the Hutterite social order people are exposed to a large number of common experiences. Their indoctrination begins in infancy and is continued by daily religious instruction and later by daily church-going. Hutterites spend their entire life within a small and stable group. Their homes consist only of bedrooms, all furnished in an almost identical manner. The women take turns cooking and baking for everybody. Everyone wears the same kind of clothes; the women, for example, all let their hair grow without cutting, part it in the middle and cover it with a black kerchief with white polka dots. The Hutterite religion provides definite answers for many of the problems that come up. (1953:37)

In spite of this great cultural homogeneity and stability, the Hutterites do have mental illness. Eaton and Weil discovered in 1950 that about one in forty-three individuals either had active symptoms or had recovered from mental illness. Although this incidence is not particularly high, it is somewhat greater than many other less homogeneous groups with which they were compared by the investigators. It is of interest that very few of these cases ever manifested delusions, hallucinations, or other schizophrenic symptoms. There was, however, a high incidence of manic-depressive reactions. To a certain extent it is possible to find an explanation for this in the ideological system of these people. Eaton and Weil explain it this way:

> There was much evidence of irrational guilt feelings, self blame, withdrawal from normal social relations and marked slowing of mental and motor activities . . . Religion is the focus of the Hutterite way of life. Their whole educational system, beginning with nursery school, orients the people to look for blame and guilt within themselves rather than in others. (1953:34)

PERSONALITY AND CULTURAL CHANGE

One of the characteristics of modal or representative personality is that it is subject to change. In the most stable societies the social, technological, and ideological environment is never quite the same for any two generations of people. A generation ago the average Samoan child grew up in a large extended family, was educated to be a good fisherman and agriculturalist, and participated in a world where rank and ceremony were focal points. Service and obedience were required of young untitled men, and dignity, responsibility, and wisdom were synonymous with chiefly rank. Samoan children today come of age in a very different world. European technology and economics have created new values. Instead of looking forward to the time when he may become the chief of his extended family, administer family lands and properties, and participate in the sacred ceremonies of old Samoa, many a Samoan young man is looking forward to a trade or even a college education and a job in government or industry. He finds the old system of communal ownership of land stifling and life in his remote village dull. His travels to the port towns of his archipelago show him what luxuries money can buy and these are often more attractive to him than the security and prestige he can attain by remaining within the traditional system. Since the young man is literally a part of a different cultural world from his father, it is little wonder that he thinks and behaves in a different manner. There are a number of behavior patterns learned in childhood that tend to dominate the young man's actions even now, but many of his childhood values do not bring rewards in the European world and thus they are modified or replaced.

Teton Personality Change

Esther Goldfrank (1943) has given us an excellent example of personality change under changing external conditions in Teton Indian society in the nineteenth century. In analyzing patterns of cooperation and hostility among these people, Goldfrank found that prior to 1850, when the white man was not yet a threat, there was a great deal of in-group violence growing out of rivalries between individuals for war and hunting honors.

Between 1850 and 1877 caravan travel west brought immigrants into the area, who killed the buffalo and thus threatened the Indians' basic economy. Faced with this common threat from outside, the Teton neither fought nor quarreled among themselves and instead developed a sense of tribal solidarity where individuals took greater pride in giving than getting.

The period of 1877 to 1885 was one in which the spirit of the tribe was broken. The buffalo had disappeared and thus their traditional economy was gone. The people were poverty stricken. With the complete collapse of the tribal structure, the sense of cooperation and tribal solidarity also disappeared and internal strife, even to the point of a series of murders, once more developed.

From 1885 on, the Teton again managed to develop a sense of solidarity. The people were now one in their economic deprivation. It was a matter of helping each other or none would survive. Hospitality became a cardinal virtue and the church became an important institution in that it provided both solace for the bulk of the Teton and opportunity for prestige for those young men who entered the ministry.

Ashley Montagu believes that personality is a pattern of behavior that can change not only from one generation to another but within the same person in a single generation. He points out that history stands as a strong ally for his position. Montagu writes:

Consider . . . the seafaring Scandinavians of the Bronze Age, undoubtedly the ancestors of the modern Scandinavians: how different is the cultural behavior of the modern relatively sedentary Scandinavians [who have not fought a war in more than 148 years] from that of their raiding forbears!

The boisterous joy in life of the English of Elizabeth I's period is very different from the attitudes of the English in the reign of Elizabeth II. The lusty libertinism of the Restoration contrasts sharply with the prudery of the Victorian Age. The Englishman's "nature" was different in the sixteenth as compared with that which he exhibited in the seventeenth century. In the centuries preceding the middle half of the nineteenth the English were among the most aggressive and violent peoples on the face of the earth, today they are among the most law-abiding. (1956:77–78)

Many anthropologists would agree that the people of Fiji are among the happiest, friendliest, and most cooperative and peaceful in the world. And yet, as late as 1878 Fijians were still practicing cannibalism, raiding their neighbors, schooling their children in revenge, and making a specialty of massacring shipwrecked mariners. How such a drastic change in attitude and action came about in less than a century is a mystery. Norman Cousins (1964) suggests that perhaps the Fijians might be persuaded to send missionaries to the rest of the world and inform all of us how we might also develop their pacifistic personality traits.

It is still possible to use the old cliché that "You can't change human nature," for that can be done through evolution alone. But cultural nature, the product of given cultures at given times, is as dynamic as culture itself.

SUGGESTED READINGS

EATON, JOSEPH W., and WEIL, ROBERT J. "The Mental Health of the Hutterites," *Scientific American*, December, 1953. (Discusses social and cultural milieu of Hutterite communities and analyzes the causes for their higher than expected incidence of mental illness.)

GILLIN, JOHN. "Personality in Preliterate Societies," *American Sociological Review*, 4:681, 1939. (Summary of the pioneer studies in psychological anthropology. Excellent bibliography.)

HENRY, JULES, et al. "Symposium on Projective Testing in Ethnology," *American Anthropologist*, 57:245, 1955. (Deals with evaluation of usefulness of Rorschach test in cross-cultural research in culture and personality.)

LINDESMITH, A. R., and STRAUSS, ANSELM. "A Critique of Culture-Personality Writings," *American Sociological Review*, **15**:587, 1950. (Criticism of the methods and theoretical frame of reference of Benedict, Mead, Kluckhohn, DuBois, and others by two sociologists.)

LINTON, RALPH. "The Personality of Peoples," *Scientific American*, August, 1949. (The influence of culture and cultural change on national character.)

OPLER, MARVIN K. "Schizophrenia and Culture," *Scientific American*, August, 1957. (How different cultures—Italian and Irish—produce different forms of schizophrenia.)

SAPIR, EDWARD. "Personality," *Encyclopedia of the Social Sciences*, 1933. (Various definitions of the term personality and discussion of relationship between culture and personality.)

SEWELL, W. H. "Infant Training and the Personality of the Child," *American Journal of Sociology*, **58**:150, 1952. (The relationship between infant training and personality development is analyzed utilizing records of 162 American farm children.)

Paperbound Books

BENEDICT, RUTH. *Patterns of Culture*. The New American Library of World Literature, Inc. (A cultural and psychological characterization of four cultures.)

DuBois, CORA. *The People of Alor*. Vols. I and II, Harper and Row. (A pioneer sociopsychological study of an East Indian island.)

ERIKSON, ERIK. *Childhood and Society*. W. W. Norton. (Psychoanalytic approach in culture and personality.)

GORER, GEOFFREY, and RICKMAN, JOHN. *The People of Great Russia*. W. W. Norton. (National character study of Russian peasants.)

LINTON, RALPH. *Cultural Background of Personality*. Appleton-Century-Crofts. (Interdisciplinary approach to personality.)

MALINOWSKI, BRONISLAW. *Sex and Repression in a Savage Society*. World Publishing Co. (Oedipus complex tested cross-culturally.)

MEAD, MARGARET. *Coming of Age in Samoa*. The New American Library of World Literature, Inc. (Psychological study of adolescent Samoan girls.)

WALLACE, ANTHONY F. C. *Culture and Personality*. Random House. (Past and present theories of culture and personality; the psychology of culture change.)

WHITING, J. W. M., and CHILDS, I. L. *Child Training and Personality*. Yale University Press. (Relationship of childhood experience to anxiety and illness in seventy-five tribes.)

16

How Anthropologists
Study Man's Cultures

The life of an anthropologist, in the eyes of many, is one filled with adventure among strange and exotic people. Most people realize that it is the job of anthropologists to live in far-off places, participate in the lives of its peoples, and return with accounts of their customs and manners that will ultimately find their way into books gracing the shelves of public or college libraries. What many people do not quite understand is just why such foreign excursions are considered so essential to the perpetuation of the science of man.

There are two reasons for field trips to foreign cultures: First of all, in anthropology a field trip is considered a kind of internship experience for the budding anthropology student. It provides the student with a certain insight or "feel" into the nature of culture. When one lives his life in but one culture, he tends to take his customs for granted and is therefore rarely aware of their force in shaping behavior. If, however, the student goes to work and live in another culture, he is immediately struck by the fact that things can be done in a very different way from what he has been used to. Patterns of culture stand out and have reality to him as he compares the foreign customs with his own cultural legacy. In addition to what the field work does to the student's own scientific orientation, there is the matter of the field-worker's contribution to the discipline of anthropology itself. As has been pointed out earlier, anthropology cannot depend for its facts on the accounts of people who have not been scientifically trained[1] to observe and record the details of man's living habits and value orientations. Anthropologists know that they have to study the species man in a scientific way. Their observations must be reliable, valid, and free from bias. The facts of foreign cultures must be brought in from all corners of the world so that they may be analyzed, combined, and compared. The flow of such facts cannot stop, because cultures are constantly changing and the changes are also of vital significance. Because a culture has been studied once does not mean that the job is done.

THE HOLISTIC, RELATIVISTIC, SCIENTIFIC APPROACH TO ANTHROPOLOGY

The anthropologist does not go to another culture just to see what he can find out. He goes out with a definite theoretical frame of reference, one that has been acquired through years of college training in his discipline. We can say that his approach will undoubtedly be holistic, relativistic, and scientific. By holistic we mean that he will look for the *Gestalt* or the whole view of the society. He will look at the culture as an entity with functionally related components. Although he may be studying something quite specialized, like folklore, he knows that this aspect of culture cannot be completely understood unless he has some grasp of the total way of life. He knows, for example, that legends often constitute history for a primitive people and often regulate their political organization. Folktales and proverbs are frequently used as educational devices for training the young in the values of a society. Songs or riddles are often considered private property and lead one, therefore, into studies of economics. It is only when one approaches a culture as a consistent whole that true insights may be acquired. When

[1] Something of the value of ethnographic descriptions as produced by untrained writers may be seen in the list of character traits assigned to Samoans by early voyagers, traders, administrators, and missionaries: "happy, proud, self-opinionated, suspicious, impudent, daring, social, decorous, polished, turbulent, threatening, treacherous, ferocious, respectful of old age, fond of children and travelling, sedate and dignified when chiefs, cunning, ungrateful, full of intrigue, expedient in truth and falsehood, cruel to animals, lacking in physical sensitivity, jealous, deceitful, generous, untrustful, arrogant, egotistical, loquacious, unstable, unenterprising, lazy, vain, cowardly when alone, superstitious, boastful, assertive, generous, hospitable, communalistic, lacking in ideas, capable of being lead, unable to be bullied, subtle, diplomatic, patient, badly-treated, maladjusted . . ." (Stanner 1953:305–6). This very contradictory list compiled from early literature by Stanner gives some indication of the objectivity and the value of these reports.

The missionary Hiram Bingham upon seeing the Hawaiians for the first time records (1848:125) his doubt as to whether these strange people were even human, and if they were, would it be possible to ever civilize them.

any custom is viewed in terms of the total cultural configuration, its meaning and utility become more apparent and its bizarre and baffling qualities disappear. To the anthropologist, seeing the whole of a culture—i.e., the general configuration—is often more important than knowing all of its intricate details.

One of the most difficult attitudes for the anthropologist to assume is that of relativism, but that this be done is essential to truly good field work. By this we mean that he must try to divorce himself from those value judgments that grow out of the fact that he has been raised in a society that often has a very different set of moral, ethical, and, for that matter, sanitary standards. Even the experienced anthropologist must get over an initial "culture shock" that comes when he is forced to alter his living patterns and his tastes to those of his native hosts. Few non-Western people have value systems approximating those of Europe and America and therefore their behavior cannot be judged in terms of ideas and values entirely foreign to them. The anthropologist must maintain a liberal open-minded position at least until he discovers what the local norms of behavior are. This approach to foreign cultures has become so much a part of anthropological field work that anthropologists are often jokingly referred to as people "who have respect for every culture in the world except their own."

Although there has been some debate as to whether or not anthropology is a true science, anthropologists insist fiercely that their methods are as scientific and objective as those used in any social or behavioral science. With an eye to objectivity and careful control of data, anthropologists have, over a long period of time, developed through experimentation and experience a number of specialized methodological techniques that allow them a penetrating and accurate study of foreign cultures. While fieldworkers are constantly developing new avenues of investigation the following techniques have stood the test of time and might be said to represent the fieldworker's standard set of research tools.

Participant Observation

The most widely used technique in anthropological field research is participant observation. Essentially this amounts to living with the people, participating in their lives as much as is permitted, and keeping one's eyes and ears open. A more formal definition would be that of Florence Kluckhohn, which reads:

Participant observation is conscious and systematic sharing, in so far as circumstances permit, in the life activities and on occasion, in the interests and affects of a group of persons. Its purpose is to obtain data about behavior through direct contact and in terms of specific situations in which the distortion that results from the investigator's being an outside agent is reduced to a minimum. (1940:331)

For best results, the anthropologist prefers to secure native housing right in the middle of the village as this gives a more natural situation for observation. Without any great effort on his part he can experience the daily routine—the quarrels, disciplining of children, and entertainments of the people going on all around him.

Much can be learned about a people's way of life from observation alone, but when carefully tied in with interviewing, observation becomes even more valuable. Observations suggest questions or topics for interview as well as serving to verify interview data. Ceremonies can, for example, be described in great detail from observation alone, but what they mean or what is happening may not be completely understood. By questioning knowledgeable members of the culture, the meanings, symbolism, and function of the ceremony may be added to the description. On the other hand, misinformation about a ceremony may be corrected when the anthropologist is permitted to see the event for himself.

Since the anthropologist in the field depends for a great share of his information upon what he sees, he must be more observant than the average human being and he must also be able to organize and categorize his observations.

Participation in the society's way of life, if properly done, is an excellent way of establishing rapport, but more than that, by actually helping to build a house or canoe, by helping out with work in the fields, the anthropologist begins to understand the people's problems and his descriptions of the culture are in some degree more from their point of view.

It should be remembered, however, that participation in a culture does not add up to "going native." Regardless of what the anthropologist might believe, he can never truly become a part of the culture he is studying, and he will be more respected if he lives as a tolerant but respectable representative of his own culture, governing his behavior by his own cultural norms.

The anthropologist should be sensitive to just how far he can go in his participation. The amount of participation permitted often varies according to the sophistication of the people in regard to strangers. Even among very acculturated people there are areas of their culture that are confidential. The good fieldworker will realize this and not insist on going where he is not wanted. In comparing

his opportunity to participate in Nuer and Azande culture, E. E.
Evans-Pritchard writes:

> Azande would not allow me to live as one of themselves; Nuer would not
> allow me to live otherwise. Among Azande I was compelled to live outside
> the community; among Nuer I was compelled to be a member of it. Azande
> treated me as a superior; Nuer as an equal. (1940:15)

ACCEPTANCE BY THE GROUP. Before any field researcher can begin to
participate in the culture he must, of course, be accepted by the
people. A number of avenues of approach have been used successfully.
In Samoa, the role of the anthropologist is well known, and they welcome him as the *a'o a'o aganu'u* (one who studies the customs of the
country), but in many areas the fieldworker must communicate satisfactorily the reason why he wants to move in with his notebooks,
cameras, and tape recorder. In some cultures the role of teacher has
proved the best to assume. He tells them he wants to study their way
of life because his students are particularly interested in knowing about
them. Equally effective has been the assumption of a role of historian
who wants to write a history of the culture so their own grandchildren
may know how people lived in the "old days." This approach is becoming an increasingly effective explanation, for more and more people,
under the contact of the West, are realizing that their traditional
customs are slowly being lost.

The Language

Of equal importance with participation and observation is the
acquiring of information through interviews with native informants.
This aspect of fieldwork, of course, immediately involves us in the
rather serious problem of how this communication is to take place. The
problem is greatly increased by the fact that in ninety per cent of the
cases the people will speak languages that cannot be learned in college
courses or through the aid of language records. Some ethnographers
maintain that learning the native language is desirable but not essential, since in most areas where field work is likely to be carried on there
are school teachers or other educated persons who can serve as interpreters. The majority of anthropologists, however, feel that it is abso-
lutely essential that the ethnographer have an adequate grasp of the
native language so that checks might be made on interpreters, or even
that work might proceed in the native tongue without the use of interpreters. One Australian anthropologist, R. G. Crocombe, has stated this
quite emphatically:

It is my firm belief that top class field work cannot be done anywhere without a good knowledge of the language. I have seen many field workers try to do without it, and construct formidable rationals for not learning the language, and from an examination of their work as well as from my own experience I am of the opinion that a fieldworker who is not prepared to learn the language should not be allowed into the field (at least not sponsored by any reputable institution). (Holmes 1962:5–6)

The anthropologist's struggle with the native language is usually one of his greatest tribulations. Clyde Kluckhohn, who was one of America's most outstanding anthropologists, claimed that he spoke Navaho only imperfectly, although he had been actively involved in learning and using the language for some twenty-five years. While it is difficult for any anthropologist to attain any proficiency in a native language in a one-year field trip, there are some definite advantages in making an effort. Margaret Mead (1933) points out that a few words of greeting, a sign of recognition at the mention of a technical cliché uttered in the native tongue make all the difference as to whether the anthropologist is accepted as a sympathetic visitor or an unwanted intruder.

The Key Informant

Regardless of whether the anthropologist has decided to use an interpreter or handle the language by himself, he must solve the rather knotty problem of whom to get his information from. It is seldom that an anthropological field worker must proceed in the manner of the sociologist—ascertaining the composition of the population and making up a representative sample. In a small primitive community composed of say three hundred people almost any intelligent knowledgeable person will know much of the way of life of his community and will represent to a certain extent a representative sample of the people. Great care must be exercised in choosing such people since it is always possible to use a deviant who will not share the values of other societal members.

There is no rule of thumb as to how many informants must be used to ensure a good study. This depends to a great extent on the knowledge of the informants and the nature of the research. If the anthropologist is primarily interested in magicomedical lore and there is only one practitioner in the society, then that person will of necessity represent his sole informant. In most studies, however, it is advisable to use several persons for cross-checks and verification of data. Since the anthropologist is essentially concerned with documenting regularities and shared behavior patterns, he feels that a few well-chosen key informants are sufficient to communicate to him the general cultural patterns that prevail within the society. The success of the research does not depend so much on how many informants are used but rather on their proper selection.

As the research with a few well-chosen informants proceeds, it will often be necessary to consult certain specialists. In many societies there

The author interviewing a key informant in American Samoa.

are religious specialists, professional fishermen, commercial traders, or specially qualified craftsmen. While one's key informant will probably know how to build a house, he doesn't know the fine details that are known only to professional carpenters. A good key informant will often inform the anthropologist as to who is best able to provide accurate and detailed information in these specialized areas. It is not unusual that, in time, the research will become a collaboration between the anthropologist and his key informants. While working with the ethnographer, many informants develop a very keen interest in their own culture and do everything in their power to help the field worker describe it accurately and completely.

Nondirective and Directive Interviewing

In his work with his informants the ethnographer utilizes two types of interview, (1) the nondirective or open-ended interview and (2) the directive. The first type involves asking the informant to discuss a general area of culture. Typical questions might be "Tell me about your life as a child" or "Explain to me how your family is organized." "Describe the religious beliefs of your people."

The nondirective interview is frequently used in the early phases of research as it allows the informant to discuss freely the things that interest him and seem inportant to him. It brings to light many things that the anthropologist might overlook because of a lack of an equivalent situation in his own culture. One type of nondirective procedure is the collection of autobiographical material. When invited to tell the anthropologist his life story, the informant has the opportunity to reveal his own personality. It represents for the anthropologist a personal document of one individual's values, goals, and motivations. When a variety of such personal documents have been collected, it is possible to describe the norms of the society as well as the extent to which persons are permitted to deviate. Invaluable in Culture and Personality research, autobiographies also have had great value in discovering dominant patterns of culture.

The directive, or structured, interview involves asking a series of prepared questions that systematically attempts to cover a specific area of the culture. After the anthropologist has a general "feel" of the culture by letting his informants talk about broad general aspects of culture, it is necessary to ask detailed questions about customs or traditions that might have been mentioned only briefly in the nondirective interviews. The ethnographer's daily observations will also prompt these specific questions.

Over a period of many years several publications such as *Notes and Queries on Anthropology* (1874), *Outline of Cultural Materials* (1950), *Field Guide to the Ethnological Study of Child Life* (1960), and others have been developed to aid the anthropologist in framing his questions and in making sure that his questions are exhaustive in scope. These outlines of cultural content serve as handy *aide-memoire* for the trained anthropologist and it is seldom that questions are taken directly from the books as each culture must have its own custom tailored schedule of questions. A paragraph from *Notes and Queries* will, however, give the reader a vague idea of the kind of questions asked in the directive interview. On the subject of cooking the structured interview might run something like this:

> What articles of food are eaten raw? Is food preferred fresh or "high"? Is meat preferred slightly or well cooked? Are there any spots where it is definitely forbidden to cook? Is cooking performed exclusively by one sex, and are there any rites or beliefs connected with it? Is the food for men and women cooked together or separately? (1951:242–3)

In spite of the many aids to interviewing that have been published, it must be pointed out that structured interrogation in a foreign culture involves many pitfalls for the inexperienced ethnographer. An example of the kind of thing that can occur has been related by S. J. Campbell, who worked in the Tonga Islands of the South Pacific. He warns that in response to a question like "Weren't these slabs used for burials?" the native would probably answer "Yes" but actually mean that they were not. Campbell points out (Holmes 1962:12) that in a case like this "The 'Yes' agrees with your statement equivalent which was 'These slabs were not used for burials.'" Another problem involved in getting accurate information is, strangely enough, the amiability of the natives. Most primitive informants are very friendly and anxious to please. If they think the interrogator would like a certain answer, they are quite willing to give it in order to make him happy even if it is incorrect. To avoid this kind of thing, the ethnographer must always avoid the leading question.

HYPOTHETICAL SITUATION

As part of the interview situation the ethnographer can often use the "hypothetical situation" to good advantage. This technique, which has been discussed at some length by veteran ethnographer M. J. Herskovits, represents a method of getting information about practices or traditions without making reference to specific persons, places, or events. It is, for example, more judicial to ask "What would happen if a boy were caught stealing bananas from someone's land?" than to ask "I understand your cousin got caught stealing last year. What happened to him?"

Herskovits points out that the hypothetical situation:

> . . . brings forth responses that are in the nature of projections of the informant's experience against the background of his culture, it affords the

investigator a heightened sensitivity to those relations of person to person in the group being studied . . .

By this method the informant is:

. . . released to tell of happenings to himself as to others that, in any other terms, he would be loath to reveal were he naming "actual" persons. Thus both in the personal and the cultural sense, he can go further, and will go further in expressing reactions than conventions of approved conduct would otherwise permit. (1950:40)

Success in interview is not so much a matter of using specific techniques, however, as it is developing good rapport between the interrogator and his informants. As Pacific ethnographer R. G. Crocombe has put it, "The only information of value is that which people give freely. People do not speak freely unless they feel at home with the interviewer" (Holmes 1962:8).

QUANTIFICATION

Traditionally, cultural anthropology has fallen far short of her sister discipline sociology in the quantification of data. There has never been a strong tradition in cultural anthropology of framing problems in quantitative terms, and many anthropologists, interested in humanistic or historical problems, have expressed contempt for quantitative field measurements. In general, however, anthropology is becoming more scientific and more quantitative. More and more anthropologists are maintaining that if anthropology is ever to make a major contribution to the knowledge of human behavior, data must be more comparable and measurable.

Although there have been early examples of statistical analysis of cultural materials (Tylor's adhesions in 1889 and Boas' use of Chi square in folklore analysis in 1895), it has not been until quite recently that there has been a major breakthrough in the use of truly scientific methods of control and analysis of field data.

In Clyde Kluckhohn's study of Navaho ceremonial participation he states why a quantitative field approach is necessary. He writes:

In anthropological literature one continually reads such statements as the following: "The Navaho are a very religious people," or more specifically, "The Navaho spend a great deal of their time in ceremonials." It would seem to me interesting and perhaps useful to examine such statements as these on the basis of fairly full information about this particular group of Navaho during a particular period of time. (1938:359)

In his research on this subject, Kluckhohn found:

1. One summer forty-one individuals spent a total of ninety-three days attending four different Enemy Way ceremonials.
2. From March 15 to September 15 nine singers spent sixty-two days in conducting twenty ceremonials.
3. Twenty out of sixty-nine adult men of the community conduct ceremonials and nine women and seven men serve as diagnosticians in the healing ceremonies.
4. The most popular ceremonial singer participated in twenty-nine ceremonials, totally eighty-one days, during the six month's period.
5. In this period there were one hundred forty-eight ceremonials with a time involvement of three hundred eighty-nine nights (more than one might be going on in a single night).

As a result of his detailed observations and interviews, Kluckhohn could do more than just comment in a general way on Navaho religiosity or ceremonial involvement. It was possible instead to state ". . . During this six month period, the average adult man in the community spent 0.32 of his waking hours in ceremonial activity, the average adult woman, 0.18" (1938:364).

Quantitative measurement of a different type but no less important was that utilized by Oscar Lewis of the daily round of activities of a Mexican family in Tepoztlan. He carefully recorded the activities of each and every member of the family throughout the day giving precise amounts of time devoted to each of their activities. In presentation of this data in the form of a chart it is possible for anyone to see at a glance (1) the family division of labor, (2) tasks performed individually or shared by the family, (3) exact time allotted to work, rest, and recreation, etc. This method is much more effective than the usual type of generalization that appears in most anthropological monographs. While the generalizations may be correct, they often lack the precise quality that will make them valuable in comparative analysis.

One of the major incentives for collecting measurable and more comparable data has been the availability of machines such as the IBM, Univac, or Alwac electronic computers. Anthropologists Murdock and Whiting see the use of these devices as vital additions to the science of man. They state:

We believe that the day is past when we can depend on an analysis of single cases or single societies to give us scientific answers. We feel that hypotheses suggested by the exploratory studies of individual societies should be tested by quantitative methods in a large number of societies. (1951:32)

With the use of the computer great masses of data can be fed into the machine and calculations concerning trait distributions, kinship variables, etc., which used to take months of laborious work can now be done in a few hours.

THE GENEALOGICAL METHOD

Another traditional method that allows a concrete and analytical approach to abstract phenomena is the genealogical method developed by W. H. R. Rivers, a British anthropologist, in 1910. The method consists of diagramming (see Fig. 10–1) the kinship relationships of every individual in the group as many generations back as they can remember, noting those living and dead, as well as those residing outside the community. The value of this method is, in River's own words, as follows:

The genealogical method makes it possible to investigate abstract problems on a purely concrete basis. It is even possible by its means to formulate laws regulating the lives of people which they have probably never formulated for themselves. (1910:*passim*)

With the genealogical method it is possible to study marriage regulations, laws of descent and property inheritance, succession to chieftainship, ceremonial functions of particular relatives, and even such biological data as ratio of sexes, fecundity, and mortality. Aside from the concrete information it provides, the genealogical method gives the anthropologist a wealth of general background data and also aids him in establishing rapport with his subjects. As *Notes and Queries* states,

The data in the genealogies will not only give the investigator the names and relationship to one another of all those whom he will meet in daily work, but will further give him information about individuals not present in the community. Such knowledge is a great asset. There are few people who are not flattered by the personal attention that is shown to them when greeted by their correct names; the skilled fieldworker will use the data he has gained from a few informants to make many more personal contacts. (1951:50)

VILLAGE MAPPING

A valuable companion to the genealogical diagram is the village or regional map that the anthropologist constructs to record the plan of village housing, agricultural land, and fishing or hunting territories of the group. If there is individually or family-owned land ownership or use, the boundaries or divisions are carefully plotted and related to genealogical or census data. Where aerial photographs are available,

Table 5. A synchronic record of the activities of each member of a Tepoztlan family (Lewis 1951:63).

	Father	Mother	Eldest daughter	Second daughter	Youngest daughter
A.M.					
6:00–6:30	In bed	Rises, makes fire and coffee	In bed	In bed	In bed
6:30–7:00	Rises, feeds cattle, takes them to pasture	Goes to buy bread, sweeps patio	Rises, sweeps kitchen, prepares utensils	Rises, goes for milk	In bed
7:00–7:30	Drinks coffee	Serves husband and self coffee	Grinds corn, makes tortillas	Drinks coffee, cuts and stores fish	Rises, washes, combs hair
7:30–8:00	Hauls water, shells corn for mules	Resumes sweeping patio	Grinds corn, makes tortillas	Smooths and folds laundered clothes	Breakfasts
8:00–8:30	Breakfasts	Combs hair, breakfasts, serves others	Grinds corn, makes tortillas	Breakfasts	Goes to school
8:30–9:00	Talks with investigator	Cuts squash for animals, cooks squash, shells corn	Grinds corn, makes tortillas	Makes beds	At school
9:00–9:30	Goes to bed	Arranges squash in market basket	Breakfasts	Sweeps porch	At school
9:30–10:00	In bed	Arranges squash in market basket	Washes dishes	Washes arms and feet, combs hair	At school
10:00–10:30	In bed	Goes to market to sell corn and squash	Prepares corn for grinding	Accompanies mother to market to make purchases	At school
10:30–11:00	In bed	At market	Prepares and cooks stew	At market	At school
11:00–11:30	In bed	At market	Prepares and cooks stew	At market	At school
11:30–12:00	In bed	At market	Prepares and cooks stew	Returns home, polishes nails	At school

P.M.					
12:00–12:30	Feeds mules	At market	Grinds corn	Talks with recorder	Returns home
12:30–1:00	Rests	At market	Makes tortillas	Feeds chickens	Does nothing
1:00–1:30	Rests	Returns home, prepares lunch	Makes tortillas	Helps making tortillas	Does nothing
1:30–2:00	Eats and talks with recorder	Serves and eats	Makes tortillas	Eats	Eats
2:00–2:30	Eats and talks with recorder	Serves and eats	Eats	Eats	Goes to school
2:30–3:00	Reads prayers	Serves and eats	Eats	Sews	At school
3:00–3:30	Goes to bed	Hauls water for animals	Washes dishes	Sews	At school
3:30–4:00	In bed	In bed	Washes dishes	Sews	At school
4:00–4:30	In bed	Cleans dried gourds	Shells corn, prepares dough	Sews	At school
4:30–5:00	Reads prayers	Cleans dried gourds	Shells corn, prepares dough	Sews	At school
5:00–5:30	In bed	Cleans dried gourds	Mends her clothes	Sews	Returns home
5:30–6:00	In bed	Feeds turkeys	Mends her clothes	Sews	Reads
6:00–6:30	In bed	Cuts squash for animals	Knits	Sews	Talks to friends
6:30–7:00	In bed	Mends blouse	Knits	Sews	Talks to friends
7:00–7:30	In bed	Goes to visit mother	Grinds corn	Goes for bread	Knits
7:30–8:00	In bed	Sits in kitchen, talks with girls	Makes tortillas	Prepares coffee	Knits
8:00–8:30	Gets up for coffee	Serves coffee to family and self	Eats	Eats	Eats
8:30–9:00	Goes to bed, takes medicine and foot bath	Prepares medicinal drink and foot bath for husband	Washes dishes	Knits	Knits
9:00–9:30	In bed	Goes to bed	Goes to bed	Knits	Knits
9:30–10:00	In bed	In bed	In bed	Goes to bed	Goes to bed

maps of this type may be constructed for quite large areas. Maps can be valuable contributions to field data for a number of reasons. They force the anthropologist to analyze closely the spatial dimensions of his village, the precise arrangements of habitations of kinsmen, the number, size, and variety of buildings, and the natural features of the area.

The maps included in this chapter, one by the author, of a Samoan village and two by Raymond Firth of a village in Tikopia record quite different details and show how maps can supplement ethnographic field reports. In the sketch of Ta'u village the reader will note the different symbols for houses of traditional native construction and those utilizing European materials and design. Since the latter type of construction represents a departure from indigenous culture methods,

VILLAGE LAND OWNERSHIP

The following numbers correspond to numbers on the village map and indicate the various families who own the village plots.

1. Lauofo	29. Nua	57. Niumata
2. Seu	30. Mailo	58. Tuumalo
3. Salausa	31. Salevao	59. Aiasau
4. Mua	32. Tuia'ana	60. Seumae
5. Talavale	33. Solia	61. Atiu
6. Su'afo'a	34. Faaea	62. Tafa
7. Mailo	35. Tufele	63. Pese
8. Aufotu	36. Upega	64. Fuatuua
9. Ulugalu	37. Saveena	65. Tulifua
10. Atuelua	38. Lauofo	66. Tago'a'i
11. Salevao	39. Liliu	67. Vivao
12. Leaai	40. Pomele	68. Mua
13. Fualau	41. Liliu	69. Ale
14. Salausa	42. Tuialu'ulu'u	70. Togotogo
15. Tuito'elau	43. Leui	71. Moliga
16. Pomelo	44. Mau'u	72. Tuimanufili
17. Li	45. Faumina	73. Tunupopo
18. Fiame	46. Gaoā	74. Ui
19. Aufotu	47. Siva	75. Taula
20. Savini	48. Manulauti	76. Ale
21. Pomele	49. Ioelu	77. Tauala
22. Seu	50. Tiāligo	78. Gogo
23. Aufotu	51. Lepolo	79. Maui
24. Mua	52. Taule'ale'a	80. Moliga
25. Atuelua	53. Milo	81. Ve'a
26. Sei	54. Lemau	82. Vivao
27. Lefiti	55. Faumina	83. Ve'a
28. Se'a	56. Taua	

Fig. 16–1 (from Holmes 1957).

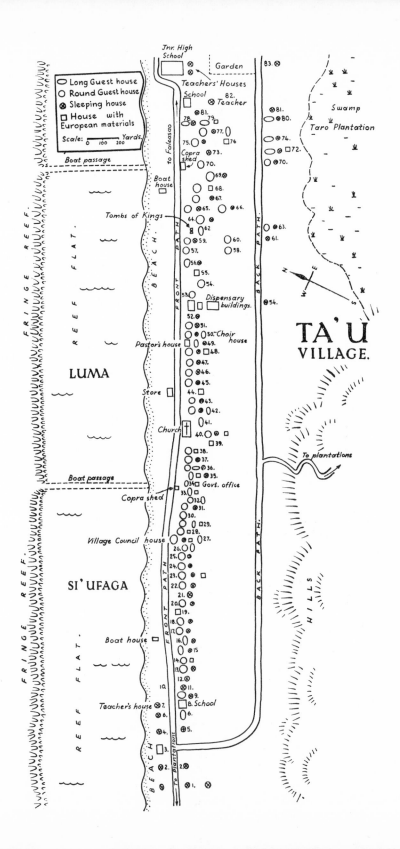

TA'U
VILLAGE.

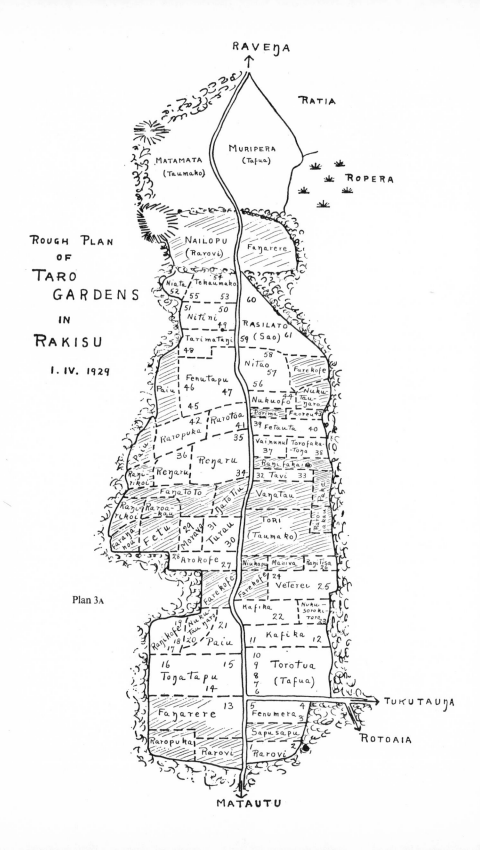

RAVEŊA

RATIA

MURIPERA
(Tafua)

MATAMATA
(Taumako)

ROPERA

ROUGH PLAN
OF
TARO
GARDENS
IN
RAKISU

1. IV. 1929

NAILOPU
(Rarovi)

Faŋarere

Niata Tehaumako 54
52 55 53 60
51 50
Nitini 49
Tarimataŋi 59 RASILATO 61
48 (Sao)
58
Fenutapu NiTao 57
Paiu 46 56 Farekofe
47 Nuku-
45 Nukuofo 44 Tau-
Porima Faoreu 43
42 Rarotoa 39 Fetauta 40
Raropuka 41
35 Vainunul Torofaka-
36 Reŋaru 37 -Toŋa 38
Raŋi rikoi Reŋaru 34 Raŋi fakaia
Fanatoto 32 Tavi 33
Raŋi Raroa- Ŋatotiu Vaŋatau
rikoi bau
Taraŋa noa Fetu 29 31 Turau TORI
Morava 30 (Taumako)
28 Arokofe 27 Niuhapu Mauiva Raŋitisa
Farekofe 24 26
Plan 3A Farekofe Veterei 25
Kafika 22 Nuku-
soroki-
Raŋi kofe 19 Nuku taro
18 20 Tau yaro 21 11 Kafika 12
17 Paiu
16 15 10
9 Torotua
ToŋaTapu 14 8 (Tafua)
7
Faŋarere 13 5 Fenumera 4
Sapusapu 3
Raropuka
Rarovi Rarovi

TUKUTAUŊA

ROTOAIA

MATAUTU

the map is useful in measuring one aspect of cultural change. A series of such maps drawn for the same village over a period of years could show the rate of change as well as its direction. Numbers appearing on the map represent separate households. Thus an analysis of the number and type of structures in each household gives some indication of its relative prosperity.

The Tikopia maps are valuable in the study of land tenure, ecology, and the physical-environmental aspects of the culture and the change that can take place in land usage over a period of twenty-three years.

TECHNICAL AIDS TO RESEARCH

Western technology has provided the field anthropologist with a number of devices to increase his efficiency in recording ethnographic data. In recent years cameras and tape recorders have become considered almost essential equipment for, in a manner of speaking, they allow the anthropologist to bring a little bit of the culture home with him. Both still and motion pictures capture events that can be studied again and again. Many times they will provide him with information that he neglected to note while in the field. If, for example, he failed to see how a certain type of lashing was made in house construction, he can have his pictures of housing enlarged and study this technique in detail. Many times a complete set of photographs can be useful to others doing cross-cultural comparisons of certain cultural features. An example of this might be the study of comparative motor behavior from motion pictures with a number of sequences showing native peoples dancing or working. Although the anthropologist who originally recorded the sequences may not have been interested in this aspect of the culture at all, he makes it possible for others to analyze this facet of culture without actually going to the area themselves.

No matter how carefully an anthropologist tries to record the details of an intricate ceremony, he can never hope to match the documentary capabilities of the motion picture camera. With his photographic record he has, in effect, a set of notes that will allow him the ultimate in precision in writing descriptions of the proceedings. One anthropologist confessed that he "couldn't make head nor tail" out of a particular weaving process he observed and therefore took a movie of the whole procedure so he could figure it out when he got home.

Margaret Mead has also shown that photographs can be extremely useful in the study of native personality. In her study of Balinese

---

Fig. 16–2 (from Firth 1959). (*Continued on page 340.*)

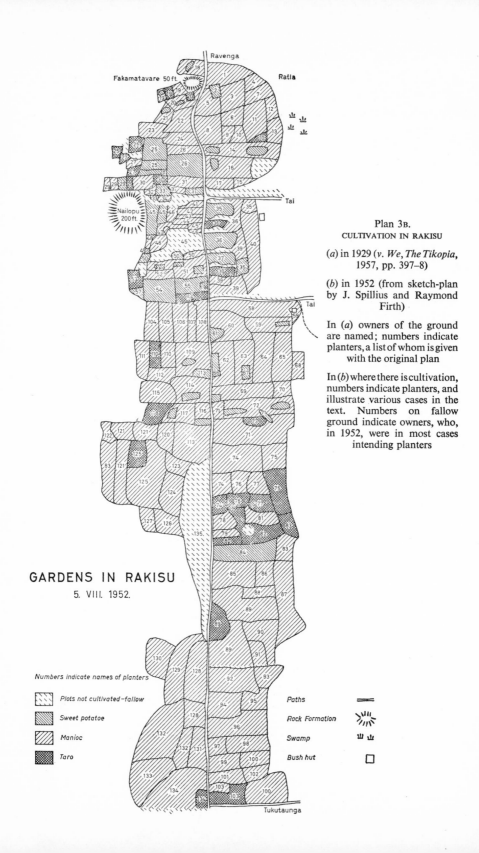

Plan 3B.
CULTIVATION IN RAKISU

(a) in 1929 (v. We, *The Tikopia*, 1957, pp. 397–8)

(b) in 1952 (from sketch-plan by J. Spillius and Raymond Firth)

In (a) owners of the ground are named; numbers indicate planters, a list of whom is given with the original plan

In (b) where there is cultivation, numbers indicate planters, and illustrate various cases in the text. Numbers on fallow ground indicate owners, who, in 1952, were in most cases intending planters

GARDENS IN RAKISU
5. VIII. 1952.

Numbers indicate names of planters

	Plots not cultivated–fallow		Paths
	Sweet potatoe		Rock Formation
	Manioc		Swamp
	Taro		Bush hut

personality she took hundreds of photographs of body attitudes and facial expressions of people as they expressed love, sympathy, fear, anxiety, or hatred.

A set of still pictures or a reel of movies can become, in effect, museum specimens recording aspects of a culture that have disappeared upon increased contact with the Western world. Many of the details of American Indian house types and costumes are known to modern anthropologists only because of ancient yellowing photographs that have been preserved in museum archives. An interesting set of photographs in this respect is that to be found in Margaret Mead's book *New Lives From Old*. Between her visits in 1928 and in 1953, revolutionary changes took place in the Manus island community described in this volume. The then-and-now photographs clearly show the changes and record for all time the culture of 1928, which is no more.

The tape recorder is a newer addition to the field worker's set of scientific gadgets, but it has great research possibilities. Kenneth Emory of Bishop Museum in Honolulu states that "the tape recorder is the greatest boon to the field worker" (Holmes 1962:6). He points out that a recorder enables the anthropologist to get native text (useful in linguistic analysis) and samples of music for ethnomusicological research. Emory also suggests that the tape recorder might prove extremely valuable in the interview situation, especially if the fieldworker is having difficulty using the native language. He recommends, "Let them talk freely. You can miss much at the start before you have the language in hand, but later you can go back on this record" (*Ibid.*). While the fieldworker frequently finds himself in an area where electrical power is not available, this is no great obstacle to using a recorder, since a number of small battery-operated instruments have been developed which are adequate for research purposes.

THE GOAL OF ANTHROPOLOGICAL RESEARCH

We have mentioned only a few of the more traditional anthropological field methods; there are many others and as anthropology matures

---

Fig. 16–2. (Continued.)

In (a) (page 338) owners of the ground are named; numbers indicate planters, a list of whom is given with the original plan.

In (b) where there is cultivation, numbers indicate planters, and illustrate various cases in the text. Numbers on fallow ground indicate owners, who, in 1952, were in most cases intending planters.

as a discipline many more methods will be developed to ensure more penetrating and productive research. Although the ways and means of studying man's cultures may be refined, the anthropologist will continue to pursue the goal that was described as early as 1922, by the British anthropologist Malinowski. It is:

. . . to grasp the native's point of view, his relation to life, to realise *his* vision of *his* world. We have to study man, and we must study what concerns him most intimately, that is, the hold which life has on him. In each culture, the values are slightly different; people aspire after different aims, follow different impulses, yearn after a different form of happiness. In each culture, we find different institutions in which man pursues his life-interest, different customs by which he satisfies his aspirations, different codes of law and morality which reward his virtues or punish his defections. To study the institutions, customs, and codes or to study the behaviour and mentality without the subjective desire of feeling by what these people live, of realising the substance of their happiness—is, in my opinion, to miss the greatest reward which we can hope to obtain from the study of man. (1961:25)

SUGGESTED READINGS

BENNETT, J. W. "The Study of Cultures: A Survey of Technique and Methodology in Fieldwork," *American Sociological Review,* 13:672, 1948. (A survey of the more important methods used in studies of non-literate societies, urban neighborhoods, or rural villages.)

BOAS, FRANZ. "The Aims of Anthropological Research," *Science,* 76:605, 1932. (Presents anthropology as an historical science rather than one primarily concerned with establishing general laws of human behavior.)

DuBois, CORA. "Some Psychological Objectives and Techniques in Ethnology," *The Journal of Social Psychology,* 8:285, 1937. (Deals with problems which must be solved by all cultural anthropologists in the field—use of the native language, establishing rapport, and carrying on effective interviews.)

KLUCKHOHN, F. R. "The Participant Observer Technique in Small Communities," *American Journal of Sociology,* 46:331, 1940. (Manner in which range, relevance, and reliability of field data may be increased through participation in community activities.)

MURDOCK, GEORGE PETER. "The Cross-Cultural Survey," *American Sociological Review,* 5:361, 1940. (Description of the Human Relations Area File system developed by Yale University to organize and classify the great body of cultural data.)

————. "World Ethnographic Sample," *American Anthropologist,* 59:664, 1957. (A representative sample of the world's cultures is classified according to standard ethnographic categories.)

WARNER, W. L. "Social Anthropology and the Modern Community; Method of Community Study," *American Journal of Sociology,* 46:785, 1941. (The value of social status classification as a method in community studies.)

Paperbound Books

CASAGRANDE, JOSEPH (ed.). *In the Company of Man.* Harper and Row. (Profiles of key informants by a number of ethnographers.)

BEALS, ALAN R., and HITCHCOCK, JOHN T. *Field Guide to India.* Publication 704 (1960), National Academy of Sciences, National Research Council.

BEARDSLEY, RICHARD. *Field Guide to Japan.* Publication 716 (1959), National Academy of Sciences, National Research Council.

HUTCHINSON, H. W. *Field Guide to Brazil.* Publication 908 (1961), National Academy of Sciences, National Research Council.

WOLFE, ALVIN. *Field Guide to West and Central Africa.* Publication 702 (1959), National Academy of Sciences, National Research Council.

(The above field guides have been prepared to aid the novice research worker in establishing a favorable working climate for himself and in selecting the most effective methods of field investigation.)

17

Understanding
Other Cultures

Among the Australian aborigines when a stranger is encountered by a hunting band, he is immediately considered an enemy unless he can discover some kinsman among the party and thus establish some common basis for understanding. If he cannot, he will be quickly driven off or killed. While this rather narrow and unfriendly point of view has been unanimously condemned by the Western world on the grounds that it is quite uncivilized, the West has given little indication that its learned enlightenment has led it to develop adequate means for understanding the strange and different cultures of the world. It would seem that the tendency to look down on other people with different ways of life as inferiors or even as potential enemies in order to bolster one's own personal or national ego is as old as time itself. Cicero once wrote Attilus, advising him thus: "Whatever you do, do not buy English slaves, for the English people are so dull and stupid that they are not fit to be slaves . . ." This, of course, was during a period of Roman domination, but at an earlier period, when the Greeks were in a position of power, they referred to the Romans as "barbarians, good enough to kill and fight, but devoid of culture and having base souls." Going back even farther in history we find that the Egyptians felt that the Greeks "are but children . . . who . . . have no history, no past, no adequate civilization."

Usually the claims of superiority have been based on evidence of cultural differences and always there is the underlying feeling that if another people are of equal quality why do they behave so differently. When European peoples first observed the behavior of nonindustrial people living in the remote and isolated corners of the world, they saw very little to admire in their way of life and categorically labeled them "savages," "barbarians," and "primitives." Although the latter term is used by anthropologists even today, it *does* carry overtones of crudeness and childlikeness, and many anthropologists prefer more objective labels such as "preliterate" or "nonliterate." When we turn to the early accounts of primitive people written by explorers, government administrators, and even scientists, we find no end of derogatory assessments of native minds as judged by native manners.

In the late eighteenth century the French naturalist Comte de Buffon described the North American Indians as having "no vivacity, no activity of mind; the activity of his body is less an exercise, a voluntary motion, than a necessary action caused by want; relieve him of hunger and thirst, and you deprive him of the active principle of all his movements; he will rest stupidly upon his legs or lying down entire days" (1866:464).

In 1839 the American scientist Samuel G. Morton wrote that "the mental faculties of the Eskimo from infancy to old age, present a continued childhood; they reach a certain limit and expand no further." Of the Australian aborigine he said "It is not probable that this people as a body are capable of any other than their slight degree of civilization" (1839 *Passim*).

Some scholars have couched their derogatory views of primitive people in elaborate theories. One social philosopher, Lucien Levy-Bruhl, actually became an authority on the subject of primitive mentality. It was his position that primitive people are prelogical. This meant that their minds were entirely governed by waves of emotional force developed in ritual activities. They did not therefore analyze and they did not seek explanations. Primitives, he felt, did not understand cause-and-effect relationships. Western man, on the other hand, had been able to progress because he had been able to develop a purely rational and scientific pattern of thought, totally divorced from the pressures of emotion. Even today there are many seemingly intelligent people who feel that the majority of aborigines justifiably warrant the name "primitive" because they are more emotional, less reasonable and rational than we.

LABELS

As is true of many social problems, much of the difficulty in cross-cultural understanding arises out of the use of labels and stereotypes. Although there are quite detailed and objective definitions of such terms as "primitive" and "civilized," Western man often thinks of the latter term as symbolic of total cultural superiority and lets it go at that. It is no wonder that anthropologists like Goldenweiser, in trying to tip the balance, suggested that civilization should be synonomous with culture. In keeping with this idea, he makes reference to "Australian civilization," "Hopi civilization," and "Masai civilization" in his writing.

V. Gordon Childe (1950) has drawn up a very adequate set of criteria for recognizing a civilization. They are (1) a great increase in the size of the settlement, (2) the institution of tribute or taxation with resulting central accumulation of capital, (3) monumental public works, (4) the art of writing, (5) the beginnings of such exact and predictive sciences as arithmetic, geometry, and astronomy, (6) developed economic institutions making possible a greatly expanded foreign trade, (7) full-time technical specialists, (8) a privileged ruling class, and (9) the state. It will be noted that at least six of these criteria depend greatly on technological advance. If we define civilization in terms of advanced technology, there can be little quarrel that the industrial cultures of the West are more civilized than those aboriginal populations of Africa, Asia, Oceania, or the Americas. If we use civilization as a mere term of classification (similar to industrial), there is no real problem. If, however, we define civilization as an overall superiority in all aspects of culture, then there might be some serious question as to the civilized nature of the West. Man cannot live by gadgets alone and there is no reason why technology should be a yardstick for evaluating the quality of a culture. It would seem logical that a truly advanced culture should exhibit a high development of philosophy, literature, the arts, and government. Yet we are embarrassed to read that Hindu intellectuals consider Americans incredibly "boorish," "materialistic," "unintellectual," and "uncivilized." While Hindu culture has never been exceptionally noteworthy for its technological developments, it has been renowned for centuries for its high development of music, literature, art, and philosophy.

CULTURAL RELATIVISM

Closely associated with the proper evaluation of the quality of cultures is the concept of *cultural relativism*. This concept, which has become a dominant theme in anthropology, is defined by Redfield as follows:

Cultural relativism means that the values expressed in any culture are to be both understood and themselves valued only according to the way the people who carry that culture see things. In looking at a polygamous society and a monogamous society, we have no valid way to assert that the one is better than the other. Both systems provide for human needs; each has values discoverable only when we look at marriage from the point of view of the man who lives under the one system or the other. (1958:144)

Cultural relativism represents a rejection of the bigotry and self-centeredness that quite naturally develops in all cultures. This self- or group-centeredness, commonly known as *ethnocentrism*, is a very natural human reaction, and within limits, a rather essential requirement for group solidarity. If the members of a particular group had no preference for their own group, there would be nothing to hold it together. When this ingroup feeling develops to the extent that the members of a particular society feel that their way of life is so superior to all others that it is their duty to change other people to their way of thinking and doing (if necessary by force), then this attitude becomes a menace.

Cultural Relativism at the United Nations

Believing that the tolerance that comes from an understanding and application of a relativistic point of view is vital to harmonious human

The United Nations—unity in spite of infinite cultural diversity.

relations, the Executive Board of the American Anthropological Association submitted in 1947 the following statement to the Commission on Human Rights of the United Nations:

1. The individual realizes his personality through his culture: hence respect for individual differences entails a respect for cultural differences.

2. Respect for differences between cultures is validated by the scientific fact that no technique of qualitatively evaluating cultures has been discovered.

3. Standards and values are relative to the culture from which they derive, so that any attempt to formulate postulates that grow out of the beliefs or moral codes of one culture must to that extent detract from the applicability of any Declaration of Human Rights to mankind as a whole.

What this statement basically attempts to convey is that it is unfair and undemocratic for any one society to declare that it alone has the right cultural road. It reminds people of all nations that each society should be free to solve certain cultural problems according to their own time-tested methods without condemnation from those who would choose different solutions. It pleads, in essence, not to think too harshly of the Eskimo or Bushman mother who has no other choice but to put a new-born child to death if it is born before its sibling is old enough to fend for itself. The practice of infanticide undoubtedly tears the heart out of the mother, but there is no choice if the group as a whole is to survive. Hunters who live constantly on the edge of starvation cannot be burdened with surplus helpless children. This practice, which we would define as murder, is not too foreign from our own concepts of behavior, however, when we are faced with a matter of individual versus group survival. During time of war there have been numerous occasions when it was necessary to sacrifice an individual rather than to put the lives of an entire company of soldiers or a whole ship's crew in jeopardy.

The relativistic statement submitted to the United Nations further points up the fact that primitives who believe in animistic gods do so because they were raised to believe in them, and it is the cultural deviant who rejects his indigenous religion. Cultural relativism also says that a man raised in Africa has a basic human right to follow the norms of his society and practice plural marriage; it brands as irresponsible such dogmatic proclamations as that of an American industrialist who queried in a graduation address, "How can we hope to sit down at a conference table and work out a satisfactory agreement for peace with men who have more than one wife?"

DIFFICULTIES OF INTERPRETATION. The United Nations statement on Human Rights is a good one from the standpoint that it strongly condemns bigotry and ethnocentric attitudes. On the other hand, the statement if taken literally proclaims that all cultures are equally good and all forms of behavior, no matter how destructive or inhumane they might be, should be respected. It implies that the people of New Guinea have a perfect right to take a neighbor's head as part of an ordeal validating manhood, and it would sanction the destruction of all village property standing in the way of the litter on which the corpse of a Samoan king is carried. The statement taken literally gives the nod of approval to *suttee* and other forms of ceremonial human sacrifice. The statement leaves no room for condemnation of racial segregation in America, or Apartheid in South Africa, or even of the killing of millions of Jews in Germany during the Nazi regime. The majority of the world's peoples would surely hesitate to sanction much of this behavior, but a strict position of cultural relativism would demand that they respect all customs and cultures as equally good.

Faced with a position of bigoted ethnocentrism at one pole and uncritical cultural relativism at the other, the student of social science often stands bewildered, trying to locate himself on the continuum. Is it possible, he asks, to prefer the benefits of modern medicine to the practices of the bush doctor and still be an objective observer of human culture? Any number of scholars would answer "Yes."

ARE SOME CULTURES MORE ADVANCED?

Kroeber for one has stated that there is validity in maintaining that some cultures are indeed more advanced intellectually and have progressed farther than others. In a rather daring attack on the problem he has arrived at "three approaches that seem to yield at least a partial standard of what constitutes 'higher' or more advanced culture, apart from mere quantity of it" (1948:298). His three criteria for assessing cultural level are concerned with (1) magic and superstition, (2) obtrusion of physiological or anatomical considerations in social situations, and (3) cumulative quality of technology, mechanics, and science.

Magic and Superstition

Kroeber feels that

. . . in proportion as a culture disengages itself from reliance on these, it may be said to have registered an advance . . . When the sane and well in one culture believe what only the most ignorant, warped, and insane believe in another, there would seem to be some warrant for rating the first culture lower and the second higher. (*Ibid.*)

While our own Western society can hardly claim vast superiority over the primitive in the realm of magic and superstition, many primitive societies assign the cause of all physical illness to witchcraft and sorcery; and while certain societies believe that charms and rituals can solve all of their problems, there should also be a certain stigma attached to a society that refuses to give up its magical practices and superstitions when its science has proved these invalid. Many of the large medical centers in the United States boast the most advanced therapy and facilities and yet there is not a hospital in our country that has a room or floor 13 for patient use. While nearly every large newspaper in the United States has considered dropping their astrology feature, few have had the courage to do so and face the fury of its sizeable public.

On April 25, 1961, a United Press International release from London read as follows:

Dr. Gerald Gardner, a self-proclaimed witch, said Monday the world situation is so precarious the witches of Britain may have to "raise a cone of power" against a nuclear war.

A well-known anthropologist when he is not engaged in witchcraft, Gardner, 77, said that at least three times before in history British witches have massed their powers to prevent harm to the nation.

"The first time we know of was in 1588 when witches 'willed' the failure of the Spanish Armada," he said.

"The witches also worked against Napoleon in the days when he was assembling invasion barges on the French coast. And the word went out again during the last war to concentrate on the mind of Adolf Hitler and keep him from going through with his plan to invade England. Whether the witches helped or not I will leave it to others to judge—but the fact is that in all three cases the things the witches did not want to happen, did not happen."

Physiological and Anatomical Obtrusions

Kroeber feels that a high culture is one that has been able to throw off a pre-occupation with blood, death, and decay. Some of the practices that he feels are characteristic of a less advanced culture are blood and animal sacrifice, segregation of menstruating women, anatomical mutilations, puberty rites, mummification, human sacrifice, head-hunting, and cannibalism. Civilized people, he maintains, tend to look upon such practices with "aversion, disgust, revulsion, or the shame of bad taste" (1948:300).

Technology and Science

The area in which progress can best be measured is that of technology. Whereas it is difficult to say objectively that monogamy is more progressive than polygamy or that monotheism is more progressive than polytheism, it is possible to say that a steel axe is a better tool than a stone axe and a gun is a better weapon than a spear. The important consideration is the function of the tool. If it is to chop down a tree and a steel axe can do it in one-tenth the time it takes with one made of stone, then the former is the more advanced tool. While it can definitely be shown that European cultures are far more advanced technologically than African or Oceanic ones, this does not necessarily imply superiority in all aspects of culture. Although the West was able to develop an atomic bomb, the act of dropping it on Japanese cities is considered by some a more savage thing than the sporadic headhunting activities of some primitives. It is somewhat embarrassing to read, in an account by Lowie, of the Eskimo who stated a desire to send missionaries to teach the white man how foolish (and primitive?) it is to go to war with one another.

Kroeber comes to a final conclusion that there *are* more advanced (or adult) cultures and also infantile ones. He believes that with civilization comes a greater concern for humaneness—e.g., opposition to slavery, torture, and capital punishment and slaughter of prisoners of war. When any of these things are done by a supposedly civilized people (the Nazis, for example), we are more horrified than if they were carried out by some South American bush tribe.

Primitive cultures have been so much maligned that the anthropologist, somewhat unscientifically, will take an overly relativistic position and will not admit that Western culture is in any way superior to those of the African, American Indians, or South Sea islanders. But J. C. Furnas, a very anthropologically minded journalist, has made a point that we are forced to consider. He writes:

For generations the western world has bitterly blamed western man for the crime of not understanding the savage. It seems never to occur to anyone that, other things being equal, it would be equally fair to blame the savage for not understanding western man. Since that would obviously be absurd, the two sets of cultures are unmistakably on different levels, a statement that can be made without specifying higher or lower. Western man has something which neither the preliterate nor any of his ancestors possess or ever did possess, something that imposes the privilege and complicating duty of intellectual integrity, self-criticism, and generalized disinterestedness. If there is such a thing as the white man's burden, this is it. (1937:488)

Thus, we arrive at what Redfield describes as a "double standard of ethical judgment toward primitive peoples." In such a system, he explains:

We do not expect the preliterate person to cultivate and protect individual freedom of thought as we expect civilized people to do. We do not blame the Veddah for failing to have a subtle graphic art. We understand how it is that the Siriono husband leaves his wife to die alone in the jungle, and we do not condemn him as we condemn the suburban husband who leaves his wife to die in a snowdrift. We do not expect a people to have a moral norm that their material conditions of life make impossible. (1953:163)

The important thing to consider is the fact that because we find a custom or two offensive is no reason for rejecting the entire culture as backward and incapable of growth and development. We cannot always condemn the primitive for following inhumane ways or for lacking respect for human life. His scope of thought has been stunted by isolation and shackled by vested interests, supernatural taboos, and fear of change. He has not had the opportunity of freely selecting or rejecting the ideas of thousands of minds like those of Einstein, Goethe, Aristotle, or Jefferson. We cannot condemn his head-hunting, infanticide, or cruelty, but we can prefer the enlightened heritage of civilization. If we can respect limitations, understand differences, and emphasize those things held in common, we then have, in essence, a skeleton for developing world understanding.

COMPROMISE POSITIONS

Often the cause of failures in cross-cultural understanding is the tendency to dwell too much upon cultural differences rather than attempting to discover common denominators among them. On first acquaintance with any foreign people there is a temptation to be overly impressed with differences in language, dress, food, and customs, but many an anthropologist after studying a group of people for an extended period of time has discovered that in the more important aspects of daily living people are much the same the world over.

There is in fact a tenable position between a completely ethnocentric and a completely relativistic point of view, and that is to respect those cultures whose practices tend to correspond to a universal system of ethics, and look with disfavor on those who have developed, in one way or another, customs that ignore or violate those common principles that men the world over observe in order to promote the welfare of their group and species.

In an essay summarizing these worldwide ethical uniformities Ralph Linton states:

The resemblances in ethical concepts so far outweigh the differences that a sound basis for mutual understanding between groups of different cultures is already in existence. The present difficulties seem to stem from two main sources: the first is that societies which share the same values often differ considerably in the relative importance which they attach to them. To judge from historic evidence on the changes which have taken place in various cultures, such differences are by no means insurmountable. A greater difficulty lies in the age-old tendency of every society's members to assume that ethical systems apply only within their own tribe or nation. This attitude is difficult to overcome but the modern world is witnessing a rapid expansion of social horizons. When people learn to think of themselves as members of a single world society, it will be easy for them to agree on a single ethical system. (1952:660)

Universal Ethics

One of the claims frequently laid on primitive people by Europeans is that they are dishonest not only in their dealings with strangers but with each other. Although the first allegation is often true, it should be remembered that all people have a strong sense of in-group as opposed to out-group. This is certainly true in our own society as evidenced by the grocer who will set aside the best produce for his friends, relatives, and good customers but will sell the poorer quality goods to strangers and occasional shoppers. Among many peoples it is actually considered good fun to cheat the outsider. Linton points out that within the in-group, however, "theft is everywhere regarded as a crime and is severely punished" (1952:656). He adds that:

. . . all societies recognize economic obligations of the sort involved in exchange of goods and services and the individual who fails to live up to them is punished simply but effectively by exclusion from future exchanges. Attitudes with respect to sharp practices show more diversity but each society defines the areas in which such practices are permitted and usually has rules as to what techniques are and are not permissible." (1952:657)

Closely associated with dishonesty, at least in the minds of Europeans, is the practice of lying. While few societies set such a high value on telling the truth as we do, Linton's research reveals that all societies demand truth in certain areas of personal interaction and some even go so far as to demand that its members take oaths.

The statement is often made that "life is cheap" in primitive societies, but killing or maiming without justification is universally condemned. Again the problem we face is the in-group out-group differentiation. While no headhunter would wantonly take the head of a next door neighbor, he often feels quite justified in taking one in the next village occupied by a different tribe. He, of course, would strenuously object to a "turn about is fair play" policy. And here it is believed that the anthropologist is justified in condemning a people for imposing practices on other people that they do not sanction within their own group. In this respect warfare as carried on by modern nations is as reprehensible as headhunting. When our side kills the enemy it is glorious, but when our soldiers are killed it is an atrocity.

While the attitudes toward sexual behavior vary widely from one society to another, each feels that it must regulate sex behavior. Every society prohibits incest, abhors rape, and punishes adulterers, but beyond this, what constitutes sexual morality is a matter of divergent definition. Sometimes the codes of sexual morality are stricter than those in European society but lay emphasis on entirely different things.

It also appears that every society admires the "good family man" and responsible parent. Linton writes that

. . . Lifelong union of spouses is everywhere the ideal no matter how easy and frequent separations may be in practice . . . Each parent must make certain contributions toward the economic life of the family (and) loyalty to the spouse is expected in most societies . . . (1952:652)

Other phases of intrafamily behavior appear universally similar also. While ideas on discipline vary widely, sadistic and irresponsible punishment of children by parents is everywhere condemned and violence toward a parent is usually a major crime. Every society nourishes its in-group feelings, but the family is the tightest in-group of them all. Feelings that "blood is thicker than water" are standard and ensure family stability and security for its members the world over.

Not only does man everywhere feel a responsibility to family but we can find similar feelings for fellow group members and for the group as a whole. There are always recognized ways of caring for poor and unfortunate individuals, and as Linton points out:

Among the values involved in ethical systems, that of insuring the perpetuation and successful functioning of the society always takes first place. Acts which threaten the group are condemned and punished with greater severity than those which threaten only individuals . . . All societies also recognize that there is a point beyond which the interests of the individual must be made subordinate to those of the state. (1952:659)

Real and Ideal Behavior

One of the factors that often brings about intolerance and hostility toward other cultures is the common tendency to compare the worst in another culture with the best in one's own. There is also the tendency, particularly on the part of Europeans, to compare primitive *real* behavior with the *ideal* standards of the West. In Samoa it is often alleged by Americans and Englishmen alike that Samoans are "not a religious people" in spite of their faithful church attendance, tithing-plus practices, and almost fanatical church-building activities. It is maintained that the Samoans only like the ceremonial nature of the church services, and as for their church-building, it is only a method of gaining prestige for themselves and their villages. While some of this may be true, one can hardly speak disparagingly of Samoan Christianity when one comes from a culture where a large percentage of people go to church only on Easter, and then only to show off their new spring attire.

The same principle would apply to Polynesian morality. While ideally sex activity is confined to marriage in American culture, a number of studies have shown that this is far from the truth, and if the actual figures could be obtained they would probably show that in his erotic behavior the average American youth differs little from his South Sea island counterpart. The people of West Africa are often bitterly criticized for their custom of plural marriage but whether one has several wives at once or several, one after the other, as we sometimes find in America, seems only a technicality.

ONE WORLD OR SEVERAL

In a book carrying the same title as this chapter, Ina Corinne Brown writes the following solemn warning:

> Our only hope of a peaceful, just and reasonably orderly world lies in the development of sufficient knowledge, insight, understanding, and maturity on the part of enough people so that we can respect differences, be willing to live and let live, and work together to solve the common problems that are involved when two and one half billion people attempt to share an ever-shrinking globe. (1958:v)

Many people have felt that if the whole world were one culturally, our problems of maintaining the peace would be over. The cultural uniformity of America was of little help in maintaining peace in 1860, nor did our common cultural heritage keep us from war with Great Britain in 1775 or 1812. Thus stressing the cultural similarities between all peoples does not really guarantee that we will be able to live together in peace. It has often been said that America and the Soviet Union have trouble getting along not because they have such different cultures but rather because they are so similar. Both are products of revolutions, both have great national pride, both are technologically minded, both are anxious to spread their political doctrine, and both yearn to be world leaders.

Unity Through Diversity

Although for many years man has been recognized as part of the animal kingdom, there is a great tendency to consider him apart from the world of nature. Diversity is the rule of nature; in our complex world no two leaves, snowflakes, sets of fingerprints, or individuals are exactly alike. To expect all mankind to practice the same set of customs, hold the same values, and be equally motivated by common situations is contrary to this rule of nature.

The anthropologist feels that the only answer to world harmony is unity through diversity, achievable only by an attitude of live and let live. Since all cultures have something to offer mankind, the greatest good can accrue to man from recognizing the value of each and every culture, and through this proper evaluation of their worth then profiting from cross-cultural fertilization of these different points of view rather than trying to change them to a single pattern of thought and action.

WHERE TO START

Just "knowing" man is not the ultimate answer in achieving a peaceful world, but it is surely a start. We have to learn to get along with each other, but the greater share of this is knowing man and thus being able to predict his behavior. No civil engineer builds a bridge and then runs a train over it to test its strength. First he painstakingly investigates the characteristics of every piece of material which will go into the structure. He predicts where the greatest stresses and strains will occur and compensates for this in his material. The anthropologist believes that a peaceful world can be achieved only by a thorough knowledge of man as he functions in his many cultures.

A number of years ago Mark Twain said that everyone complains about the weather but no one does anything about it. Today through the science of meteorology things are being done about it. Perhaps the actual weather can be changed very little but through accurate prediction, the disastrous effects of its flare-ups can be minimized. In like manner the science of anthropology attempts to understand man, predict his actions, and reduce points of tension. If men are to live together successfully in an atomic age, they are going to have to learn to do it and the greater share of this learning centers on knowing the nature of culture and the nature of man.

We are often tempted to ask why we must worry about understanding and respecting the way of life of all these primitives anyway. There are two reasons: One is the moral reason that these people have a right to be respected as human beings of worth, the same as we. If there is to be any freedom or dignity of mankind, it must be shared equally by all human beings and not be considered the heritage of a fortunate few. The other reason for our understanding foreign and primitive

Cross-cultural understanding—a basic Peace Corps principle. (Courtesy of John and Bini Moss for *Black Star*.)

people is a practical one. If we do not learn to live with them, we may one day have to defend our lives against them. As the wealthiest and most powerful nation in the world, the United States is, whether we like it or not, an example. Whether it is a good or bad one depends on us. We have made a great point of the supposition that our democratic way of life is better than all other forms, as it has at its heart the ideas of the equality and fraternity of all men. Many of the people of Africa, Asia, and Oceania were only yesterday dominated by foreign colonial powers but today they are free. As members of newly emerging countries they can follow the way of the free democratic world or choose totalitarianism in its many forms. If democracy advocates that all people regardless of color or culture can live together peacefully respecting each other's rights, we must show them that this is in truth the way it works. It is not enough to groom a few dedicated young people in a Peace Corps effort. We must accept the responsibilities of democracy as a nation and as individuals in our relations and attitudes to people of the whole world. Democracy depends on responsible citizens who are well informed on the issues. The issues of cross-cultural understanding are now of vital importance. Let us hope that through the scientific and humanitarian influence of anthropology and its related sciences we can learn to think clearly and feel deeply about the species man in all his cultural variety.

SUGGESTED READINGS

COUSINS, NORMAN. "Confrontation," *Saturday Review,* March 25, 1961. (Describes the shocking discovery that other cultures are conspicuously different in values and standard of living.)

———. "A Plea to the Fijians," *Saturday Review,* July 25, 1964. (How we can take a lesson from the Fijians, who in less than one hundred years have changed from warlike cannibals to one of the most friendly and cooperative people known to anthropologists.)

EISELEY, LOREN. "An Evolutionist Looks at Modern Man," *Saturday Evening Post,* April 26, 1958. (The key to human survival—love and understanding.)

HALL, EDWARD T. "The Anthropology of Manners," *Scientific American,* April, 1955. (The importance of understanding and respecting cultural variation.)

HONIGMANN, J. J. "White Man's New Burden; What Anthropology Indicates as the Best Colonial Policy," *Commonweal,* March 12, 1943. Entreats us to respect the right of other cultures to be different and points out that we do not have the right even to force beneficial change.

USEEM, JOHN. "Americans as Governors of Natives in the Pacific," *Journal of Social Issues,* August, 1946. (How inability to adjust to the values of a foreign culture can lead to administrative problems.)

Paperbound Books

BOHANNAN, LAURA M. *Return to Laughter.* Doubleday. (How an anthropologist's wife learns to accept a native people for what they are.)

BROWN, INA CORINNE. *Understanding Other Cultures.* Prentice-Hall. (Explores the problem of how cultural differences can be resolved and lived with.)

DIAMOND, STANLEY (ed.). *Primitive Views of the World.* Columbia University Press. (Essays dealing with definitions of primitive processes, descriptions of primitive societies and critiques of civilization in anthropological perspective.)

HALL, EDWARD T. *The Silent Language.* Fawcett Publications. (Deals with the language of behavior, a source of misunderstanding in intercultural communication.)

MALINOWSKI, BRONISLAW. *Freedom and Civilization.* Indiana University Press. (Problems of peace and war analyzed cross-culturally.)

Literature Cited

ACKERKNECHT, ERWIN H. 1953. "Paleopathology," in KROEBER, A. L. (ed.), *Anthropology Today*. Chicago, University of Chicago Press.

ALLPORT, FLOYD. 1934. "The J-Curve Hypothesis of Conforming Behavior," *Journal of Social Psychology*, 5:141–83.

ARGYLE, MICHAEL. 1959. *Religious Behavior*. Glencoe, Ill., Free Press.

ATTWOOD, WILLIAM. 1958. "The American Male: Why Does He Work so Hard?" *Look*, 22:70–75 (March 4).

BARKER, GORDON H. 1940. "Family Factors in the Ecology of Juvenile Delinquency," *Journal of Criminal Law and Criminology*, 30:681–91.

BASCOM, WILLIAM R. 1948. "West Africa and the Complexity of Primitive Cultures," *American Anthropologist*, 50:18–23.

BATESON, GREGORY, and MEAD, MARGARET. 1942. *Balinese Character, a Photographic Analysis*. New York, New York Academy of Sciences.

BEALS, ALAN. 1962. *Gopalpur: A South Indian Village*. New York, Holt, Rinehart & Winston.

BEALS, RALPH L., and HOIJER, HARRY. 1959. *An Introduction to Anthropology*. New York, Macmillan.

BENEDICT, RUTH. 1938. "Continuities and Discontinuities in Cultural Conditioning," *Psychiatry*, 1:161–67.

————. 1943. *Thai Culture and Behavior*. (Mimeographed. Distributed by the Institute for Intercultural Studies, Inc.)

————. 1959. *Patterns of Culture*. (Preface by Margaret Mead.) New York, New American Library. Copyright 1934, Houghton Mifflin.

BENNETT, JOHN W. 1946. "The Interpretation of Pueblo Culture," *Southwestern Journal of Anthropology*, 24:361–74.

BENNETT, JOHN W., and WOLFF, KURT H. 1956. "Toward Communication between Sociology and Anthropology," in THOMAS, WILLIAM L., JR. (ed.). *Current Anthropology*. Chicago, University of Chicago Press.

BINGHAM, HIRAM. 1848. *A Residence of Twenty-One Years in the Sandwich Islands*. Hartford, Hezekiah Huntington.

361

BOAS, FRANZ. 1895. *Indianische Sagen von der Nord-Pacifischen Kuste Amerikas.* Berlin, A. Asher and Co.

————. 1908. "Decorative Designs of Alaskan Needle Cases: A Study in the History of Conventional Designs, Based on Materials in the U. S. National Museum," *Proceedings of the U. S. National Museum,* 34:321–44.

———— (ed.). 1938. *General Anthropology.* New York, Heath.

————. 1948. *Race, Language and Culture.* New York, Macmillan.

————. 1955. *Primitive Art.* New York, Dover.

BOOTH, CHARLES. 1891. *Life and Labour of the People of London* (4 vols.). London, Williams and Norgate.

BROWN, INA CORINNE. 1958. *Understanding Other Cultures.* Cincinnati. This edition was produced for women's study groups in the Methodist church and is now out of print. A revision has been published under the same title (1963) by Prentice-Hall. Englewood Cliffs, N. J.

BUCK, SIR PETER. 1950. *The Coming of the Maori.* Wellington, Maori Purposes Fund Board, Whitcombe and Tombs.

BUFFON, GEORGE LOUIS LECLERC, COMTE DE. 1866. *A Natural History. General and Particular; containing the history and theory of the earth, a general history of man, the brute creation, vegetables, minerals, etc.* Vol. I. (WILLIAM SMELLIE, trans.). London, Thomas Kelly and Co.

BUNZEL, RUTH. 1938. "Art," in BOAS, FRANZ (ed.), *General Anthropology.* New York, Heath.

CHAPPLE, ELIOT D., and CARLETON, S. COON. 1942. *Principles of Anthropology.* New York, Holt.

CHILDE, V. GORDON. 1946. *What Happened in History.* Harmondsworth, Middlesex, England, Penguin.

————. 1950. "The Urban Revolution," *Town Planning Review,* 21:3–17.

————. 1951. *Man Makes Himself.* New York, New American Library. Copyright C. A. Watts and Company, Ltd., London.

CLARK, WILFRED E. LE GROS. 1959. "The Crucial Evidence for Human Evolution," *American Scientist,* 47:299–313.

COHEN, YEHUDI. 1961. *Social Structure and Personality.* New York, Holt, Rinehart, & Winston.

Consumer Reports. 1958. "Confessions of an Appliance Salesman," 23:546.

COON, CARLETON, GARN, STANLEY M., and BIRDSELL, JOSEPH B. 1950. *Races: A Study of the Problems of Race Formation.* Springfield, Ill., Charles C Thomas.

COUSINS, NORMAN. 1964. "A Plea to the Fijians," *Saturday Review,* July 25, pp. 14–15.

COVARRUBIAS, MIGUEL. 1937. *The Island of Bali.* New York, Knopf.

DANIELSSON, BENGT. 1956. *Love in the South Seas.* New York, Reynal.

DART, R. A. 1957. *"The Osteodontokeratic Culture of Australopithecus Africanus.* Transvaal Museum Memoir No. 10.

DARWIN, CHARLES. 1846. *Journal of Researches . . . during the Voyage of HMS Beagle round the World . . .* New York, Harper & Bros.

————. 1859. *Origin of Species.* London, Murray.

DAVIS, MAXINE. 1956. *The Sexual Responsibility of Woman.* New York, Dial Press.

DE TOCQUEVILLE, ALEXIS. 1945. *Democracy in America.* Vol. II, New York, Knopf. (Vintage ed. 1954)

DOBZHANSKY, THEODOSIUS. 1955. *Evolution, Genetics, and Man.* New York, Wiley & Sons.

DORJAHN, VERNON. 1960. "The Changing Political System of the Temne," *Africa,* **30**:110–39. (Oxford University Press.)

DOZIER, EDWARD. 1956. "The Concepts of 'Primitive' and 'Native' in Anthropology," in THOMAS, WILLIAM L. (ed.), *Current Anthropology.* Chicago, University of Chicago Press.

DuBOIS, CORA. 1961. *The People of Alor.* 2 vols. New York, Harper & Bros. Copyright 1944 by the University of Minnesota.

DURKHEIM, EMILE. 1915. *The Elementary Forms of the Religious Life* (J. W. SWAIN trans.). London, Routledge and Kegan Paul.

EATON, JOSEPH W., and WEIL, ROBERT. 1953. "Mental Health of the Hutterites," *Scientific American,* **189**:31–37.

EINZIG, PAUL. 1951. *Primitive Money.* London, Eyre & Spottiswoode.

EVANS-PRITCHARD, E. E. 1940. *The Nuer.* Oxford, Clarendon Press.

————. 1956. *Social Anthropology.* Glencoe, Ill., Free Press.

EVANS-PRITCHARD, E. E., *et al.* 1961. *Institutions of Primitive Society.* Glencoe, Ill., Free Press.

FINEGAN, JACK. 1952. *The Archaeology of World Religions.* Princeton, copyright by Princeton University Press.

FIRTH, RAYMOND. 1929. *Primitive Economics of the New Zealand Maori.* New York, Dutton.

————. 1958. *Human Types.* New York (Mentor Books), New American Library. Copyright 1956 by Thomas Nelson & Sons, London.

————. 1959. *Social Change in Tikopia.* London, Allen & Unwin.

FITCH, JAMES M., and BRANCH, DANIEL P. 1960. "Primitive Architecture and Climate," *Scientific American,* **203**:134–44.

FLETCHER, A. C., and LA FLECHE, F. 1911. *The Omaha Tribe.* 27th Annual Report, Bureau of American Ethnology. Washington, D. C.

FORDE, DARYLL. 1954. "Foraging, Hunting and Fishing," in SINGER, CHARLES, HOLMYARD, E. J., and HALL, A. R. (eds.). *A History of Technology.* Vol. I. New York, Oxford Univ. Press.

FORSTER, GEORGE. 1777. *A Voyage round the World . . . Sloop Resolution, Commanded by Captain James Cook.* 2 Vols. London, B. White.

FORSTER, JOHN REINHOLD. 1778. *Observations made during a Voyage round the World, on Physical Geography, Natural History, and Ethic Philosophy . . . (Resolution).* London, Printed for G. Robinson.

FORTES, MEYER, and EVANS-PRITCHARD, E. E. (ed.). 1940. *African Political Systems.* London, Oxford University Press.

FRANKFORT, H. 1948. *Kingship and the Gods.* Chicago, University of Chicago Press.

FRAZER, SIR JAMES. 1958. *The Golden Bough.* New York, Macmillan.

FREEMAN, DEREK. 1962. Review of *Trance in Bali, Journal of the Polynesian Society,* **71**:270–73.

FRIED, MORTON. 1959. *Readings in Anthropology.* Vol. II. New York, Crowell.

FURNAS, J. C. 1948. *Anatomy of Paradise.* New York, William Sloane Associates.

GEARING, FRED. 1962. *Priests and Warriors.* Memoir No. 93, American Anthropological Association.

GIDE, ANDRE. 1931. *The Counterfeiters*. New York, Modern Library.

GILLIN, JOHN. 1948. *The Ways of Men*. New York, Appleton-Century. Quoted by permission of author and publisher.

————. 1948. "Magical Fright," *Psychiatry*, 11:387–400.

GOLDEN, HARRY. 1955. "Personal Journal," *The Carolina Israelite*, May.

GOLDFRANK, ESTHER. 1943. "Historic Change and Social Character: A Study of the Teton Dakota," *American Anthropologist*, 45:67–83.

GOLDSCHMIDT, WALTER. 1960. *Exploring the Ways of Mankind*. New York, Holt, Rinehart & Winston.

GOODE, WILLIAM J. 1951. *Religion Among the Primitives*. Glencoe, Free Press.

GORER, GEOFFREY. 1948. *The American People*. New York, W. W. Norton. Copyright 1948 by Geoffrey Gorer. Revised ed. copyright © 1964. Reprinted by permission.

GORER, GEOFFREY, and JOHN RICKMAN. 1949. *The People of Great Russia*. London, Cresset Press.

GOUGH, KATHLEEN. 1959. "The Nayars and the Definition of Marriage," *Journal of the Royal Anthropological Institute*, 89:23–34.

GRAEBNER, ROBERT FRITZ. 1911. *Methode der Ethnologie*. Heidelberg, C. Winter.

GRANT, MADISON. 1916. *Passing of a Great Race*. New York, C. Scribner's Sons.

GREEN, RICHARD, and MONEY, JOHN. 1961. "Effeminacy in Prepubertal Boys," *Pediatrics*, 27:286–91.

HART, C. W. M. 1954. "The Sons of Turimpi," *American Anthropologist*, 56:242–61.

HENRY, JULES, and SPIRO, MELFORD E. 1953. "Psychological Techniques: Projective Tests in Field Work," in Kroeber, A. L. (ed.). *Anthropology Today*. Chicago, University of Chicago Press.

HERODOTUS. 1928. "Euterpe," in *The History of Herodotus* (Rawlinson, trans.). New York, Dial Press.

HERSKOVITS, M. J. 1949. *Man and His Works*. New York, Knopf.

————. 1950. "The Hypothetical Situation," *Southwestern Journal of Anthropology*, 6:32–40.

————. 1952. *Economic Anthropology*. New York, Knopf.

————. 1953. *Franz Boas: The Science of Man in the Making*. New York, Charles Scribner's Sons.

HILGER, INEZ. 1960. *Field Guide to the Ethnological Study of Child Life*. New Haven, Human Relations Area Files Press.

HOBHOUSE, LEONARD T. 1924. *Social Development*. New York, Holt, Rinehart & Winston.

HOCKETT, CHARLES F., and ASCHER, ROBERT. 1964. "The Human Revolution," *Current Anthropology*, 5:135–47.

HOGBIN, H. IAN. 1938–39. "Tillage and Collection, a New Guinea Economy," *Oceania*, 9:127–51, 286–325.

HOLMES, LOWELL D. 1958. *Ta'u: Stability and Change in a Samoan Village*. Reprint No. 7, Polynesian Society. Wellington.

————. 1962. *Methods in Polynesian Ethnography*. (University Studies, No. 50) Wichita, University of Wichita.

HONIGMANN, JOHN J. 1954. *Culture and Personality*. New York, Harper & Bros.

HOOK, SIDNEY. 1950. *Reason, Social Myths and Democracy*. New York, Humanities Press.

HOOTON, EARNEST. 1945. *A Survey in Seating*. Gardner, Mass., Heywood-Wakefield Co.

HOWELLS, WILLIAM W. 1944. *Mankind So Far*. Garden City, N. Y., Doubleday. Quoted by permission of the author and publisher.

――――. 1948. *The Heathens*. Garden City, N. Y. Doubleday.

HSU, FRANCIS L. K. 1953. *Americans and Chinese: Two Ways of Life*. New York, Schuman.

――――. 1958 "Taboo," *What's New*, 206:12–15. Abbott Laboratories Publication. North Chicago.

――――. 1961. "American Core Value and National Character," in Hsu, F. L. K. (ed.), *Psychological Anthropology*. Homewood, Ill., Dorsey Press.

Institute of Human Relations. 1950. *Outline of Cultural Materials*. 3rd ed. New Haven, Yale University Press.

KARDINER, ABRAM, and PREBLE, EDWARD. 1961. *They Studied Man*. Cleveland, World.

KEESING, FELIX. 1953. *Culture Change*. Stanford, Stanford University Press.

――――. 1953b. *Cultural Dynamics and Administration* Proceedings, Seventh Pacific Science Congress. Auckland, New Zealand.

――――. 1958. *Cultural Anthropology*. New York, Holt, Rinehart, & Winston.

KITTO, H. D. F. 1951. *The Greeks*. Harmondsworth, Middlesex, England, Penguin.

KLUCKHOHN, CLYDE. 1938. "Participation in Ceremonials in a Navaho Community," *American Anthropologist*, 40:359–69.

――――. 1949. *Mirror for Man*. New York, McGraw-Hill.

KLUCKHOHN, CLYDE and MURRAY, HENRY (eds.). 1949. *Personality in Nature, Society, and Culture*. New York, Knopf.

KLUCKHOHN, FLORENCE. 1940. "Participant Observer Technique in Small Communities," *American Journal of Sociology*, 46:331–42.

KROEBER, A. L. 1917. "The Superorganic," *American Anthropologist*, 19:41–54.

――――. 1948. *Anthropology*. New York, Harcourt, Brace.

――――. 1959. "The History of the Personality of Anthropology," *American Anthropologist*, 61:398–404.

LANDES, RUTH. 1938. "The Abnormal among the Ojibwa Indians," *Journal of Abnormal Psychology*, 33:14–33.

LAYARD, JOHN. 1954. "The Family and Kinship," in Evans-Pritchard, E. E., et al., *The Institutions of Primitive Society*. Glencoe, Ill., Free Press.

LEACH, E. R. 1954. "Aesthetics," in Evans-Pritchard, E. E., et al. *The Institutions of Primitive Society*. Glencoe, Ill., Free Press.

LEBON, J. H. G. 1952. *An Introduction to Human Geography*. London, Hutchinson.

LEE, DOROTHY. 1959. *Freedom and Culture*. Englewood Cliffs, N.J. Prentice-Hall.

Quotes from *Freedom and Culture* (page 17) by permission of Harper and Row, publisher of *Integrity and Compromise* (MacIver, R. M., ed.) 1957; page 167 by permission of The Ronald Press, publisher of *Religious Perspectives in College Teaching* (FAIRCHILD, H. N., ed.) 1952.

LESSA, WILLIAM A., and VOGT, EVON Z. 1958. *Reader in Comparative Religion.* Evanston, Ill., Row, Peterson.

LEWIS, JOHN. 1961. *Anthropology Made Simple.* Garden City, N.Y. Doubleday.

LEWIS, OSCAR. 1951. *Life in a Mexican Village: Tepoztlan Restudied.* Urbana, University of Illinois Press.

LINTON, RALPH. 1924. "Totemism in the A.E.F.," *American Anthropologist,* 26:296–300.

———. 1936. *The Study of Man.* New York, Appleton-Century-Crofts. Quoted by permission of publisher.

———. 1952. "Universal Ethical Principles," in ANSHEN, R. (ed.), *Moral Principles of Action.* New York, Harper and Row.

———. 1955. *Tree of Culture.* New York, Knopf.

LIN, YUTANG. 1935. *My Country and My People.* New York, John Day.

LIPS, JULIUS. 1956. *The Origin of Things.* New York, Fawcett Publications. Copyright by A. A. Wyn, Inc.

LISITZKY, GENE. 1960. *Four Ways of Being Human.* New York, Viking Press.

LIVINGSTON, DAVID. 1858. *Missionary Travels and Researches in South Africa.* New York, Harper & Bros.

LLEWELLYN, KARL N., and HOEBEL, E. ADAMSON. 1941. *The Cheyenne Way.* Norman, University of Oklahoma Press.

LOMAX, ALAN. 1959. "Folk Song Style," *American Anthropologist,* 61: 927–54.

———. 1962. "Song Structure and Social Structure," *Ethnology,* 1:425–51.

LOWIE, ROBERT. 1937. *History of Ethnological Theory.* New York, Holt, Rinehart & Winston.

———. 1948. *Social Organization.* New York, Holt, Rinehart & Winston.

———. 1952. *Primitive Religion.* New York, Liveright.

LUCRETIUS. 1873. *De Rerum Natura.* 5th Book (Munro, H. A. J., trans.). New York, Deighton, Bell & Co.

LYND, ROBERT S., and LYND, HELEN M. 1929. *Middletown, A Study in Contemporary American Culture.* New York, Harcourt, Brace.

MAIR, LUCY. 1962. *Primitive Government.* Harmondsworth, England, Penguin.

MAITLAND, F. W. 1911. "The Body Politic," in *Collected Papers,* Vol. III. Cambridge, Cambridge University Press.

MALINOWSKI, BRONISLAW. 1929. *Sexual Life of Savages.* London, Routledge and Kegan Paul.

———. 1931. "Culture," *Encyclopedia of the Social Sciences.* New York, Macmillan.

———. 1935. *Coral Gardens and their Magic.* London, Allen & Unwin.

———. 1961. *Argonauts of the Western Pacific.* New York, Dutton & Company.

MANDELBAUM, DAVID. 1956. "Social Groupings," in SHAPIRO, HARRY (ed.), *Man, Culture and Society.* New York, Oxford University Press.

MARX, KARL. 1867. *Das Kapital.* New York, L. W. Schmidt.

MAYO, ELTON. 1933. *The Human Problems of an Industrial Civilization.* New York, Macmillan.

MEAD, MARGARET. 1939. "Native Languages as Field Work Tools," *American Anthropologist,* 41:189–205.

———. 1953. "National Character," in KROEBER, A. L. (ed.), *Anthropology Today.* Chicago, University of Chicago Press.

———. 1957. "The Pattern of Leisure in Contemporary American Culture," in DOUGLASS, PAUL F., HUTCHINSON, JOHN L., and SUTHERLAND, WILLARD C. (eds.) *The Annuals of the American Academy of Political Science; Recreation in the Age of Automation* (September). Philadelphia.

———. 1956. *New Lives For Old; Cultural Transformation-Manus, 1928–1953.* New York, Morrow.

———. 1959. *Coming of Age in Samoa.* New York, New American Library. Copyright 1932 by William Morrow & Co.

MILL, JOHN STUART. 1898. *Principles of Political Economy* (abridged by J. Laurence Laughlin). New York, D. Appleton and Company.

MONTAGU, ASHLEY. 1956. *The Biosocial Nature of Man.* New York, Grove Press.

MONTESQUIEU, CHARLES LOUIS DE SECONDAT, BARON DE. 1756. *The Spirit of Laws.* Aberdeen, Scotland, F. Douglass and W. Murry.

MORGAN, LEWIS HENRY. 1877. *Ancient Society.* New York, H. Holt.

MORTON, SAMUEL G. 1839. "Varieties of the Human Species" (preface to), *Crania Americana.* Philadelphia, J. Dobson.

MOSKIN, ROBERT. 1958. "The American Male: Why Do Women Dominate Him?" *Look,* 22:76–80 (Feb. 4).

MURDOCK, GEORGE P. 1937. "Comparative Data on Division of Labor by Sex," *Social Forces,* 15: 551–53 (University of North Carolina Press).

MURDOCK, GEORGE P., and WHITING, JOHN W. M. 1951. "Cultural Determination of Parental Attitudes," in SENN, M. J. E. (ed.), *Problems of Infancy and Childhood.* New York, Josiah Macy, Jr., Foundation.

NADEL, S. F. 1953. "Social Control and Self Regulation," *Social Forces,* 31: 265–73 (University of North Carolina Press).

NAPIER, JOHN. 1964. "The Evolution of Man," *Discovery,* 25:32–36 (June).

NAROLL, RAOUL S. 1950. "A Draft Map of the Culture Areas of Asia," *Southwestern Journal of Anthropology,* 6:183–87.

NEWMAN, HORATIO, FREEMAN, FRANK N., and HOLZINGER, KARL. 1937. *Twins: A Study of Heredity and Environment.* Chicago, University of Chicago Press.

NEWTON, NILES. 1955. *Maternal Emotions.* New York, Harper & Row.

NORBECK, EDWARD. 1961. *Religion in Primitive Society.* New York, Harper & Row.

OAKLEY, KENNETH. 1957. *Man the Tool Maker.* Chicago, University of Chicago Press.

OGBURN, WILLIAM, and NIMKOFF, MEYER. 1964. *Sociology.* Boston, Houghton Mifflin.

PERRY, W. J. 1923. *Children of the Sun.* London, Methuen.

RADCLIFFE-BROWN, A. R. 1948. *Andaman Islanders.* Glencoe, Ill., Free Press.

RADIN, PAUL. 1957. *Primitive Religion.* New York, Dover Publications.

REDFIELD, ROBERT. 1953. *The Primitive World and Its Transformations.* Ithaca, Cornell University Press. Quoted by permission.

———. 1956. "How Society Operates," in SHAPIRO, HARRY (ed.), *Man, Culture and Society.* New York, Oxford University Press.

REICHARD, GLADYS. 1938. "Social Life," in BOAS, FRANZ (ed.), *General Anthropology.* New York, Heath.

RIESMAN, DAVID, GLAZER, NATHAN, and DENNEY, REUEL. 1950. *The Lonely Crowd.* New Haven, Yale University Press.

RIVERS, W. H. R. 1910. "The Genealogical Method of Anthropological Inquiry," *The Sociological Review*, 3:1–12.

ROBINSON, C. H. 1896. *Hausaland.* London, S. Low, Marston and Company.

ROYAL ANTHROPOLOGICAL INSTITUTE OF GREAT BRITAIN AND IRELAND. 1951. *Notes and Queries on Anthropology.* London, Routledge and Kegan Paul. Copyright 1874.

SAHLINS, MARSHALL. 1960. "The Origin of Society," *Scientific American*, 203:76–87.

SCHAPERA, ISAAC. 1930. *The Khoisan Peoples of South Africa.* London, Routledge and Kegan Paul.

———. 1956. *Government and Politics in Tribal Societies.* London, Watts.

SCHMIDT, WILHELM. 1939. *The Culture Historical Method of Ethnology.* New York, Fortuny.

SHAPIRO, HARRY L. 1953. *Race Mixture.* Paris, UNESCO.

SHARP, LAURISTON. 1952. "Steel Axes for Stone Age Australians," in SPICER, EDWARD H. (ed.), *Human Problems in Technological Change.* New York, Russell Sage Foundation.

SHELDON, WILLIAM H. 1940. *The Varieties of Human Physique.* New York, Harper & Bros.

———. 1942. *The Varieties of Temperament.* New York, Harper & Bros.

SIMS, NEWELL LeRoy. 1939. *The Problem of Social Change.* New York, Crowell.

SMITH, GRAFTON ELLIOT. 1915. *The Migrations of Early Culture.* London, New York, Longmans, Green & Co.

———. 1916. *The Influence of Ancient Egyptian Civilization in the East and in America.* New York, Longmans, Green & Co.

SMITH, HARVEY. 1949. *Sociological Study of Hospitals.* Unpublished Ph.D. dissertation, Dept. of Sociology, University of Chicago.

STANNER, W. E. H. 1953. *The South Seas in Transition.* Sydney, Australasia Publ. Co. Quoted by permission of Australian Institute of International Affairs.

STEWARD, J. H. 1949. "Cultural Causality and Law: A Trial Formulation of the Development of Early Civilizations," *American Anthropologist*, 51:1–27.

———. 1956. *Theory of Culture Change.* New York.

SUMNER, WILLIAM GRAHAM. 1906. *Folkways.* Boston, Ginn & Co.

TACITUS. 1942. *The Complete Works of Tacitus.* (A. J. Church, trans.) New York, Random House.

THOMAS, WILLIAM JR. (ed.). 1956. *Current Anthropology.* Chicago, University of Chicago Press.

TOMARS, ADOLPH S. 1943. "Rural Survivals in American Urban Life," *Rural Sociology*, 8:378–86.

TYLOR, SIR EDWARD BURVETT. 1871. *Primitive Culture*. London, J. Murray.

TYLOR, EDWARD B. 1889. "On the Method of Investigating the Development of Institutions . . ." *Journal of the Royal Anthropological Institute*, 18: 245–69.

————. 1894. *Anthropology*. New York, D. Appleton.

UNDERHILL, RUTH. 1953. *Red Man's America*. Chicago, University of Chicago Press.

UNESCO. 1952. *What is Race?* Paris.

VAILLANT, GEORGE C. 1962. *The Aztecs of Mexico*. Garden City, N.Y., Doubleday.

VEBLEN, THORSTEIN. 1912. *The Theory of the Leisure Class*. New York, Macmillan.

WALLACE, ANTHONY F. C. 1952. *The Modal Personality Structure of the Tuscarora Indians, as Revealed by the Rorschach Test*. Bulletin 150, Bureau of American Ethnology, Washington, D.C.

WARNER, WILLIAM LLOYD. 1937. *A Black Civilization*. New York, Harper & Bros.

WASHBURN, SHERWOOD L. 1960. "Tools and Human Evolution," *Scientific American*, 203:62–75.

WEINBERG, S. KIRSON. 1952. *Society and Personality Disorders*. New York, Prentice-Hall.

WHITE, LESLIE. 1959. *The Evolution of Culture*. New York, McGraw-Hill.

WHYTE, WILLIAM F. 1955. *Street Corner Society*. Chicago, University of Chicago Press.

WHYTE, WILLIAM H., JR. 1952. "Help Wanted—Sales," *Fortune* (May).

WILLIAMS, ROGER. 1958. "Chemical Anthropology," *American Scientist*, 46: 1–23.

WINICK, CHARLES. 1958. *Dictionary of Anthropology*. New York, Philosophical Library.

WISSLER, CLARK. 1923. *Man and Culture*. New York, Crowell.

Index

371